D1521172

Soviet Nuclear Weapons Policy

About the Book and Author

This book assesses both Western and Soviet literature on Soviet nuclear weapons policy. The author
discusses the development of the various Western schools
of interpretation and their effect on U.S. policy and
provides an introduction to Soviet sources (Russian
language as well as translated material). Analytical
chapters are followed by comprehensive annotated
listings of a broad range of civilian and military
publications.

Dr. William C. Green is senior analyst at Orion
Engineering in Arlington, Virginia.

Soviet Nuclear Weapons Policy

A Research and
Bibliographic Guide

William C. Green

Westview Press / Boulder and London

016.3550947

G79&

Westview Special Studies in National Security and Defense Policy

This Westview softcover edition is printed on acid-free paper and bound in
softcovers that carry the highest rating of the National Association of
State Textbook Administrators, in consultation with the Association of
American Publishers and the Book Manufacturers' Institute.

All rights reserved. No part of this publication may be reproduced or
transmitted in any form or by any means, electronic or mechanical, including
photocopy, recording, or any information storage and retrieval system,
without permission in writing from the publisher.

Copyright © 1987 by Westview Press, Inc.

Published in 1987 in the United States of America by Westview Press, Inc.;
Frederick A. Praeger, Publisher; 5500 Central Avenue, Boulder, Colorado 80301

Library of Congress Cataloging-in-Publication Data
Green, William, 1956-
    Soviet nuclear weapons policy.
    (Westview special studies in national security and
defense policy)
    Includes bibliographies and indexes.
    1. Soviet Union--Military policy. 2. Atomic weapons.
3. Strategic forces--Soviet Union. I. Title.
UA770.G735 1987   355'.0217'0947   83-23273
ISBN 0-86531-817-4

Composition for this book was provided by the author.
This book was produced without formal editing by the publisher.

Printed and bound in the United States of America

∞   The paper used in this publication meets the requirements
     of the American National Standard for Permanence of Paper
     for Printed Library Materials Z39.48-1984.

6   5   4   3   2   1

This book is dedicated to Robert Reeves.
Without his encouragement and support,
it would never have been completed.

UNIVERSITY LIBRARIES
CARNEGIE-MELLON UNIVERSITY
PITTSBURGH, PENNSYLVANIA 15213

Contents

Preface

This research guide is intended primarily for two groups of specialists. The first consists of Sovietologists interested in acquiring a more complete knowledge of Soviet strategic and military policy. The second includes strategic analysts interested in expanding their expertise to cover Soviet strategy and thinking. However, it was assembled so as to be useful as well for non-specialists interested in investigating Soviet nuclear weapons policy.

The book falls into three main sections: an analytical essay; a bibliographic guide to scholarly, professional, and journalistic sources on Soviet nuclear weapons policy and related issues; and a guide to the primary Soviet source material. It begins with an initial chapter outlining major trends and themes in the interpretation of Soviet nuclear weapons policy by various U.S. analysts. This is followed by six chapters of abstracts taken from the various publications in which Western interpretations of Soviet nuclear weapons policy have appeared. These abstracts have been sorted according to topic: general works and overviews; works on Soviet strategy and doctrine; works on Soviet strategic defense; Soviet theater, tactical, and naval nuclear weapons policy; works discussing three closely-related topics; and anthologies and bibliographies. The book concludes with a chapter that includes essays on the primary Soviet strategic literature as well as a guide to Soviet sources available in English translation.

The abstracts provided in Chapters 2 through 7 are not meant to evaluate the various works. Instead, they are intended to convey the substance of the material as the authors would express it. One exception should be noted -- the Penkovsky Papers. This work was and remains an important source on Soviet nuclear weapons policy of the 1960s. However, in recent congressional testimony, representatives of the Central Intelligence Agency revealed that the book was prepared by the CIA after GRU Colonel Oleg Penkovskiy's death, from a variety of sources. They were careful to state that only material actually attributed to Penkovskiy in the text was derived from his reports and debriefings. The remainder, about half the total, presumably reflects the views of the CIA analysts who prepared the book.

Several of the journals I consulted in the preparation of this research guide publish abstracts of the articles appearing in them. They include <u>Strategic Review</u>, <u>Comparative Strategy</u>, <u>Problems of Communism</u>, and a number of others. Since these abstracts were presumably written by or approved by the authors, I have used them rather than produce new ones. Research performed under federal contract is always abstracted, and I have used these whenever they are available.

The abstracts do not use a standard Russian transliteration system. Instead, transliteration of Russian names and terminology corresponds to that used in the original publication. In all other parts of the research guide, however, transliteration follows the Bureau of Geographic Names system.

Three additional matters should be explained here in the foreward. The first is that after investigating a variety of formats, I concluded that a simple index listing each abstracted source in alphabetical order by author would be most helpful to the reader. The second is that no systematic attempt to gather reviews was made in the preparation of this research guide, but I included those I came across. Finally, the three related subjects included in Chapter 6 were not selected randomly; as noted in the first Chapter, they bear directly on the question of the validity of the Soviet source material. As can be readily verified, many of them were written by the authors of works directly addressing the issue of Soviet nuclear weapons policy.

William C. Green

Acknowledgments

I would like to acknowledge the support of the scores of individuals who eased my way in producing this book. My special thanks go to the Hon. Regina C. McGraney and to Karen Joy Tarcza, whose editorial help was essential to completing it. Raymond Garthoff, Daniel Goure, Leon Goure, Al Graham, Floyd Kennedy, James McConnell, William F. Scott, Harriet Fast Scott, Rebecca Strode, John Thomas, Joseph D. Douglass, Jr., David B. Rivkin, Jr., Dennis Gormley, Henry Sokolsky, and Douglas Graham all helped provide me with or directed me towards source materials. Patrick Vaughan showed much forbearance and understanding during the inevitable last minute production deadlines. Finally, I would like to thank my former colleagues at Delex Systems, Inc., for their help and encouragement, including Jim Ferro, Sandra Dye, Thomas Dollard, Susan Buchanan, Kathrine Jenkins, and especially Robert Reeves, to whom this book is dedicated.

It is traditional to absolve one's collaborators and supporters from any flaws or shortcomings of the book. This is a good custom, for no one is more aware of a book's faults than its author. I take full responsibility for any errors or omissions in this work. However, if it proves useful to the defense and Sovietological communities, I may be able to amend any flaws in a revised and expanded edition. In fact, I've already started a notebook...

1

The Interpretation of
Soviet Nuclear Weapons Policy

This research guide emphasizes interpretations of Soviet
nuclear weapons policy by Western authors rather than original
Soviet sources. It includes a chapter which discusses Soviet
publications on nuclear weapons and gives a listing of translated
Soviet materials on the subject. But Soviet sources are
incomplete and contradictory, ranging from assertions of the
nonutility of nuclear weapons to detailed assessments of their
utility in tactical combat. As a result, they can be read in
many different ways, depending upon one's basic premises about
the Soviet Union.

The Western interpretative works abstracted in this
research guide differ greatly in the descriptions they give of
Soviet nuclear weapons policy. Their competing and discordant
voices might well confuse the reader. Hence, to assist in understanding the conflicting messages, this first chapter is offered
as a means of placing the individual works abstracted for this
book in the context of an entire body of literature. By tracing
the issues, themes, and debates emphasized as this body of
literature developed, the premises of each author and the information available to him will become clear.

THE FIRST YEARS: 1945 TO 1953

The years 1945 to 1953 span the period from the end of
the Second World War to the death of Stalin. During this period
few if any U.S. analysts attempted to discern Soviet atomic
weapons policy from published Soviet sources, largely because
such sources were scarce and seemingly uninformative. After
Stalin's death, when Soviet publications became more plentiful,
U.S. analysts working with this literature tried to fashion
explanations for its earlier paucity. The most widely circulated
explanation for this phenomenon significantly affected later
interpretations of subsequent Soviet strategic literature.

The most extensively researched and widely cited work on the Soviet military from this early post-war period is Raymond Garthoff's book <u>Soviet Military Doctrine</u>.[1] Garthoff, a RAND Corporation analyst, mentioned atomic weapons only once in this work, in a short section subtitled "The Fallacy of the Single Weapon."[2] In this section he discussed the Soviet military's rejection of reliance on any one type of combat force, and its emphasis on a combined arms approach -- using all types of forces on the basis of their particular characteristics. He noted that Soviet military spokesmen insisted that this principle also applied to atomic weapons, and deprecated American assertions and policies based on the premise that the atomic bomb was an "ultimate" weapon.

Garthoff's brief discussion is the closest that can be found to an interpretation of Soviet nuclear weapons policy from this period.[3] Soviet strategic literature became much more plentiful and detailed after Stalin's death, shifting its focus from marked indifference to intense interest in all aspects of nuclear weapons. It is not surprising that several U.S. analysts of Soviet strategic literature attempted to account for its scarcity during the immediate post-war period. In a subsequent work, <u>Soviet Strategy in the Nuclear Age</u>, Raymond Garthoff (who by this time had left RAND for government service) stated emphatically that lack of Soviet commentary on atomic and nuclear issues reflected a complete absence of any planning for nuclear war under Stalin.[4] Herbert Dinerstein, another RAND corporation analyst, arrived at the same conclusion in his 1959 book, <u>War and the Soviet Union</u>.[5] Their position was based on their perception that Stalinist military principles exerted a stranglehold on discussion of nuclear doctrine and strategy, and they found further evidence to support this in the speedy abandonment of these principles after Stalin's death.

By contrast, in his well-known <u>Nuclear Weapons and Foreign Policy</u>, Henry Kissinger pointed out that it was not in the Soviet Union's interest to discuss its atomic weapons policy at a time when it lagged behind the United States in development, testing, and delivery capacity.[6] Acknowledging U.S. atomic superiority would have weakened the Soviet Union's position and might have created morale problems for the Armed Forces. Many later writers have confirmed Kissinger's view by describing important Soviet nuclear policies and programs begun under Stalin. Thomas Wolfe, of the RAND Corporation, and William F. and Harriet Fast Scott, have reported on behind-the-scenes planning of nuclear weapons policy during this period that had important influence on its course after Stalin's death.[7] More recently, William T. Lee and Richard Staar have provided an in-depth review of important programs and organizational changes made with Stalin's direct approval.[8]

Despite this, however, numerous authors have followed Garthoff and Dinerstein in attributing to Stalin a totally negative

influence on the development of Soviet nuclear weapons policy.[9]
This interpretation's chief effect has been to create an impression that the Soviet Union suffers from a "doctrinal lag."
According to this view, the United States began to examine the
implications of the nuclear age from its beginnings in 1945. The
Soviet Union, however, was not able to begin this process until
after Stalin's death. As Henry Kissinger put it: "...the Soviet
officers simply went through the process about five years after
their Western counterparts in each phase."[10]

THE SOVIET UNION INVESTIGATES NEW CONCEPTS: 1953 TO 1959

The years 1953 to 1959 were characterized by a great
increase in published Soviet discussions of nuclear weapons.
The marked changes in Soviet strategic literature between Stalin's
death in March 1953 and the 20th Party Congress in February
1956 led U.S. analysts to investigate their meaning. One of the
first of these was by Col. G.C. Reinhardt, U.S. Army Corps of
Engineers, who co-authored an early study of tactical nuclear
weapons.[11] Shortly after it appeared, Reinhardt contributed an
essay on Soviet nuclear weapons policy to a collection of articles
entitled The Red Army.[12] Reinhardt noted the "growing role of
surprise attack" in Soviet strategic literature as a means of
neutralizing an opponent's nuclear weapons.[13] He viewed this as
over-publicized bluff; in the event of an actual war, he assumed
that the Soviet Union would employ nuclear weapons in support
of the tactics it developed during the Second World War.

Henry Kissinger reached exactly opposite conclusions;
the Soviet emphasis on the massive retaliatory force of nuclear
weapons "may indicate a realization that the greatest vulnerability of the Soviet armed forces is in the area of limited nuclear
war."[14] In his view, the Soviet political and military leadership
had not yet undertaken the fundamental alteration of tactics
which nuclear war requires, and faced what they knew to be a
difficult task.

The changes in Soviet strategic literature were more
closely observed and analyzed by analysts at the RAND corporation. In a series of RAND papers and memoranda, Raymond
Garthoff, Herbert Dinerstein, and other analysts evaluated the
unfolding Soviet events.[15] This work was disrupted by an organizational change at RAND which resulted in Garthoff's leaving for
government service in 1956. However, he summarized his RAND
work in his second book, Soviet Strategy in the Nuclear Era,
which he completed late in 1957.[16] Garthoff organized this book
around a central theme: since 1953 the Soviet military had slowly
been evolving its thinking and organization to fit the realities of
the nuclear age. It was based on a Soviet recognition of the

realities of mutual deterrence. In short, the Soviet military employed its nuclear forces to deter war, but if war were to come it would be fought along classical lines.

In 1959 Garthoff published a short monograph entitled The Soviet Image of Future War.[17] He explained in the introduction that he wished to expand and emphasize the conclusions of his previous book. He felt it important to emphasize his view that Soviet strategy had not changed significantly since the death of Stalin, despite its rhetoric about surprise and nuclear weapons, which he attributed to the recently disgraced Marshal Zhukov. It was Garthoff's belief that doctrinal innovation had greatly decreased since Zhukov's ouster, and that the Soviet military was reverting to World War II concepts of warfare. It saw strategic nuclear weapons as useful only for deterring conflict between the superpowers.

Dinerstein gave a preliminary view of his evalution of the changes in Soviet nuclear weapons policy in an article he published in January 1958. He drew on changes in both Soviet strategic writings and the Soviet political leadership to conclude that the introduction of nuclear weapons had revolutionized Soviet military thought. In his view, the Soviet military had adopted a strategy of fighting a preemptive war.[18] Dinerstein pointed out that at present this was defensive, since the Soviet Union had no hope, in its first strike, of hitting U.S. strategic forces effectively enough to preclude retaliation. However, if this capability were attained, the Soviet leadership would be presented with extremely favorable policy alternatives.[19]

In 1959 Herbert Dinerstein published War and the Soviet Union, an expansion and extention of his earlier article.[20] Dinerstein subtitled his work "Nuclear Weapons and the Revolution in Soviet Military and Political Thinking," which aptly sums up his approach and conclusion. Dinerstein's approach was to correlate the Soviet political debates and faction-fighting of the 1950s with the military debates and discussions over the role of nuclear weapons. He emphasized the role preemption had come to play in Soviet military thought, and concluded his book by predicting a reorganization of the Soviet military that would reflect the primacy of ballistic missiles.

Although few U.S. interpretations of Soviet strategic literature were published during the 1950s, they varied greatly. Two patterns emerge, however, from the examples reviewed here. The Reinhardt, Kissinger, and Garthoff interpretations each in their own way saw Soviet nuclear weapons policy as evolutionary. That is, it was built up by the addition of the nuclear factor to already existing concepts. By contrast, the Dinerstein interpretation explicitly presented the change in Soviet strategic literature as revolutionary. The new elements in Soviet military policy produced by addition of the nuclear factor were so different from what had existed before that they forced the Soviet Union to undergo a complete reexamination of its military forces and thinking.

It should be noted that both Garthoff and Dinerstein published their works prior to the formal appearance of the new Soviet doctrine in January 1960. This doctrine, and the thousands of Soviet publications that followed it in the 1960s, confirmed Dinerstein's conclusion of a complete change in Soviet military thought. The Soviet writers even used a term to describe this change very similar to the one coined by Dinerstein -- they called it "the Revolution in Military Affairs."

THE EARLY 1960s: PREEMINENT ROLE OF RAND ANALYSTS

Nikita Khrushchev formally announced the new Soviet military doctrine in January 1960. Soviet military writers maintain that this date marks the beginning of the third and current stage of the Revolution in Military Affairs. Between 1960 and 1962, Soviet writings on military art and strategy changed in order to correspond to the new doctrine. By the end of 1962 Soviet military strategy had been completely overhauled. Soviet publications, directed at a wide range of audiences, were filled with descriptions of the nuclear Revolution in Military Affairs which had made the new doctrine and strategy necessary. Soviet strategic literature was still focused on the Revolution in Military Affairs when Khrushchev was removed from office in October 1964.

Relatively few interpretations of Soviet strategic literature were published in the United States in the first years after Khrushchev announced the new Soviet military doctrine. But as major Soviet military-theoretical works appeared, the number of U.S. interpretative works increased sharply. The lack of development in open-source Soviet strategic literature prior to the appearance of Marshal V.D. Sokolovskiy's Military Strategy in late 1962 had a definite influence -- few works appeared in the West that addressed Soviet nuclear weapons policy. This effect was reinforced when, after the advent of satellite surveillance, American intelligence found it had grossly overestimated the size of the Soviet ICBM force, which created the so-called "missile gap." The Soviet Union instead had focused on the production of short-range and theater ballistic missiles.

In 1962, both Raymond Garthoff and Herbert Dinerstein published revised editions of previous works, updated to include the new Soviet military doctrine. Garthoff added a brief epilogue to his new edition, in which he concluded that Khrushchev's speech would not signal radical change.[21] By contrast, Dinerstein wrote a lengthy introduction to the second edition of

War and the Soviet Union. In it he attempted to explain why the Soviet Union had not undertaken a major production of ICBMs.[22] Dinerstein had predicted this in his earlier works, since the Soviet emphasis on nuclear preemption implied the need for a prompt, long-range delivery system -- the ICBM.

Dinerstein believed that certain cost-related factors used by other U.S. analysts of the "missile gap" were not sufficient to explain it. Instead, he offered two additional hypotheses: that the Soviet Union's procurement bureaucracy persisted in developing theater systems, although this emphasis had outlived its usefulness; or that the Soviet Union was dissatisfied with its current ICBM model (the SS-6), and would wait for a more perfected system before large-scale deployment would begin. He concluded that the Soviet Union still had an emphasis on nuclear preemption.

In 1962, another RAND analyst, Leon Goure, published a book focusing on Soviet civil defense.[23] Goure emphasized the strategic importance of Soviet civil defense, contending that it was neither a form of nuclear disaster relief, as in the West, or a hold-over from the air raid defenses of the Second World War; but instead was a contribution to the overall Soviet defense capability. Goure's evaluation was that the Soviet leadership did not need to fear a sudden surprise attack from the United States. Therefore, Soviet civil defense was intended to support the Soviet position in the event of the two most likely nuclear conflict scenarios: escalation of a local war into a global nuclear war, or a Soviet preemptive or preventive nuclear attack.[24]

U.S. analysts studying the changes in Soviet military policy were strongly affected by an authoritative Soviet publication that appeared in the fall of 1962. This work, Military Strategy, was authored by a collective of officers headed by Marshal of the Soviet Union V.D. Sokolovskiy, formerly the Chief of the General Staff.[25] The book gave much more detail on Soviet nuclear weapons policy than any work that had appeared since the doctrinal revision of 1960.

Raymond Garthoff published a translation of this book which appeared in February 1963.[26] It included an introductory essay in which Garthoff set forth his views on the book's significance. He saw it as a product of consensus reached after a factional debate between representatives of two opposing views on the nature of modern war: radicals, stressing deterrence; and conservatives, interested in meeting the requirements for waging nuclear war.[27] Garthoff felt that the debate had largely been won by the "conservative traditional" school, but that in the process their opinions had been modified: "enlightened conservatives" now wanted the Soviet military to retain large conventional forces, but use nuclear missiles in new ways.[28]

RAND analysts also translated and interpreted <u>Military Strategy</u>, releasing <u>Soviet Military Strategy</u> in June 1963.[29] This volume combined a lengthy "analytical introduction" with an annotated translation of the first edition of <u>Military Strategy</u>. The analytical introduction was credited to three RAND analysts, but was probably authored solely by Thomas W. Wolfe. He saw the Soviet military as permanently divided between two factions: Radicals or "Modernists" in favor of a strict nuclear emphasis, and Traditionalists arguing for the integration of the nuclear factor with time-tested concepts and practices. He viewed Nikita Khrushchev as backing the Modernists, primarily for reasons of economy; while the Traditionalists found their support among the leaders of heavy industry. The chief significance of <u>Military Strategy</u> was that it was an indicator of the relative strength of the two factions, and represented a compromise between them.

A sign of general Western interest in <u>Military Strategy</u> was the sponsorship of a conference in April 1963 by the Washington, D.C.-based Center for Strategic Studies to discuss the work's significance. This conference was attended by sixteen specialists in U.S. or Soviet military affairs, including Garthoff, Goure, and Wolfe; the proceedings were quickly published by the Center.[30] The transcript does not reveal any doubt among the participants that a Soviet factional debate over nuclear weapons policy was underway or that <u>Military Strategy</u> was one of its interim products. Garthoff and Wolfe made a conscious effort to merge their debate typologies, and cast doubt on the notion that any real consensus between the factions was possible.[31]

Similar conclusions were reached at another conference held at this time by the U.S. Arms Control and Disarmament Agency. Thirty-five Sovietologists and arms control specialists participated, including Dinerstein, Garthoff, and Wolfe. The chapter on the Soviet military in the conference's report used both Garthoff's and Wolfe's terminology in describing military factions. It synthesized certain differences in their views by postulating two different groups of modernists in alliance: political "moderates" and military radicals. This alliance was based on converging interests: the military modernists were interested in adapting military concepts to reflect the primacy of nuclear missiles; and the political modernists were interested in adopting a military posture of primary reliance on nuclear deterrence, in part, for the sake of political and economic benefits.[32]

The RAND and Garthoff translations stimulated an extraordinary number of derivative articles and review essays. Most of them reported on the views presented in the introductions to the translations, rather than giving independent analysis.[33] The only writer to dispute the factional debate interpretations offered in the introductions to the translations was Walter Jacobs, an associate of the Library of Congress. In an article published in Military Review, he noted that protests within the Soviet system were not normally made in the manner described by Garthoff and Wolfe.[34] Jacobs also reviewed the two translations for National Review. He expressed a fear that the introductions might "divert the reader unnecessarily," and recommended that the reader approach Sokolovskiy "without exegesis or gloss."[35]

In a monograph on the second (1963) edition of Military Strategy, Leon Goure compared the two editions as well as other Soviet publications for changes in major military themes. As a result of this comparison, Goure concluded that the Soviet debate on strategy had not been resolved.[36] He agreed with Wolfe that there was a "conservative" or "traditionalistic" element in the Soviet military that continued to resist a military strategy founded on a doctrine of nuclear emphasis. Yet he gave a very different picture of the strength of the conservative opposition than had Wolfe, concluding that no radical changes had taken place between the two editions of Military Strategy, and that it had the approval of a "very influential element of the Soviet military leadership."[37] This implied continuing Soviet readiness to fight a nuclear war if need be, preferably after having launched a preemptive strike on Western nuclear forces.

Just prior to Khrushchev's ouster in October 1964, Thomas Wolfe completed two major works that covered the period since the Cuban Missile Crisis in October 1962. The first of these was his book Soviet Strategy at the Crossroads.[38] In this work Wolfe addressed a number of issues which he felt were at the core of the unresolved Soviet military factional debate.

These issues can be reduced to what Wolfe phrased as the "difficulty stem[ming] from the nature of modern war itself, which gives rise to fundamental questions as to whether war or the threat of war can any longer be regarded as a rational instrument of policy."[39] Wolfe offered no direct conclusions as to which route the Soviet Union would take past the "crossroads," but it is clear in many places that he saw the Soviet Union evolving towards a "realistic" position, stressing the deterrent value of nuclear weapons rather than their value in direct military usage.

Wolfe wrote an article that covered Soviet strategic literature after the appearance of the second edition of Military Strategy, as a follow-on to his book.[40] In this work Wolfe discussed a number of articles by Soviet military authors that he felt indicated a resurgence of "traditionalist" influence against the "centrist" position of the Military Strategy authors. This article's chief importance is that it was the first in which Wolfe explicitly identified his "modernist-traditionalist" factional debate with Garthoff's "nuclear deterrence-nuclear warfighting" factional debate.[41]

Two points stand out in an examination of these U.S. interpretations from the early 1960s. The first is the uncertainty and lack of unanimity with which the U.S. interpreters addressed the question of preemption. Goure and Dinerstein had no difficulty accepting that the Soviet Union had a policy of preemption, while Wolfe saw Soviet discussion of preemption intended primarily as a psychological deterrent to the United States. Garthoff believed that Soviet discussion of preemption had faded out about 1957 as missiles replaced bombers. In his view, subsequent references interpreted as implying preemption probably were misunderstood. The various interpretations apparently reflected the divergent views of the analysts on a fundamental point: did nuclear weapons have a real potential for actual combat use?

The second point that stands out in this examination of U.S. interpretations is the ready acceptance of the thesis of an intramilitary debate by the Americans who wrote on the changes in Soviet military doctrine and strategy. In all the interpretations and other works from this period that were identified in the preparation of this research guide, only two -- both by Walter Jacobs -- expressed serious objections to the notion that Soviet nuclear weapons policy was the subject of a major intramilitary factional debate.

In sum, the increase in Soviet strategic literature marked by publication of Sokolovskiy's Military Strategy triggered a corresponding increase in published U.S. interpretations of Soviet strategic literature. These publications differed in their assessment of what appeared to be a key feature of Soviet military doctrine -- nuclear preemption. But they were generally in agreement on discerning an intra-military factional debate over the integration of the nuclear factor into Soviet military strategy. Some interpretations also perceived a factional debate between the political leadership and at least a large portion of the Soviet military over whether or not nuclear weapons were essentially a deterrent force.

ATTENTION WAVERS: 1965 TO 1972

After the fall of Khrushchev and the accession of the Brezhnev-Kosygin-Podgorniy "troika" regime, U.S. interpreters of Soviet nuclear weapons policy tried to assess the implications of the new leadership for the factional debates they perceived in the Soviet military. In late October 1964, immediately after Khrushchev's removal from power, a conference was held in Munich on Soviet strategy and foreign policy, sponsored by the West German Institute for the Study of the USSR. Thirty-three Western strategists participated in the conference, including Thomas Wolfe, Raymond Garthoff, Herbert Dinerstein, and Robert

Crane. According to press reports, most of the participants felt that the Soviet Union "would remain committed to the nuclear-deterrent strategy initiated by Mr. Khrushchev."[42] However, a number added that "traditionalists" in the Soviet military would use the removal of Khrushchev as an occasion to attack the "centrist" compromise, and would reopen the factional debate by demanding "a rounded military establishment as well as an attempt to achieve nuclear superiority over the West."

Raymond Garthoff expressed his view that any efforts along these lines by the Soviet military had a limited future, since they flew in the face of the reality of mutual deterrence.[43] One of the conference organizers, Nikolay Galay of the Institute for the Study of the USSR, held that mutual deterrence had led to a withering of ideology. By accomodating to this fact, the "loss of political primacy over military strategy is automatically undermining the ideological foundations of the Soviet regime."[44] Galay felt that the breakdown in ideology was responsible for much of the factional debate over Soviet nuclear weapons policy.

Immediately after returning to the United States from this conference, Thomas Wolfe presented what he saw as the major factors behind Khrushchev's ouster to the National Defense Seminar at the Harvard University Center for International Affairs. Wolfe concluded cautiously that "it seems entirely reasonable to assume that the weight of problems in the military sphere contributed in some measure to his [Khrushchev's] failure to weather this latest and most telling challenge to his leadership."[45] Of these problems, Wolfe saw the revival of 'traditionalist' resistance to the 'modernist' theories and policies associated with Khrushchev as the most important.

In the views of these interpreters of Soviet strategic literature, the continuation of intramilitary factional debate even after Khrushchev's ouster indicated that the dispute probably was irresolvable. Therefore, political-military relations were key to determining the course of Soviet nuclear weapons policy, since in the absence of a stable military consensus over nuclear weapons, the views of other elements of the Soviet leadership would likely predominate. As a result, U.S. interpretations of Soviet strategic literature began to focus on the relationship between the military and the political leadership, rather than on military views of nuclear weapons policy.

A work that marked this shift was a RAND-sponsored work by Arnold Horelick and Myron Rush (1966) that investigated the interrelation of Soviet strategic military power and foreign policy.[46] Although military factional debate and potential for conflict with the political leadership is assumed, these views and statements are not addressed in this work. The choices that the Soviet Union had to make in developing its nuclear forces are addressed in terms of how they might affect Soviet foreign policy, rather than as the product of a particular strategic theory.

To U.S. analysts searching for evidence of conflict between military factions and other elements of the Soviet leadership, popular press pieces explaining the Revolution in Military Affairs appeared to be attempts by "modernists" to subvert the "centrist" consensus by taking their cause outside military publications. An article by retired General-Major N. Talenskiy in the English-language Moscow journal International Affairs attracted particular attention. It openly stated that to think "it is possible to achieve political aims by using nuclear weapons, and at the same time survive" was a "dangerous illusion."[47] Talenskiy's article was attacked in numerous Soviet journals; perhaps the most direct rebuttal was by Col. Ye.I. Rybkin. No additional formulation about nuclear weapons such as Talenskiy had used was to be found in the Soviet press for many years.

Roman Kolkowicz, another RAND analyst, perceived a struggle extending throughout the Soviet Union and Eastern Europe between "hawks and doves."[48] He identified Rybkin as an archetype of the military "hardliner." Kolkowicz portrayed such "hawks" as determined to reverse what he considered to be the Communist Party's rejection of nuclear war as a political weapon. He noted that there was no discernable Soviet reaction to Rybkin's views.[49] However, he saw as an effective rebuttal an article published about the same time in a Polish journal.[50] This article, by a Polish professor of sociology, maintained that Western political objectives could not be achieved even through nuclear war. Kolkowicz's interpretation of a factional debate between Soviet "hawks and doves" was to become an enduring feature of many other U.S. interpretations of Soviet strategic literature.

In his next major work, The Soviet Military and the Communist Party, Kolkowicz expanded upon his view of the Soviet military as an institution with separate interests from the Party and some hostility to it. The Party leadership was aware of the military's detachment, but was not strong enough to coerce it directly. Kolkowicz evaluated Soviet Party-military relations in the ten years (1953-1963) covered by his study as far from stable, including occasional open military opposition and characterized by dialogue between two conflicting "powerful institutional bureaucracies."[51]

These works by Kolkowicz indicate how greatly RAND analysis of Soviet strategic literature had changed since the mid-1950s, when it concentrated on reporting the content of Soviet strategic literature. By contrast, since Wolfe's initial essay describing Sokolovskiy's Military Strategy, RAND publications had become involved in ever-broader efforts to discern the issues and personalities involved in Soviet factional debate over nuclear issues.

This shift was followed by the dispersal of most of RAND's analysts of Soviet nuclear weapons policy, with Thomas Wolfe remaining as the only staff analyst involved in studying Soviet strategic literature. This breakup was the result of two related changes. Secretary of Defense Robert McNamara's procurement reforms led to RAND's research agenda being set by customer demand rather than staff interest. This change came just as the Vietnam War began to absorb the U.S. government's attention and financial resources.

As a result, for the next five years RAND publications on the subject were exclusively by Thomas Wolfe. His RAND studies during this period were summarized in his next book, Soviet Strategy and Europe.[52] In it, he noted the appearance in this literature of the possibility of a conventional phase even in a general war. This he ascribed to the greater influence of "traditionalists," but he felt that, on the whole, the "centrists" had managed to maintain their position.

Wolfe's continuing presence at RAND and his prolific publications may account in part for the endurance of his interpretation of an intramilitary factional debate among "modernists" and "traditionalists." It was adopted by a large number of secondary interpreters of Soviet strategic literature and nuclear weapons policy. For example, the CIA-edited Penkovsky Papers incorporated Wolfe's interpretation into the lengthy unattributed commentary.[53] The author(s) of this commentary informed the reader that Col. Oleg Penkovskiy, an officer on the Soviet General Staff arrested for spying for the West, had delivered reports which confirmed Wolfe's thesis of a "modernist-traditionalist" debate within the Soviet military. However, examination of the statements on the Soviet military specifically attributed to Penkovskiy reveals nothing of this sort.

The attraction of interpretations of factional debate can be seen in the burgeoning arms control literature of the mid- and late 1960s. When discussing Soviet nuclear weapons policy, such works generally assumed that it was indeed subject to intense factional debate, and frequently cited Wolfe's work as a primary source of evidence for this assumption.[54]

Popular assessments of the Soviet military also tended to be cast in terms of debates or factionalism between hawks and doves.[55] Many of these articles viewed the Soviet Union as a mirror-image of the United States, and brought in many references and analogies to U.S. institutions and procedures.[56] In short, the mid-1960s saw a gradual diffusion of interpretations of debate as various commentators mirror-imaged Soviet debates paralleling those in the United States over defense, arms control, and detente. Articles appeared which assessed the Soviet view on such issues as nuclear deterrence without reference to a single Soviet military journal.[57]

The prevalence of interpretations of debate was enhanced by the absence of serious works challenging its explanation of Soviet military literature. A partial exception is provided by a lengthy article by Stefan Possony, which was entirely devoted to challenging Thomas Wolfe's contention that the Soviet Union was moving away from the use of force as an instrument of policy. Possony did not attempt to dispute that a debate between "modernists" and "traditionalists" was taking place over the issues Wolfe had described. Instead, he objected to Wolfe's writings on methodological grounds, and for his failure to reconcile his findings on Soviet nuclear strategy with Soviet global strategy as a whole. In Possony's judgement, Wolfe's conclusions did not reflect the importance of ideology as a cohesive force both for the Soviet military and for all of Soviet society.[58]

The first direct public challenge to the prevalent interpretations of factional debate was written in 1966 by a still anonymous French Defense Ministry official, identified only as XXX.[59] In this article he bluntly asserts that Soviet military writings provided an accurate picture of Soviet nuclear weapons policy, and that Soviet Ground Forces had been reconfigured to fight in a nuclear environment. He went on to charge that Western views discounting the Soviet doctrine of nuclear warfighting were based upon "very subjective interpretations" of variations between official Soviet statements. This essay was translated and reprinted in Military Review, the journal of the U.S. Army Command and Staff College.

It convinced William and Harriet Scott that they should make public the results of their own research on Soviet military policy. They had become interested in the topic in 1962, when Col. Scott began a two year tour as Air Attache in Moscow. The appearance of the XXX article encouraged Harriet Fast Scott to begin two ambitious projects. The first was the preparation of an anthology of articles from Soviet military journals to show the continuity of Soviet military thought on nuclear weapons from the Khrushchev period through the mid-1960s.[60] Her second project was the preparation of a new translation of Sokolovskiy's Military Strategy, containing not only the text of the first edition, but highlighted and bracketed entries where additions and omissions had been made in the second (1963) and third (1968) editions. In essence, it is a translation of all three editions. The Scotts had little success in rousing official or academic interest in Sokolovskiy's book, and it was not published.

In short, the few efforts made during the 1960s to challenge the prevailing interpretions of Soviet factional debate over nuclear weapons policy had little effect. The overwhelming majority of Soviet foreign policy specialists accepted the contention that the Soviet Union was progressing towards a view of nuclear weapons that recognized their unusability except as a strategic deterrent.[61]

The massive Soviet buildup in strategic capability which began to make itself evident in 1965 did not alter this view of the Soviet Union's nuclear weapons policy. It was explained as the result of the Soviet Union's desire for strategic parity, and hence, as a positive development. Carl Kaysen, former assistant for strategic nuclear policy on McGeorge Bundy's National Security Council, went so far as to urge resistance to misguided attempts by Americans to maintain U.S. strategic superiority.[62] This would merely fuel what Robert McNamara termed the "mad momentum" of the strategic arms race, and would upset stability.[63]

Behind these patterns of thinking was a strong emotional and intellectual commitment to McNamara's policy of Mutual Assured Destruction. Adherents of MAD did not react strongly to indications that Soviet military and political figures were making statements inconsistent with the theory. They attributed this to internal Soviet debates, since they saw in the Soviet Union the same struggles as were occurring between the Office of the Secretary of Defense and such military holdouts as the Strategic Air Command (SAC). These adherents believed it did not much matter what Soviet military writings actually said. "MAD imperatives" -- the inescapable fact of mutual deterrence -- would govern Soviet policy regardless of doctrine.

REACTIONS TO ARMS CONTROL, DETENTE, AND PARITY: 1973 TO 1976

A growing portion of the strategic community began to examine and challenge the premises behind MAD in the early 1970s. In particular, the rapid quantitative and qualitative buildup of Soviet nuclear forces was difficult to reconcile with the often-expressed view that the Soviet Union was coming to accept MAD. One premise this policy was founded upon was that Soviet nuclear weapons policy was the provisional product of factional debate. Hence, Soviet strategic literature was not to be taken seriously when it discussed the possible use of nuclear weapons in tactical and strategic combat, since this would change as the debate progressed. After the signing of the SALT I treaty, a small but growing number of analysts examining Soviet nuclear weapons policy had become convinced that Soviet writings on the subject were not the product of a debate, but instead represented a consensus of the military and the Party.

The University of Miami's Center for Advanced International Studies (CAIS) produced some of the first public examinations of the premises of MAD. Most of the CAIS studies produced during the early 1970s were similar in format, relying heavily on published Soviet materials, and quoting them extensively. For example, over half of the 1973 study Soviet Strategy for the Seventies consisted of excerpts from Soviet publications and speeches by Soviet leaders.[64] A later work from CAIS, The Role of Nuclear Forces in Soviet Strategy, was its first to address central strategic issues.[65] It presented them simply as evidence of the lack of compatibility in U.S. and Soviet views, and hence of the unrealistic nature of U.S. detente policy. With its publication of Leon Goure's War Survival in Soviet Strategy, CAIS finally addressed the issue of Soviet nuclear weapons policy directly. This work was an updating and expansion of Goure's earlier research, and like it, examined the place of civil defense in the overall Soviet nuclear weapons policy.[66]

Publicly available translations of Soviet military literature also began to appear at this time. One prominent example was "The Soviet View," which appeared quarterly beginning with the third issue of Strategic Review (1973). This series consisted of sometimes excerpted book chapters and journal and newspaper articles, which were offered "as examples of official pronouncement important to an appraisal of United States interest."[67] The growing demand for translations of Soviet military works encouraged Harriet Fast Scott to resubmit her translation of the three editions of Sokolovskiy's Military Strategy for publication. In 1975 it finally appeared, and is probably the single Soviet military work most widely cited in the West.[68]

The most widely disseminated source of translations, however, was the Soviet Military Thought Series, produced by the Directorate of Soviet Affairs, Air Force Intelligence Applications Section (AF/INA). The translations series began in 1972, when William Scott, then the U.S. Air Attache in Moscow, submitted to Air Force Intelligence an annotated list of what he felt were the most significant Soviet military works published over the past dozen years. As a trial effort, the first book on Col. Scott's list, Sidorenko's The Offensive, was translated and published by the Government Printing Office.[69] Many non-Russian speaking defense analysts were introduced to Soviet military theory because the Soviet Military Thought Series made this literature available. The explosion of U.S. articles and monographs discussing Soviet nuclear weapons policy over the next decade can be attributed at least partially to this series.

By 1976, many U.S. strategic analysts were rejecting interpretations of factional debate within the Soviet Union over military strategy. To a considerable extent this was due to the appearance of a fairly sizable body of translations of recent Soviet military literature, in addition to a growing impression of unprecedented expansion in Soviet nuclear warfighting capabilities. Important works based on these translations which vigorously asserted the validity of Soviet strategic literature were being published.[70]

Why did this not occur sooner? The Foreign Broadcast Information Service (FBIS) and Joint Publications Research Service (JPRS), both affiliates of the Central Intelligence Agency, were providing translations of Soviet military writings throughout this period. There are a number of reasons why their translations did not have a perceptible effect on the views of analysts dealing with Soviet nuclear weapons policy. One is that translations of Soviet military works were not being made generally available to U.S. strategic analysts. FBIS/JPRS had many audiences to reach, and this task was not a particularly high priority.

But the most important reason for the resurgence in interest among U.S. strategic analysts in Soviet strategic literature was timing. The strategic community, during the 1960s, was mired in concerns over U.S. policy in Southeast Asia. It was interested in arms control and general relaxation of tensions with the Soviet Union, not in finding evidence for Soviet belligerence. Only after these conditions changed did interpretations of Soviet strategic literature, based upon an assessment of Soviet consensus over nuclear weapons policy rather than debate, find an audience. By 1975, the United States had given up in Southeast Asia and was in disarray in many other parts of the world. It had committed itself to a detente and arms control regime based on MAD and convergence, yet the Soviet Union was actively increasing the size and effectiveness of its strategic forces. This triggered greater interest among Americans concerned with defense and foreign policy in examining and challenging fundamental assumptions about the Soviet Union.

THE SALT II DEBATE: 1977 TO 1981

Owing to a number of factors, during the second half of the 1970s many U.S. analysts and commentators began to include Soviet military literature in their assessments of overall Soviet strategic intent. A consensus developed among a wide range of these analysts that this literature presented a valid and authoritative picture of Soviet nuclear weapons policy. They felt that its emphasis on preemptive and combat use of nuclear weapons, rather than assured destruction or mutual deterrence, was an accurate depiction of the views of the entire Soviet political-military hierarchy.

As a result, Soviet military literature was widely used to attack the premises of President Jimmy Carter's strategic and arms control policy. Inevitably, analysts and policymakers supporting the Carter policies often attempted to denigrate the significance of Soviet strategic literature. This debate resulted in a polarization of U.S. interpretations of Soviet strategic intent and of Soviet nuclear weapons policy.

As the American political struggle over detente and arms control intensified in the late 1970s, the number and character of published U.S. interpretations of Soviet strategic literature increased dramatically. In fact, so many articles were produced in the late 1970s which offered interpretations of Soviet nuclear weapons policy that in 1981 no fewer than three anthologies of such works appeared. Soviet Strategy, edited by John Baylis and Gerald Segal, could be termed "dovish," in that the collection was organized around articles that tended to minimize any Soviet nuclear threat and contended that Soviet nuclear weapons policy was based upon notions of mutual deterrence.[71] Col. Graham Vernon's Soviet Perceptions of War and Peace included a number of articles, written primarily by U.S. government analysts, which stressed the continuity and coordinating functions of Soviet doctrine and strategy, while Derek Leebaert's Soviet Military Thinking included works from both perspectives.[72]

Many of the interpretations of Soviet strategic literature produced during the late 1970s continued to be published as reports on analytical research conducted for the purpose of elucidating the nature of the Soviet government, its political-military relations, or its military and arms control policy and programs. But during the SALT II debate many more were produced as polemical works in the U.S. strategic debate, for eventually a reductionist position appeared: any interpretation of Soviet strategic literature which viewed the literature as the product of a Soviet military-political consensus on nuclear weapons policy was popularly perceived as hawkish, anti-detente, and anti-arms control. An interpretation of Soviet strategic literature which rested on a description of Soviet factional debate over this issue was seen as support for U.S. detente policies and for the SALT II treaty. Another factor aiding this process was a steady increase in Soviet strategic and conventional force strength and capabilities throughout the 1970s. This forced a shift in U.S. government understanding and concern, and gave a stronger voice to those arguing against U.S. arms control and detente policies based upon the assumption that the Soviet Union was interested in promoting strategic stability.

In the late 1970s non-polemical works on Soviet strategic literature were produced by members of a much wider spectrum of defense analysts. Because of the translation program initiated by the U.S. Air Force in 1973, fluency in Russian was no longer essential to gain access to a sizable body of Soviet strategic literature. One of the first researchers to take advantage of this new access was Joseph Douglass, an engineer who had been involved in studies on tactical and theater nuclear issues in Europe. As he became aware of Soviet strategic literature, he turned to it "to identify the purposes behind the Soviet threat to NATO, the basic fundamental provisions of their military doctrine, and any changes that appear to be taking place."[73]

Douglass drew nine general conclusions from his study of Soviet unclassified military literature. He cautioned that "considerable care must be exercised in transitioning from general conclusions...to any specific situational analysis."[74] His fundamental finding was that preemption was the key to all Soviet military writing on nuclear weapons.[75] Douglass continued his research in translated Soviet military literature, and later that year discovered a large number of recently-declassified translations of Voyennaya mysl' dating from 1963 to 1969. Using this material as well as other translations that had recently appeared, he reviewed his earlier conclusions, and published an article which emphasized an additional major point: that in the European theater, Soviet nuclear weapons policy was probably oriented toward selected targeting and damage limiting, with the objective of seizing Western Europe largely intact.[76] This conclusion, he noted, contrasted strongly with what he felt was the dominant image of such massive destruction occurring in a nuclear war in Europe that the Soviet Union would be "self-deterred" from launching an attack.[77]

As a result of the SALT II debate, Douglass was led to expand his analysis to study Soviet thoughts and concepts of global nuclear war, and to contrast this with the premises behind U.S. arms control policy. In his co-authored study Soviet Strategy for Nuclear War, he concluded that "the goal of Soviet military strategy is to identify what is required in terms of organization, tactics, and systems to fight and win a nuclear war, beginning with world nuclear war, and to effect these requirements."[78] Furthermore, he could not identify any opposition to this mind-set in Soviet military literature.[79]

For the most part, Douglass' analysis presented Soviet military doctrine and strategy as it had been expressed in Soviet military writings since the early 1960s. On one important point, however, Douglass took his conclusions beyond what was stated in Soviet military literature, his original limiting parameter, and relied instead upon capability analysis. He expressed his support of the growing U.S. conviction that Soviet nuclear weapons policy emphasized preventive war, as well as preemption and retaliation.[80] Douglass has been faulted for not justifying his use of Soviet military literature from 1962 onward in any of these published assessments with insufficient regard to time sequence.[81] By not addressing this point, Douglass left himself open to the charge that he was using obsolete literature in order to extract more dramatic statements.[82]

Other authors also stressed a Soviet military and political consensus over doctrine and strategy. In 1976, Leon Goure published a monograph on Soviet civil defense, following up on his earlier work at RAND.[83] This publication examined the implications of the asymmetry in nuclear weapons policy between the United States and the Soviet Union, as typified by the disparities between their civil defense programs. Its conclusions on the extent and effectiveness of Soviet civil defense were widely circulated by the growing opposition to SALT and to Carter's reductions in the U.S. strategic program. Goure's article was subjected to rebuttals by political activists not specialists in the subject, who were interested in minimizing the effect it would have on the U.S. political debate.[84]

Other notable works from the late 1970s which emphasize the Soviet consensus over nuclear weapons policy as an analytical premise include Harriet and William Scott's The Armed Forces of the USSR, which has gone through three editions to become a standard reference work on the Soviet armed forces.[85] Another significant work was Richard Soll's article on Soviet planning for protracted nuclear war.[86] It drew heavily from Soviet military literature of the late 1960s and early 1970s in assessing the Soviet Union's concepts and planning for the events which might occur after the initial period of a nuclear war.

Benjamin Lambeth, at the RAND Corporation, also produced numerous articles during the late 1970s that addressed the issue of Soviet nuclear weapons policy. During the early 1970s he felt that SALT I "symbolized the formal acceptance by both [the United States and the Soviet Union]...of the desirability of a stable mutual deterrence relationship."[87] However, by 1975 his views shifted, and he began to voice concern about the consequences of what he now saw as a Soviet doctrine of massive nuclear preemption.[88] Lambeth spelled out his views fully in a 1978 RAND paper, How to Think About Soviet Military Doctrine.[89] In this work he divided American views on the significance of Soviet doctrine into two opposing groups: those who accepted the validity of Soviet military literature as a guide to Soviet nuclear weapons policy; and those who rejected it as a military wish-list for budgetary infighting that did not reflect the real views of the Politburo, who at bottom accepted mutual deterrence as the only solution to the East-West nuclear dilemma. Lambeth added that he "tended to treat the former view more sympathetically than the latter."[90] Throughout the remainder of this period, Lambeth addressed Soviet nuclear issues from this viewpoint.[91]

Other U.S. interpreters of Soviet strategic literature continued to have doubts about any Soviet political-military consensus over nuclear weapons policy. Chief among these were analysts applying bureaucratic politics or group politics models to Soviet behavior. Michael Deane (1977) and Timothy Colton (1979), for example, each investigated Party-military relations, and especially the role of the Main Political Administration (MPA), which is responsible for the political oversight of the Soviet Armed Forces.[92] Both concluded that the professional military had an independent voice in Soviet decision-making, and that it was often in conflict with the Party line, even when it is set at the highest levels. They both concluded that the MPA was also an independent actor, often even more "hard-line" than the professional military, and certainly not subservient to the Party.

Edward Warner, an Air Force officer assigned to the RAND Corporation, undertook a more ambitious project -- he subjected the entire Soviet military establishment to a study that in part used interest group politics models, but rested fundamentally on "assumptions and insights developed in the study of American foreign and security policy by the 'bureaucratic politics school'."[93] He judged the results of this exercise to be highly productive, despite certain shortcomings, in identifying "a series of basic viewpoints and policy preferences that are regularly expressed by members of the Ministry of Defense and appear to be actively promoted and defended by its leadership and major spokesmen."[94]

Other analysts were less optimistic about the value of such models in analyzing Soviet factional debate. Karl Spielman (1978), for example, proposed that three models be simultaneously used in evaluating Soviet military decision-making: the "strategic [rational] actor" and the "pluralistic" [bureaucratic and interest group] models, as well as a third he termed the "national leadership decision-making" model.[95] This last seems an effort to interject an element of centralized authority and national consensus into modeling techniques that otherwise rely solely on factionalism and bargaining.

Jack Snyder, a RAND analyst, agreed with the interest group and bureaucratic politics modelers that Soviet strategic literature could not be a serious expression of a general Soviet consensus on nuclear weapons policy. Snyder was even less hopeful than Spielman that Western behavioralist social science models could be successfully applied to the Soviet Union, and listed these approaches under the heading of "mirror-imaging."[96] As an alternative, he put forth the concept of a Soviet "strategic culture," which he defined as the "sum total of ideas, conditioned emotional responses, and patterns of habitual behavior that members of a national strategic community have acquired through instruction or imitation and share with each other in regard to nuclear strategy."[97] While the strategic culture provided consensus on many points, it nevertheless was made up of a number of strategic subcultures, each with "reasonably distinct beliefs and attitudes on strategic issues, with a distinct and historically traceable analytical tradition, with characteristic institutional associations, and with more or less distinct patterns of socialization to the norms of the subculture."[98] In short, strategic culture explained those elements of consensus in Soviet nuclear weapons policy, and strategic subculture provided for the factional debates.

Another set of interpretations of Soviet strategic weapons policy was produced by analysts who saw Soviet participation in both the arms control process and a major military expansion as confirmation of a major factional debate. For example, Samuel Payne felt that Soviet military opposition to and foreign affairs specialists' support of arms control was deliberately exploited by the top leadership.[99] Payne termed the supporters of strategic arms limitation "arms controllers," and the opponents "militarists."

Thomas Wolfe also contributed a lengthy work on Soviet motivations for arms control.[100] Like Payne, he identified the leading element of the "arms controllers" as members of the social science institutes of the Soviet Academy of Sciences, opposed by "military theorists" and "military spokesmen" operating "under the aegis of the MPA."[101] But Wolfe did not feel himself able to give a conclusive answer as to which faction had the greater influence on the Soviet political leadership or on Soviet nuclear weapons policy.

A number of points arise from this examination of the more prominent U.S. interpretations of Soviet strategic literature produced during the late 1970s. The first is the vastly greater number of publications that interpret the significance and validity of Soviet strategic literature. The second is the intensifying split between interpretations of debate and of consensus. Finally, there is a self-conscious air to the more analytical interpretations. Although they were produced with the intent of conducting objective scholarship, their authors could not help but be aware that they were also taking sides in a much broader and divisive U.S. political debate.

Fritz Ermarth, of the RAND Corporation, expressed this point in an article in which he spelled out three consequences of the U.S. failure to develop a unified and realistic view of Soviet doctrine.[102] The first he termed "the hawk's lament": by underestimating the competitiveness of Soviet strategic policy and its very different character from U.S. views, the United States has failed to respond adequately. This was shown both in U.S. SALT behavior under the Nixon, Ford, and Carter Administrations, and in the strategic force programs they initiated and terminated. The second consequence he termed "the dove's lament" -- by projecting its own views onto the Soviet Union and overselling the value of SALT and detente, the United States has set itself up for "profound, perhaps even hysterical, disillusionment in the years ahead" in regards to relations with the Soviet Union. The third consequence was excessive confidence in strategic stability, in which U.S. strategic behavior has actually "helped to ease the Soviet Union onto a course of more assertive international action."[103] This could lead to situations that would actually increase the operational value of preemption.

Some authors produced interpretations of Soviet strategic literature with the specific intention of influencing the U.S. political debate. This process intensified with an article published by Richard Pipes, "Why the Soviet Union Thinks It Can Fight and Win a Nuclear War" (1977).[104] Pipes was a professor of Russian history at Harvard who had been the chairman of the so-called B-Team just prior to writing this essay. The B-Team was formed in 1976 to "competitively analyze" the material to be used by the CIA in preparing the forthcoming National Intelligence Estimate on Soviet strategic forces. Its conclusions were in stark contrast to previous NIEs, and not only strongly influenced that year's NIE 11-8-76, but had a strong effect on the manner in which subsequent NIEs were prepared.[105] Therefore it is not surprising that Pipe's article should attract great public attention and controversy. It repeats a key finding of the B-Team -- that the doctrine and strategy that had been portrayed in Soviet military literature over the previous fifteen years represented a consensus of Soviet opinion. Pipes concluded that "there is something innately destablilizing in the very fact that we consider nuclear war unfeasible and suicidal for both, and our chief adversary views it as feasible and winnable for himself."[106]

A number of highly charged articles appeared in various journals in the wake of "Why the Soviet Union Thinks It Can Fight and Win a Nuclear War," which strongly took issue with its propositions. An example of the emotion it raised is provided by a mystifying article by Robert Legvold (1979), a Senior Fellow at the Council on Foreign Relations, which set up its own definition of "strategic doctrine." It then stated that since Soviet military doctrine and strategy did not meet all the terms of this definition, the Soviet Union lacked a "strategic doctrine."[107] Dennis Ross (1978) and Robert Arnett (1979) each produced articles that began by identifying American "hawks" who asserted that the Soviet Union was striving for superiority in strategic nuclear weapons and the ability to survive a nuclear war.[108] Both then cited statements from Soviet political leaders and Academy of Sciences staffers that implictly or explicitly contradicted this. As a result, they concluded that the American hawks were unjustified in their suspicions of the Soviet Union. This approach was also taken in Dubious Specter: A Skeptical Look at the Soviet Nuclear Threat, a monograph by Fred M. Kaplan, a staffer at the Institute for Policy Studies.[109]

In his article "Mutual Deterrence and Strategic Arms Limitation in Soviet Policy," Raymond Garthoff attempted to demonstrate that the Soviet military and political leaderships shared a consensus on the desirability of mutual deterrence.[110] Garthoff then examined what he saw as contradictory views about nuclear warfare in Soviet strategic literature, both military and civilian. He saw a Soviet doctrinal dilemma resulting from the Communist need to assert the inevitable victory of socialism, even were a nuclear war to occur. He felt that Soviet legitimacy would be challenged were this claim dropped.

During the SALT II debate, some proponents of the treaty began to intimate that discussion of a Soviet policy of surviving and winning a nuclear war indicated the author himself wanted the United States to adopt such a policy. Raymond Garthoff appears to have been the first to imply this, in a short article he wrote in 1978.[111] This line of reasoning was repeated even more forcefully by Dmitri Simes: "Those American strategists who originally warned that the Soviets intended to prevail in a nuclear war now argue that it is the United States which should adopt a war-winning strategy."[112]

As the foregoing discussion indicates, the U.S. debate over the correct interpretation of Soviet strategic literature played a minor but energetic part in the larger U.S. debate over the Carter Administration's defense and foreign policy. Interpretations of Soviet strategic literature based on the notion of a consensus between the Soviet military and political leaderships meshed well enough with Soviet behavior and trends in force acquisitions that key members of the Carter Administration began to accept their claims. By contrast, proponents of "debate" interpretations of Soviet strategic literature lost ground even with wide-ranging publications promoting their view.

1981 TO 1986: A RETURN TO PROFESSIONALISM

Western analyses of Soviet nuclear weapons policy began to regain a sense of professionalism after ratification of the SALT II Treaty was removed from the national agenda. This followed the Soviet invasion of Afghanistan and the election of Ronald Reagan as President. As a result, writers and publishers no longer felt a compelling need to assert their overall assessment of Soviet nuclear weapons policy -- whether it was that the Soviet leadership was divided between advocates of MAD and of a nuclear war-winning strategy, or was solidly convinced of one view or the other. Freed from this obsession, Western research on Soviet nuclear weapons policy began to focus on many issues that had not previously been seriously examined.

This trend was reinforced by many developments in the Soviet Union. To begin with, from 1982 to 1985 the Soviet Union had three changes of the top leadership. The latest of these leaders, Mikhail Gorbachev, has vigorously demonstrated his dissatisfaction with the domestic status quo. Whether this has military repercussions has yet to be conclusively demonstrated, although numerous Western analysts are diligently scrutinizing all available sources for evidence. Second, there is some indication from a variety of sources that the Soviet military is reevaluating

its doctrine and strategy, and contemplating internal reorganization. Finally, the post-Brezhnev leadership has accelerated a
"peace campaign" begun in 1977 and directed against Western
public opinion. It includes deletion of the many direct
references to the offensive use of nuclear weapons that once
were common in Soviet military writings. Whether this represents
a real change in Soviet military thinking as well is being hotly
debated in the West.

One important effect of the heightened interest in the
Soviet view of nuclear war in the late 1970s was the later
appearance of two solid retrospectives of the development of
Soviet nuclear weapons policy. The titles of these books show
that they take different stands on the question of the motivating
factor in Soviet nuclear weapons policy. The first, written by
Mark Miller, is entitled Soviet Strategic Power and Doctrine:
The Quest for Superiority.[113] The second, authored by David
Holloway, is entitled The Soviet Union and the Arms Race.[114]
In keeping with their different perspectives, the two books focus
on different motivations for Soviet nuclear weapons policy.
Miller concentrates on elucidating the purposeful growth in
Soviet strategic capability both from analyses of the patterns of
Soviet strategic force development and from close attention to
Soviet military literature. By contrast, Holloway primarily
examines the technological impulse behind Soviet force develop-
ment, both in terms of the need to respond to U.S. initiatives
and to exploit new technical capabilities. Neither Holloway nor
Miller neglects the issues covered more extensively by the other.
In addition to these comprehensive works, which extend from the
beginnings of the Soviet atomic program to the early 1980s,
articles by Raymond Garthoff, Mark Evangelista, and William
Green provide retrospectives on the early post-war Soviet
attitude to atomic weapons.[115]

Other analysts, still strongly influenced by the SALT
II-motivated politization of the question of the Soviet attitudes to
nuclear deterrence and warfighting, resolved to settle the issue
without direct reference to current U.S. policy. The journal
Strategic Review even sponsored a formal debate on the issue
between Richard Pipes and Raymond Garthoff, based on
Garthoff's 1978 article in International Security.[116] This
spurred several additional articles on the same topic by authors
anxious to add their voices to the controversy.[117] Some
additional works of this sort were produced by John Erickson;
Roman Kolkowicz; James McConnell, of the Center for Naval
Analyses; and John Dziak, of the Defense Intelligence
Agency.[118]

Another issue which analysts began to address in the
1980s was the question of how the Soviet Union viewed U.S.
strategic forces and capabilities. The most comprehensive treatment of this subject was Jonathan Lockwood's The Soviet View of
U.S. Deterrence.[119] His short book addresses the issue in a

straightforward chronological fashion. Each chapter is divided into four parts, including a brief summary of U.S. strategic policy during a given period, the Soviet propaganda line in response, the real Soviet view, and conclusions. Soviet reactions to specific U.S. policies have also been gauged by William F. Scott and Harriet Fast Scott, Jeffrey Richelson, and Leon Goure.[120] Soviet strategic defense has also been closely examined from this perspective, as a result of the U.S. Strategic Defense Initiative. Daniel Goure, Sayre Stevens, and Stephen Meyer have each contributed important preliminary views on this subject.[121]

The changing Soviet political environment and its possible effects on Soviet nuclear weapons policy are the subject of numerous works. The most in-depth of these is by Robbin Laird and Dale Herspring, The Soviet Union and Strategic Arms (1984).[122] They argue that the Soviet leadership believes the strategic relationship with the United States is based on the reality of MAD, that they have attempted to build a military force that can defeat the United States in conventional combat, and that strategic parity is the cornerstone of their military and diplomatic competition with the United States. This view is developed further in works by William Odom, Dale Herspring, and Mary FitzGerald, in connection with the dismissal of Marshal Nikolay Ogarkov from his position as Soviet Chief-of-Staff.[123] James McConnell has gone so far as to argue that the entire fabric of Soviet military doctrine is now obsolete and under revision.[124]

The question of the role of nuclear weapons in Soviet tactics and operational art is currently the subject of strong contention. Some British analysts have maintained at least since the early 1980s that Soviet planners had discarded the nuclear option in their scenarios of even the most heated NATO-Warsaw Pact conflict.[125] While not taking the matter to this extreme, John Hines and Phillip Petersen produced an influential article in 1984 concurring that the Soviet Union was now emphasizing conventional operations in its planning, even for major conflicts, while Steven Cimbala cautioned that there was an enduring nuclear dimension to the problem of conflict in Europe.[126] Michael Deane headed a collaborative study of the reorganization of Soviet military commands in the European Theater that had important implications for this subject.[127]

This brief inventory of recent research into questions of Soviet nuclear weapons policy amply demonstrates the breadth of interest currently being displayed in this field of inquiry. When compared to the moribund state of the field in the 1960s, or its obsession with the single issue of deterrence versus warfighting in the 1970s, the opportunities for impartial and conscientious research seem bright. However, the impact of research upon policy is now painfully clear to most analysts of Soviet nuclear weapons policy. The dangers of political biases once again capturing or dividing the field are still very real.

CONCLUSIONS

In this examination of the chronological development of Western study of Soviet nuclear weapons policy, the issues, themes, and debates that have characterized it are traced into the present. As a result, the user of this research guide should have an appreciation for the premises underlying the publications of which it gives abstracts. This is important, for the abstracts represent the views of the authors rather than the compiler, and indeed in some cases were prepared by the authors.

The most important issues deserve to be summarized. They include the question of whether Soviet nuclear weapons policy evolved to an acceptance of mutual deterrence or in a doctrinal revolution began to emphasize preemption as a means to victory in nuclear war; whether the Soviet military has a consensus over nuclear weapons policy and if this consensus or division is shared by the political leadership; the role of ideology in Soviet strategic decision-making; and the balance between nuclear and conventional emphasis in Soviet planning for tactical and theater conflict. Finally, one last point remains to be reiterated: the implications of the various interpretations of Soviet nuclear weapons policy are highly charged politically. The reader must always be alert to determine whose interests are being served by the conclusions of even the most copiously annotated and scholarly study.

NOTES TO CHAPTER ONE

1. Raymond L. Garthoff, Soviet Military Doctrine. Glenscoe,
    Ill.: The Free Press, 1953.

2. Ibid., pp. 174-177.

3. Other authors writing at the time on the Soviet military,
    such as Lee, Ely, or Guillaume, did not do even this much
    (See Asher Lee, The Soviet Air Force. New York: Harper
    and Brothers, 1950; L.B. Ely, The Red Army Today.
    Harrisburg, Penn.: Military Services Publishing Company,
    1949; A. Guillaume, Soviet Arms and Soviet Power. Washing-
    ton, D.C.: Infantry Journal Press, 1949). Even in an
    article with the title "The Red Army in Atomic Warfare,"
    Armor Vol. 62 No. 2 (March-April 1953), pp. 24-27, Ely
    contented himself with speculation on when the Soviet Union
    would acquire various nuclear capabilities, without addressing
    how it would be likely to employ them.

4. Raymond L. Garthoff, Soviet Strategy in the Nuclear Age.
    New York: Frederick A. Praeger, Publisher, 1958, p. 156.

5. Herbert S. Dinerstein, War and the Soviet Union. New
    York: Frederick A. Praeger, Publisher, 1959, p. 9.

6. Henry Kissinger, Nuclear Weapons and Foreign Policy. New
    York: Harper and Brothers, 1957, pp. 364-365.

7. Thomas W. Wolfe, Soviet Power and Europe: 1945-1970.
    Baltimore, Md.: Johns Hopkins Press, 1970, pp. 37-38;
    Harriet Fast Scott and William F. Scott, The Armed Forces of
    the USSR. Boulder, Colo.: Westview Press, 1979, p. 38.

8. William T. Lee and Richard F. Starr, Soviet Military Policies
    After World War II. Stanford, Calif.: The Hoover Institution
    Press, 1986.

9. J. Malcolm Mackintosh, Strategy and Tactics of Soviet For-
    eign Policy. London: Oxford University Press, 1962, pp.
    88-104; Stanley Sienkiewicz, "SALT and Soviet Nuclear
    Doctrine," International Security Vol. 2 No. 4 (Spring 1978),
    p. 85; David Holloway, The Soviet Union and the Arms
    Race. New Haven, Conn.: Yale University Press, 1983, p.
    31.

10. Kissinger, op. cit., p. 398.

11. G.C. Reinhardt and William R. Kintner, Atomic Weapons and
    Land Combat. Harrisburg, Penn.: Military Service Publish-
    ing Company, 1953.

12. G.C. Reinhardt, "Atomic Weapons and Warfare," Chapter 37 in B.H. Liddell Hart (Ed.), The Red Army. New York: Harcourt, Brace, and Company, 1956, pp. 420-438.

13. Ibid., p. 427.

14. Kissinger, op. cit., p. 397.

15. Alexander Dallin, "Red Star" on Military Affairs, 1945-52: A Selected, Annotated List of Articles in the Soviet Military Newspaper. Santa Monica, Calif.: The RAND Corporation (RM-1637), February 10, 1956; Raymond L. Garthoff, The Soviet High Command and General Staff. Santa Monica, Calif.: The RAND Corporation (P-684), May 27, 1955; Raymond L. Garthoff, Recent Trends in Soviet Military Policy. Santa Monica, Calif.: The RAND Corporation (P-726), August 30, 1955; Herbert S. Dinerstein, "The Revolution in Soviet Strategic Thinking," Foreign Affairs Vol. 36 No. 2 (January 1958), pp. 241-254; Herbert S. Dinerstein, "The Soviet Employment of Military Strength for Political Purpose," Annals of the American Academy of Political and Social Science Vol. 31 (July 1958), pp. 104-112; M.J. Ruggles and Arnold Kramish, The Soviet Union and the Atom: The Early Years. Santa Monica, Calif.: The RAND Corporation (RM-1711), April 2, 1956; M.J. Ruggles and Arnold Kramish, Soviet Atomic Policy. Santa Monica, Calif.: The RAND Corporation (P-853), May 23, 1956.

16. Garthoff, Soviet Strategy.

17. Raymond L. Garthoff, The Soviet Image of Future War. Washington, D.C.: Public Affairs Press, 1959.

18. Dinerstein, "The Revolution in Soviet Strategic Thinking," Foreign Affairs Vol. 36 No. 2 (January 1958), p. 252.

19. Ibid.

20. Herbert S. Dinerstein, War and the Soviet Union. New York: Frederick A. Praeger, Publisher, 1959.

21. Raymond L. Garthoff, Soviet Strategy in the Nuclear Age (second edition). New York: Frederick A. Praeger, Publisher, 1962.

22. Herbert S. Dinerstein, War and the Soviet Union (second edition). New York: Frederick A. Praeger, Publisher, 1962, pp. xvi-xx.

23. Leon Goure, Civil Defense in the Soviet Union. Berkeley, Calif.: University of California Press, 1962.

24. Ibid., p. 148.

25. V.D. Sokolovskiy (Ed.), Voyennaya strategiya. Moscow: Voyenizdat, 1962.

26. V.D. Sokolovsky (Ed.) (Raymond L. Garthoff, Ed. and Trans.), Military Strategy: Soviet Doctrine and Concepts. New York: Frederick A. Praeger, Publisher, 1963.

27. "Military Strategy in Perspective," ibid.

28. Ibid., p. xx.

29. V.D. Sokolovskii (Ed.) (Herbert S. Dinerstein, Leon Goure, Thomas W. Wolfe, Eds. and Trans.), Soviet Military Strategy. Eagle Cliffs, N.J.: Prentice-Hall, Inc., 1963.

30. Robert D. Crane, Soviet Military Strategy: A Critical Appraisal. Washington, D.C.: Center for Strategic Studies, 1963.

31. Ibid., p. 7, 10.

32. Alexander Dallin (Ed.), The Soviet Union, Arms Control, and Disarmament: A Study of Soviet Attitudes. New York: School of International Relations, Columbia University, 1964, p. 91.

33. David Abshire and Robert D. Crane, "Soviet Strategy in the 1960s: An Analysis of Current Russian Debate over Strategy," Army Vol. 13 (July 1965), pp. 10-12, 84, 86; Harold W. Baldwin, "The View From Red Army Headquarters," New York Times Review of Books, Part VII, June 16, 1963, p. 3; Murray Green, "Soviet Military Strategy," Air Force Magazine Vol. 46 No. 3 (March 1963), pp. 38-42; William Zimmerman, "Sokolovskii and His Critics: A Review," Journal of Conflict Resolution Vol. 8 No. 3 (September 1964), pp. 322-328.

34. Walter D. Jacobs, "Sokolovskiy's Strategy," Military Review Vol. 43 No. 7 (July 1963), pp. 8-12.

35. Walter D. Jacobs, "Straight From the Horsé's Mouth," National Review No. 15, July 30, 1963, p. 69.

36. Leon Goure, Notes on the Second Edition of Marshal V.D. Sokolovskii's "Military Strategy". Santa Monica, Calif.: The RAND Corporation (RM-3972-PR), February 1964.

37. Ibid., p. 5.

38. Thomas W. Wolfe, Soviet Strategy at the Crossroads. Cambridge, Mass.: Harvard University Press, 1964.

39. Ibid., p. 24.

40. Thomas W. Wolfe, "Some New Developments in the Soviet Military Debate," Orbis Vol. 8 No. 3 (Fall 1964), pp. 550-562.

41. Ibid., p. 555.

42. A.J. Olsen, "Soviet Seen Firm in Military Field: But Specialist Predict No Adventurist Moves," New York Times, October 24, 1964, p. 1.

43. Ibid., p. 6; also see Raymond L. Garthoff, "Military Power in Soviet Policy," in John Erickson (Ed.), The Military-Technical Revolution: Its Impact on Strategy and Foreign Policy. New York: Frederick A. Praeger, Publisher, 1966.

44. Hanson W. Baldwin, "Soviet Seen Firm in Military Field: Ideology Said to Suffer," New York Times, October 24, 1964, p. 6; also see Nikolay Galay, "The Soviet Approach to the Modern Military Revolution," in John Erickson, ibid., pp. 20-34.

45. Thomas W. Wolfe, "Impact of Khrushchev's Downfall on Soviet Military Policy and Detente," Appendix to Eleanor L. Dulles and Robert Dixon Crane (Eds.), Detente: Cold War Strategies in Transition. New York: Frederick A. Praeger, Publisher, 1965, p. 290.

46. Arnold Horelick and Myron Rush, Strategic Power and Soviet Foreign Policy. Chicago: University of Chicago Press, 1966.

47. N. Talenskii, "The Late War: Some Reflections," International Affairs No. 5 (May 1965), pp. 12-18.

48. Roman Kolkowicz, The Red "Hawks" on the Rationality of Nuclear War. Santa Monica, Calif.: The RAND Corporation (RM-4899-PR), March 1966.

49. Ye.I. Rybkin, "O sushchnosti mirovoy raketno-yadernoy voyny" (On the Nature of World Nuclear Rocket War), Kommunist vooruzhennykh sil No. 17 (September 1965), pp. 50-56.

50. J.J. Wiatr, "Szanza instnienia" (The Chance of Survival), Politika No. 45 (November 6, 1965).

51. Roman Kolkowicz, The Soviet Military and the Communist Party. Princeton, N.J.: Princeton University Press, 1967, p. 15.

52. Thomas W. Wolfe, Soviet Power and Europe: 1945-1970. Baltimore, Md.: Johns Hopkins Press, 1970.

53. Peter Deriabin (Ed.), The Penkovsky Papers. New York: Doubleday and Company, 1965, pp. 132-138.

54. C.f. Lincoln P. Bloomfield, Walter C. Clemens, and Franklyn Griffiths, Khrushchev and the Arms Race: Soviet Interests in Arms Control and Disarmament, 1954-1964. Cambridge, Mass.: The MIT Press, 1966; Roman Kolkowicz, Matthew P. Gallagher, and Benjamin S. Lambeth, The Soviet Union and Arms Control: A Superpower Dilemma. Baltimore, Md.: Johns Hopkins Press, 1970.

55. C.f. Bernard Gwertzman, "Russians Debate Nuclear 'Victory'," Washington Evening Star, February 21, 1967, p. 23.

56. C.f. Victor Zorza, "Soviet Armed Forces Renew Fight Against Party Control," Washington Post, January 8, 1969; Joseph Alsop, "Concern Stirred by Seeming Rise of Soviet Military Over Civilians," Washington Post, January 10, 1969, p. A23.

57. C.f. Frederick H. Gareau, "Nuclear Deterrence: The Soviet Position," Orbis Vol. 8 No. 4 (Winter 1965), pp. 922-936.

58. Stefan T. Possony, "U.S. Intelligence at the Crossroads," Orbis Vol. 9 No. 3 (Fall 1965).

59. XXX, "L'Adaptation des Forces Terrestres Sovietiques a une Guerre Nucleaire," Revue de Defense Nationale, February 1966. Reprinted as "The Adaptation of Ground Forces to Nuclear War," Military Review Vol. 46 No. 9 (September 1966).

60. William Kintner and Harriet Fast Scott, The Nuclear Revolution in Soviet Strategy. Norman, Okla.: University of Oklahoma Press, 1968, p. v.

61. C.f. Raymond L. Garthoff, "Military Theory and Practice," in Milorad D. Drachkovitch (Ed.), Fifty Years of Communism in Russia. Pennsylvania State University Press, 1968, pp. 213-243; William Zimmerman, Soviet Perspectives on International Relations, 1956-1967. Princeton, N.J.: Princeton University Press, 1969, pp. 219-241.

62. Carl Kaysen, "Keeping the Strategic Balance," Foreign Affairs Vol. 46 No. 4 (July 1968), pp. 671-674.

63. Robert S. McNamara, Address to Editors and Publishers of United Press International, San Francisco, September 18, 1967, Reprinted in Mark E. Smith and Claude J. Johns, Jr. (Eds.), American Defense Policy (Second edition). Baltimore, Md.: Johns Hopkins Press, 1968, pp. 131-132.

64. Foy D. Kohler, Mose L. Harvey, Leon Goure, and Richard Soll, Soviet Strategy for the Seventies: From Cold War to Peaceful Coexistence. Coral Gables, Fla.: University of Miami Center for Advanced International Studies, 1973.

65. Leon Goure, Foy D. Kohler, and Mose L. Harvey, The Role of Nuclear Forces in Soviet Strategy. Coral Gables, Fla.: University of Miami Center for Advanced International Studies, 1974.

66. Leon Goure, War Survival in Soviet Strategy: USSR Civil Defense. Coral Gables, Fla.: University of Miami Center for Advanced International Studies, 1976.

67. John Erickson, "The Soviet View," Strategic Review Vol. 1 No. 3 (Summer 1973), p. 69.

68. V.D. Sokolovskiy (Ed.) (Harriet Fast Scott, Ed. and Trans.), Soviet Military Strategy. New York: Crane, Russak, Inc., 1975.

69. Sidorenko, The Offensive. Washington, D.C.: Government Printing Office, 1973.

70. C.f. William R. Van Cleave, "Soviet Doctrine and Strategy: A Developing American View," in Lawrence L. Whetten (Ed.), The Future of Soviet Military Power. New York: Crane, Russak, and Co., 1976, pp. 41-71; William F. Scott, "Soviet Military Doctrinal Strategy: Realities and Misunderstandings," Strategic Review Vol. 3 No. 3 (Summer 1975), pp. 57-66; Paul Nitze, "Deterring Our Deterrent," Foreign Policy No. 21 (Winter 1976-1977).

71. John Baylis and Gerald Segal (Eds.), Soviet Strategy. London: Croon Helm, Ltd., 1981.

72. Derek Leebaert (Ed.), Soviet Military Thinking. London: George Allen and Unwin, 1981.

73. Joseph D. Douglass, Jr., The Soviet Theater Nuclear Offensive. Washington, D.C.: Government Printing Office, 1976, p. 2.

74. Ibid., p. 3.

75. Ibid., p. 121.

76. Joseph D. Douglass, Jr., "Soviet Nuclear Strategy in Europe: A Selective Targeting Doctrine?" Strategic Review Vol. 5 No. 4 (Fall 1977), pp. 19-32.

77. Ibid., p. 20.

78. Joseph D. Douglass, Jr., and Amoretta Hoeber, Soviet Strategy for Nuclear War. Stanford, Calif.: Hoover Institution Press, 1979, p. 8.

79. Ibid., p. 5.

80. Ibid., p. 101.

81. Benjamin S. Lambeth, The State of Western Research on Soviet Military Strategy and Policy. Santa Monica, Calif.: The RAND Corporation (R-2230-AF), October 1984, pp. 14-17.

82. C.f. Ibid., p. 16.

83. Goure, Ibid., 1976.

84. See Les Aspin, "Soviet Civil Defense: Myth and Reality," Arms Control Today Vol. 6 No. 9 (September 1976), pp. 1-4; Fred M. Kaplan, "Soviet Civil Defense: Some Myths in the Western Debate," Survival Vol. 20 No. 3 (May-June 1978), pp. 113-120.

85. Scott and Scott, Ibid., 1979.

86. Richard S. Soll, "The Soviet Union and Protracted Nuclear War," Strategic Review Vol. 8 No. 4 (Fall 1980), pp. 15-28.

87. Benjamin S. Lambeth, "The Soviet Strategic Challenge Under SALT I," Current History Vol. 63 No. 374 (October 1972), pp. 150-155.

88. Benjamin S. Lambeth, "The Evolving Soviet Strategic Threat," Current History Vol. 66 No. 410 (October 1975).

89. Benjamin S. Lambeth, How to Think About Soviet Military Doctrine. Santa Monica, Calif.: The RAND Corporation (P-5939), February 1978.

90. Ibid., p. 3.

91. C.f. Benjamin S. Lambeth: "The Political Potential of Soviet Equivalence," International Security Vol. 4 No. 2 (Fall 1979), pp. 22-39; Elements of Soviet Strategic Policy. Santa Monica, Calif.: The RAND Corporation (P-6389), September 1979; Soviet Strategic Conduct and the Prospects for Stability. Santa Monica, Calif.: The RAND Corporation (R-2579-AF), December 1980.

92. Michael Deane, Political Control of the Soviet Armed Forces. New York: Crane, Russak, and Company, 1977; Timothy Colton, Commissars, Commanders, and Civilian Authority. Cambridge, Mass.: Harvard University Press, 1979.

34

93. Edward L. Warner, _The Military in Contemporary Soviet Politics: An Institutional Analysis_. New York: Praeger Publishers, 1977.

94. _Ibid._, p. 268.

95. Karl F. Spielman, _Analyzing Soviet Strategic Arms Decisions_. Boulder, Colo.: Westview Press, 1978.

96. Jack Snyder, _Soviet Strategic Culture: Implications for LNOs_. Santa Monica, Calif.: The RAND Corporation (R-2154-AF), September 1977, p. 5.

97. _Ibid._, p. 8.

98. _Ibid._, p. 10.

99. Samuel Payne, _The Soviet Union and SALT_. Cambridge, Mass.: The MIT Press, 1980, pp. 8-9.

100. Thomas W. Wolfe, _The SALT Experience_. Cambridge, Mass.: Ballinger Publishing Company, 1979.

101. _Ibid._, pp. 166-167.

102. Fritz W. Ermath, "Contrasts in American and Soviet Strategic Thought," _International Security_ Vol. 3 No. 2 (Fall 1978), pp. 138-155.

103. _Ibid._, p. 154.

104. Richard Pipes, "Why the Soviet Union Thinks It Can Fight and Win a Nuclear War," _Commentary_ Vol. 64 No. 1 (July 1977), pp. 21-34.

105. D. Binder, "New CIA Estimate Finds Soviet Seeks Superiority in Arms," _New York Times_, December 26, 1976, p. 1.

106. Pipes, _op. cit._, p. 31.

107. Robert Legvold, "Strategic 'Doctrine' and SALT: Soviet and American Views," _Survival_ Vol. 21 No. 1 (January-February 1979), pp. 8-13.

108. Robert Arnett, "Soviet Attitudes Toward Nuclear War: Do They Really Think They Can Win?", _Journal of Strategic Studies_ Vol. 2 No. 2 (September 1979), pp. 172-191; and Dennis Ross, "Rethinking Soviet Strategic Policy: Imputs and Implications," _Journal of Strategic Studies_ Vol. 1 No. 1 (May 1978), pp. 3-30.

35

109. Fred M. Kaplan, <u>Dubious Specter: A Skeptical Look at the Soviet Nuclear Threat</u>. Washington, D.C.: Institute for Policy Studies, 1980.

110. Raymond L. Garthoff, "Mutual Deterrence and Strategic Arms Limitation in Soviet Policy," <u>International Security</u> Vol. 3 No. 1 (Summer 1978), pp. 112-147.

111. Raymond L. Garthoff, "On Estimating and Imputing Intentions," <u>International Security</u> Vol. 2 No. 2 (Winter 1978), pp. 28-29.

112. Dmitri Simes, "Deterrence and Coercion in Soviet Policy," <u>International Security</u> Vol. 5 No. 3 (Winter 1980/81), p. 80.

113. Mark E. Miller, <u>Soviet Strategic Power and Doctrine: The Quest for Superiority</u>. Washington, D.C.: Advanced International Studies Institute, 1982.

114. David Holloway, <u>The Soviet Union and the Arms Race</u>. New Haven, Conn.: Yale Unversity Press, 1983.

115. Raymond L. Garthoff, "The Death of Stalin and the Birth of Mutual Deterrence," <u>Survey</u> Vol. 25 No. 2 (Spring 1980), pp. 10-16; Matthew A. Evangelista, "Stalin's Postwar Army Reappraised," <u>International Security</u> Vol. 7 No. 3 (Winter 1982-83), pp. 110-138; William C. Green, "The Early Formulation of Soviet Strategic Nuclear Doctrine," <u>Comparative Strategy</u> Vol. 4 No. 4 (1984), pp. 369-386.

116. "A Garthoff-Pipes Debate on Soviet Strategic Doctrine," <u>Strategic Review</u> Vol. 10 No. 4 (Fall 1982), pp. 36-63. The original article was Garthoff's "Mutual Deterrence and Strategic Arms Limitations in Soviet Policy," <u>International Security</u> Vol. 2 No. 1 (Summer 1978), pp. 112-147.

117. Albert L. Weeks, "The Garthoff-Pipes Debate on Soviet Doctrine: Another Perspective," <u>Strategic Review</u> Vol. 11 No. 1 (Winter 1983), pp. 57-64; Gerhard Wettig, "The Garthoff-Pipes Debate on Soviet Strategic Doctrine: A European Perspective," <u>Strategic Review</u> Vol. 11 No. 2 (Spring 1983), pp. 68-78.

118. John Erickson, "The Soviet View of Deterrence: A General Survey," <u>Survival</u> Vol. 24 No. 6 (November-December 1982), pp. 242-251; Roman Kolkowicz, "U.S. and Soviet Approaches to Military Strategy: Theory vs. Experience," <u>Orbis</u> Vol. 25 No. 2 (Summer 1981), pp. 307-330; James M. McConnell, <u>Soviet and American Strategic Doctrine: One More Time</u>. Alexandria, Va.: Center for Naval Analyses (PP-271), January 1980; John

Dziak, Soviet Perceptions of Military Power: The Inter-action of Theory and Practice. New York: Crane, Rus-sak and Co., 1981.

119. Jonathan S. Lockwood, The Soviet View of U.S. Strategic Doctrine: Implications for Decision-Making. New Bruns-wick, N.J.: Transaction Books, 1983.

120. William F. Scott and Harriet Fast Scott, "U.S. Perceptions of U.S. Military Strategies and Forces," Chapter 6 in Graham Vernon (Ed.), Soviet Perceptions of War and Peace. Washington, D.C.: National Defense University Press, 1981, pp. 97-112; Jeffrey T. Richelson, "Soviet Responses to MX," Political Science Quarterly Vol. 96 No. 3 (Fall 1981), pp. 401-410; Leon Goure, "The U.S. 'Countervailing Strategy' in Soviet Perception," Strategic Review Vol. 9 No. 4 (Fall 1981), pp. 51-64.

121. Daniel Goure, "The Strategic Competition and SDI," in Zbigniew Brzezinski et al. (Eds.), Promise or Peril: The Strategic Defense Defense Initiative. Washington, D.C.: Ethics and Public Policy Center, 1986, pp. 227-236; Stephen M. Meyer, "Soviet Strategic Programs and the U.S. SDI," Survival Vol. 27 No. 6 (November-December 1985), pp. 274-292; Sayre Stevens, "The Soviet BMD Program," Chapter 5 in Ashton Carter and David Schwartz (Eds.), Ballistic Missile Defense. Washington, D.C.: The Brookings Institution, 1984, pp. 182-220.

122. Robbin F. Laird and Dale R. Herspring, The Soviet Union and Strategic Arms. Boulder, Colo.: Westview Press, 1984.

123. William E. Odom, "Soviet Force Posture: Dilemmas and Directions," Problems of Communism Vol. 34 No. 4 (July/August 1985), pp. 1-14; Dale R. Herspring, "Marshal Akhromeyev and the Future of the Soviet Armed Forces," Survival Vol. 28 No. 6 (November-December 1986), pp. 524-535; Mary C. FitzGerald, "Marshal Ogarkov on the Modern Theater Operation," Naval War College Review Vol. 39 No. 4 (Autumn 1986), pp. 6-25.

124. James M. McConnell, "The Irrelevance Today of Sokolovskiy's Book Military Strategy," Defense Analysis Vol. 1 No. 4 (1985), pp. 243-254.

125. Christopher N. Donnelly, "The 'March' in Soviet Tactical Doctrine," RUSI Journal Vol. 119 No. 3 (September 1974), pp. 77-79; Peter Vigor, The Soviet Blitzkrieg Theory, 1983.

126. John G. Hines and Phillip A. Petersen, "The Soviet Conventional Offensive in Europe," Military Review Vol.

64 No. 4 (April 1984), pp. 2-28; Stephen J. Cimbala, "Soviet 'Blitzkrieg' in Europe: The Abiding Nuclear Dimension," <u>Strategic Review</u> Vol. 14 No. 3 (Summer 1986), pp. 67-76.

127.   Michael Deane et al., "The Soviet Command Structure in Transformation," <u>Strategic Review</u> Vol. 12 No. 2 (Spring 1984), pp. 55-70.

2

Overviews of Soviet
Nuclear Weapons Policy

A. NUCLEAR WEAPONS AND SOVIET POLICY

Soviet Global Policy and Grand Strategy

No. 1. Adomeit, Hannes.
Soviet Risk-Taking and Crisis Behavior: From Confrontation to
Co-existence?
London: International Institute for Strategic Studies (Adelphi
Paper No. 101), Autumn 1973, 40 p.

This work examines two aspects of Soviet behavior under nuclear
parity. The first concerns the purposes and conditions under
which the Soviet leaders are prepared to take risks, and the
second addresses the optimism in some Western quarters that
present East-West relations are fundamentally different from the
short-lived Spirits of Geneva, Camp David, and Glassboro. Part
I considers the theoretical and conceptual aspects of risk and
crisis and classifies specific cases of crisis after the Second
World War. This is followed in Part II by a review of some of
the major propositions and hypotheses about Soviet behavior
advanced in the West and by a review of empirical evidence.
Part III analyzes the relevance of three possible determinants of
Soviet risk-taking and crisis behavior: Soviet ideology; military-
strategic and conventional military factors and the military
doctrine governing their use; and the preferences, priorities,
and constraints of the Soviet domestic system. Finally, in Part
IV the relative weight of these determinants is evaluated and
used in a projection of the future direction of Soviet risk-
taking. Western predictions that superpower status would
require the Soviet Union to undertake risky expansionist adven-
tures have not been fulfilled. But Western policies based on the
conviction of a fundamental transformation of Soviet foreign
policy would increase temptations for the Soviet leader ship to
exploit unstable conditions.

40

Reprinted as Chapter 7 in John Baylis and Gerald Segal (Eds.), Soviet Strategy (Montclair, N.J.: Allanfeld, Osmun and Company, 1981), pp. 185-202.

No. 2. Aspaturian, Vernon V.
"Detente and the Strategic Balance."
Chapter 1 in Michael MccGwire and John McDonnell (Eds.), Soviet Naval Influences: Domestic and Foreign Dimensions. New York: Praeger Publishers, 1977, pp. 3-30.

Since the Vietnam War, U.S. Presidents have been unable either to mobilize the political support needed to sustain a posture of strategic superiority or to inspire sufficient public confidence in the President to enable him to execute policies based upon strategic parity effectively. It must not be assumed that the USSR is similiarly afflicted. While in the U.S. view, parity is a goal that ought to be sought and maintained by both parties, the Soviet concept is that it is up to each side to uphold its end or accept the political consequences that flow from weakness. The Soviet leadership appreciates that U.S. weakness is transitory -- reflecting a confusion of purpose and weakness of will -- and know that a single imprudent seizure of opportunistic advantage could regalvanize American unity of purpose.

No. 3. Aspaturian, Vernon V.
"Soviet Global Power and the Correlation of Forces."
Problems of Communism Vol. 29 No. 3 (May-June 1980), pp. 1-18.

During recent years, the USSR has pursued a global policy that is something less than a "grand design" but something more than a response to targets of opportunity. As part of this policy, it has demanded treatment as an equal of the United States, but it has recognized that in fact, if not in propaganda claims, it has not yet achieved equality. Moscow now fears that its assertiveness since the mid-1970s, and especially the Soviet invasion of Afghanistan, will cause Washington to take advantage of America's superior productive potential to counter the military capabilities that underlie the Soviet claims to equality.

No. 4. Beloff, Max.
"The Military Factor in Soviet Foreign Policy."
Problems of Communism Vol. 30 No. 1 (January-February 1981), pp. 70-73.

This essay-review critically analyses the following: Prospects of Soviet Power in the 1980s, Christoph Bertram (Ed.); Present Danger: Towards a Foreign Policy, Robert Conquest; Zur Aufwerung der Aussenpolitischen Rolle der Sowjetchen Militarmacht (Toward an Assessment of the Foreign Policy Role of Soviet

Military Power), Peer Lange; and Soviet Military Power and Performance, John Erickson and E.J. Feuchtwanger (Eds.). The essay concludes that after an effort spanning almost two decades, the Soviet Union has succeeded in creating a capacity to project its power around the world. Soviet leaders have not failed to exploit this capability in their conduct of Soviet foreign policy. In the 1980s, they will continue to seek the maximum political and economic advantages from the Soviet Union's enhanced position of military strength.

No. 5. Brodie, Bernard.
The Communist Reach for Empire.
Santa Monica, Calif.: The RAND Corporation (P-2916), June 1964, 19 p.

A consideration of the fact that, because of specialized study of the Soviet Union and Communist China which has developed in universities and research institutions like RAND, we have at our disposal a number of realistic formulations by which to direct our dealings with the Communist world. To illustrate, the author surveys some recent scholarly developments and applies them to an analysis of the Cuban crisis and the Sino-Soviet split. He also suggests ways in which U.S. policy might avail itself of this new knowledge.

No. 6. Clark, Donald L.
"Soviet Strategy for the Seventies."
Air University Review Vol. 22 No. 1 (January-February 1971), pp. 3-18.

Although a minority of the Soviet leadership believes that capitalism and communism can co-exist, the majority believes that a more aggressive world-wide strategy will have to be developed in the seventies. The soft line of Dr. Andrei Sakharov contrasts with the hard line of Marshal Nikolai Krylov who believes that war with the West is inevitable and that the Red Army must be prepared to insure victory when it comes. A compromise policy of detente-expansion will provide the USSR with the means of attaining as many goals as possible, considering its present problems. With their detente-expansion strategy, the Soviets should be able to: insure their survivability, avoid nuclear war, maintain their East European community, resolve the China problem, maintain nuclear parity with the United States while extending their economic growth, replace the U.S. presence on their periphery with Soviet influence, and strengthen their international communist leadership. A detente-expansionist strategy precludes a first-strike strategy, which must be prohibitively costly. However, the detente-expansion strategy should accomplish the same results.

42

No. 7. Erickson, John.
"Soviet Military Policy in the 1980s."
Current History Vol. 75 No. 440 (October 1978), pp. 97-99,
135-138.

While generally satisfied with the outcome of SALT I, Soviet
military leaders must be concerned with the strategic nuclear
balance and the course of the SALT II negotiations. Meanwhile,
the Soviet strategic weapons program can count up some impressive achievements, with force structures configured to furnish a
first strike capability or to circumvent the neutralization of
Soviet systems with the advent of the MX ICBM and the Trident
SLBM. The many developments in strategic defense probably do
not provide a "post-attack recovery capability." The Ground
Forces will continue to modernize in spite of a projected demographic slump in the 1980s, while there is visible evidence of
qualitative and quantitative improvement in the Soviet Air Force.
The Soviet Navy can point to the diversification of its effort
toward strategic attack, anti-submarine warfare, and anti-ship
capabilities in the open oceans. A new Eurasian strategy is
emerging, with a certain stability in the West (Europe), consolidation and buildup in the East (vis-a-vis China), and penetration to the South. The Soviet military understands detente as a
means to manage any dangerous collisions that might induce
nuclear war, but the search will continue for the means to "win"
any war at any level of weapons.

No. 8. Ermath, Fritz.
Internationalism, Security, and Legitimacy: The Challenge to
Soviet Interests in East Europe.
Santa Monica, Calif.: The RAND Corporation (RM-5909-PR),
March 1969, 162 p.

An analysis of Soviet policies in Eastern Europe during 1964-68,
which culminated in the invasion of Czechoslovakia. Post-war
Soviet dominance of East Europe has depended on three fundamental values: 1) internationalism -- the system of shared
values and political inducements used to bring East European
socialist states to accept Soviet hegemony; 2) security -- the
preservation of East-West political balance of power; 3)
legitimacy -- the means by which the Communist Party maintains
its monopoly within the states. From 1963 to 1967, Rumania
challenged both internationalism and security by adopting a more
independent foreign policy, and by establishing diplomatic
relations with West Germany. In 1968, Prague's demands for
political liberalization were a recognized threat to all Soviet
interests in Eastern Europe, including the legitimacy of internal
Communist rule, and the Soviets elected to invade Czechoslovakia
to prevent further challenges to their hegemony. However, the
Soviet Union must still face the forces of nationalism, modernization, and liberalism that are acting to change its relationships in
Europe. Future policy must choose between defense of Soviet

hegemony and expanded influence in West Europe. It may well be affected by reform within the political system as the Soviet Union becomes increasingly unable to cope with these forces.

No. 9. "Five Keys to Soviet Strategy: A Special Report." Air Force Magazine Vol. 44 No. 10 (October 1961), pp. 29-32.

Soviet policy at times seems complex. It zigs and zags, blows hot and cold. But the central aim is simple -- total world domination through decisive superiority in nuclear weaponry. Assessments of this aim can be sharpened by examining the broad outlines of present day Communist strategy, as disclosed by the Kremlin conflict-managers themselves: 1) current Kremlin strategy is predicated on a need to wage unceasing warfare on a variety of fronts by an assortment of methods; 2) fanning the current war scare over Berlin is the Soviet Union's way of achieving several time urgent short-range and long-range goals simultaneously; 3) top Soviet priority has been assigned to a new push to win the weapons lead-time race with the United States; 4) while the Kremlin's hard line ostensibly may soften, basic decisions -- already taken -- to accelerate preparations for the final nuclear showdown will not be altered; and 5) hard-headed realism about nuclear weapons is the only effective response the United States may any longer afford. If these indicators are ignored and policies not adopted to render them ineffective, eventual U.S. capitulation will have to be attributed to the unrealistic U.S. complacency.

No. 10. Garrett, Banning N.; and Bonnie S. Glaser. Soviet and Chinese Strategic Perceptions in Peacetime and War. Washington, D.C.: Defense Nuclear Agency (DNA-TR-81-262), October 31, 1982, 190 p.

This report on Soviet and Chinese perceptions of the strategic environment examines Soviet perceptions of the threat posed by China on Sino-American security ties; Chinese perceptions of the Soviet threat and the role of the strategic cooperation with the U.S. and Chinese strategy; and Soviet and Chinese perceptions of the character of war, including protracted nuclear war and post-war recovery. The study also develops a peacetime/wartime framework for evaluating perceptions of the balance of power.

No. 11. Garthoff, Raymond L. "War and Peace in Soviet Policy." Russian Review Vol. 20 No. 2 (April 1961), pp. 121-133.

Soviet global strategy may be summarized as follows: to advance the power of the USSR in whatever ways are most expedient so long as the survival of Soviet power itself is not endangered. Soviet leaders have decided that general war would not be in their interest for the foreseeable future -- "peaceful coexistence" means a vigorous policy of expanding power and influence by means short of general war. Mutual deterrence is not fragile -- the Soviet leaders recognize the risks and consequences of a global nuclear holocaust. The Soviet Union seeks to take advantage of this strategic stalemate to pursue policies to its own advantage. The United States must remain aware of the many facets of the overall Soviet threat so that in countering one aspect of it, it does not ignore or even indirectly facilitate others.

Reprinted in John Erickson et al. (Eds.), The Military-Technical Revolution (New York: Frederick A. Praeger, Publisher, 1966), pp. 239-257.

No. 12.   Garthoff, Raymond L.
Detente and Cooperation.
Washington, D.C.: The Brookings Institution, 1985, 1147 p.

The United States and the Soviet Union are rivals and adversaries, yet in the nuclear age they face the imperitive of coexistence. A detente in relations was reached in 1972, but from 1975 to 1979 this detente gradually eroded until it collapsed in the wake of the Soviet occupation of Afghanistan. Differences in ideology, aims, and interests have been key determinants of both U.S. and Soviet policies. Involvements of the rival powers in Europe, China, and the Third World have further entangled their relations. And each sees the other as harboring hostile intentions and building military and other capabilities to support such aims. This study analyzes the development of U.S.-Soviet relations from 1969 through 1984, taking into account both the broader context of world politics as well as internal political considerations and developments. Nuclear weapons and arms control policies are closely related as a major factor in both areas.

No. 13.   Goldhammer, H.
The Soviet Union in a Period of Strategic Parity.
Santa Monica, Calif.: The RAND Corporation (R-889-PR), October 1971, 78 p.

The high priority objectives of the Soviet Union in the 1970s will be broader integrity, adhesion of East Europe, Party defense, and strength of its armed forces. No consistent pattern of past Soviet behavior emerges; aggressiveness and caution exist together, although the former is preferred. In the 1970s, the Soviet Union will be greatly influenced by its two-front position between the U.S. and Communist China; it will continue a forward policy in the Third World, its naval activity, and the pursuit of strategic parity/superiority; seek economic commitments from the industrial powers; and negotiate over issues

already open, i.e., SALT, European troop reduction, European
security, and Berlin. Over the long term, provided the U.S.
demonstrates the military, political, and moral ability to counter
aggressive moves, the Soviet Union will choose a collaborative
policy. In this case, relations with Communist China, rather
than acquisition of nuclear parity or superiority, will dominate
the Soviet policy in the 1970s.

No. 14. Holloway, David.
"The View from the Kremlin."
Wilson Quarterly Vol. 7 No. 5 (Winter 1983), pp. 102-111.

The Soviet Union has moved from a position of military inferiority to parity with the United States. Contrary to some Western
analyses, the Soviet Union has not built up its armed forces
simply in reaction to moves by the West. Rather, the growth of
Soviet military strength has its roots in historic Russian fears of
militarily superior foreign powers, being with the Mongols. The
Soviet press argues that increasing Soviet strength was what
made detente possible. On the other hand, it has driven the
main adversaries of the Soviet Union together. The failure of
detente has created serious problems for the Soviet Union. The
fact that these troubles are, in large measure, of the Soviet
Union's own making does not make them any easier for the
Kremlin leaders to contemplate.

No. 15. Hsieh, Alice Langley.
The Sino-Soviet Nuclear Dialogue: 1963.
Santa Monica, Calif.: The RAND Corporation (P-2852), January
1964, 40 p.

A close analysis of Chinese and Soviet statements about military
matters affecting the West. Their postures diverge on the
following: war and peace, proliferation of nuclear weapons, and
Soviet military assistance to China. The Chinese, though aware
of nuclear destructiveness, and sensitive to their own military
weakness, are less cautious about war than the Soviet Union.
The Chinese want nuclear weapons; the Soviet Union prefers for
other socialist states to rely on Soviet might. China has decided
to go it alone rather than pay the price of Soviet military assistance. Looking to the future, it is difficult to envisage even a
partial restoration of military cooperation.

No. 16. Jacobsen, Carl G.
"Soviet-American Policy: New Strategic Uncertainties."
Current History Vol. 81 No. 477 (October 1982).

The Reagan Adminstration's arms policies are creating controversy about the U.S.-USSR balance of power. The primary
area of concern is the Artic region, an area the Soviet Union

has extensively researched. By the 1970s, the region was
becoming a part of Soviet home waters. More important to the
balance of power, however, were advances being made in
submarine-launched ballistic missile technology. It seemed that
the United States and Soviet Union had established the equality
implied in the SALT negotiations, and that the Mutual Assured
Destruction concept would be used as a point of departure for
arms control and reduction talks in the 1980s. The U.S. administration, however, claiming the USSR had achieved superiority in
technology and was spending large sums on defense, set out to
regain past U.S. superiority. This was accepted at first, but
critics have begun debating such activities and relations within
NATO have entered a period of crisis.

No. 17. Kupperman, Charles M.
"The Soviet World View."
Policy Review No. 7 (Winter 1979), pp. 45-67.

The Soviet concept of what is "strategic" is much broader and
more dynamic than its U.S. counterpart, and stems from the
Soviet Union's view of the world as a single strategic theater for
the historic clash between capitalism and socialism. There is no
inconsistency for the Soviet Union to follow the policy of
"detente" while engaging in the most massive strategic nuclear
buildup in history. Detente, in their view, was forced upon the
United States by the increase in Soviet power, and will come to
an end if the United States chooses to resist Soviet initiatives.
The most important asymmetry between Soviet and American
strategic doctrine is the Soviet Union's policy to design its
strategic forces to fight and "win" a general nuclear war. Thus
far, detente is working to the advantage of the Soviet Union,
since it has made few if any concessions and secured the West's
acceptance of the Soviet right to expand its sphere of influence
with means that would have been totally unacceptable in the days
of "cold war."

No. 18. Laird, Robbin F.; and Dale R. Herspring.
The Soviet Union and Strategic Arms.
Boulder, Colo.: Westview Press, 1984, 160 p.

This book provides a comprehensive overview of the role of
strategic nuclear weapons in Soviet military and foreign policy,
focusing primarily on an assessment of Soviet policy and perspectives since 1970 -- the period of strategic parity. Three
themes are stressed: first, that the Soviet Union believes the
strategic relationship with the United States is forged around the
reality of mutual assured destruction; second, that although
Soviet leaders have accepted this objective reality, they have
nevertheless attempted to build a military force that could defeat
the United States in war without resorting to strategic nuclear
weapons; and finally, that the Soviet Union considers strategic

parity to be the cornerstone of its military and diplomatic competition with the United States. The book discusses the Soviet
concept of strategic parity in terms of Soviet perceptions of the
American challenge and in terms of their bargaining behavior in
arms control negotiations with the United States, concluding with
an assessment of the future of the strategic arms race.

No. 19. Legvold, Robert.
"The Nature of Soviet Power."
Foreign Affairs Vol. 56 No. 1 (October 1977), pp. 49-71.

International politics are changing -- fewer and fewer of our
problems are caused by the Soviet Union or can be solved by it,
save for the ultimate matter of nuclear war. Yet amidst the
loosening of the old order there is the distracting spectacle of
ever expanding Soviet military power. For many, the next step
is obvious: if intellectually the Soviet leaders acknowledge the
utility of force, and if practically they are dependent on it, then
not surprisingly they appear bent on achieving the largest possible margins of military advantage. Viewed like this, it is no
wonder that the Soviet-American relationship is soon largely
reduced to its military dimension. Were Soviet participation in
detente a tactical expedient, this view might be justifiable. But
detente is a profound and long-term commitment dictated by the
Soviet leaders' three elemental objectives: 1) restraining the
changes the Soviet Union fears and easing those it desires; 2)
sanctifying the Soviet Union's status as a global power coequal
with the United States; and 3) securing the economic and technological benefits of the "international division of labor,"
engaging itself in the interdependent world. A search for new
and untried standards for a restructured Soviet-American
relationship will allow each to trust to the advantages of a
moderated contest.

No. 20. Mackintosh, J. Malcolm.
"Soviet Strategic Policy."
World Today Vol. 25 No. 7 (July 1970), pp. 269-276.

This study of Soviet strategic policy examines Soviet capabilities
and intentions in the military field from knowledge of the Soviet
Union, of Soviet and Russian national tradition, of the importance of Communist ideology, and the impact of the nuclear age.
Soviet strategic policy may be defined as the military aspect of
the measures taken by the Soviet government to deter war, to
deal with the rest of the world from a position of strength as a
super-power, and to win any war if deterrence fails. There are
several main factors to this strategic policy: 1) the size and
geographical position of the USSR; 2) the dual nature of the
Soviet system, which serves both as a national government and
as leader of world Communism; and 3) the impact of nuclear and
missile weapons on warfare. To these factors an economic one

48

can be added: that military spending enjoys a position of great
privilege in the allocation of resources. Soviet strategic policy
can be divided into four component parts: the strategic confrontation with the United States; the European theater, the China
theater, and the peacetime use of military forces to support
overseas policy. It is important to emphasize that the main
priorities in ˙ Soviet strategic policy are deterrence, and the
ability to protect the homeland and wage general war if deterrence fails.

No. 21. Mackintosh, J. Malcolm.
"Russia's Defense: A Question of Quality."
Interplay, February 1971, pp. 14-18.

During the 1970s the Soviet Union will continue to give priority
to the protection and enhancement of its position as one of two
superpowers. It will try to keep its strategic power close to
that of the United States by avoiding another arms race, which
might leave it worse off than it is now, and by concluding a
SALT agreement which would allow both countries to retain
sufficient offensive and defensive weapons for deterrence. No
restrictions of military research and development are likely to be
acceptable to the Soviet government. Futhermore, the Soviet
Union is unlikely to allow Eastern Europe to change its political
status, and it will maintain a military presence there for
defensive as well as potentially offensive purposes. Soviet
defense policy in the 1970s could seek to force Western Europe
to face Soviet military power not only in the East, but also in
the South, based on sea power in the Mediterranean and growing
land and air power in North Africa. The Soviet Union will also
develop realistic military policies to ensure its military superiority over Chinese conventional and nuclear forces, although it
foresees improved relations with China after the departure of
Mao Tse Tung. It will expand the use of its military forces to
support its overseas policy in peacetime, as well as to limit the
options of Western powers in local crises. These policies will not
require any radical reorganization of Russia's forces, but only
qualitative improvements in weapons systems and force management. In sum, the present Soviet leadership is in an expansionist mood; and its current decisions will give Soviet forces at
the end of the decade the hardware to continue Russia's present
superpower policies.

No. 22. Mackintosh, Malcolm.
"The Soviet Military: Influence on Foreign Policy."
Problems of Communism Vol. 22 No. 5 (September-October 1973),
pp. 1-11.

It is the purpose of this article to explore the nature and extent
of the influence of the Soviet military on foreign policy decision-
making. Some basic issues for analysis of this subject include:

1) the difference in the roles of the military in influencing
defense policy on the one hand and foreign policy on the other,
since defense is the military's business while foreign policy is
the military's business only if the Party leadership invites it to
participate; 2) the growth of the Soviet armed forces' capabilities
since the Second World War, which has helped the Soviet Union
into superpower status; and 3) the problem of military access to
the decision-makers -- does access necessarily mean influence?
The case studies examined in this article tend to support the
view that the military establishment favors hardline policies when
issues concerning the defense of the homeland or the Soviet
position in Eastern Europe are at stake. On the other hand,
when a proposed foreign policy may involve the commitment of
Soviet armed forces beyond these areas, the military tends to
react on the side of caution. The present military leaders want
influence over a strong foreign policy, but they do not want the
responsibility of formulating Soviet foreign policy itself.

Reprinted as "The Soviet Military's Influence on Foreign Policy,"
Chapter 2 in Michael MccGwire et al., Soviet Naval Policy: Ob
jectives and Contraints (New York: Praeger Publishers, 1977),
pp. 23-39.

No. 23. McConnell, Robert B.
Conventional Military Force and Soviet Foreign Policy.
Monterey, Calif.: The Naval Postgraduate School, June 1978.

The Soviet Union has, historically, always maintained a large
standing army, primarily for defensive purposes. However,
after World War II and with the advent of nuclear weapons, the
Soviet Armed Forces have undergone tremendous change. This
paper traces the changes in Soviet attitudes towards conventional
military force since World War II, and attempts to illustrate the
role of conventional forces in Soviet foreign policy. Postwar
Soviet military development is traced through four distinct
periods: 1945-1953 was a period in which the Soviet military was
generally a continental land army; 1954-1959 saw the introduction
of nuclear weapons but little or no change in strategy and
doctrine; the period 1960-1967 saw the birth of the Strategic
Rocket Forces and primary emphasis on nuclear warfare; and
since 1968 the Soviet Union has been developing both a strong
nuclear capability as well as a modern conventional force capable
of global deployment. In addition to historical surveys of the
phases in military development, detailed analyses are presented
of Soviet military interventions.

No. 24. Odom, William E.
"Who Controls Whom in Moscow?"
Foreign Policy No. 19 (Summer 1975).

Striving for military power and the exercise of that power have been key elements of Soviet policy, but this has not meant that military officers have become the key decision-makers in Soviet foreign policy. This becomes clear when the military's role in Soviet foreign policy is viewed from four perspectives: 1) political/cultural; 2) economic; 3) technological; and 4) elite/institutional. A number of conclusions may be drawn from this assessment. The first is that the Party chief is never a purely military leader; martial preferences are not limited to marshals. The second is that the Soviet leader's policy choices are not analogous to U.S. policy choices. He is not trying to shift present capacity to non-military activities. His arms control policies are aimed precisely at avoiding basic changes in the command economy, and at minimizing the uncertainty imposed on Soviet military planners by the arms race. Opposition to detente and arms control is less likely to be found in the military than in other parts of the Soviet elite.

Abridged in Survival Vol. 17 No. 6 (November/December 1975), pp. 276-281.

No. 25. Pipes, Richard.
The Correlation of Forces in Soviet Usage -- Its Meaning and Implications.
Menlo Park, Calif.: SRI International Technical Note (SSC-TN-43832), March 1978.

This technical note assesses in the Soviet context, the operational significance of the concept "correlation of forces" and draws implications for U.S. policymakers. In the discussion, the concept is examined for its utility in making rational assessments of complex socio-political phenomena both at a global and regional level of analysis. It is argued, on the basis of a survey of Soviet publications, that the concept "correlation of forces" does not lend itself to quantitative assessment, but rather by virtue of its holistic connotations, represents a highly complex and changing array of factors best expressed in generalized terms.

No. 26. Sallagar, F.M.
An Overview of the Soviet Strategic Threat.
Santa Monica, Calif.: The RAND Corporation (R-2580-AF), February 1980, 32 pp.

Current U.S. strategic planning rests on an assumption that the most likely course of a major war with the Soviet Union would be a Soviet military attack on the United States or its European allies. This Project AIR FORCE report questions the validity of that assumption. The author examines the Soviet policy of "peaceful coexistance" against the backdrop of the Soviet military buildup over the past fifteen years, and offers an alternative hypothesis for the source of war. He argues that the changing military balance has allowed the Soviet Union to adopt a policy designed to undermine the strategic position of the United States by means short of a direct attack. Effects of this policy are to disrupt global stability and encourage situations in critical areas that might bring about American intervention. This could precipitate a military confrontation with the Soviet or Soviet-supported forces, and become a more likely source of war between the two super-powers than a direct Soviet attack on the United States or its allies. U.S. defense policy has not made adequate allowance for this contingency.

No. 27. Simes, Dimitri K.
Detente and Conflict: Soviet Foreign Policy, 1972-1977.
Washington, D.C.: Center for Strategic and International Studies (The Washington Papers No. 44), 1977, 64 p.

Detente has not brought about real reconciliation or even significantly modified the U.S.-USSR superpower rivalry. But the question is whether the Soviet Union ever intended this as its outcome. This study addresses the question of the balance between accommodation and confrontation in contemporary Soviet foreign policy, emphasizing the domestic contraints of detente in the USSR.

No. 28. Vernon, Graham D.
"Controlled Conflict: Soviet Perceptions of Peaceful Coexistence."
Orbis Vol 23 No. 2 (Summer 1977).

Peaceful coexistence, or detente, is a term often used by both U.S. and Soviet leaders, yet with apparently different definitions. Leaders in the United States have suggested that Soviet actions in Africa, for example, are not compatible with detente. The Soviets have argued that there is no conflict. While it might be difficult, given the hetrogeneity of American political statements, to accurately define the U.S. concept of peaceful coexistence, the same does not apply to the Soviet Union. In this chapter, peaceful coexistence is traced from its genesis, soon after the Bolshevik revolution, to the present day. Although the policy has received varying emphases depending on the international situation, the rationale behind it and the purpose peaceful coexistence is designed to accomplish have been remarkably consistent.

Also printed as Chapter 7 in Graham D. Vernon (Ed.), Soviet Perceptions of Peace and War (Washington, D.C.: National Defense University Press, 1981), pp. 113-142.

No. 29. Wolfe, Thomas W.
The Soviet Union Six Months After Khrushchev's Fall.
Santa Monica, Calif.: The RAND Corporation (R-3720), April 1965, 27 p.

An examination of the record of the new regime in various important policy areas: the status of collective leadership, problems of economy and defense, attitudes toward the intelligentsia, and foreign policy developments. The major difficulties concern conflicting central policy alternatives: 1) the need to mount an effective attack on basic internal problems; and 2) the need to repair the Soviet position in the power struggle with the West and within the Communist world.

No. 30. Wolfe, Thomas W.
Soviet Power in the Setting of a Changing Power Balance.
Santa Monica, Calif.: The RAND Corporation (P-4055), March 1969, 20 p.

A consideration of the possible effects of the shift in the American-Soviet strategic balance and the Soviet transformation form a continental military power to a global one in the last five years. Both economic and political considerations give good reason to believe that Soviet leadership would be satisfied with strategic parity with the United States instead of seeking superiority. If so, Soviet interest in arms limitation talks might reflect a genuine willingness to achieve agreement on strategic force levels. On the other hand, Soviet leaders might be reluctant to drop the opportunity to gain political leverage by forging ahead of the United States. If so, Soviet interest in the talks might be to prolong them so as to pursue force improvements while inhibiting the United States from funding any of its own. The more favorable power balance could tempt the USSR to pursue bolder policies and to accept a wider range of risks. But ingrained Soviet caution toward the risk of war might prevail. At the heart of questions of future Soviet conduct is the direction in which the system is moving. It may prepare leaders either to play a more responsible and stabilizing role in international politics, or to follow the well-trod path of promoting global ferment and discord.

No. 31. Wolfe, Thomas W.
Soviet Foreign and Defense Policy Under the Brezhnev-Kosygin Regime.
Santa Monica, Calif.: The RAND Corporation (P-4227), October 1969, 19 p.

Discussion of trends under the leadership of Brezhnev and Kosygin since the 1964 Khrushchev ouster. Whether as a result of decisions to increase the political-military competition with the U.S. for global influence, or because of major unforeseen crises such as the Middle East war -- or both -- the Soviet Union has made larger commitments for resources and prestige. It has gradually whittled down the U.S. edge in strategic arms superiority. It has held the line in Eastern Europe, extended overtures in the Middle East, and may be attempting to change the

Warsaw Pact from an alliance facing westward against NATO Europe to one facing eastward against China. Yet the tacit survival pact with the U.S. remains intact, signaling a recognition of mutual interest in crisis control, if not yet formal accommodation. The Soviet Union faces a decision on policy priorities in an environment of shifting alignments.

No. 32. Wolfe, Thomas W.
The Global Strategic Perspective from Moscow.
Santa Monica, Calif.: The RAND Corporation (P-4978), March 1973, 17 p.

An appraisal of the foreign policy and strategic considerations that help shape the USSR's posture in the seventies and its strategic relationship with the United States in the SALT negotiations. The international setting of two rival superpowers in a nuclear age has been replaced by unclarified conditions of global competition and adjustment. The Soviet Union's recourse to detente and intricate negotiations reflects its intent to take advantage of new opportunities, while consolidating old Soviet positions and easing domestic difficulties. One major consideration is who came out best in the SALT I negotiations. Did the U.S. allay the Soviet Union's fear of Safeguard, while giving it headroom in ICBMs and SLBMs to develop an even greater threat to the survivability of U.S. forces? Another question is whether, despite the ABM treaty, the Soviets have fully embraced the American concept of mutual assured destruction. Prepared for presentation at the National Defense College, Kingston, Ontario, April 3, 1973.

Soviet Views on the Political Utility of Military Force

No. 33. Alexiev, Alex R.
The Use of Force in Soviet Policy and the West.
Santa Monica, Calif.: The RAND Corporation (P-6466), March 1980, 9 p.

Examines Soviet theory and practice regarding the use of force in international relations and argues that the invasion of Afghanistan was neither unprecedented nor particularly surprising. The Soviet Union has used military force for political purposes on many occasions in the past and the primary rationale guiding the use of force has been the likelihood of accomplishing the given political objective expeditiously and with relative impunity. In recent years the Soviet Union has continued and intensified its military buildup while the United States has sought to enhance its security primarily through arms control. In view of the rapidly growing Soviet military capacities and the Kremlin's unshakable belief in the continuing political utility of military

power, which is contrasted with Western indecisiveness and
perceived loss of political will, the outlook for the West is
uncertain unless far-reaching remedial measures are taken soon.

No. 34. Aspin, Les.
"What Are the Russians Up To?"
International Security Vol. 3 No. 1 (Summer 1978), pp. 30-54.

In the current defense debate, much attention is being focused
on the most alarming view: that the Soviets, using detente as a
smokescreen, are striving for military superiority. To underscore the imminent danger, its proponents draw a parallel
between the Soviet military expansion today and the Nazi military
buildup leading to World War II. Behind this rhetoric lies the
reasonable point that inferences about intentions can be drawn
by examining trends in capabilities. This study compares the
military growth in six countries over a five year period in which
they have been found to be threatened or threatening: the
Soviet Union, 1972-76; Nazi Germany, 1935-39; Egypt and Syria
combined, 1968-72; Israel, 1968-72; China, 1967-71; North
Korea, 1971-75. The analysis shows that Soviet capabilities have
been increasing at a time when U.S. military power has been
declining. But Soviet growth is not only nowhere near as
marked as that of Nazi Germany, it is not even the largest
since. As far as Soviet intentions can be deduced from the
trends in their military programs, they are not as hostile as
some have portrayed them.

No. 35. Baritz, Joseph J.
"The Soviet Strategy of Flexible Response."
Bulletin of the Institute for Study of the USSR Vol. 16 No. 4
(April 1969), pp. 25-35.

Nuclear weapons represent such a powerful strategic force that
they cannot be used directly for the attainment of political goals.
War remains an instrument of politics, being conducted: a) as
local wars limited by geography, objectives, and the military
means employed; b) on the periphery of the area of interest of
one or another great power; and c) in escalated steps carefully
controlled by the superpowers. With the fall of Khrushchev, the
area of military policy based on threats of full-scale nuclear war
came to an end. In the course of the last several years, Soviet
military doctrine has undergone a number of changes: 1) escalation in local war can be controlled to prevent world war from
occurring; 2) the search for greater flexibility in local conflicts
has led to greater balance in the armed forces; 3) anti-missile
defense has become an essential element of Soviet military
doctrine; and 4) a discussion has been conducted in the Soviet
military press on the need for a "supreme military-political
organ" to coordinate all national resources. These changes in
doctrine have resulted in a great increase in the development

and production of conventional weaponry, and of transport and combat aircraft. The operating radius of the navy has been increased, and the reorganization of the marines is being carried out. The Soviet Union is also trying to catch up with the United States in ballistic missiles. This trend in Soviet military strategy gives ground for supposing the Soviet Union will become more active in localized conflicts.

No. 36. Baxter, William P.
"Soviet Perceptions of the Laws of War."
Chapter 2 in Graham Vernon (Ed.), Soviet Perceptions of Peace and War.
Washington, D.C.: National Defense University Press, 1981, pp. 17-26.

The Soviet Union is a closed society run by a centrally directed Party that is the sole guardian of the single true political, social, and military orthodoxy. Right thinking of the military profession is controlled by a well-organized philosophical structure which assures that the decision-making process in military affairs supports Party national and international politics. By telling the Soviet military profession what to think and how to think, the philosophical structure guides perceptions of military theory and policy.

No. 37. Deane, Michael J.
"The Soviet Assessment of the 'Correlation of World Forces': Implications for American Foreign Policy."
Orbis Vol. 20 No. 3 (Fall 1976), pp. 628-636.

The Soviet leadership contends that Communism can attain its "inevitable victory" even without war, because the correlation of world forces is shifting in its favor. The most recent shift, in their view, transpired about 1969-1970, and is closely connected with their attainment of strategic parity. The capitalist states, especially the United States, were supposedly compelled to re-appraise their policy of acting from a position of strength and to enter into "an era of negotiations." As a result, the main com-petition between the two systems shifted away from the military confrontation toward the economic, political, and ideological spheres. U.S. policy matters are insensitive to the magnitude of the conflict and unprepared to cope with innovative Soviet non-military actions against Western spheres of influence.

No. 38. Dinerstein, Herbert S.
"The Soviet Employment of Military Strength for Political Purpose."
Annals of the American Academy of Political and Social Science Vol. 318 (July 1958), pp. 104-112.

Although traditionally the Soviet Union has thought in terms of
capitalist encirclement, increased Soviet military and political
strength has now made them feel that it is they who are on the
offensive and the capitalist world which is on the defensive. As
a result of Soviet advances, many people who profess no faith in
the Marxist god of history seem to accept the Soviet hopes and
expectations for the future, as, in part at least, inevitable.
They feel that we can no longer delude ourselves by viewing the
Soviet Union as a second-rate power. Russia is strong, both
politically and militarily, and since this is an accepted fact, it
would be unrealistic to oppose the Soviet Union at every point
where it wishes to advance. Thus go the arguments which have
resulted in mounting pressures to negotiate with the Soviet
Union. The aim of this paper is to demonstrate that appre-
hensions and counsels of despair about present Soviet strength
are without adequate foundation. It is argued here that changes
in the nature of war -- the potentiality for a nuclear holocaust --
and in the political organization of the world -- the ideological
polarization of international politics -- make it much more
difficult for the Soviet Union to expand politically and territor-
ially than it was for Germany and Japan. Further, the
doctrinaire Marxist belief that communism must rise as capitalism
wanes -- for this is how they read the Book of History --
reinforces the caution and conservatism dictated by military
and political considerations.

Also printed as RAND Paper P-1317 (1958), 22 p.

No. 39. Dinerstein, Herbert S.
"Soviet Goals and Military Force."
Orbis Vol. 7 No. 4 (Winter 1962), pp. 425-436.

As Soviet military strength has grown in recent years, the
Soviet Union has been making political capital by: 1) demon-
strating the existence of its military power; 2) threatening to
use this power; and 3) selling conventional weapons to other
countries. Soviet possession of nuclear weapons is used to
intimidate the NATO allies into considering exclusion of nuclear
weapons from their territories as a means of reducing the
danger of destruction. In this connection, however, Berlin
poses a dilemma for the Soviet Union (namely, pressure on
Berlin enhances the attractiveness of NATO protection, while
relative passivity encourages resistance to Soviet demands. As
to the sale of weapons, in every case the purchaser could have
been expected to use them militarily or politically against a
member of NATO, CENTO, or SEATO. Aid to emergent nations
is considered a blow to Western imperialism, and therefore a
means of weakening capitalism and of fostering Socialism and
ultimately Communism.

Also printed as RAND Memorandum RM-2771 (June 2, 1961),
23 p.

No. 40. Dinerstein, Herbert S.
The United States and the Soviet Union: Standoff or Confrontation?
Santa Monica, Calif.: The RAND Corporation (P-3046), January
1965, 25 p.

An examination of the present relations between the Soviet Union
and the United States and a projection into the future. Emphasis
is on factors affecting the balance of power between these two
countries and the systems of states of which they are the chief
members.

Reprinted in John Erickson et al (Eds.), The Military-Technical
Revolution (New York: Frederick A. Praeger, Publisher, 1966),
pp. 270-284.

No. 41. Erickson, John.
"The Soviet Military, Soviet Policy, and Soviet Politics: A
Lecture at the U.S. Army War College."
Strategic Review Vol. 2 No. 4 (Fall 1973), pp. 23-36.

The Soviet emphasis on military strength does not conflict with
its policy of detente, for the Soviet Union sees a rough strategic
parity with the United States as its prerequisite. It views both
military strength and detente as essential ingredients of its
security. It defines detente simply as a means of gaining time
until it attains military superiority over the United States; its
military policy is motivated by a desire to retain its superpower
status and to reap its benefits. Another aspect is to build the
kind of force which will enable it to survive a nuclear war
should deterrence fail; thus, it has a spread of forces designed
to cope with both war-waging and war-avoiding. To meet this
dual "job," the Soviet Union has concentrated on building the
largest possible standing force, both strategic and tactical.
There has been a constant improvement in the quality of its
entire military system. Regarding the "strategic balance," the
Soviet Union leads in both delivery vehicles and megatons, while
it is narrowing the U.S. lead in MIRVs. Soviet military strategy
and capabilities can be characterized as having an offensive bias
but not truly designed for a first-strike. The buildup reflects
the Soviet effort to reinforce its scientific-technological elements
and to intensify its R&D programs. At the same time the Soviet
Union has increased its ground forces, not sacrificing the
European front because of the buildup on the Chinese border.
The Soviet military command is also undergoing change; younger
men with better technical training and expertise are replacing
older veterans of the Second World War.

Reprinted as United States Strategic Institute Report 73-3
(1983).

No. 42. Erickson, John.
"Soviet Military Capabilities."
Current History Vol. 71 No. 420 (October 1976), pp. 97-100,
128, 135-137.

"Military buildup" could signify the immediacy of resorting to
war, a means to fend off or meet such an onslaught, or it could
signal some long-term but indeterminate process, even
bureaucratic mindlessness, in the propagation and management of
complex weapons programs. In view of the relativism of military
strength, a build-up could even been related to an opponent's
run-down. Over the past two decades, there has been a
strangely regular periodization to the Soviet military program:
begun in the mid-1950s, the military build-up passed through its
own ten-year cycle, followed in the mid-1960s by a massive
numerical expansion and qualitative improvement that is now
showing formidable results, with signs that a third, most
complex phase is about to be launched to bring men and
machines into closer and more effective alignment. This projected
phase could prove to be the most demanding upon Soviet
resources; it tests the systems and demands "performance."
Today it is clear that performance is not all that it should be.

No. 43. "Foremost Soviet Military Journal Emphasizes Crucial
Role of War and Military Might."
Soviet World Outlook, February 13, 1976.

The November 1975 issue of Communist of the Armed Forces
carried an article on Soviet war doctrine that is notable for the
clarity and succinctness of its exposition of standard Soviet
positions on war in the nuclear age. Contrary to much Western
thinking, the article once more affirmed Moscow's acceptance of
the permissibility of nuclear war, its commitments to support
"liberation" wars, and its emphasis on the "conditions and means
of ensuring victory" in a nuclear war. The key point of the
article is that, despite revolutionary increases in the destructive
power of weapons, Moscow continues to view war as an instrument of policy.

No. 44. Garthoff, Raymond L.
Soviet Military Policy: A Historical Analysis.
New York: Frederick A. Praeger, Publisher, 1966, 276 p.

This book places the author's earlier analyses of Soviet military
doctrine and Soviet strategy in the nuclear age in a broader
frame of reference. It traces the many ways military power
enters into Soviet society, ideology, internal and foreign policy,
and policy-making by coordinating historical, political, sociological, strategic, and "Kremlinological" approaches. The USSR
has developed into the world's second most powerful country by
placing its interest above those of the World Communist movement

whenever they conflicted. It has used its military potential for political purposes, as is demonstrated through the examination of several important crises. The trend of current Soviet policy is toward limited, indirect exploitation of military power. Because the Soviet leaders are Communists, they expect the Communist revolution to arise from failure in the capitalist world rather than in the aftermath of nuclear war.

Chapter 4, "Ideology and the Balance of Power," pp. 65-76 (first half), earlier printed as "Ideological Concepts in Soviet Foreign Policy," Problems of Communism Vol. 2 No. 5 (1953), pp. 1-18; Chapter 4, pp. 77-94 (second half), as "The Concept of Power in Soviet Policy Making," World Politics Vol. 4 No. 1 (October 1951), pp. 85-111; Chapter 8, "The Military in Soviet Politics," in Problems of Communism (November-December 1957).

No. 45. Gray, Colin S.
"Soviet-American Strategic Competition: Instruments, Doctrines, and Purposes."
In Robert J. Pranger and Roger P. Labrie (Eds.), Nuclear Strategy and National Security: Points of View.
Washington, D.C.: American Enterprise Institute (Studies in Defense Policy), 1977, pp. 278-301.

This analysis of Soviet strategic programs concludes that the Soviet Union is seeking nuclear superiority over the United States. In the past there was incongruity between Soviet doctrine and Soviet weapons capabilities, but recent Soviet weapons acquisitions and civil defense efforts have allowed that gap to be narrowed considerably. Two basic issues are developed: the failure of defense analysts in the United States to recognize the trend in Soviet strategic programs for what it is, namely, an attempt by the Soviet Union to exploit for political advantage the asymmetries between its strategic capabilities and those of the United States; and the vulnerability of silo-based ICBMs. Soviet doctrine maintains that a superiority in arms can be employed coercively in a crisis. Should war occur, such superiority, together with extensive civil defense preparedness, would ensure victory.

No. 46. Gray, Colin S.
"Soviet Rocket Forces: Military Capability, Political Utility."
Air Force Magazine (Soviet Aerospace Almanac No. 4) Vol. 61 No. 3 (March 1978), pp. 49-55.

Soviet behavior strongly suggests that the Soviet Union is seeking strategic superiority, which it deems politically useful. Soviet thinking on military power does not draw the distinction between usable and unusable weapons that permeates Western theorizing and policy. Deterrence flows from anticipated war-fighting competence, and war, at any level, can and should be won. The Soviet Union adheres to a balanced, combined arms approach to politico-military problem. The Strategic Rocket Forces, for all of their impressive technology, derive much of their political clout from the combat capability of the other armed services. Thus, circumstances of threatened or actual strategic nuclear use should be determined by the relative competence of the Soviet Ground and Air Forces. The SRF has the following political utility: to deter strong moves by the United States in response to a challenge, military action by the United States during a crisis, and escalation of a theater conflict to the intercontinental level.

No. 47. Horelick, Arnold L., and Myron Rush.
Strategic Power and Soviet Foreign Policy.
Chicago: University of Chicago Press, 1966, 237 p.

A study of the interrelation of Soviet strategic military power and foreign policy. Discussed are: 1) the concern of Soviet leaders, after Stalin's death, with the political potentialities, as well as dangers, of nuclear weapons; 2) the Soviet attempt to deceive the West by politically exploiting strategic weapons; 3) the differences between the military-political actions Soviet leaders threatened to take and the actions they really could take; and 4) alternative Soviet military policies with their strategic consequences. The conclusion of the book considers the role of strategic power in relation to other factors in forming future Soviet foreign policy.

Also printed as RAND study R-434-PR (1965), 350 p.

No. 48. Jacobsen, C.G.
"The Emergence of a Soviet Doctrine of Flexible Response?"
Atlantic Community Quarterly Vol. 12 No. 2 (Summer 1974), pp. 233-238.

The early 1970s have witnessed a perceptible evolution of Soviet strategic thought. Limited war scenarios, both conventional and nuclear, are coming to the fore. The composite of recent Soviet deliberation on the utility of surplus strategic capabilities and on the efficacy of her increasingly mobile and "lean" non-strategic forces, coupled with a less constricting appreciation of the nature of conflict, does indeed amount to an embryonic doctrine of flexible response. There are three essential levels at which Soviet forces can operate: the nuclear scenario, the conventional scenario, and Third World interventionary-type prospects. It is too facile to equate Soviet military writers demands for superiority with counterforce capabilities; they have long evinced profound appreciation of the political value of military force, stressing the role of perception as distinct from reality. In days of relative parity on the strategic and non-strategic levels, the ability to command the support of revolutionary aspirations could prove crucial. Need the United States always concede the force of national and egalitarian aspirations to the USSR?

No. 49. Jonas, Anne M.
"Changes in Soviet Conflict Doctrine."
Chapter 13 in Walter F. Hahn and John C. Neff (Eds.), American Strategy for the Nuclear Age.
Garden City, N.J.: Doubleday and Company, Inc., 1960, pp. 152-168.

The Soviet Union is adapting, within the framework of Communist orthodoxy, its strategy and tactics to the realities of the technological world revolution. These broad shifts can be attributed to two factors: 1) the Soviet Union has acquired new weapons -- nuclear explosives and advanced means of delivery; and 2) possession of greater fundamental strength than before -- economic, technological, and psychopolitical. An examination of four crucial factors -- the role of nuclear weapons, the role of peaceful revolution, the role of war, and the correlations for initiating war -- may provide a partial answer to the question of whether the Soviet Union will succeed in its attempts to extend Communist power without unleashing nuclear war. It seems to be combining nuclear strategy and revolutionary theory, in the best dialectic tradition, into a synthesis conflict strategy.

No. 50. Jones, W.M.
Soviet Leadership Politics and Leadership Views on the Use of Military Force.
Santa Monica, Calif.: The RAND Corporation (N-1210-AF), July 1979, 24 p.

Soviet military doctrinal writings emphasize the value of preemptive attacks carried through to the complete defeat of the enemy. An examination of histories of various Soviet leaders reveals a recurrent pattern. A dominant leader is replaced by a group of successors which, in turn, devolves into competition ending only when one competitor has established dominance. In the dominant leader phase, aspirants to the top position enhance their power by building a coterie of proteges. Once the competition flares into direct conflict, the ultimate winner has preemptively attacked his opponents and their coterie, and carried through until eliminated as a future threat. Assuming that Soviet leaders would view the prospect of major superpower war as being analogous to top level political power struggle, their history and experience would tend them toward preemption in force with intention of carrying through until the enemy is eliminated as a threat.

No. 51. Kime, Steve F.
"The Soviet View of War."
Comparative Strategy Vol. 2 No. 3 (1980), pp. 205-221.

For the peoples of the Soviet Union, war is a very real possibility. They live on past battlefields and realize that, in the event
of another major war, their country will be a battlefield once
again. Consequently, theoretical contrasts designed primarily
for maintaining the peace rather than dominating the battlefield
do not satisfy their desire for a strong defense. Unlike many
Western military analysts who focus on how a war might begin,
Soviet strategists are more concerned with examining how it
would end.

No. 52. Kime, Steve F.
"Power Projection, Soviet Style."
Air Force Magazine Vol. 63 No. 12 (December 1980), pp. 50-54.

The Soviet Union's record at projecting its power beyond the
Eurasian periphery is a mixed one. Soviet staying power is not
great; given the rate at which former colonial powers have been
withdrawing during the last quarter of a century, it is amazing
that the Soviet Union has not done much better. Yet a fundamental change is underway: first, the U.S.-Soviet military
relationship has changed, most dramatically in the balance of
strategic nuclear power. Second, there is an important change
in global perceptions of U.S. resolve. Third, mainly because of
the two previously mentioned changes, Soviet evalutions of the
dangers of a more aggressive policy in the world are changing.
This essay deemphasizes distant projections and stresses
continental projections of Soviet military power, because they
have two different natures. In Eurasia and its maritime
approaches, the use of Soviet military power is inextricably
intertwined with the totality of Soviet power. At distances from
the USSR, the use of military power is much more disconnected.

No. 53. Kober, Stanley.
"Causes of the Soviet Military Buildup."
In Kenneth M. Currie and Gregory Varhall (Eds.), The Soviet
Union: What Lies Ahead?
Washington, D.C.: Government Printing Office (Studies in Com-
munist Affairs Vol. 6), 1985, pp. 314-323.

This article, citing Soviet sources, notes three purposes behind
the growth in Soviet military power: the political effect which it
produces in the event of war; the political effect it has upon the
Western powers in peacetime -- i.e., a moderation in their
activities vis-a-vis the USSR; and the political effect it has upon
the nonaligned states in terms of persuading these countries that
the "prevailing wind blows from the East." It concludes that
Soviet military power is not an action-reaction phenomenon or an

exaggeration of the Tsarist military legacy but the product of definite and relatively specific political goals.

No. 54. Lambeth, Benjamin S.
"The Political Potential of Soviet Equivalence."
International Security Vol. 4 No. 2 (Fall 1979), pp. 22-39.

Explores Soviet perceptions regarding the political significance of the parity relationship that has come to characterize the East-West strategic confrontation and the opportunities which attainment of equivalance may imply for future Soviet action. The paper describes Soviet approaches toward weighing the strategic balance (which differ fundamentally from most currently fashionable Western indices), examines possible Soviet views on the adequacy of current Soviet forces for a variety of political and military tasks, and concludes with a brief overview of how our NATO allies perceive their own security requirements, imperatives, and options to have been affected by the shifts that have occurred in the Soviet-American relationship during the past decade.

Also printed as RAND Paper P-6167, The Political Potential of Equivalence: The View From Moscow and Europe, August 1978, 27 p.

No. 55. MccGwire, Michael.
"The Overseas Role of the 'Soviet Military Presence'."
Chapter 2 in Michael MccGwire and John McDonnell (Eds.), Soviet Naval Influences: Domestic and Foreign Dimensions. New York: Praeger Publishers, 1977, pp. 31-40.

A double shift in Soviet policy occurred between 1969 and 1973 on the use of armed forces in support of international goals. Soviet leaders initially decided to commit Soviet forces overseas in support of foreign policy objectives, and this deicison was reflected in the assignment of air defense systems to Egypt in 1970. By early 1972, the policy was modified, leading to the withdrawal of the main body of forces from Egypt. A further decision was made in May 1973 to limit direct overseas Soviet involvement to advisers, weapons, and strategic logistics support. Factors contributing to the final decision probably were heavy foreign aid burdens, negative U.S. experience in Vietnam, bad Soviet experiences with overseas regimes, and a desire to upgrade the domestic standard of living. A change in naval priorities also contributed to the policy change. During the SALT negotiations of 1970 Soviet leaders probably perceived for the first time that the United States had never seriously considered initiating nuclear war against the USSR and was seriously concerned with the danger of nuclear escalation.

No. 56. McConnell, James M.
"Ideology and Soviet Military Strategy."
In Richard F. Staar (Ed.), Aspects of Modern Communism.
University of South Carolina Press, 1968.

Discusses the fluctuations in Soviet military strategy since 1917
as a consequence of shifts in the Soviet ideological action
program. The defensive strategy of the Leninist era stems from
the concept of permanent revolution; and the return to strategic
defense in the post-Stalinist period flows logically from the
notion of peaceful coexistence.

No. 57. Pelliccia, Antonio.
"Clausewitz and Soviet Politico-Military Thinking."
NATO's Fifteen Nations Vol. 20 No. 6 (December 1975-January
1976), pp. 18-21; 24-26; 28-29; 32.

The Soviet concept of war is the same as Clausewitz's. The
social content of the original has been expanded, and in the
definition of the essence of war the unmeasurable and uncertain
element represented by chance and the probability factor has
been eliminated to make the concept less metaphysical and more
scientific. The Soviet Union has thus gone beyond Clausewitz's
concept, in that it considers violence to be the one essential
element of war. Therefore it acknowledges only the absolute
form of war, war as an instrument of Soviet politics, aimed at
achieving Russia's ideological goals after sufficient economic,
technical, and industrial progress has been made to launch the
final, decisive conflict against the biggest capitalist power: the
United States of America. These intentions, set forth officially
in unambiguous terms, are matched by the weapons already
available or which are being prepared: by military doctrine, the
training of military cadres, the training and psychological
conditioning of men, and by the slow, inexorable progress of
communist ideology throughout the world.

No. 58. Pipes, Richard.
Some Operational Principles of Soviet Foreign Policy. (Memoran-
dum prepared at the request of the Subcommittee on National
Security and International Operations, Committee on Government
Operations, U.S. Senate.)
Washington, D.C.: Government Printing Office, 1972.

The language of Soviet politics is permeated with militarisms, for
Soviet theory does not distinguish sharply between military and
political forms of activity. Both are regarded as variant ways of
waging conflict which the Soviet Union regards as the essence of
history. The term "art of operations," a military concept that
stresses coordinated, uninterrupted assault, admirably describes
the most characteristic feature of Soviet foreign policy. The
Soviet government conducts a "total" foreign policy which draws

on essential distinction between diplomatic, economic, psychological, or military means of operation; or for that matter,
between domestic and foreign relations. Analysis of the "correlation" of forces is one of the basic ingredients in the formulation of Soviet foreign policy; that is, the determination of the
actual capability of the contending parties to inflict harm on each
other. Knowledge of this allows one to decide whether to act
more aggressively or less, and which means to employ. If the
Soviet Union were to discard cautious probing based on weighing
of the correlation of forces in order to engage in "world politics" -- pursuing power for its own sake, other operative
principles in the conduct of foreign relations would have to be
worked out.

Reprinted as "Operational Principles of Soviet Foreign Policy."
Survey Vol. 19 No. 2 (Spring 1973), pp. 41-61; in Michael
Confino and Shimon Shamir (Eds.), The Soviet Union and the
Middle East (New York: 1973); Richard Pipes (Ed.), U.S.-
Soviet Relations in the Era of Detente (Boulder, Colo.: West-
view Press, 1981), pp. 19-46.

No. 59. Pipes, Richard.
"Militarism and the Soviet State."
Daedalus Vol. 109 No. 4 (Fall 1980), pp. 1-12.

This essay deals with the role of militarism in the Soviet system.
It seeks to indicate how deeply embedded militarism is in
Communist theory and practice and how broad is its scope. It is
meant to counteract a notion widespread in the West that the
Soviet Union, a country with a socialist ideology, acute internal
problems, and a history of appalling losses from war, resorts to
militarism reluctantly, out of fear of foreign invasions or encirclement. This notion reflects a propensity of Westerners to impose
their values and experiences on Soviet Russia. Nuclear weapons
acquire particular relevance in Soviet thinking, since their
ability to destroy the home front signifies in Soviet doctrine
that, more than ever, intelligent preparation for the contingency
of war requires that one's own "rear" be merged with the front.

Reprinted in Richard Pipes (Ed.), U.S.-Soviet Relations in the
Era of Detente (Boulder, Colo.: Westview Press, 1981), pp.
195-213.

No. 60. Porter, Richard E.
"Correlation of Forces: Revolutionary Legacy."
Air University Review Vol. 27 No. 3 (March-April 1977), pp.
24-32.

The Russian meaning of "correlation of forces" has an ideological
flavor that makes it unique as a "balance of power" concept.
The purpose of this article is to determine the Soviet meaning of

66

the term, discover its philosophical and historical origins, and survey its significance in contemporary Soviet defense and foreign policy decision-making. The calculation of the correlation of forces appears to play no major role in Soviet decision-makers daily attempts to determine appropriate action. Why then, do the Soviets continue to imply that it does? The answer is that the concept is both useful and necessary. Within the concept there is inherent optimism: in the end socialism will triumph. Setbacks are not deviations from historical course but temporary tactical actions based on the current correlation of forces. The concept of the correlation of forces is one of the few remaining Soviet revolutionary standards. It allows for complete freedom of decision-making within an ideological context, and eliminates public debate and outside accountability.

No. 61. Scribner, Jeffrey L.
"Soviet Military Buildup: A New Dimension in Foreign Policy."
Military Review Vol. 51 No. 8 (August 1971), pp. 53-62.

Historically the foreign policy of the Soviet Union has been marked by a pragmatic use of the instruments available at any given period either to protect and consolidate the current Soviet position or to expand it to a new level which could be then protected and consolidated until the opportunity for further expansion appeared. This historical pattern of alternate expansion and consolidation continues its progression through the present moment and will do so in the future. At present, the Soviet Union is ending a period of consolidaton and beginning a period of expansion. This is because the Soviet leadership has reached what it regards as a state of strategic nuclear parity with the United States. This gives them an umbrella under which they can pursue the expansion of Soviet political, military, and economic influence throughout the world.

No. 62. Simes, Dimitri K.
"Disciplining Soviet Power."
Foreign Policy No. 43 (Summer 1981), pp. 33-52.

For the geopolitical rivalry to result in a code of conduct rather than a catastrophic superpower confrontation, two conditions have to prevail. First, the United States must determine what it considers unacceptable Soviet behavior. Second, the superpowers must develop and maintain a modicum of cooperation in the bilateral relationship. This cooperative track would remain subordinate in the framework of U.S.-Soviet relations. The U.S. political process cannot support such a complex, two-dimensional policy towards the Soviet Union if it remains in a position of perceived weakness. But if the United States felt confident on the world stage, it would not suffer from a reflexive urge to disrupt cooperative arrangements every time the Soviet Union became involved in a foreign crisis or arrested a dissident. The Soviet Union, of course, would not welcome this new U.S. policy. But if the alternative is an unworkable containment likely to encourage superpower confrontation, then a temporary Soviet uproar is a price worth playing.

No. 63. Vigor, Peter H.
The Soviet View of War, Peace, and Neutrality.
London: Routledge and Kegan Paul, 1975, 256 p.

Soviet views on war, peace, and neutrality can be summarized into three theories: 1) Until such time as Communism is established over the whole globe, war will continue to be regarded by the Soviet Union as a useful tool of Soviet foreign policy and as a valuable aspect of the world-wide revolutionary process. But although valuable as a tool, war will still only be selected by the Kremlin leaders for solving particular problems if it seems to be the tool best suited for securing the objective; 2) Between socialist and capitalist countries "peace" can be no more than an absence of fighting. The Soviet Union will resort to peace with the capitalist countries when an open struggle seems unprofitable, or when it is desirable for the Soviet Union to take an opportunity to regroup, replenish, or reinforce her armies; and 3) Marxist theory rejects neutrality -- he who is not with me is against me. In practice, several sorts of neutrality are recognized. They comprise an option the Soviet Union resorts to when it must operate from a position of weakness to the area or issue concerned.

A precis appears as "The Soviet View of War," Chapter Two in Michael MccGwire (Ed.), Soviet Naval Developments: Capability and Context (New York: Praeger Publishers, 1973), pp. 16-30.

Reviewed by Ralph N. Channel, Naval War College Review Vol. 30 No. 4 (Spring 1977), pp. 130-132; Francois Perround, Studies in Strategic Thought Vol. 18 No. 1 (February 1977), p. 83; William Scott, Strategic Review Vol. 4 No. 2 (Spring 1976), pp. 107-108.

No. 64. Wolfe, Thomas W.
The Communist Outlook on War.
Santa Monica, Calif.: The RAND Corporation (P-3640), August 1967, 47 p.

A discussion of the Communist concept of war and how it differs from Western ideas on the subject. The diversity of Western views on the causes, functions, and potential eradicability of war in human society is contrasted with the relatively narrow but more cohesive Communist interpretation. The development of Communist views on the relationship of war to revolution and politics is considered, as well as the Marxist-Leninist classifica-

tion or typology of war and the question of prescribed Communist attitudes toward wars of various types.

Reprinted as Chapter 12 in Vernon V. Asparurian (Ed.), Process
and Power in Soviet Foreign Policy (Boston: Little, Brown and
Company, 1971), pp. 401-425.

No. 65. Wolfe, Thomas W.
Statement by Dr. Thomas W. Wolfe at Hearings of the Subcom-
mittee on National Security Policy and Scientific Developments,
House Foreign Affairs Committee, July 22, 1969.
Washington, D.C.: Government Printing Office, 1969.

Testimony before a House Foreign Affairs subcommittee regarding
Soviet strategic attitudes and policy priorities. Despite the
Brezhnev-Kosygin regime's placement of a high priority on
increased economic growth, it has successively increased the
military budget at the expense of economic gains. A shift in the
Soviet-American strategic balance has resulted as the USSR has
changed from an essentially continental military power under
Stalin into a truely global one under the current leadership.
Whether the Soviets will be content to rest with the strategic
gains thus far, or whether they will press for a still more favorable power position may be answered in the upcoming SALT
controls upon MIRV and the means of inspecting them.

Also printed as a RAND Paper (P-4215), October 1969, 11 p.

Soviet Views of Arms Control and Disarmament

No. 66. Barnet, Richard J.
"The Soviet Attitude on Disarmament."
Problems of Communism, May-June 1961, pp. 32-37.

The basic Soviet attitude toward disarmament is difficult to
discern. During fifteen years of disarmament negotiations, the
Communists have insisted that all Western inspection proposals
were devices for espionage on Soviet territory. Mr. Khrushchev
has said, however, that the USSR will accept fully any Western
inspection scheme after disarmament is an accomplished fact.
The Soviet Union has likewise objected to Western proposals to
stablize arms at approximately present levels in the interests of
mutual deterrence, even though Western spokesmen have insisted
that this is a necessary prerequiste to actual arms reduction.
The basic question for attempting to understand the Soviet
attitude is whether it is in the Soviet interest to negotiate some
form of disarmament.

Reprinted as Chapter 9 in Ernest Lefever (Ed.), Arms and Arms Control (New York: Frederick A. Praeger, Publishers, 1962), pp. 32-37.

No. 67. Becker, Abraham S.
Strategic Breakout as a Soviet Policy Option.
Santa Monica, Calif.: The RAND Corporation (R-2097-ACDA), 1977, 56 p.

An assessment of the assumption that the Soviet Union is not likely to violate the SALT agreement because any incentive to do so would be overridden by the military and political costs of breeching the agreements and the far greater benefits of compliance. This report suggests that there are indeed Soviet incentives for covert and overt buildup within or without treaty constraints. This analysis of strategic breakout (defined here as a large-scale violation of the SALT treaty) is concerned with objectives and motivations for such an action, and the conditions fostering a change in direction. An important factor is an understanding of Soviet military decision-making, which is discussed in some detail. It is noted that even without a formal treaty, breakout may be defined as a form of military buildup "breaking away" from an informal strategic accommodation with the United States.

No. 68. Caldwell, Lawrence T.
"The Soviet Union and Arms Control."
Current History Vol. 67 No. 398 (October 1974), pp. 150-154, 178-180.

Below the hardware issues deadlocking the SALT II negotiations are political issues of far greater importance. These include the purpose of U.S. strategic doctrine and its derivative military force and their justification in a world of detente. If the United States accepts strategic parity with the USSR, of what value is its guarantee to protect Western Europe from invasion and diplomatic blackmail by the umbrella of its deterrent force? Thus the question of strategic parity triggers a second range of questions about security in Europe. The resolution of these issues lies in negotiation with the Soviet Union. SALT II and Mutual Force Reduction agreements should not be sacrificed for elusive, if desirable, goals like the alteration of the political system of the USSR. To accept that goal, even in terms of "freer movement of peoples and ideas," is to regress toward the cold war and toward an incalculably more dangerous world.

No. 69. Dallin, Alexander, and others.
The Soviet Union, Arms Control, and Disarmament: A Study of Soviet Attitudes.

New York: Columbia University School of International Relations,
1964, 282 p.

This book is the product of a study undertaken by a group of
scholars at the invitation of the U.S. Arms Control and Disarmament Agency. These scholars met in late 1963 over several
weeks in an environment that amounted to an immersion of a
group of leading specialists in a wide pool of problems, ranging
from "Kremlinology" to future trends in weapons systems. These
meetings confirmed the initial premise, that there were few
experts fully conversant with Soviet affairs and with the
intricacies of arms control. This report summarizes their views
on the basic factors of the greatest relevance to an understanding of Soviet attitudes toward arms control and disarmament.

No. 70. Frank, Lewis A.
Arms Limitations and Strategic Operations--A Soviet Perspective.
Falls Church, Va.: Analytical Services Inc. (ANSER Strategic
Division Note SDN 75-1), November 1975, revised January 1976.

Provides a much-needed interpretation of factors influencing the
future development of the strategic-nuclear forces of the USSR.
Written from the viewpoint of a hypothetical Kremlin expert, the
book reviews the effect of SALT on these forces through the
mid-1980s. The USSR is shown to have two major variables in
its power equation -- the size and composition of its forces in
relation to those of the United States, and the effect of SALT on
this comparative strength. It concludes that, in order to
maintain a favorable balance for the USSR, the planner would
recommend at least a threefold increase in Soviet strategic-
nuclear warheads by the 1980s. With this buildup, the USSR
would try to achieve SALT agreements that would reduce the
threat of new American strategic systems -- perhaps by trading
off older Soviet airborne and undersea weapons in exchange for
a halt in the Trident, B-1, and Cruise Missile programs and a
'go-slow' in upgrading other U.S. systems. And these agreements in turn could lead to a reduction in the SALT ceiling of
2,400 strategic delivery vehicles allowed each side by the 1974
Vladivostok accord.

Reviewed by Patrick Murphey, Perspective: Reviews of New
Books Vol. 6 No. 4 (May 1977), p. 87; Ronald Roberge, Parameters Vol. 7 No. 1 (1977), pp. 97-98.

Also printed as Soviet Nuclear Planning: A Point of View on
SALT (Washington, D.C.: The American Enterprise Institute,
AEI Studies 140, Defense Policy 1, 1977), 63 p.; and under the
same title as a chapter in Robert J. Pranger and Roger P.
Labrie (Eds.), Nuclear Strategy and National Security: Points
of View (Washington, D.C.; American Enterprise Institute
Studies in Defense Policy, 1977), pp. 439-464.

No. 71. Garthoff, Raymond L.
"Negotiating With the Russians: Some Lessons from SALT."
International Security Vol. 1 No. 4 (Spring 1977), pp. 3-24.

SALT I, which culminated in the ABM Treaty and an Interim
Agreement on strategic offensive missile limits, offers a wealth of
lessons on how to negotiate -- and on how not to negotiate --
with the Russians. This article discusses and summarizes these
lessons, stressing above all the need in negotiating with the
Russians for firm leadership, direction, and support for the
negotiation from the President on down. It concludes that the
most important element in the success of negotiation with the
Soviet Union is the extent of shared or congruent -- not necessarily identical -- objectives and interests. Greater equality
between the power of the Soviet Union and the United States in
the recent years has led not to greater intransigence and over-
bearing Soviet behavior, but generally to more responsible and
business-like negotiation.

Response by Abraham Becker and reply by Raymond Garthoff,
International Security Vol. 2 No. 1 (Summer 1977), pp. 106-109.

No. 72. Holloway, David.
War, Militarism, and the Soviet State.
New York: Institute for World Order (World Order Models
Project Working Paper No. 17), 1981, 26 p.

This paper surveys the obstacles to disarmament in the Soviet
Union, and analyses both internal and external factors of Soviet
militarism, the role of Russian political/military tradition, and the
centrality of the defense sector to Soviet society. Although the
sources of militarism are strong, the author argues that they are
not absolute, and that there is scope for demilitarization initiatives. Most of the demilitarizing tendencies will come from
internal influences and the working out of internal contradictions, such as that between declining economic growth and an
increased military burden. Nevertheless, the West should not
foreclose through their own policies the possibility of Soviet
moves toward disarmament.

No. 73. Holst, Johan Jorgen.
Comparative U.S. and Soviet Deployments, Doctrines, and Arms
Limitation.
Chicago: University of Chicago Center for Policy Study Occasional
Paper, 1971, 60 p.

Strategic weapons may be viewed as largely irrelevant to the
solution or management of important international issues and
largely inconvertable into political currency. Part of the difficulty confronting an analyst in this context is mapping the
distribution of this attitude both between the superpowers and

72

within the decision-making systems of each. Mutually "nego-tiated" doctrinal convergence may amount to a "doctrinal freeze." It might come to prevent desirable adjustments to new oppor-tunities.

No. 74. Kolkowicz, Roman.
The Role of Disarmament in Soviet Policy: A Means or an End?
Santa Monica, Calif.: The RAND Corporation (P-2952), August 1964, 15 p.

A discussion of Soviet attitudes toward disarmament within the context of Soviet policy objectives: 1) the distant goal of world communism as determined by the ideology; and 2) the more immediate and pragmatic objectives related to the conduct of current policy.

Also published as "The Role of Disarmament in Soviet Policy." In James E. Dougherty (Ed.), The Prospects for Arms Control (New York: Macfadden-Bartell Corporation, 1965).

No. 75. Kolt, George.
"Soviet and American Perceptions of Arms Control."
In Kenneth M. Currie and Gregory Varhall (Eds.), The Soviet Union: What Lies Ahead?
Washington, D.C.: Government Printing Office (Studies in Communist Affairs Vol. 6), 1985, pp. 142-147.

This article examines the differing Soviet and U.S. attitudes toward arms control. Using Fred Ikle's negotiation classification scheme, it argues that while the United States pursues innova-tion, the Soviet Union variously seeks redistribution of burdens and effects, extension of the status quo, or side effects such as propaganda. It urges a wider appreciation for these differences; the result will be to lessen U.S. impatience with slow results and increase the prospects for sound agreements.

No. 76. Lambeth, Benjamin S.
Soviet Strategic Conduct and the Prospects for Stability.
Santa Monica, Calif.: The RAND Corporation (R-2579-AF), December 1980, 15 p.

Throughout the past decade, the Soviets have refused to enter-tain SALT proposals that would require the Soviet Union to become an active partner in increasing its own vulnerabilities. They have also revealed a penchant for immoderate levels of arms acquisition, which raises disturbing questions about their willingness to settle for a strategic posture "essentially equiva-lent" to that of the United States. These features of Soviet strategic style constitute major obstacles in the path of achieving a cooperative solution to the security dilemma traditionally espoused by Western theories of mutual assured destruction. If the United States is to endure as a respectable player in the strategic arms competition, it will have to begin imposing measures conducive to stability through a strategy that appeals primarily to Soviet sensitivities, rather than to the doubtful prospect of eventual Soviet convergence with the preferred concepts of the West.

Earlier version published in The Future of Strategic Deterrence, Part II (London: International Institute for Strategic Studies, Adelphi Paper No. 161, Autumn 1980), pp. 27-38.

No. 77. Osgood, Eugenia V.
"Soviet Perceptions of Arms Control."
In Kenneth M. Currie and Gregory Varhall (Eds.), The Soviet Union: What Lies Ahead?
Washington, D.C.: Government Printing Office (Studies in Communist Affairs Vol. 6), 1985, pp. 106-141.

This article notes that disarmament -- the idea if not the substance -- has been a central feature of Soviet foreign policy since the Revolution. There continue to be divergences of opinion within the Soviet leadership over the questions of deterrence, nuclear war, parity, and superiority. These differences reflect the interest groups from which they originate. Continued Soviet interest in strategic arms control will depend upon the "delicate balance" between military and civilian interests, the direction of Soviet power projection, and U.S. military and political behavior.

No. 78. Payne, Keith B.; and Dan L. Strode.
"Arms Control: The Soviet Approach and Its Implications."
Soviet Union/Union Sovietique No. 10 Pts. 2-3 (1983), pp. 218-243.

The Soviet approach to arms control focuses upon four generic objectives, the priority of which can fluctuate over time: to help reduce the probability that the United States will confront Soviet foreign policy initiatives; to help undermine NATO alliance solidarity, and in particular to divide the United States from its NATO allies; help manage the American-Soviet relationship; and help provide a force posture and strategic balance compatible with the operational requirements stemming from Soviet strategy. The strategic arms control process will not cause the Soviet Union to alter its approach to nuclear weapons. Understanding the Soviet approach to arms control should facilitate the avoidance of potential pitfalls by the United States. It may well be that the transition to strategic defense envisaged by President Reagan will provide a basis for deep offensive force level reductions.

No. 79. Payne, Samuel B., Jr.
The Soviet Union and SALT.
Cambridge, Mass.: The MIT Press, 1980, 155 p.

At the root of Soviet-American hostilities is a mutual distrust of basic motives. The problem of assessing the Soviet Union's military posture is compounded by the secrecy surrounding political decision-making and the frequent contradictory and always political statements in the Soviet press. This book presents the Soviet attitude toward strategic arms limitation. It describes and analyzes the character, content, issues, and tactics of the Soviet proponents and opponents of arms control, since 1968, as expressed primarily in published Soviet statements and writings. It brings out both the intra-elite policy conflicts, and the general agreement on objectives -- how best to employ the new Soviet accretion of strength to advance Soviet goals -- shared by all elements of the ruling elite.

Reviewed by William J. Barlow, Air University Review Vol. 32 No. 6 (September-October 1981), p. 125.

No. 80. Sienkiewicz, Stanley.
"SALT and Soviet Nuclear Doctrine."
International Security Vol. 2 No. 4 (Spring 1978), pp. 84-100.

Two important factors have largely determined the evolution of Soviet nuclear doctrine. One is the inhibiting effect of the Marxist-Leninist doctrinal context within which all Soviet intellectual activity occurs. The other is the strong influence produced by the exclusive authority of the Soviet military over virtually all military activity below the major Politburo-level choices. For Soviet nuclear doctrine to become more like that of the United States requires a class of strategic thinkers freed both from professional military perspectives and Marxist-Leninist constraints. The absence of such conditions has resulted in a fundamental difference between U.S. and Soviet strategic theory. Soviet doctrine does not dismiss deterrence, but denies the American formulation of stability -- the absence of threats to each other's punitive capabilities. It has been the basis for the development of Soviet strategic forces which today appear to pose exactly the threat which Soviet doctrinal debates of two decades ago made it clear they would like to pose. In the absence of doctrinal convergence, the United States can proceed with SALT only on pragmatic case by case bargaining, rather than a search for a formal common understanding on strategic principles.

Reprinted as Chapter 4 in Derek Leebaert (Ed.), Soviet Military Thinking (London: George Allen and Unwin, 1981), pp. 73-91.

No. 81. Strode, Dan.
"Arms Control and Sino-Soviet Relations."
Orbis Vol. 28 No. 1 (Spring 1984), pp. 163-188.

Soviet attempts to use arms control as an instrument of policy
vis-a-vis China have been largely unsuccessful. The Soviet
Union was unable to prevent China from becoming a nuclear
power, and it has failed to draw the United States into a cooperative arrangement directed against China. Soviet arms control
negotiations with the United States were insufficient to prevent
Sino-U.S. rapprochement. Finally, Soviet proposals for discussions of mutual troop reductions and confidence-building
measures have not induced the Chinese to abandon their five
conditions for better relations. Yet Soviet analysts remain
confident that in the long term China and the United States will
draw apart due to different interests and that in the short term
the Soviet Union needs to make concessions to neither. If
Chinese and U.S. interests do drive the two nations apart and
Sino-Soviet relations do not improve, the Soviet Union will
probably again advance proposals designed to establish a superpower compact at the expense of China.

No. 82. Wolfe, Thomas W.
"Khrushchev's Disarmament Strategy."
Orbis Vol. 4 No. 1 (Spring 1960), pp. 13-27.

Soviet disarmament proposals are an integral part of a strategy
aimed at degrading Western strengths and reducing the risks of
nuclear war while the Soviet Union builds up its own overall
power position. Soviet disarmament proposals fall into two
categories: the "full and complete" disarmament scheme, and a
group of partial-disarmament measures. The sweeping general
disarmament proposal is meant to put the West on the defensive,
while the partial disarmament proposals are clearly calculated to
advance Soviet military and political objectives. Despite the
mutual incompatibility of Soviet and Western goals, there is some
possibility that the Soviet Union might be brought to accept
genuine arms control measures. Concern over accidental war,
economic pressure, or a desire to reduce potential sources of
internal stability might motivate Soviet interest. Still, their is
no reason to assume that Soviet leaders are less hardheaded and
calculating about arms control than their forerunner Lenin.

Also printed as "Soviet Strategy of Disarmament," Chapter 12 in
Walter Hahn and John Neff (Eds.), American Strategy for the
Nuclear Age (Garden City, N.Y.: Doubleday Press, 1960), pp.
139-151.

No. 83. Wolfe, Thomas W.
Some Factors Bearing on Soviet Attitudes Toward Disarmament.
Santa Monica, Calif.: The RAND Corporation (P-2766), July
1963, 22 p.

76

A presentation of possibly relevant factors bearing on Soviet attitudes toward disarmament under two broad categories: pro -- considerations which may furnish motivations for "genuine" Soviet interest in arms control and disarmament, and con -- considerations which argue against real Soviet interest. The paper is intended primarily as a check list and basis for discussion; no conclusions are drawn.

No. 84. Wolfe, Thomas W.
Soviet Influences on an Arms Control Environment.
Santa Monica, Calif.: The RAND Corporation (P-2995), October 1964, 17 p.

A discussion of the Soviet concept of arms control and disarmament and its influence on an arms control environment. Considerations motivating a genuine Soviet interest in arms control are contrasted with those arguing against serious Soviet interest in disarmament programs. Long- and short-term prospects for progress in arms control and disarmament are discussed.

No. 85. Wolfe, Thomas W.
The Soviet Union and Arms Control.
Santa Monica, Calif.: The RAND Corporation (P-3337), April 1966, 41 p.

A discussion of arms control, limited war, and peacekeeping as they relate to current Soviet disarmament policy and to Soviet general aims and behavior in international affairs. The paper includes comments on GCD (General and Complete Disarmament) as disclosed at the Geneva Conference, the feasibility of partial measures, nonproliferation, and other facets of the problem. It also discusses possibilities of change within the USSR itself and the resulting effects on the arms question.

No. 86. Wolfe, Thomas W.
The SALT Experience.
Cambridge, Mass.: Ballinger Publishing Company, 1979, 405 p.

Explores the political and strategic impact of the Strategic Arms Limitation Talks upon relations between the United States and the Soviet Union, and upon national decision-making in the two countries. This book covers the entire era of SALT I and II, but focuses on the SALT II period, treating it in both historical and analytical terms. This analysis covers four main areas: SALT I, how and why it came about and the agreements it produced; the institutional setting pertinent to SALT-related planning and negotiating activities of the United States and Soviet Union; the evolution of strategic policies of the two superpowers during the SALT era and their interaction with the SALT process; and the pursuit of a SALT II accord under successive

American administrations with the focus on issues that arose and how they were handled. The final chapter presents the author's closing reflections on the SALT experience, and a forecast of changes and problems that could occur during the SALT III period.

B. GENERAL WORKS ON THE SOVIET MILITARY

No. 87. Cockburn, Andrew.
The Threat: Inside the Soviet Military Machine.
New York: Random House, 1983, 338 p.

Never in the postwar era has the Soviet threat been depicted in more alarming colors than today. This threat is used to justify soaring U.S. military spending. Despite the billions of dollars the American people furnish to meet the threat, the reality of Soviet military power is little known. This book presents the real balance of military power: how Pentagon analysts count Soviet patrol boats as a threat to the U.S. coastline, how no Soviet weapon is too obsolete or worn out for inclusion in the "threat estimate," how the combat effectiveness of the Soviet forces has actually declined in the last decade. Despite what Soviet and American generals claim, the Soviet nuclear forces are no more capable of actually fighting and winning a nuclear war than those of the United States.

Reviewed by: Kenneth R. Whiting, Air University Review Vol. 35 No. 1 (November-December 1983), p. 112; G. Murphy Donovan, Naval War College Review Vol. 38 No. 5 (September-October 1985), 102-103; Andrew C. Goldberg, Political Science Quarterly Vol. 99 No. 2 (Summer 1984), pp. 351-353.

No. 88. Garder, Michael.
A History of the Soviet Army.
New York: Frederick A. Praeger, Publisher, 1966, 226 p.

The Soviet Army of today has evolved from the celebrated Red Army of Workers and Peasants, and represents, in Communist doctrine, the "armed section" of the world proletariat. That, indeed, is its avowed function, and at every level the impress of the Party is unmistakably clear. Yet it is at the same time a "national" army, continuing many of the traditions of the old imperial army. Thus it has a dual nature: it is both the armed force of the state and the military instrument of the CPSU. This book traces the military system of the Soviet Union from the October Revolution to the fall of Khrushchev. Within the frame- work of this historical narrative, it analyzes the organizational structure, the armament and operational theory of the Soviet Army at the different periods; and assesses developments in

78

Soviet military doctrine and the Kremlin's global strategy. In describing the social and ethnic composition of the USSR's armed forces and, in particular, the status of officers and society, evidence is presented which leads many observers to think that eventually the army will form the nucleus of a new class structure.

Translated from the French edition, Historie de l'Armee Sovietique (Paris: Librairie Plon, 1959).

Reviewed by Raymond Garthoff, East Europe Vol. 16 No. 6 (June 1967), p. 52.

No. 89. Gervasi, Tom.
The Myth of Soviet Military Supremacy.
New York: Harper and Row, Publishers, 1986, 545 p.

The Reagan Administration and its supporters have claimed that its rearmament program has been necessary to counter a growing threat, and have even claimed that the Soviet Union holds a margin of superiority. All the best evidence indicates that these claims are false. This book shows how the administration created the impression it desired by systematically misrepresenting the balance of power between East and West, and how the mainstream media disseminated this impression without carefully questioning it. This is demonstrated through evidence available in the public domain on the strategic balance of forces between the United States and the Soviet Union, and on the theater nuclear and conventional balances of power in Europe through the first five years of the Reagan Administration.

Reviewed by William S. Lind, "Of Myths and Missiles," Washington Post, August 22, 1986.

No. 90. Lambeth, Benjamin S.
Trends in Soviet Military Policy.
Santa Monica, Calif.: The RAND Corporation (P-6819), October 1982, 33 p.

The paper reviews the major doctrinal inputs into Soviet military policy, indicates important distinctions between Soviet and American approaches where appropriate, and surveys the changing nature of Soviet military capabilities so as to underscore their growing congruence with long-standing Soviet strategy. The paper discusses the doctrinal basis of Soviet defense policy, the impact of doctrine on force posture, the character and goals of the Soviet military buildup, and the developments in combat missions and forces.

No. 91. Leites, Nathan.
Soviet Style in War.
New York: Crane, Russak & Company, 1982, 398 p.

This book addresses the question: What are the distinctive
properties in Soviet warfighting (particularly on the ground)?
An answer is arrived at by examining both Soviet memoirs of the
war and German and Soviet military publications since then.   It
is suggested that in substantial measure, Soviet peculiarities in
warfighting are attempts to ward off undesirable tendencies
which Soviet leaders perceive in their subordinates as well as in
themselves.   A separate chapter is devoted to nuclear issues.

Also issued as a RAND report (R-2615-NA), April 1982, 398 p.

Reviewed by Milan Vego, Air University Review Vol. 35 No. 1
(November-December 1983), p. 120.

No. 92. Mackintosh, J. Malcolm.
Juggernaut: A History of the Soviet Armed Forces.
New York: MacMillan, 1967, 320 p.

This general history of the Soviet Armed Forces is based upon
Western and Soviet standard histories, as well as both popular
and specialized periodical publications.   Its fourteen chapters
trace the Red Army from its foundation during the Russian Civil
War (1918-1920) up to the date of publication.   Its last two
chapters cover the Soviet military under Stalin after World War
II and under Khrushchev and his successors.   The book includes
maps and photographs, as well as a short selected bibliography
of sources in English.

Reviewed by Raymond L. Garthoff, The Russian Review Vol. 27
No. 2 (April 1968), p. 260.

No. 93. Scott, Harriet Fast; and William F. Scott.
The Armed Forces of the USSR.
Boulder, Colo.: Westview Press, 1979, 400 p.; 2nd rev. ed.,
1981, 439 p.; 3rd rev. ed., 1984, 475 p.

The authors of this book draw on thousands of Soviet Ministry
of Defense publications -- only a very few of which have been
translated into English -- and four years of research in the
USSR to portray the fundamentals of Soviet military doctrine and
strategy.   They fully cover the postwar development of the
Soviet military, looking at the high command, each of the five
services, combat formations, and supporting agencies, and give
a comprehensive account of the Soviet military-industrial
complex, military training of Soviet youth, military manpower,
mobilization, and the Soviet officer corps.   Their discussion of

the relationship between the Party and the Armed Forces, based on Soviet data, includes an examination of popular Western myths about internal Soviet military debates and military-party splits. This reference book includes numerous notes, tables, figures, and a wealth of other data -- all based exclusively on primary sources.

No. 94. Wolfe, Thomas W.
"Problems of Soviet Defense Policy Under the New Regime."
Slavic Review Vol. 24 No. 2 (June 1965), pp. 175-188.

An examination of current problems of Soviet defense policy. Discussed are: 1) resource allocation and defense; 2) the modernist-traditionalist controversy on the role of the military in formulating defense policy; 3) size of the Soviet armed forces; 4) strategic power position in relation to the United States; and 5) attitudes toward local or limited wars and national liberation conflicts.

Also printed as a RAND paper (P-3098), March 1965, 27 p.

No. 95. Wolfe, Thomas W.
Soviet Military Policy Under Khrushchev's Successors.
Santa Monica Calif.: The RAND Corporation (P-3193), August 1965, 34 p.

An examination of the various issues of military policy and strategy which presently confront Khrushchev's successors. The general problem of resource allocation, i.e., how much of Soviet resources should be spent on defense measures, is discussed in detail. Size and strength of the Soviet armed forces, the strategic power relationship between the USSR and the U.S., and the search for a suitable Soviet policy position toward distant local wars are also covered. The author suggests that Khrushchev's successors have not yet found it feasible to make clear-cut choices between policy alternatives.

Reprinted as "Military Policy: A Soviet Dilemma," Current History Vol. 49 No. 290 (October 1965), pp. 201-245.

No. 96. Wolfe, Thomas W.
Soviet Military Policy Trends Under the Brezhnev-Kosygin Regime.
Santa Monica, Calif.: The RAND Corporation (P-3556), May 1967, 29 p.

A review of Soviet military trends since October 1964 when Khrushchev was removed from power. There has been no radical change of direction in Soviet defense preparations or in the strategic philosophy underlying them. Among the major issues of the Brezhnev-Kosygin regime is that of defense claims on Soviet resources -- a perennial question sharpened by the new regime's commitment to domestic economic reform and improvement. Indications are that the present Soviet leadership considers a major war between the United States and the USSR as unlikely; war as an instrument of policy in the nuclear age is one of the main issues in Sino-Soviet differences. Soviet leaders also seem to be considering the strategic balance and the issue of military supervisory via the arms control route rather than relying solely on further unilateral buildup of offensive and defensive strategic forces. Despite the demands of the war in Vietnam and the Soviet Union's increasing stake in Asian affairs, priority is given to maintaining the USSR/European power position in dealing with the political and military problems of Europe -- in particular, that of keeping a resurgent Germany in check.

No. 97. Wolfe, Thomas W.
Soviet Military Policy at the Fifty-Year Mark.
Santa Monica, Calif.: The RAND Corporation (RM-5443-PR), September 1967, 48 p.

During the fifty years' existence of the Soviet Union, its leaders have sought to turn growing military power to political advantage. Although there has been no radical change of direction in Soviet defense preparations or in strategic philosophy, the present government has undertaken a substantial buildup in strategic delivery forces and ABM defenses. The possibility of involvement in "local" wars is admitted, but how far the Soviet Union is prepared to go in committing forces and resources remains a critical question. The perennial problems that attend the relations of Soviet leaders with their own military remain: maintaining political control over the armed forces in times of crisis; meshing industrial and military planning; and balancing their traditional reluctance to grant the military an influential voice in policy formation against their growing need for the military's professional expertise.

No. 98. Wolfe, Thomas W.
"The Soviet Military Since Khrushchev."
Current History, October 1969, pp. 220-227.

Soviet military strategy traditionally coincides with Soviet foreign policy as conceived by the political leadership of the USSR. Where Stalin's foreign and military policy was limited to continental ambitions, Khrushchev sought to expand Soviet influence and interests throughout the world. Khrushchev, however, experienced only limited success because his foreign policy was not backed up by sufficient military strength. His successors have attempted to fortify Soviet foreign policy ambitions by expanding Soviet military strength. Current Soviet military

82

policy is premised on avoiding a general nuclear war by maintaining a strategic deterrent. Strategic policy depends essentially on an increased delivery capability, coupled with a great emphasis on strategic defense. The Soviet Navy now provides an instrument for the global support of Soviet interests, rather than an adjunct to land power as during the Khrushchev era. Finally, the Warsaw Pact continues to figure prominently in Soviet continental military strategy. It serves as a counterweight to NATO, while at the same time providing an intrabloc mechanism for the control and discipline of recalcitrant satellites. The Pact provides the legal rationale for maintaining Soviet troops in East Europe to keep the Western front quiet while Russia concentrates on its border with China. Current Soviet military policy is merely part of the world's two superpowers, and that new status still needs to be legitimized by developing a stable relationship with the U.S. The impending SALT talks may represent the method by which Soviet power and influence will be delineated on a global level and serve also as a guideline for future U.S.-USSR relations.

No. 99. Wolfe, Thomas W.
"Soviet Military Strategy and Policy."
In Kurt London (Ed.), The Soviet Impact on World Politics. New York: Hawthorn Books, 1974, pp. 237-268.

This paper describes the USSR's emergence as a global power, the buildup of its strategic and general purpose forces, and some alternative future possibilities. Detente rather than confrontation may reflect the fact that past Soviet pressure often prompted the West to close ranks. Despite SALT agreements, a gulf remains between the U.S. concept of "mutual assured destruction" and Soviet dedication to a strategic philosophy which emphasizes warfighting and survival, and continues to reject the "balance of terror". Emerging as a major naval power, the Soviets optimized their capabilities by a combination of surface, subsurface, and air-launched missiles and have gained U.S. assent to their numerical superiority in missiles. Military aid programs opened formerly closed doors to Soviet influence and provided valuable overseas experience for Soviet military and administrative personnel. A dynamic and markedly self-righteous energy continues to animate the Soviet world outlook and behavior.

Also printed as RAND Paper P-5008, "Worldwide Soviet Military Strategy and Policy," (April 1973), 38 p.

No. 100. Wolfe, Thomas W.
"Military Power and Soviet Policy."
In William E. Griffith (Ed.), The Soviet Empire: Expansion and Detente.
Lexington, Mass.: Lexington Books, 1976, pp. 145-216.

For more than a decade the Soviet Union has been making an extraordinary effort to increase its military power. In the strategic field, the outline SALT agreement reached at Vladivostok in November 1974 may signify that an end to the quantitative buildup of Soviet strategic forces is in sight, though as yet neither a complete accord has ensued from the Vladivostok transaction, nor have Soviet strategic programs slowed down. In the field of ground-air theater forces and naval forces, programs to improve these aspects of Soviet military power are also continuing and appear relatively insensitive to changes in the political environment under detente. This paper examines various factors which influence the formation of Soviet military policy, and identifies some of the salient military policy issues growing out of current Soviet unilateral programs, as well as the negotiations on limitation of strategic arms and the talks on reduction of theater forces in Europe.

Also printed as RAND Paper (P-5388), March 1975, 82 p.

C.   SOVIET VIEWS ON NUCLEAR DETERRENCE/WARFIGHTING

The Soviet View of Deterrence

No. 101.   Arnett, Robert L.
"Soviet Attitudes Toward Nuclear War: Do They Really Think They Can Win?"
Journal of Strategic Studies Vol. 2 No. 2 (September 1979), pp. 172-191.

Two types of evidence are used to support the contention that the Soviet Union has the capacity to survive and win a nuclear war: analyses of relative U.S.-Soviet nuclear capabilities, and analyses of Soviet attitudes on nuclear war.   The second type of evidence requires more attention, since it is crucial for determining the credibility of the U.S. deterrent.   It requires a review of Soviet statements on nuclear war as an instrument of policy, victory in a nuclear war, and the consequences of such a war.   What Soviet spokesmen say about nuclear war does not support the claims of Western analysts who argue that the Soviet Union believes it can win and survive a nuclear war.   Soviet statements proclaiming that victory in such a war is possible are necessary to keep up morale and are required by Marxist-Leninist ideology.   They are contradicted by many other Soviet statements on nuclear war.

Reprinted as Chapter 2 in John Baylis and Gerald Segal (Eds.), Soviet Strategy (Montclair, N.J.:   Allanfeld, Osmon, and Co., 1980), pp. 55-74.

No. 102. Banerjee, Jyotirmoy.
"Arms and Ideology in Soviet Foreign Policy."
Institute for Defense Studies and Analyses Journal Vol. 5 No. 2
(October 1972), pp. 277-300.

The overtaking of the United States by the USSR in the number
of strategic missiles on the one hand and the stepped-up Soviet
naval activities on the other have led both academic and government circles in the West to devote a great deal of attention to
such questions as: whether it has been the policy of the USSR
to acquire a first-strike capability and thereby to threaten the
precarious nuclear "balance"; has the increased Soviet nuclear
power, coupled with a more assertive naval policy, caused
perceptable shifts in the Soviet politico-strategic doctrine; and,
if so, are such doctrinal shifts a prelude to a more vigorous,
even aggressive, Soviet policy posture. The overall impression
conveyed by the Soviet arms buildup policy, politico-military
doctrine, and operative policy is that of an obsessive concern
for the security of the USSR. Hence, there appears to be no
"threat" as such to the global balance of power from the Soviet
side; recent Soviet endeavors have been geared to equalization
with the Western powers.

No. 103. Erickson, John.
"The Chimera of Mutual Deterrence."
Strategic Review Vol. 6 No. 2 (Spring 1978), pp. 11-17.

Western concepts of "mutual deterrence" lean heavily on models
drawn from economics, in which "rationality" is related to self-
interest and "utility" represents its maximization. The central
assumption holds that it would not be "rational" to act against
one's major self-interest by inviting one's own self-destruction.
Yet, Soviet strategy is motivated by starkly different conceptions of self-interest -- i.e., "rationality." These conceptions
reject Western notions of "balance" and the equation of deterrence with vulnerability -- with "mutual assured destruction."
The American "management" approach thus clashes with the
Soviet "military" inclination. Ironically, while the United States
has pressed to "educate" the Soviets in the nuclear facts of life,
it may well be that it will have to learn from them what is
involved in effective unilateral deterrence.

No. 104. Erickson, John.
"The Soviet View of Deterrence: A General Survey."
Survival Vol. 24 No. 6 (November-December 1982), pp. 242-251.

The Soviet Union terms the Western deterrent concept
ustrashenie (threatening intimidation), while its own is registered by the word sderzhivanie (constraining and restraining).
This is more than semantics -- from the outset the Soviet Union
was not inclined to accept the metaphysics of deterrence, in its

view arcane scholasticism screening the U.S. policy of containment. In the Soviet view, U.S. capabilities were being developed beyond those which could be identified with "deterrence through punishment," and therefore it was impossible to accept the mutuality of "assured destruction" when military reality suggested further expansion of U.S. counterforce capability. It was no part of Soviet policy to increase Soviet vulnerability -- mutual deterrence had to be stripped of U.S. attempts at coercion. Many Western circles became confused, because certain American attitudes professed war avoidance and the "unthinkability" of nuclear war, while the Soviet Union adopted on war-prevention coupled with the acceptance of the possibility of nuclear war. This led them to conclude that the Soviet Union had an implacable quest for unchallenged military superiority, which demolished deterrence and undermined any mutuality.

No. 105.   Gareau, Frederick H.
"Nuclear Deterrence: The Soviet Position."
Orbis Vol. 8 No. 4 (Winter 1965), pp. 922-936.

The purpose of this article is to review the Soviet literature on nuclear deterrence up to 1963 in order to relate it to the general literature on the subject.   Soviet literature has two distinctive features which tend to put it in a class by itself: a liberal infusion of ideology and an essential uniformity modified to some degree by the circumstances and objectives of a given pronouncement.   Since Soviet writers reject bilateral deterrence, they must be classified as "nuclear skeptics."   They maintain that a world war would result in a victory for Communism, denying the assumptions of most Western partisans of deterrence that neither contestant can win.   Soviet spokesmen espouse a form of unilateral deterrence which restrains the West only.   It is not based primarily on weapons of mass destruction, but is a balanced deterrent including conventional military forces, a superior socialist economy, and the allegience of the "people." It is designed to hold the West at bay while the inexorable process of history spells the doom of capitalism.

No. 106.   Garthoff, Raymond L.
"The Soviet Challenge."
Army Vol. 11 No. 2 (September 1960), pp. 30-32.

It is true that the Communists are dangerous double-dealers out for world domination, but this is not an adequate depiction of their threat and challenge.   The Soviet leaders seek to expand their power and influence beyond the Communist bloc, but they also give their primary attention to maintaining the security and power of the Soviet state.   This means: 1) that the Soviet leaders have decided that general war is not in their interests; 2) that they will avoid the serious risk of general war; 3) that they will pursue a policy of expansion by means short of major

war; and 4) that within this general policy they will be alert to
neutralize the U.S. deterrent in certain local challenges. Mutual
deterrence has already resulted from the U.S. and Soviet
acquisition of global thermonuclear striking power. The Soviet
leaders do not subscribe to the view that mutual devastation
spells mutual defeat. But this does not mean that they are so
certain of success and so indifferent to costs and risks that they
would launch a general war in the foreseeable future. The
United States needs a military policy and posture that provides
for local use of nuclear or conventional forces to meet local
aggression and provocation.

No. 107. Garthoff, Raymond L.
"Mutual Deterrence and Strategic Arms Limitations in Soviet
Policy."
International Security Vol. 2 No. 1 (Summer 1978), pp. 112-147.

The basis for possible strategic arms limitation has sometimes
been questioned on the grounds that the Soviet Union does not
accept the concept of mutual deterrence. This essay seeks to
illuminate Soviet thinking on this subject, concluding that since
the late 1960s, when SALT was launched, the Soviet political and
military leadership has recognized that the strategic balance
provides mutual deterrence, that the strategic balance is
basically stable, but requires continuing military efforts to
assure its continuation; and that strategic arms limitations can
make a significant contribution to reducing otherwise necessary
military efforts. More broadly, the Soviet leaders believe that
peaceful coexistence is the preferable alternative to an unrestrained arms race and to recurring high-risk politico-military
confrontation.

Reprinted in Strategic Review Vol. 10 No. 4 (Fall 1982), pp.
36-63 as part of the "Garthoff-Pipes Debate" (q.v.); and as
Chapter 5 in Derek Leebaert (Ed.), Soviet Military Thinking
(London: George Allen and Unwin, 1981), pp. 92-124.

Response by Donald Brennan, International Security Vol. 3
(Summer 1978) pp. 193-198; Raymond Garthoff, "A Reply to
Donald Brennan," International Security Vol. 3 No. 4 (Spring
1979), pp. 197-199.

No. 108. Garthoff, Raymond L.
"On Estimating and Imputing Intentions."
International Security Vol. 2 No. 3 (Winter 1978), pp. 22-32.

It is most important to try to understand the perceptions, aims,
decisions, and actions of the Soviet Union, and to make the
attempt for this purpose, rather than to serve any other. Ten
common fallacies in estimating intentions -- in particular, with
respect to Soviet military and international political activity --

are identified and briefly discussed in this article: 1) when in doubt, assume the worst; 2) never estimate intentions, only capabilities; 3) the mirror image; 4) the double mirror image; 5) the Soviets never mean what they say and/or the Soviets always mean what they say; 6) U.S. national security basically means military security against the Soviet Union; 7) Soviet capabilities are larger than needed for deterrence; 8) the enemy seeks military superiority; 9) "just give me the facts"; and 10) "bad news" is public news. Estimating intentions is difficult, and surely important enough not to be burdened by permitting fallacies such as these to enter the process. It deserves the best U.S. efforts, rather than being used to dramatize U.S. forebodings.

No. 109. Garthoff, Raymond L.
Perspectives on the Strategic Balance.
Washington, D.C.: The Brookings Institution, 1983, 34 p.

There is no single measurable military or strategic balance appropriate to all purposes. Assessments of the balanced relationship of forces, and still more of capabilities, are heavily dependent on conditions and purposes (or, in analysis, on assumptions based on contingent assumptions about intentions and scenarios. Finally, the different perspectives of adversaries arrayed on opposing sides leads to significant differences in perceptions of the military balance. As a result, public representations of the balance are bound to differ even when not intentionally manipulated. It is nonetheless necessary to estimate military balances for various purposes. A broad strategic balance is stressed by the Soviet Union, with its approach centered on the political significance of military power, whereas in the United States the tendency is to view the strategic balance much more in analytical terms. Each side must evaluate the strategic balance for itself, but each should also attempt to understand the perspective of the other.

No. 110. Ground Zero.
What About the Russians -- And Nuclear War?
New York: Pocket Books, 1983, 237 p.

This book seeks to show the historical and present condition of the Soviet Union and the U.S.-Soviet relationship. The historical picture is one with roots deep in the Russian past, and more shallowly set in events of the recent past, from the Revolution to the U.S. and Soviet efforts to defuse the stains of the Cold War. The Soviet Union built a massive strategic and conventional military capability even as it sought to develop a favorable relationship with the United States through the process of detente, and in particular through arms control. It seems unlikely that a perceived ideological imperative has evolved in some meaningful way into a substantial real belief in a strategic possibility of "winning" among those individuals in the Kremlin who will ultimately make the decision as to how, why, and when the Soviet Union will choose to fight a nuclear war.

No. 111. Kaplan, Fred M.
Dubious Specter: A Skeptical Look at the Soviet Nuclear Threat.
Washington, D.C.:   Institute for Policy Studies, 1980, 93 p.

This book is about the strategic nuclear balance between the United States and the Soviet Union -- and, implicitly, about whether the state of this balance, for now and in the forseeable future, has any implications for international politics, broadly speaking.   It analyzes the increasingly widespread contention that the Soviet Union's strategic nuclear forces are "superior" to those of the United States and that the Soviets are aiming to fight and win a nuclear war.   Its aim is to challenge and try to dispel some hard-won myths that have recently gained an extraordinary amount of attention -- and, in turn public credence -- and to put some widely publicized facts into a broader perspective.   At the same time, it summarizes and examines some basic issues of defense policy and strategy, which have been badly misunderstood by many analysts (on the left, right and center) and without which a discussion of something called a "military balance" is pointless and abstract.

No. 112. Kober, Stanley.
"Interpreting Soviet Strategic Policy."
Comparative Strategy Vol. 4 No. 1 (1983), pp. 65-74.

This review begins by assessing John Baylis and Gerald Segal, (Eds.), Soviet Strategy (Totowa, N.J.:   Allanheld, Osmun & Co., 1981); Derek Leebaert, (Ed.), Soviet Military Thinking (Winchester, Mass.:   Allen & Unwin, 1981); and Samuel B. Payne, The Soviet Union and SALT (Cambridge, Mass.:   The M.I.T.   Press, 1980).   There are many questions about the Soviet Union that Western policy makers need to have answered. What has prompted the vast Soviet military buildup, and what spurs its continuing growth?   Can arms control play a significant role in countering or reversing Soviet accumulation of military power?   Will the Soviet Union be content with parity, or is it determined to achieve superiority?   The books under discussion serve as a starting point for examination of these questions. But, although they provide some useful information and analysis, they seem to have too ready an acceptance of Soviet vulnerability and insecurity.   The review demonstrates that there are many reasons for challenging this assumption.

Comment from Raymond L. Garthoff with response by Stanley Kober.

No. 113.   Lambeth, Benjamin S.
"Deterrence in the MIRV Era."
World Politics Vol. 24 No. 2 (January 1972), pp. 221-242.

The dialectic of the Soviet-American strategic relationship has become firmly immobilized by the durability of mutual deterrence. As a result, this essay tries to lay out a systematic case in favor of arms control, dominated not by apocalyptic warnings but by the suggestion that it would defy common sense to do otherwise.   If the United States wishes to achieve a negotiated arms-limitation accord with the Soviet Union it must openly abandon its pursuit of superiority in favor of nuclear equality.   A promising step in this direction is the concept of "sufficiency" as the proper premise upon which U.S. strategic policy should be based, since the term has enough semantic ambiguity to serve as a value-free slogan for both superpowers.

No. 114.   Legvold, Robert.
"Strategic 'Doctrine' and SALT: Soviet and American Views."
Survival Vol. 21 No. 1 (January-February 1979), pp. 8-13.

Those studying the contrast between Soviet and American approaches to strategic thought have often made the United States the great adherent of deterrence and the Soviet Union of defense, giving rise to the notion that the Soviet Union is preoccupied with ways of waging nuclear war, and the United States with ways of avoiding it.   But this impression is inexact -- neither side believes in distinguishing deterrence from defense. Rather, the critical difference arises out of the conception of deterrence that each side embraces.   The United States has, or aspires to have, a strategic doctrine; the Soviet Union does not. As a result, where the American strategic deterrent is made to cope with a broad range of threat beyond that of nuclear attack, the Soviet Union tends to expect its strategic nuclear forces only to deter others' resorting to (strategic) nuclear war.   To the extent that the Soviet leaders persist in seeing the United States as determined to fuse its force planning and arms controlling, they will treat with utmost suspicion the numbers, the forces, and the formulas the United States advances in SALT.

No. 115.   Questor, George H.
"On the Identification of Real and Pretended Communist Military Doctrine."
Journal of Conflict Resolution Vol. 10 No. 2 (June 1966), pp. 172-179.

Communist regimes may really have understood the military problems arising with nuclear weapons since 1945, so their seemingly unrealistic pronouncements can be explained as deliberate dissimulations required by the strategic enviroment. The Russians and Chinese have clearly been liars when dis-

cussing their perceptions of strategic questions, for their views
in reality are likely to resemble our own.

No. 116. Ross, Dennis.
Rethinking Soviet Strategic Policy: Inputs and Implications.
Los Angeles, Calif.: UCLA Advanced Center for International
Studies (Working Paper No. 5), June 1977.

By interpreting Soviet strategic behavior according to Western
logic or preconceptions, American strategists necessarily draw
overly negative conclusions -- for example, according to how the
United States would logically or theoretically use them, the
Soviet development of big missiles can only be interpreted in an
offensive, threatening manner. Aside from almost mindlessly
linking intentions with capabilities, the problem with such an
interpretation is that it blithely ignores the possibility that the
Soviet Union may believe big missiles make deterrence more, not
less secure. That the Soviet Union could have such a different
view of deterrence highlights the need to come to grips with the
attitudes that underpin Soviet strategic policy. This paper
characterizes the values of those primarily responsible for
formulating Soviet strategic thinking, and will also show how
these values relate to ideological and historical factors. The
central argument of this essay is that although different
subjective inputs yield a Soviet strategic mind-set different than
that of the United States, the disparities: 1) need not be
destabilizing if understood, 2) allow Soviet strategic behavior to
be explained in terms of deterrence, and 3) indicate that even in
the abstract Soviet capabilities should not be interpreted in a
totally offensive, threatening light. Although Soviet deployment
policies will eventually ensure Soviet superiority in certain
dynamic and static measures of nuclear power, the United States
can afford to practice restraint, since "superiority" or asymmetries in the nuclear balance are neither militarily destabilizing
nor politically detrimental.

Also printed in the Journal of Strategic Studies Vol. 1 (May
1978), pp. 3-30; and as Chapter 5 in John Baylis and Gerald
Segal (Eds.), Soviet Strategy (Montclair, N.J.: Allanfeld,
Osmun, and Co., 1981), pp. 124-153.

No. 117. Shenfield, Stephen.
"Soviet Thinking About the Unthinkable."
Bulletin of the Atomic Scientists, February 1985.

That there will be no victors in a nuclear war is nowadays a
commonplace in Soviet public statements. Some Western analysts
dismiss all the Soviet talk on the impossibility of winning a
nuclear war as no more than a shift in propaganda tactics,
pointing to continuing evidence that Soviet leaders still believe
they could win a nuclear war. All theories that assume a united

"Soviet view" can be rejected with fair confidence. Scientific
and dynamic views on nuclear war probably coexist in the Soviet
mind, although there has been enormous progress in official
Soviet perceptions of its consequences. While the political
leadership continues to be divided in its attitude on this subject,
efforts to convince them of the truth of their own propaganda
are by no means wasted.

An earlier version of this article was published in Detente,
January 1985.

No. 118. Simes, Dimitri K.
"Deterrence and Coercion in Soviet Policy."
International Security Vol. 5 No. 3 (Winter 1980-1981), pp.
80-103.

The privileged position of the Soviet military is not set in
concrete. A combination of economic slowdown, energy shor-
tages, and consumer pressures, coupled with fears of a growing
technological gap with the West, may persuade a future leadership to contrain military appetites. But for this to happen, the
leadership that will succeed Brezhnev will have to resist a temp-
tation to enhance domestic legitimacy through a global diplomacy
of force. In addition, any attempt to eliminate the warfighting
aspects of the Soviet strategic traditions would encounter considerable bureaucratic and cultural odds. The dual nature of the
Soviet view of deterrence, emphasizing both offense and war-
avoidance, is not a result of the Soviet Union's lack of sophistication or of its bureaucratic inertia and confusion. Soviet
coercive deterrence represents a logical outcome of Soviet conceptions of national security on the one hand and of domestic
political organization on the other.

No. 119. Snow, Donald M.
"Strategic Uncertainty and Nuclear Deterrence."
Naval War College Review Vol. 34 No. 6 (November-December
1981), pp. 27-41.

This article discusses the advances that the Soviet Union has
made in weapons development and points out that this force
expansion has produced a capability that exceeds the need for
an assured destruction strategy. It reviews the assumptions
underlying assured destruction, including a mixture of strategic
bombing theory, a regard for the destructive capability of
nuclear weapons, and an acceptance of the limits of ballistic
missiles. Although the strategy of assured destruction appeared
to replace the calculation of gain with the certainty of a lethal
response to aggression, sources of uncertainty are present.
Traditional sources of uncertainty are examined in the article as
well as new technological sources of uncertainty. These new

sources include increased missile accuracy and potential break-
throughs in ballistic missile defense.

No. 120. Van Oudenaren, John.
Potential Threats to U.S.-Soviet Deterrence: The Political Dimension.
Santa Monica, Calif.: The RAND Corporation (P-6826), November 1982, 36 p.

This paper analyzes the stability of U.S.-Soviet deterrence
against the background of a changing global environment. It
argues that a potential cause of instability is the clash between
U.S. and Soviet views on the role of the "unrealized" military
potential (in the form of economic power) outside the hands of
the two superpowers. Soviet interests are served by the
development of a special relationship with the U.S. in which the
latter in effect "polices" its allies to prevent them from challenging Soviet "equality." From the American perspective, however, it grows increasingly difficult to both defend third areas
against the Soviet Union while at the same time policing these
areas on behalf of the Soviet Union. Hence the American
disillusionment with detente. The paper then suggests three
possible ways in which the international order might develop so
that the conflicting views of the U.S. and the USSR on the
meaning of "equality" do not threaten deterrence.

Also published as a National Defense University Research Directorate study (Washington, D.C.: National Defense University
Press, 1979), 27 p.

No. 121. Van Oudenaren, John.
Deterrence, Warfighting and Soviet Military Doctrine.
London: International Institute for Strategic Studies (Adelphi
Papers No. 210), Summer 1986, 47 p.

This paper explores the hypothesis that both Soviet and American
doctrines are attempts to resolve dilemmas inherent in the nuclear
competition that cannot be reduced to a simple set of propositions. These dilemmas arise from the different and in many
ways contradictory aspects of nuclear weapons: deterrent,
warfighting, and political. The paper examines three broad
topics to disentangle these aspects of the nuclear competition:
the concept of "doctrine," the question of how the problem of
security in the nuclear age is reflected in doctrine, and certain
basic features of the Soviet system which may motivate the
apparent drive to maximize Soviet security through the pursuit
of warfighting capabilities. Perhaps the most important lesson of
this analysis concerns the widening gap between Soviet ideological pretentions and reality.

The Soviet View of Nuclear Warfighting

No. 122. Arbeiter, Jurgen B.
"A Transparent Figleaf--The Offensive Nature of Soviet Military Doctrine."
Air University Review Vol. 31 No. 6 (November-December 1980), pp. 93-98.

There is a clear interconnection between Soviet foreign policy and Soviet military policy -- both are identical in long-term goals, but differ in their implementation. Soviet military science considers that two main categories of war between countries of the two social systems are possible: world-wide nuclear war and limited war without deployment of nuclear arms. Soviet soldiers are prepared and trained for both types of war. Soviet forces must at all times be capable of hitting the enemy hard, especially at the beginning of a war, causing the enemy to sustain heavy losses by smashing his main forces and nuclear weapons, annihilating strategic industrial plants, and destroying the political and military command system. The Soviet leadership's only concern is to win, not to deter.

No. 123. Boileau, Oliver C.
"Can Strategic Deterrence Prevent a Nuclear War?"
National Defense Vol. 61 No. 2 (March-April 1977), pp. 370-373.

If mutual assured destruction has rendered strategic superiority meaningless, why is the Soviet Union investing so heavily not only in achieving numerical nuclear superiority, but in increasing it? How willing would the Soviet leaders be to accept the risk of millions of Soviet casualties in threatening an attack on U.S. strategic forces? Two factors must be considered here. One is the difference in the values placed on human life by the Soviet Union and the United States. The second is the Soviet estimate of the cost of a nuclear exchange in Soviet lives lost and property destroyed. An official Soviet estimate claims there would be about ten million casualties -- only one half to one third as many casualties as the Soviet leaders inflicted on their own people in consolidating their internal political control. Behind these Soviet calculations -- and similar ones regarding the survival of industry --lies an intensive civil defense program.

No. 124. Crommelin, Quentin, Jr.; and David Sullivan.
Soviet Military Supremacy: The Untold Facts About the New Danger to America.
Los Angeles, Calif.: University of Southern California Defense and Strategic Studies Program, 1985, 164 p.

This book addresses how the rhetoric of American policy does not match the reality of the U.S. strategic position. In particular it focuses on several impressions subtly "sold" by the American news media and government: that the Soviet military buildup is due to the Soviet Union's belief that it must match U.S. military strength to be safe from nuclear attack; that the United States and the Soviet Union are equally menacing; that the military power of both nations is roughly equivalent; and that each side would be able to destroy the other in the event of nuclear war. In fact, the Soviet Union has focused its entire national effort, sacrificing everything except the most basic needs, to achieve the capability to survive a nuclear war and defeat any combination of opponents.

No. 125. Goure, Leon; Foy D. Kohler, and Mose L. Harvey. The Role of Nuclear Forces in Current Soviet Strategy. University of Miami: Center for Advanced International Studies, 1974, 148 p.

This study analyzes, on the basis of open Soviet sources, Moscow's current views on the military and political utility of its nuclear forces, the question of nuclear sufficiency and the future expansion of Soviet armed forces and the concepts of the use of nuclear weapons for strategic and theater war purposes. The discussion points out the critical differences in Soviet doctrine, perceptions and military planning from those of the United States, with special reference to such questions as stable deterrence vs. a war-fighting capability, controlled vs. uncontrolled use of nuclear weapons, strategic parity vs. superiority, and mutual assured destruction vs. a war-winning strategy.

Reviewed by: William G. Hanne, Military Review Vol. 55 No. 2 (February 1975), pp. 105-106; Matthew P. Gallagher, "Moscow and Detente," Problems of Communism Vol. 24 No. 2 (March/April 1975), pp. 77-79; Air Force Policy Literature for Commanders No. 9 (September 1978), pp. 31-34.

No. 126. Hamlett, Bruce D. "SALT: The Illusion and the Reality." Strategic Review Vol. 3 No. 3 (Summer 1975), pp. 67-78.

There are major differences in the Soviet and the American concepts of deterrence and strategic forces, as well as in their understanding of the requirements and implications of detente. While the Soviet defense posture emphasizes both war-avoidance and war-waging capabilities via assured survival, the United States' approach concentrates on war-avoidance through assured destruction capabilities. While the Soviets view detente as a tactic to be used in the process of changing the status quo, the Americans view detente as a desired end. Because of these differences, the SALT negotiations and agreements have resulted in an international situation offering clear threats to long-run American security. An evaluation of SALT thus far must conclude that: 1) concern with presidential electoral politics have caused both Ford and Nixon to make unwise and unnecessary concessions to the Soviet Union; 2) nuclear parity has provided the Soviets with superiority in the "correlation of forces"; 3) through the process of nuclear arms control negotiation, the Soviet Union has moved from a position of inferiority in capabilities to a position of clear potential superiority; and 4) the Soviet Union is now in a position to resist any American pressure for its withdrawal from conflicts in the Middle East, Asia, and Europe.

No. 127. Hoeber, Amoretta.
"Soviet Strategic Intentions."
In Kenneth M. Currie and Gregory Varhall (Eds.), The Soviet Union: What Lies Ahead?
Washington, D.C.: Government Printing Office (Studies in Communist Affairs Vol. 6), 1985, pp. 661-669.

This article urges a greater understanding of Soviet intentions and strategy in order to develop appropriate and effective counter-strategies. It contends that domination coupled with political and military victory appear to be serious, long-term Soviet aims. While the Soviet Union may not desire war, it will be prepared for its contingency. In order to do this, the Soviet Union emphasizes surprise, force superiority, war survival measures, and specific plans for the occupation and control of enemy territory. The Soviet Union's goal in war is its own postwar recovery, as well as political domination of a defeated West.

No. 128. Hoeber, Francis P.; and Amoretta Hoeber.
"The Soviet View of Deterrence: Who Whom?"
Survey Vol. 25 No. 2 (Spring 1980), pp. 17-24.

The problem with the mutual deterrence approach to nuclear strategy is that it does only make sense when it is mutual; yet the views attributed by it to the Soviet Union are not the real core of Soviet thought. This is not to say that the Soviet Union desires war, or that it does not understand the brutal implications of a nuclear conflict. The Soviet Union has striven to acquire both the military and political dimensions of strategic superiority. The whole Soviet thrust is toward building credible threats while denying credibility to U.S. threats. The U.S. policy of placing itself in hostage to Soviet deterrent forces and seeking mutual deterrence is based on ascribing U.S. policy views to the Soviet Union. However, its words, programs, and actions indicate otherwise.

No. 129. Holman, Paul.
"Deterrence vs. War-Fighting: The Soviet Preference."

Air Force Magazine (Soviet Aerospace Almanac No. 7) Vol. 64
No. 3 (March 1981), pp. 50-54.

The Soviet Union draws an indelible line between deterrence and
war-fighting; the first being the province of the diplomat and
propagandist, while the second is the pursuit of the military
strategist. Because U.S. observers have been slow to appreciate Soviet war-fighting preferences, the Soviet concept of
strategic superiority has been often dismissed, and Soviet statements about victory in nuclear war are excluded from consideration. But the single most important fact about Soviet military
doctrine is its striking congruence with Soviet force posture.
This article examines Soviet nuclear strategy from the perspective of a dichotomy between two extreme goals, deterrence and
war-fighting. Deterrence seems likely to remain in the 1980s
what it has always been for the Soviet Union -- an alien strategy, wholly inadequate as a basis for military doctrine and
force posture. War-fighting, with all its advantages and
pitfalls, will remain Moscow's strategy.

Also published in Kenneth M. Currie and Gregory Varhill
(Eds.), The Soviet Union: What Lies Ahead? (Washington,
D.C.: Government Printing Office, Studies in Communist Affairs
Vol. 6, 1985), pp. 693-705.

Also printed as a RAND paper (RM-3779-PR), September 1963,
73 p.

No. 130. Hughes, Peter C.; and M.R. Edwards.
"Nuclear War in Soviet Thinking -- The Implications for U.S.
Security."
Journal of Social and Political Studies Vol. 2 No. 2 (April 1976),
pp. 113-130.

The popular belief in the United States, nourished by statements
from public officials, is that nuclear war would mean an Arma-
geddon without a victor and without survivors. Therefore,
stability between the superpowers exists through Mutual Assured
Destruction. In Soviet politico-military thought, by contrast,
nuclear war is not only thinkable, but perhaps inevitable. The
Soviet Union has undertaken a massive military buildup in conventional and strategic forces; it is making rapid technological
advances in strategic arms, and it has undertaken an intensive
civil defense program. Given current strategic realities, any
Western leader might hesitate to challenge a direct Soviet military
threat, much less employ strategic weapons in the event of
lower-level Soviet aggression. This posture must be questioned.
The time has come to reassess U.S. strategic thinking and
educate the U.S. public to the realities of the nuclear age.

No. 131. Jenson, John W.
"Nuclear Strategy: Differences in Soviet and American Thinking."
Air University Review Vol. 30 No. 2 (March-April 1979), pp. 2-17.

Soviet military strategy and doctrine, like their Western counterparts, have been designed to lessen the likelihood of a general nuclear conflict. But Soviet doctrine and strategy reflect the essential differences between the Soviet and American political systems, ideologies, historical experiences, geographic positions, and economic and technical capabilities, and differing perceptions of themselves and the world at large. Soviet strategy is designed to provide both a deterrent and a war-winning capability and ensure a peacetime environment in which the political objectives of the Soviet Union can be freely pursued. Therefore, it seems doubtful that the Soviet Union will opt for any military posture short of superiority over its enemies.

No. 132. Keegan, George J.
"An Editorial in the Form of a Letter."
Strategic Review Vol. 5 No. 2 (Spring 1977), pp. 6-11.

The suggestion that Soviet strategic objectives can best be understood within the context of U.S. strategic policy is a rather substantial error. The Soviet view has been that any kind of conflict can be won. American policy-makers, where the nuclear weapon is involved, perceive no solution except the prevention of war, never seriously entertaining the thought that there might be methods that could successfully counter and neutralize the nuclear weapon. The difference is a profound one. Successive U.S. administrations have imposed restraint on military programs in the hope of inviting similar restraint on the Soviet side. The Soviet Union appears to believe that war is more likely than not, and that under these circumstances it is necessary to be able to wage it and win it, whatever the level of intensity. The assumptions under which the United States has pursued arms control with the Soviet Union are faulty, both in their basic premises and their implementation. Arms control has served the Soviet Union to enhance its own power. The noble U.S. experiment with strategic restraint is leading to the very abyss it was designed to avoid.

No. 133. King, Peter.
"Two Eyes for a Tooth: The State of Soviet Strategic Doctrine."
Survey Vol. 24 No. 1 (Winter 1970), pp. 45-56.

Soviet strategic theory lags behind that of the United States because institutional military influences prevent it from coming to grips with the fact that nuclear war would mean the cancellation of politics. The diplomatic exploitation of force, or any other use of military force besides "victory", is missing from this literature. Taking Soviet strategic doctrine at face value as praxis for managing holocaust, three standards suggest themselves for a critique of it: 1) are the elements of the doctrine -- concerning ends and means in strategic combat, as well as forecasts of its likely course -- consistent?; 2) is the doctrine pragmatically sound -- that is, are recommended means related to specified ends in a rational fashion?; and 3) is the doctrine sound from a patriotic, ideological, and ethical point of view? The execution of total preemptive nuclear retaliation remains an absurdity from a strategic point of view for the Soviet Union, and until it addresses the realities of nuclear combat, Soviet strategy will be a thing of little worth and considerable risk.

No. 134.   Luce, Clare Booth.
"Two Doctrines of War."
Strategic Review Vol. 6 No. 4 (Fall 1974), pp. 12-14

The Soviet doctrine of war advocates the calculated selection of time and place to initiate hostilities, and holds that war with the West is necesary and inevitable. Soviet military planning favors offensive operations, avoiding the use of force until victory is assured. The American doctrine of war renounces the right to initiate hostilities to defend its ideals and interests and holds that the only moral, justifiable war is one fought in self-defense, in which the enemy has been the aggressor. This purely defensive American doctrine of moral ascendancy gives the enemy the absolute initiative and relies upon a deterrence posture and diplomacy for the protection of American interests and the avoidance of conflict. Present Soviet-U.S. military trends presage a preponderance of war-winning capability -- nuclear and conventional -- in favor of the Soviets. Steadily declining U.S. power and credibility thus invite Soviet assault.

No. 135.   MccGwire, Michael.
"Soviet Strategic Weapons Policy, 1955-70."
Chapter 27 in Michael MccGwire et al. (Eds.), Soviet Naval Policy: Objectives and Constraints.
New York: Praeger Publishers, 1975, pp. 486-503.

The purpose of this chapter is to examine the policies that would logically flow from the meanings that the Soviet military attaches to such concepts as "world war" and "deterrence." It then compares the postulated requirements with what the Soviet Union has already produced, built, and deployed. There is an impressive range and diversity of evidence that point to an affirmative conclusion. A large gap often exists between Soviet doctrinally derived requirements and the actual capability to fulfil them. Bu Soviet willingness to expend substantial resources in attempting to meet such requirements should be borne in mind, even when the likely returns are low and the chances of success seem small.

No. 136. Millett, Stephen M.
Soviet Perceptions of Nuclear Strategy and Implications for U.S. Deterrence.
Columbus, Ohio: Battelle Economics and Policy Analysis Occasional Paper No. 18 (April 1981), 23 p.

One must first understand Soviet ideology, especially the concept of the "correlation of forces," before one can grasp the fundamentals of Soviet nuclear doctrine, and understand the significance of Soviet open literature only in its context of intellectual paradigms. They understand deterrence to mean the prevention of imperialist attack in an attempt to reverse the continuous shift in the correlation of forces, and hence must be prepared to wage nuclear war with the West. Recent Soviet propaganda campaigns have underlined their great apprehension that the United States is moving to a first-strike posture. If the Soviets reject the concept of the second strike, the United States faces the great hazard of a Soviet preemptive strike calculated to "beat the Americans to the punch." The safest policy for the United States is to strengthen its second-strike capabilities and minimize its first strike threat to the Soviet Union.

Republished in Air University Review Vol. 33 No. 3 (March–April 1982), pp. 50-61.

No. 137. Nicholson, Arthur Donald, Jr.
The Soviet Union and Strategic Nuclear War.
Monterey, Calif.: The Naval Postgraduate School, 1980, 154 p.

The strategic relationship which exists between the United States and the Soviet Union is an important consideration in charting the course of international relations in the remainder of this century. To understand the nature of this relationship, especially as it evolves in the SALT era, one must understand three fundamental realities of Soviet strategic policy. First, the interests of the Soviet Union, and the means selected in pursuit of those interests, are conditioned by an experience which is unique to Soviet Russia. This experience lacks sufficient commonality with that of the United States for it to serve as a basis for mutual cooperation and accommodation. Second, developments in the Soviet nuclear arsenal are designed to secure a position of strategic dominance from which Soviet influence can be exercised with relative impunity. Third, the Soviet view of nuclear war differs radically from that of the United States. Soviet nuclear doctrine represents a realistic military approach to the problems of nuclear war, and consists of a set of war fighting guidelines which capitalize on the key principles of surprise, early seizure of the strategic initiative, and decisive use of nuclear weapons.

100

This research, completed in June 1977, examines each of these three guides.

No. 138.   Olsen, Gerald E.
The U.S. Concept of Deterrence--Versus the Challenging Soviet Military Power of the 1970s.
Maxwell Air Force Base, Ala.:   Air Command and Staff College (0527u--Research Study), 1972, 72 p.

The purpose of this paper is to evaluate the United States strategy of deterrence and the growing Soviet military threat that faces the United States in the future. This report first reviews the changing concept of deterrence that the United States has followed in an effort to maintain national security and prevent nuclear war. It then examines the significant trends which reflect the Soviet Union's drive for an overwhelming military superiority, and quite possibly a first-strike capability. The conclusion points out the seriousness of this threat and makes recommendations that would improve the national security of the United States.

No. 139.   Pipes, Richard.
"Why the Soviet Union Thinks It Could Fight and Win a Nuclear War."
Commentary Vol. 64 No. 1 (July 1977), pp. 21-34.

American and Soviet nuclear doctrines are starkly at odds. The prevalent U.S. doctrine holds that an all-out war between countries in possession of sizeable nuclear arsenals would be so destructive as to leave no winner. Soviet doctrine asserts that while an all-out nuclear war would indeed prove extremely destructive to both parties, the country better prepared for it and in possession of a superior strategy could win and emerge a viable society. The American strategic community usually dismisses Soviet doctrine with the explanation that it is clearly backwards; given time and patient "education," the Soviet Union will surely adopt a "rational" strategy based on mutual deterrence. Soviet doctrine has five related elements: 1) preemption (first strike), 2) quantitative superiority in arms, 3) counterforce targeting, 4) combined-arms operations, and 5) defense. The differences between American and Soviet strategic doctrines may be summarized by stating that whereas the United States views nuclear weapons as a deterrent, the Soviet Union sees them as a "compellant." As long as the Soviet Union adheres to this strategy, mutual deterrence does not really exist; for unilateral deterrence to succeed, the United States must understand the Soviet war-winning strategy and make it impossible to succeed.

Reprinted in Air Force Magazine Vol. 60 No. 9 (September 1977), pp. 54-66; Quadrant Vol. 21 No. 9 (September 1977), pp. 10-22;

Richard Pipes (Ed.), U.S.-Soviet Relations in the Era of Detente (Boulder, Colo.: Westview Press, 1981), pp. 135-170.

Responses from Paul Roberts, Thomas Downey, Bernard Brodie, Melvin Goodman, B. Bruce-Briggs, Irwin Stark, Fred Kaplan, Stanley Page, and Elias Schwarzburt in Commentary Vol. 64 No. 3 (September 1977), pp. 5-26.

Reviewed in the Wilson Quarterly Vol. 1 No. 5 (Autumn 1977), pp. 21-22.

No. 140. Ra'anan, Uri.
"Soviet Strategic Doctrine and the Soviet-American Global Contest."
Annals, The American Academy of Political and Social Science, No. 457 (September 1981), pp. 8-17.

Soviet Military Doctrine, despite the exigencies of the thermo-nuclear age, continues to follow Clausewitz in viewing war as a continuation of policies by other means. Accordingly, war is regarded both as feasible and winnable, provided the USSR continues to maintain the initiative, to pursue the offensive, and to utilize surprise and deception. These factors mean that an initial blow against an adversary may prove ultimately decisive, but without ensuring that conflict necessarily would be short. Preparations have to be adequate for protracted warfare, with particular emphasis on reserves, military and economic. Pacifist rejection of wars as such is condemned in the USSR for failing to distinguish between just and unjust conflicts that are judged by their class content -- not by the question of who started the fighting. There is little evidence for the view that Soviet Military Doctrine is the product of military rather than civilian (Party) leaders. In accordance with the dialectic, the USSR believes that balance, or stalemate, is unfeasible as a long-term concept since, ultimately, there are only victors and the defeated.

No. 141. Rand, Robert.
Soviet Commentary on Winning a Nuclear War.
Munich: Radio Liberty Research, 1980, 4 p.

Statements found in Soviet military writings support the view that the Kremlin's strategic doctrines rest on the belief that it can fight and win a nuclear war. Some American analysts contend that such military writings are a form of psychological warfare that should be taken with a grain of salt. Others believe that they are produced strictly for internal consumption among the Soviet Union's military and political establishment. Still others maintain that they should be taken at face value and warn that a failure to do so would place U.S. national security in jeopardy. The U.S. decision to adopt a new strategic doctrine shows that the Carter Adminstration believes that such Soviet military statements are cause for alarm.

No. 142. Report of a Study Group of the Institute for the Study of Conflict.
London: ISC Special Report, March 1978, 39 p.

This report considers the consequences of the SALT II negotiations against the backdrop of the SALT I and Vladivostok agreements, and whether the strategic balance has been altered to Moscow's advantage. It examines Soviet decision-making and military doctrine, especially in terms of how they effect procurement of weapons systems. The principles of procurement include preemption, quantitative superiority, combined operations, counterforce, and active defense.

No. 143. Vick, Alan J.
"Soviet Military Forces and Strategy Come of Age: Implications for American Deterrence Theory."
Air University Review Vol. 32 No. 2 (January-February 1981), pp. 17-26.

It is essential that Western analysts appreciate this key point: Soviet military leaders do not accept academic theories of deterrence presented by American civilians. They are, however, impressed by high-quality military forces combined with the political wherewithal to use them. Thus, given first-rate Soviet military forces and strategy and increased political power for the military elite, a reasonable American response would be to procure weapons and develop strategies designed to meet military requirements for retaliation at the sub-SIOP and single integrated operational plan (SIOP) levels. Such an approach would not only make a Soviet first-strike less likely, but in the event deterrence fails, would enhance intrawar deterrence, enabling the United States to prosecute and terminate the war below the SIOP level.

No. 144. Ward, Chester C.
"The 'New Myths' and 'Old Realities' of Nuclear War."
Orbis Vol. 8 No. 2 (Summer 1964), pp. 255-291.

It has recently become fashionable to talk about the old myths and new realities of American foreign policy. The makers of new myths assert that a strategic stalemate has developed between the United States and the Soviet Union and that, therefore, nuclear war is unthinkable. Among the well-briefed realities being discarded is the all-too-real Soviet objective of world conquest. It is alleged that the Soviets themselves no longer seriously consider the attainment of this goal, particularly as it can be achieved only by the use of nuclear weapons. The time has come to assess the new and the old myths, the new and old realities. Western statesmen have gradually convinced themselves and their citizens of the "unthinkability" of general war. But they give little consideration to the possibility that the Soviet Union might have both the intent and capability to break out of the strategic stalemate, building forces designed to annihilate 150 to 180 million Americans and wreck the U.S. retaliatory force. The only way the United States can avoid the stark alternatives of suicide or surrender is to halt the trend toward a minimum deterrence posture.

No. 145. Yinon, Oded.
"The Soviet Doctrine of Total War."
Midstream Vol. 27 No. 10 (December 1981), pp. 7-11.

In the 1960s, the Soviet Union began to build a military force in dimensions the world had never known before. The objective of this giant effort has been: 1) a Soviet victory in total war, 2) survival of the Soviet bloc to enjoy the fruits of victory and, 3) enslavement of the remains of the capitalist bloc. The Soviet viewpoint since the advent of Leonid Brezhnev differs qualitatively from the earlier Soviet concept, which maintained that a nuclear war would have no value for the realization of Communism and that their purpose would be achieved by worldwide guerrilla warfare. The Soviet Union's present complex theorizing and planning derives from two basic assumptions: that the Soviet Union is capable of surviving, winning, and benefiting from a massive-scale nuclear war; and that as war is simply a continuation of politics in another form, nuclear warfare is no different from any other type of war. The Soviet plan for total war consists of five principle phases, ending with the establishment of Soviet-style regimes everywhere.

3

Soviet Strategy and Doctrine

A. SOVIET MILITARY DOCTRINE AND STRATEGY

Descriptions of Soviet Military Doctrine and Strategy

No. 146. Baker, John C.
"Continuity and Change in Soviet Nuclear Strategy."
In Kenneth M. Currie and Gregory Varhall (Eds.), The Soviet Union: What Lies Ahead?
Washington, D.C.: Government Printing Office (Studies in Communist Affairs Vol. 6), 1985, pp. 636-660.

This article describes the general continuity of Soviet military doctrine. This has been conditioned by historical factors, the Soviet Union's role as a continental land power, and the consequent dominance of the Soviet Ground Forces in Soviet military planning. As a result, even with the advent of nuclear weapons, the USSR still has a conservative approach towards modern military strategy. The article probes the sources of Soviet military thought, the nature of its nuclear strategy, and the possibility for changes in that strategy during the 1980s.

No. 147. Barlow, William J.
"Soviet Damage-Denial: Strategy, Systems, SALT, and Solution."
Air University Review Vol. 32 No. 5 (September-October 1981), pp. 2-20.

This article proposes a methodology to examine Soviet nuclear objectives. It takes the hypothesis that the fundamental Soviet nuclear strategic concept and objective is "damage-denial." The Soviet Union categorizes the nuclear threat from the United States as: 1) ICBMs; 2) submarine missiles; 3) bomber-launched Short Range Attack Missiles; and 4) Theater aircraft from NATO and Korea, including carrier aviation (Forward Based Systems). Soviet strategic nuclear planning focuses on neutralizing these threats. The implications of this for arms control and planning are discussed.

No. 148. Beukel, Erik.
"Analyzing the Views of Soviet Leaders on Nuclear Weapons."
Cooperation and Conflict Vol. 15 (June 1980), pp. 71-84.

The Soviet view on the role of nuclear weapons is of critical interest and therefore widely discussed not only in strategic but also foreign policy circles. This paper analyses the views of three Soviet personalities who are central to any such discussion: Secretary General Brezhnev, the former Minister of Defense Grechko, and Foreign Minister Gromyko. It is shown that the views of these persons differ substantially, with the former Minister of Defense appearing as the most divergent. Several explanations for these differences are considered, and various clues for future interpretations are offered. Caution is urged against the propensities to use Soviet pronouncements to sub-stantiate assertions either that the Soviet leadership perceives nuclear weapons in "war-fighting" or in deterrence terms. It is suggested that statements must be evaluated in their particular context.

No. 149. Cade, David J.
"Russian Military Strategy: A Fresh Look."
Air University Review Vol. 29 No. 6 (September-October 1978), pp. 18-27.

From 1963 to the present, Soviet strategic military thinking has remained essentially as presented in Military Strategy, an important collective work published under the leadership of Marshal V.D. Sokolovskiy. Brezhnev proved to be a proponent of its combined arms concept and pushed for an upgrading of conventional as well as strategic forces. He has shown a clear appreciation for the risks of nuclear war as well as for the application and use for force short of war, with strategic nuclear missiles providing the umbrella under which all Soviet politico-military actions are taken. Although the Soviet military may be satisfied with strategic nuclear parity, it probably will maintain its drive for clear superiority in the area of general purpose forces to override perceived U.S. advantages in other areas, primarily economic and technological.

No. 150. Caravelli, John N.
"The Role of Surprise and Preemption in Soviet Military Strategy."
International Security Review Vol. 6 No. 2 (Summer 1981), pp. 209-233.

A close examination of Soviet military thought since the Second World War reveals that the Soviet military has historically been preoccupied with working out the details of a damage limitation strategy based on a successful preemptive strike. This study examines chronologically the development of several key elements of Soviet military thought associated with the initial period of a strategic war: surprise attack, preemptive first strike, and superiority. A preemptive strike links the key elements of Soviet war-fighting strategy in the following manner: 1) by seizing the initiative the Soviet Union can decrease the effects if not (ideally) totally prevent a retaliatory strike; and 2) a preemptive first strike also provides the best opportunity for the Soviet military to achieve superiority in the correlation of forces after the initial exchange.

No. 151. Cimbala, Steven J.
"Soviet Nuclear Strategies: Will They Do the Expected?"
Strategic Review Vol. 13 No. 4 (Fall 1985), pp. 67-77.

American strategic analysis and policies have come to focus ever more sharply on warfighting and survivability capabilities as necessary parts of a credible deterrent posture. In the process, four principal Soviet nuclear strategies have commonly been deduced from Soviet writings and deployments -- strategies under the headings of coercion, attrition, annihilation, and decapitation. Yet, there is a fifth alternative consistent with Soviet doctrine and posture: a blitzkrieg strike waged within the abatement of crisis. If the alternative is palpable, it has substantial implications for U.S. strategic modernization programs, particularly those related to improvements in command, control and communications, and to the Strategic Defense Initiative.

No. 152. Dinerstein, Herbert S.
"The Revolution in Soviet Strategic Thinking."
Foreign Affairs Vol. 36 No. 2 (January 1958), pp. 241-252.

Soviet military thinkers have radically altered some of their hoary ideas about warfare. Differences in military policies played an important role in the political crises terminated by Malenkov's demotion in February 1955. They were resolved by the decision to have not only a deterrent capability, but also a war-making capability. If the Soviet Union should continue to gain technologically while the NATO alliance made little progress, the Soviet Union would be able to make war without fear of the consequences. It will be difficult to attain the ability to eliminate the opponent's nuclear striking forces in a single blow. But that is the goal which the Soviet leaders must strain to reach. If they should acquire such preponderant military strength, they would have policy alternatives even more attractive than the initiation of nuclear war. By flaunting presumably invincible strength, the Soviet Union could compel piecemeal capitulation of the democracies.

Also printed by the RAND Corporation, 1957.

No. 153. Dinerstein, Herbert S.
The Soviet Military Posture as a Reflection of Soviet Strategy.
Santa Monica, Calif.: The RAND Corporation (RM-2102), 24 March 1958, 22 p.

An attempt to determine the extent to which Soviet armed forces reflect the changes in Soviet strategic conceptions dating from 1954 to 1955, and to show the consistency of the design of Soviet ground, air, and naval forces from 1945 to 1953 with a notion of war in which total mobilization occured gradually as the war continued. Since early 1955, official Soviet policy has required readiness to fight a war in which nuclear weapons would be used and has stressed that the side which strikes first enjoys great if not decisive advantages. It is concluded that the Soviet Union is seeking a retaliation-proof capability designed to make the initial nuclear blow, whether or not it is thinking in terms of preventive war.

No. 154. Donnelly, Christopher N.
"The Development of Soviet Military Doctrine."
International Defense Review Vol. 14 No. 12 (December 1981), pp. 1589-1596.

Soviet military doctrine is an all-embracing military philosophy which is applied to the whole military system as the military element of Marxist-Leninist doctrine. Thus the principles of Soviet military doctrine are applied uniformly across the whole spectrum of military affairs. The Soviets consider their military doctrine to be one of their greatest assets as the concentration and distillation of military wisdom and experience, constantly refined and improved by experiment, exercise, and reevaluation. Four main factors which have contributed to the mold of modern Soviet military doctrine can be identified: 1) Marxist-Leninist ideology; 2) the effects of the Russian environment and the Tsarist tradition; 3) the experience of the Revolutionary War and the 1941-45 War; and 4) the impact of modern technology.

Reprinted in Military Review Vol. 62 No. 8 (August 1982), pp. 38-51.

No. 155. Douglass, Joseph D., Jr.; and Amoretta M. Hoeber.
Soviet Strategy for Nuclear War.
Stanford, Calif.: Hoover Institution Press, 1979, 138 p.

The methodology used in this study was to read Soviet military literature extensively so as to understand the Soviet mind-set and isolate the basic principles that dominate Soviet military thought. In contrast to Western military literature, the Soviet literature is seriously directed to the problems of fighting and winning a nuclear war. There is no evidence of the existence of opposing schools of military thought as are found in the West. Soviet thought about and concepts of global nuclear war present a coherent pattern linking party policy, military doctrine and strategy, and force development. Soviet force deployments and characteristics match their doctrine and strategy; where discrepancies occur, it appears that the implied force capabilities often require time to emerge completely.

Reviewed by: Steward Menaul, "How the Soviets Would Fight a Nuclear War -- And Win," (London: Foreign Affairs Research Institute Report 15/1979), 8 p.

Reviewed by Laura Hutchinson, The Friday Review of Defense Literature (82-6), February 12, 1982, pp. 3-4.

No. 156. Frank, Lewis A.
"Soviet Power After SALT I: A Strategic Coercive Capability?"
Strategic Review Vol. 2 No. 2 (Spring 1974), pp. 54-60.

The October 1973 Mideast War demonstrated the capacity and readiness of the Soviet Union to strengthen its beachhead in the Middle East. This action culminated a long buildup of Soviet military power following the embarrassing Cuban missile confrontation of 1962. Readiness of the USSR to use its military power in a time of "parity" raises grave questions about its prospective action when it enjoys superiority. SALT I did not inhibit the Soviet growth rate. There is enough latitude in the agreements to accommodate planned Soviet weapons development, on land and at sea. Soviet policy appears designed to achieve a successful nuclear war-waging capability, including an intrawar strategic-coercive capability of potentially decisive dimensions. The declining throw-weight of the U.S. and the growing throw weight of the USSR argue that the Soviet Union may achieve its strategic-coercive capability under the provisions of SALT I. The prospect raises grave questions for U.S. allies heretofore dependent upon the U.S. nuclear deterrent for survival. There is growing evidence that Soviet leadership is prepared to use nuclear advantage for political gain. Thus the provisions of SALT I are a charter not for the stability which U.S. diplomacy has proclaimed but for instability and possibly for war.

No. 157. Galay, Nikolai.
"The Soviet Approach to the Modern Military Revolution."
In John Erickson (Ed.), The Military-Technical Revolution.
New York: Frederick A. Praeger, Publisher, 1966, pp. 20-31.

Although it took seventeen years for the Soviet Union to accept the influence of the modern military revolution, its effect was powerful from the outset. The Soviet leaders foresaw the shock it would produce on Communist political and social doctrine, which explains their reluctance to accept it. First, it inflicted a severe blow on Communist ideology by disproving the Marxist thesis that capitalism was doomed because it had already exhausted all possibilities for development of productive forces. Second, it created a political barrier to Communist expansion because nuclear weapons made war no longer a feasible instrument of politics. Finally, the need to acquire nuclear weapons meant conceding a certain degree of freedom of thought and initiative among the people and in the Party. The military revolution has upset the relationship between Soviet politics and strategy to the advantage of the latter. The loss of political primacy over military strategy is undermining the ideological foundations of the Soviet regime and is leading to a revulsion against Communist dogmas and a certain revival of naked militarism born of the pressure exerted by aggressive military policy and strategy. The two future alternatives are either eventual abandonment of ideological dogmas or total militarization of Soviet society.

No. 158. "A Garthoff-Pipes Debate on Soviet Strategic Doctrine."
Strategic Review Vol. 10 No. 4 (Fall 1982), pp. 36-63.

In its Summer 1978 issue, the journal International Security published a lengthy article by Raymond L. Garthoff, then U.S. Ambassador to Bulgaria, in which he described fundamental Soviet attitudes toward strategic deterrence, nuclear warfighting, and arms control. Recently Dr. Richard Pipes, a member of the National Security Council staff on leave from Harvard University, submitted to Strategic Review a critique of Ambassador Garthoff's article. Even though the debate centers on an article that appeared more than four years ago, it nevertheless reflects an abiding controversy in an area that is both fundamental and crucial to America's security concerns and policies. For this compelling reason, the editors of Strategic Review have agreed to bring the debate to its readers. What follows is the original article by Ambassador Garthoff, "Mutual Deterrence and Strategic Arms Limitation in Soviet Policy" (abridged by him and adapted to the style of Strategic Review); the critique by Dr. Pipes, "Soviet Strategic Doctrine: Another View"; and a rebuttal by Ambassador Garthoff.

Reprinted as "A Debate Between Raymond L. Garthoff and Richard Pipes on Soviet Nuclear Strategy," Chapter 25 in P. Edward Haley et al. (Eds.), Nuclear Strategy, Arms Control, and the Future (Boulder, Colo.: Westview Press, 1985), pp. 169-178.

No. 159. Garthoff, Raymond L.
Soviet Strategy in the Nuclear Age.
New York: Frederick A. Praeger, Publisher, 1958, 283 p.

The main part of this work is devoted to a presentation of the
"Soviet principles of war." Among those discussed are the
offensive, the salient thrust, annihilation, encirclement, morale,
training, and leadership. It concludes with a study of the uses
to which these principles are put at various levels of command
and in all the branches of the Soviet service.

Revised edition published in 1962, reprinted by Greenwood Press
(Westport, Conn.) in 1974. Chapter 5, "Soviet Views on Limited
War;" also printed in Military Review Vol. 37 No. 9 (December
1957), pp. 3-12; Chapter 8, "Air Power in Soviet Strategy," also
in Air University Quarterly Review Vol. 9 No. 4 (Winter 1957-
1958), pp. 80-97; and as Chapter 69 in Eugene M. Emme (Ed.),
The Impact of Air Power (Princeton, N.J.: D. Van Nostrand
Co., Inc., 1959), pp. 526-540; also an earlier version printed as
Soviet Attitudes Toward Modern Air Power (Santa Monica, Calif.:
The RAND Corporation, P-603, November 29, 1945, 11 p.), and
in Military Affairs, Summer 1955; Chapter 10, "Missiles in Soviet
Strategy," condensed in Air Force Magazine Vol. 41 No. 7 (July
1958), pp. 91-92.

Reviewed by James F. Sunderman, "The De-Stalinization of
Soviet Military Strategy," Orbis Vol. 2 No. 4 (Winter 1959), pp.
492-496.

No. 160. Garthoff, Raymond L.
The Soviet Image of Future War.
Washington, D.C.: Public Affairs Press, 1959, 136 p.

This volume supplements and extends an earlier study, Soviet
Strategy in the Nuclear Age, with more detailed analysis of the
development and current state of thinking on the role of the
basic economic, military, political and morale factors in war, and
the evaluation of surprise, blitzkrieg, and preventive and preemptive strikes. It also presents, as appendices, three recent
significant Soviet discussions of military doctrine on the nature
of future war, in full translation: Colonel I. Baz, "Soviet Military
Science on the Character of Contemporary War," Voennyi vestnik
No. 6 (June 1958); Colonel I. Korotkov, "On the Fundamental
Factors Which Determine the Course and Outcome of Wars,"
Soviet Aviation, August 12, 1958; and Colonel P. Sidorov, "The
Creative Character of Soviet Military Science," Sovetskii flot,
December 11, 1958.

Chapter 2, "Decisive Factors in Modern War," also printed as
"Soviet Doctrine on the Decisive Factors in Modern War," in
Military Review Vol. 39 No. 4 (July 1959), p. 3-22; adapted in

"Soviet Strategy: Flexibility, Firepower, Follow-up," _Army_ Vol. 10 No. 1 (August 1959), pp. 38-42.

Reviewed by Alvin J. Cottrell, "The Soviet Threat: General or Limited War?", _Orbis_ Vol. 4 No. 1 (Spring 1960), pp. 93-100.

No. 161. Jacobsen, C.G.
"Soviet Attitudes to 'Controlled Strategic Conflict'."
Current Comment No. 10 (May 1976), pp. 14-23.

This study concentrates on current evolutions of Soviet strategic thinking, especially the possible role of "controlled conflict options." The surfacing in the early 1970s of new Soviet appreciation for historical "withholding strategies," the tentative indications that a "hold-back" of Soviet naval potentials might be contemplated, the talk of vaguely defined but apparently less than all-out "nuclear exchanges," and the talk of the need to ensure continued protection of residual strategic means after the initiation of a "nuclear exchange" must hence be seen as having reflected confidence that the physical requisites for such concepts were becoming available. Yet the Soviet Union's perceptions of a possible "controlled nuclear conflict" are different indeed from those of U.S. Secretary of Defense Schlesinger. It insists that the "Schlesinger doctrine" is an extention of "flexible response," imbued with the same logical inconsistency and hence uncontrollability. The Soviet Union's thoughts on "withholding" seem to have qualitatively different premises.

No. 162. Jacobsen, C.G.
Soviet Strategic Initiatives: Challenge and Response.
New York: Praeger Publishers, 1979, 168 p. (Second edition, 1981).

This book examines Soviet strategy and doctrine, relating the evolving biases of Soviet strategic literature to the evidence of emerging capabilities and to the potentials of strategic trends. The Soviet Union has sought novel ways of circumventing the restrictions of the established strategic balance, but even greater importance can be attached to its innovative search for a viable ballistic missile defense, aimed at negating the fundamental Western deterrent. There is a similar discrepancy between Western concerns and Soviet aspirations in the more conventional balance of power and in interventionary warfare. The ultimate flanks of the high Arctic and the southern hemisphere have received more Soviet attention, in theory and investment, than the immediate flanks of Europe. The Soviet definition of strategy, transcending the purely military component of power and incorporating the potentials of economic and other elements, serves as a unifying theme. Appendices present an in-depth analysis of Soviet Party-military relations and Soviet policy toward China by focusing on documentable trends, on ascertainable change, and on the aspirations and uncertainty that underline change. This book attempts to construct a spectrum of likely Soviet objectives and capabilities over the next two decades.

No. 163. Kolkowicz, Roman.
"U.S. and Soviet Approaches to Military Strategy: Theory vs. Experience."
Orbis Vol. 25 No. 2 (Summer 1981), pp. 307-330.

Despite a number of similarities, the United States and Soviet Union diverge sharply on many fundamental issues regarding the uses, limitations, and purposes of military power. Soviet analyses find Western strategic sophistries objectionable on several grounds: 1) the apolitical nature of Western military doctrines; 2) the status quo-supportive nature of deterrence and limited-war theory; and 3) the interdependent, controllable, mutually balanced, and self-constrained nature of Western doctrines of war. Soviet foreign policy and military doctrine have converged, supporting three primary goals: 1) stabilized relations with the West, 2) containment and isolation of China, and 3) exploration and expansion in the Third World, generally to the south of Russia. The Soviet strategic-nuclear shield is to provide stable deterrence; limited war-doctrines and forces, both nuclear and non-nuclear, are to provide additional deterrence and warfighting capabilities on the flanks of the Soviet Union, and the conventional, projective capabilities are to provide the cutting edge and perspective presence in support of expansive and exploratory policies. Given the American tradition described in this article and the newly acquired Soviet might, it is not unreasonable that the superpowers are headed for a collision in the 1980s.

No. 164. Lambeth, Benjamin S.
Selective Nuclear Operations and Soviet Strategy.
Santa Monica, Calif.: The RAND Corporation (P-5506), September 1975, p. 25.

Discusses Soviet doctrinal views on nuclear targeting restraint, the Soviet public reaction to the U.S. pursuit of limited nuclear options, and possible private Soviet attitudes regarding selective nuclear employment. Although it publicly rejects the feasibility of controlled nuclear warfare and dwells heavily on massive nuclear operations with an implied endorsement of preemption, the Soviet Union is currently acquiring a force posture capable of more measured applications of force as well. There is a reasonable presumption, therefore, that whatever it says in its public pronouncements, the Soviet Union will gradually develop its own options for controlled nuclear warfare and may be disposed in certain situations to implement improvised strategies inconsistent with its enunciated doctrinal principles. It is unlikely, however, that these strategies will constitute mirror images of currently evolving U.S. nuclear options. Rather, they will probably represent unique Soviet force application schemes, conceived in an ethnocentric Soviet frame of reference and heavily infused with idiosyncratic Soviet strategic perceptions and priorities.

Reprinted as Chapter 4 in Johan J. Holst and Uwe Nerlich (Eds.), Beyond Nuclear Deterrence: New Aims, New Arms (New York: Crane, Russak, and Co., 1977), pp. 79-104.

No. 165. Lambeth, Benjamin S.
"The Evolving Soviet Strategic Threat."
Current History Vol. 66 No. 410 (October 1975), pp. 121-125, 152-153.

Argues that the emerging Soviet strategic force posture is becoming increasingly congruent with long-established Soviet military doctrine. The Soviet Union appears to be within range of acquiring a credible first-strike disarming capability against the U.S. Minuteman force, coupled with a large reserve second-strike posture which could be withheld for intrawar coercion. If its ICBMs are MIRVed to the limit of the Vladivostok under-standings, it may eventually acquire as many as 7800 RVs. This arsenal could underwrite a whole range of specialized strategies and options in addition to the officially declared massive pre-emption doctrine. If, however, the Soviet Union chooses to follow its enunciated doctrine, there is the disturbing possibility that it could do so with devasting effectiveness. Realization of this possibility constitutes a major factor underlying the dynamic changes currently underway in U.S. strategic planning.

Also printed as RAND Paper P-5493 (August 1975), 20 p.

No. 166. Lambeth, Benjamin S.
Selective Nuclear Options in American and Soviet Strategic Policy.
Santa Monica, Calif.: The RAND Corporation (R-2034-DDRE), December 1976, 56 p.

Whatever behavior the Soviet Union might pursue in a nuclear crisis, the desirability of maintaining a U.S. selective options strategy need not hinge exclusively on the course and outcome of future developments in Soviet nuclear planning. Flexibility is a valuable asset to have whatever the other side does. Posses-sion of selective options neither commits the United States to limited nuclear use in a crisis nor requires an expectation that the Soviet Union will comply with the norm of restraint. Flexible options can provide U.S. leaders with valuable capabilities (or valuable points of departure for improvising) in the unlikely but consequential event that U.S.-Soviet relations deteriorated into a crisis in which neither the SIOP nor its Soviet equivalent would be usable. Flexible options are more a low-cost investment against a remote possibility than a venture doomed to failure should the Soviet Union continue to follow a different strategic doctrine. References.

Also printed in Johan J. Holst and Uwe Nerlich (Eds.), Beyond Nuclear Deterrence (New York: Crane, Russak, and Co., 1977).

No. 167. Lambeth, Benjamin S.
On Thresholds in Soviet Military Thought.
Santa Monica, Calif.: The RAND Corporation (P-6860), March 1983, 17 p.

Since the early 1960s, American strategic theory has dwelled heavily on the question of conflict "thresholds" and their significance in determining the advisability of various U.S. options in crises. This paper reflects on how the Soviets have come to think about "thresholds" in their own strategic planning. It reviews what appear to be the principal conflict "thresholds" in Soviet military thinking, identifies the more notable contrasts between these views and those that have long held sway in the United States, and touches on some of their implications for Western strategic planning.

Reprinted in The Washington Quarterly Vol. 7 No. 2 (Spring 1984), pp. 69-76.

No. 168. Lee, William T.
"Soviet Targeting Strategy and SALT."
Air Force Magazine Vol. 60 No. 9 (September 1978), pp. 120-129.

The USSR's negotiating positions at SALT have been, and will continue to be based on the Soviet concept of how they would use nuclear weapons in war. Understanding that concept, which is drastically different from U.S. nuclear strategy, is one key to assessing Soviet SALT II objectives. This article is an abridgement of a chapter in Steven Rosefielde and Joseph Leutz (Eds.), Contemporary Problems of Comparative Communism.

No. 169. Lewis, K.N.
The U.S.-Soviet Strategic Balance: Can We Meet the Challenge?
Santa Monica, Calif.: The RAND Corporation (P-6657), August 1981, 25 p.

A discussion of the overall U.S.-Soviet strategic competition. The author describes the context in which the "balance" is defined. Next, he points out one current problem with the

116

balance -- how the use of nuclear weapons can support our national objectives -- and suggests that the United States must commit itself to increased funding for its strategic forces. While the United States has been building up its nuclear attack capability, it has let its relative defense capabilities slide. For example, it does not make any difference if the United States has excellent hard target killing potential if its forces could be wiped out by an enemy first strike. Nuclear forces are only a part of the defense posture. Nuclear war probably is more likely to come as a result of escalation from lower "levels" of fighting. To the degree that superior conventional capabilities and enhanced provisions for readiness and mobilization can head off nuclear warfare, we must be very careful as we divide up the defense budget.

No. 170. MccGwire, Michael.
"Commentary: Soviet Intentions."
International Security Vol. 4 No. 1 (Summer 1979), pp. 139-143.

In the Spring 1979 issue, Professor MccGwire published "Naval Power and Soviet Global Strategy." This article takes off from its predecessor to consider what the past record of Soviet naval developments has to suggest about the wider questions concerning the Soviet Union's military posture and its willingness to wage nuclear war. Soviet military planners take the possibility of nuclear war seriously and plan to fight such a war should deterrence fail. The evidence does not, however, support the thesis that there is an urge towards war, nor is the navy poised to fight such a war. Except for the SSBN force, there has not been a general build-up of naval forces: surface building programs have been running at relatively modest levels. The construction of attack submarines is lower than forecasted; and although the navy's capability has progressively increased, it is still not able to meet its requirements fully. As for peacetime aspirations, the evidence argues that past developments have been the result of incrementalism and opportunism but gives no guidance for the future.

No. 171. McConnell, James.
Soviet and American Strategic Doctrine: One More Time.
Alexandria, Va.: Center for Naval Analyses (PP-271), January 1980, 43 p.

In recent years, in connection with the SALT debate and concern over the implications of emerging Soviet capabilities, there has been a revival of interest in comparing Soviet and American doctrines. In spite of the sharpness of these Western discussions, there is a certain consensus among the participants, as to both doctrinal similarities and doctrinal differences. All seem to agree that war is not regarded as an expedient policy by either Moscow or Washington, and that the common objective is the peacetime political manipulation of force -- i.e.: deterrence, bargaining from strength, etc.

No. 172. McConnell, James M.
Briefing: Soviet Doctrine, Past, Present, and Future.
Alexandria, Va.: Center for Naval Analyses (M 1050), March 1980, 29 p.

This report discusses how the Soviet Union views doctrine and for how long the Soviet doctrinal statements hold good, and how far doctrine looks ahead. It then discusses the general evolution of Soviet military doctrine over the past twenty years, mainly through examination of Soviet statements. Finally, it briefly reviews Soviet doctrinal evolution over the past twenty years to determine if patterns denoting some strategy of development can be discerned. This will help in anticipating doctrinal developments instead of reacting to them.

No. 173. McConnell, James M.
The Interacting Evolution of Soviet and American Military Doctrine.
Alexandria, Va.: Center for Naval Analyses (PP 472), September 1980, 119 p.

This paper traces the evolution of Soviet strategy from 1960 and identifies the likely course of this evolution beyond 1980. It draws on statements in the military literature of the Soviet Union and correlates them with what is known of Soviet force capabilities through operations and exercises. The timing of major changes in Soviet military doctrine suggests that these changes coincide with the USSR's five-year plans. The evident objective is the addition of a new military option in each five-year period. In the first half of the 1960s, the Soviet leadership apparently felt it had only one practical strategy -- all-out nuclear war. At the turn of 1965-66, another possibility -- conventional local war -- was added to underpin a diplomacy of force in the Third World. At the turn of 1970-71, Soviet statements began to point to a policy of limited counterforce strikes by land-based ballistic missiles, and the withholding of submarine-launched ballistic missiles. Finally, at the turn of 1975-76, evidence began to accumulate of a policy of counterforce strikes limited to targets in Europe. Apparently the long-term objective of more recent policies is the development of forces that can win limited conflicts so that the Soviet Union will not be forced to choose between massive nuclear exchange and capitulation. The next Soviet steps may therefore be to develop doctrines and forces for sustained operations in tactical-nuclear war and conventional war.

No. 174. McConnell, James M.
The Soviet Shift in Emphasis from Nuclear to Conventional.
Alexandria, Va.: Center for Naval Analyses (CRC 490), June 1983.

These two volumes detail the shift over time in the Soviet selection of military options. Volume I deals with changes in long-term Soviet perspectives on military development. Having achieved a nuclear counter to the U.S. strategy of massive retaliation in the early 1960s, the Soviet Union at first favored a long-term conventional emphasis as a follow-on, but abandoned this in 1965 in favor of nuclear options. However, in 1976-77, the Soviet Union returned to a primary conventional orientation, rounded out recently with a declared policy of no first use of nuclear weapons. All of these shifts seem to have been reflected in changes in Soviet deterrence criteria and, considering their character and timing, may perhaps be best explained as asymmetrical reactions to concurrent U.S. plans. Volume II deals with the implementation of the long-term perspective in mid-term doctrinal increments that coincide with the five-year plans. In each of the doctrinal periods since 1960, the Soviet Union has managed to introduce a new independent option: all-out nuclear war (1960-65), a conventional local war in the Third World (1966-70), limited intercontinental nuclear warfare (1971-75), theater nuclear war (1976-80), and protracted conventional war between the two coalitions (1980-85).

No. 175. McDonald, Lawrence P.
"On Defense: A Talk With Major General George Keegan."
American Opinion Vol. 20 No. 8 (September 1977), pp. 1-4; 71-82.

In this article, Congressman Larry McDonald reports on a lengthy interview with the recently retired Chief of Air Force Intelligence, Major General George Keegan. Since his retirement, General Keegan has been trying to get a considerable number of messages having to do with national security, which are presented in this article, to the American people. In virtually every way, the strategic equation has grown steadily worse over the years -- all with the full knowledge and approval of U.S. leaders. This, in McDonald's opinion, is due to a common ideological outlook at the top level of U.S. society, which includes a reasonably well agreed upon scheme for a New World Order.

No. 176. Meyer, Stephen M.
"Soviet Perspectives on the Paths to Nuclear War."
Chapter 7 in Graham T. Allison, Albert Carnesale, and Joseph S. Nye, Jr. (Eds.), Hawks, Doves, and Owls: An Agenda for Avoiding Nuclear War.
New York: W.W. Norton and Company, 1985, pp. 167-205.

This work explores some aspects of the Soviet perspective on the paths to U.S.-Soviet nuclear war. It examines questions such as which paths does the Soviet leadership perceive as most likely to lead to nuclear war, what its proclivities are towards escalation or limitation in conflicts, how Soviet military sources have been structured in reaction to these paths, and what responses are planned for them. This work's sources include Soviet military planning literature, Soviet military historical analyses, Soviet diplomatic behavior, Soviet military force structure and deployment data, and memoir material. While few of these sources speak directly to the issue of paths to nuclear war, all are affected by assumptions about such paths. This examination makes it clear that there is no single Soviet strategy for waging nuclear war. Instead, there is a progression of options: preemption, launch on tactical warning, launch under attack, and second strike. The choice of which to implement will depend upon circumstances.

No. 177. Miller, Mark E.
"Soviet Strategic Thought: The End of an Era?"
International Security Review Vol. 5 No. 4 (Winter 1980-1981), pp. 447-510.

Is Soviet strategic philosophy, as some argue, in profound transition from the attainment of victory through such classical principles of military art as surprise and superiority over the economy to a regime "more suited" to the nuclear age, stressing deterrence through mutual vulnerability? In the 1970s a Soviet strategic posture emerged that strongly suggests a rational plan for translating the requirements for a war-winning posture based on offensive-defensive damage limitation capabilities into military realities. It can justifiably be assumed that the Soviet strategic buildup and its underlying rationale reflect a high-level political consensus. A breakdown of this consensus cannot be ruled out, but the institutional clout of the Soviet military-defense industrial grouping makes it unlikely that the fundamentals of Soviet policy will be altered in the foreseeable future.

No. 178. Scott, Harriet Fast.
"The Soviet Drive for Strategic Superiority."
Air University Review Vol. 19 No 4 (May-June 1968), pp. 59-62.

The 1967 edition of Colonel P.T. Astashenkov's book Soviet Rocket Troops gives many insights into significant changes in the Soviet Armed Forces, especially when compared with the 1964 edition. To begin with, it is clear that no basic change in doctrine and strategy followed Nikita Khrushchev's ouster in late 1964. It also expands upon the descriptions of the "technical revolution" that compelled the reorganization of the Soviet military in 1960. The primacy of the Strategic Rocket Forces is stressed, as is the role of rocket capabilities in the other four Soviet

120

services. The book should be studied carefully by officers concerned with a technologically inferior opponent. If the Soviet drive for strategic and nuclear superiority is achieved, or if even parity is reached, the United States will be able to risk far less in its international behavior.

No. 179. Scott, William F.
"The Contrast in Chinese and Soviet Military Doctrines."
Air University Review Vol. 19 No. 2 (January-February 1968), pp. 57-63.

On most issues of strategy, tactics, and weapons systems, the Soviet Union and Communist China have diametrically opposite views. An analysis of these views should be of particular importance at this time. The Soviet military maintains that technology is the key to military power. The Communist Chinese leaders claim that masses of people, properly indoctrinated, are the decisive force. These opposing beliefs of the Soviet Union and China are their most significant difference, as far as warfare is concerned, and are a major issue in the striving of each nation for leadership in the Communist World.

No. 180. Scott, William F.
"Soviet Concepts of War."
Air Force Magazine (Soviet Aerospace Almanac No. 11) Vol. 68 No. 3 (March 1985), pp. 48-52.

The Soviet Party-military leadership teaches that there are certain "laws" that determine victory or defeat in war. They assert that Marxist-Leninist teaching has proven that the cause of war, like all other social phenomena, is a process governed by definite laws. Soviet strategists distinguish between general "laws of war," "laws of armed conflict," and subordinate laws of military actions at strategic, operational, and tactical levels. Soviet strategists state that the fifth general law of war -- relative combat power of the opposing sides -- will continue to operate in nuclear war. The mere presence of nuclear weapons will "increase the contradiction between the tendency to concentrate troops and to disperse them." Concentration leaves them vulnerable to nuclear attack, while dispersal makes it difficult to defeat the enemy. The answer is quick concentration for an attack, followed by a dispersal. The Western belief that primary Soviet attention has shifted to deep non-nuclear thrusts into an opponent's territory is wishful thinking. Soviet forces facing NATO are equipped to fight with either conventional or nuclear weapons.

No. 181. Soll, Richard S.
"The Soviet Union and Protracted Nuclear War."
Strategic Review Vol. 8 No. 4 (Fall 1980), pp. 15-28.

Soviet broadsides against reported changes in the U.S. targeting doctrine represent, ironically, flailings against a mirror image. The theme has been consistant in two decades of Soviet military writings and posture evaluation: Nuclear war, if it should come, must eventuate in victory (not "war termination" as in the U.S. parlance), and while the initial massive exchange many decisively shape the conflict, it will be consummated by subsequent phases found with combined arms. The concept of an extended nuclear conflict drives the echeloned organization of Soviet forces, the emphasis on strategic reserves, and the preoccupation with peacetime stockpiling. The United States is only beginning -- with gingerly reluctance -- to contemplate the terrain of nuclear warfighting.

No. 182. Weeks, Albert L.
"The Garthoff-Pipes Debate on Soviet Doctrine: Another Perspective."
Strategic Review Vol. 11 No. 1 (Winter 1983), pp. 57-64.

The debate between Ambassador Raymond Garthoff and Dr. Richard Pipes (Fall 1982 issue of Strategic Review) illuminated major premises in the continuing controversy over Soviet strategic doctrine and intentions, but failed to address squarely some salient and time-honored themes in Soviet military writings: the insistence on superiority in all military sectors, the primacy of the political and military offensive, and a continuing prescription that rings disturbingly of preemptive war (if not necessarily reflecting a ready strategy-in-place for such a conflict). These themes seem to drown out any adduced symptoms of belated Soviet interest in the concepts of mutual deterrence and U.S.-Soviet strategic parity; such more recent symptoms may also reflect the priorities of the Soviet peace offensive. While the Soviet enigma continues to bar a truly definitive assessment by anyone of Moscow's ultimate strategic intentions, nevertheless prudence and the available evidence, against the backdrop of the awesome penalities of error in the nuclear age, must incline sober analysis in the direction of some "worst case" assumptions.

No. 183. Wettig, Gerhard.
"The Garthoff-Pipes Debate on Soviet Strategic Doctrine: A European Perspective."
Strategic Review Vol. 11 No. 2 (Spring 1983), pp. 68-78.

The debate between Ambassador Garthoff and Professor Pipes over Soviet strategic doctrine (Fall 1982 issue, Strategic Review) demonstrates how differing interpretations can be drawn from the same Soviet sources: it also illuminates the dangers of reading into Soviet statements the same motives and concepts that shape Western strategic views and hopes. For reasons both of ideology and historical experience, the Soviets cannot accept any notion

of shared security with their opponents, be that "mutual deterrence" or Mutual Assured Destruction. Nor can they accept a
theory of armed force that, once invoked, is directed at anything short of victory. Indeed, behind the Soviet drive for
military superiority is the concept of "freedom from dangers" --
the achievement of the ability to deal with all contingencies and
risks, including those on the battlefield. This concept is
dominant in the Soviet military buildup and strategy with respect
to Europe and other rimlands of Eurasia. To be sure, at the
level of the strategic nuclear relationship with the United States,
the Soviets recognize the massive difficulties standing in the way
of translating this concept into achievable reality.

The Formulation of Soviet Doctrine and Strategy

No. 184. Dinerstein, Herbert S.
War and the Soviet Union: Nuclear Weapons and the Revolution
in Soviet Military and Political Thinking.
New York: Frederick A. Praeger, Publisher, 1958, 268 p.

A description of the revolution in Soviet ideas about war since
Stalin's death. These new ideas have appeared primarily as a
result of a careful reassessment of the importance of nuclear
weapons and of the improvements in the means of delivering
them. The book discusses: 1) the Soviet controversy in military
theory that occurred between the fall of 1953 and the spring of
1955; 2) whether and to what extent the Soviet leaders rely on
the military balance to deter their presumptive enemy, the United
States; 3) a few cases in which the domestic dispute over
military policy played an important role in Soviet politics at the
highest level; 4) Soviet views on preemptive attack and its
relationship to preemptive war; and 5) the roles assigned to the
various military arms in the execution of Soviet strategy. At
present, the guiding Soviet principle of war is readiness to fight
any kind of war in the most effective way. The basis of Soviet
doctrine is that the awful consequences of war can be reduced
by the creation and thorough training of a differentiated force
ready for every contingency. The Soviet leaders believe that in
some circumstances it may be desirable to strike an initial
nuclear blow, and they mean to have a military establishment
suited to that end.

Also printed as RAND study R-326 (August 11, 1958), 276 p.
Revised edition printed in 1962 (q.v.), reprinted in 1976 by
Greenwood Press.

Reviewed by Raymond Garthoff, Army Vol. 10 No. 4 (November
1959), pp. 72-73; Alvin J. Cottrell, "The Soviet Threat: General
or Limited War?", Orbis Vol. 4 No. 1 (Spring 1960), pp. 93-100.

No. 185. Dinerstein, Herbert S.
Introduction to the Second Edition of "War and the Soviet Union".
Santa Monica, Calif.: The RAND Corporation (P-2620), August 1962, 14 p.

An introduction to the new edition of War and the Soviet Union. The author discusses in a general way the most important new developments in Soviet military thinking since the appearance of the first edition of the book. Among the topics are nuclear power, delivery systems, and the strategy of pre-emptive war.

No. 186. Dziak, John J.
"The Institutional Foundations of Soviet Military Doctrine."
International Security Review Vol. 4 No. 4 (Winter 1979-1980), pp. 317-332.

Soviet military doctrine is the Party's guide to the strategic structure and future direction of the military. It is the intellectual and programmatic framework that informs war planning and guides force acquisition. Essentially a party pronouncement, it dictates the broad guidance for more specific planning and establishes the armament norms and weapons acquisition policies for the Soviet armed forces. It is not the product of an unconstrained military elite chaffing at Party restraint and control. Doctrine and associated force structure derive from a fairly rational institutional process, initiated, and controlled by the Party, in the pursuit of articulated political objectives. Politics, the Party presence, and Party control overlay the whole military-thought process. The players in that process -- the Party, military, industry, and security organs -- are not simply competing institutions fused together through Party punitive measures; their identities are shaded by a fusion which characterizes these elites. Their principal objectives are perpetuating their exclusive position at society's expense and producting politically useful military power.

Reprinted as Chapter 1 in Graham D. Vernon (Ed.), Soviet Perceptions of War and Peace. (Washington, D.C.: National Defense University Press, 1981), pp. 3-16.

No. 187. Dziak, John J.
Soviet Perceptions of Military Power: The Interaction of Theory and Practice.
New York: National Strategy Information Center, 1981, 72 p.

Soviet military doctrine is the Party's guide to the strategic structure and future direction of the Soviet military. The prolific doctrinal writings of high-ranking Soviet military officers show that Soviet military doctrine is not, as is sometimes thought in the West, the product of an unconstrained military resistant to Party restraint and control. Doctrine and associated force structure derive from a fairly rational institutional process, initiated and controlled by the Party, in the pursuit of articulated political objectives. Politics, the Party presence, and Party control overlie the whole military thought process. The players in this process -- the Party, military, industrial, and security elites -- are not simply competing institutions fused together through Party punitive measures. Their identities are shaded by a fusion which leaves uncertain boundaries. A commonality of interests centered on Party political concerns characterizes these elites. Their principal objectives are the perpetuation of their exclusive position at society's expense coupled with the production of politically useful military power for international gains.

No. 188. Garthoff, Raymond L.
"On Soviet Military Strategy and Capabilities."
World Politics Vol. 3 No. 1 (October 1950), pp. 114-129.

This article is concerned with the military establishment and begins by assessing three recent works: General Augustin Gullaume's Soviet Arms and Soviet Power (Washington, D.C.: Infantry Journal Press, 1949); Colonel Louis B. Ely's The Red Army Today (Harrisburg, Penn.: Military Service Publishing Company, 1949); and Asher Lee The Soviet Air Force (New York: Harper and Brothers, 1950). It goes on to compile a summary listing of thirty-three strategic and tactical operating principles of particular prominence in Soviet military doctrine.

No. 189. Garthoff, Raymond L.
Soviet Military Doctrine.
Glencoe, Ill.: The Free Press, 1953, 587 p.

This study constructs the pattern of Soviet military doctrine and offers interpretations of its basis through discovering and clarifying what is taught, believed, and intended by the Soviets as the basis for their conduct of war. It not only determines manifest Soviet doctrine, but also makes explicit those tenets which are not recognized by the Soviets as part of their official doctrine, but which nevertheless play a substantial role in it. Part I is concerned with the relation between Soviet military doctrine and Soviet political doctrine and strategy, as well as Soviet concepts of military art. It concludes: 1) Marxism-Leninism exerted relatively little direct influence on Soviet military doctrine per se, 2) the influence of the Imperial Russian army and its doctrine is considerable; and 3) foreign military influences have also contributed. The fifteen chapters of Part II distill and analyze the current basic Soviet principles of war. Part III is a more detailed examination of the operational, tactical, and organizational field doctrine of the various combat arms of the Soviet armed forces. The study contains an exten-

sive bibliography of Soviet and Western services as well as a
glossary of Soviet military terms.

Also printed as RAND study R-223 (May 1, 1953); British edition
under the title How Russia Makes War: Soviet Military Doctrine.
(London: George Allen and Unwin, 1954). Summary published
as "Significant Features of Soviet Military Doctrine," Military
Review Vol 34 No. 12 (March 1955), pp. 3-13.

Reviewed by John J. Earley, Military Review Vol. 34 No. 2 (May
1954), p. 109.

No. 190. Kissinger, Henry A.
Nuclear Weapons and Foreign Policy.
New York: Harper and Brothers, 1957, 463 p.

This book shows how U.S. military strength can support its
political objectives without excessive risk of all-out war. It
discusses the diplomacy and the strategy necessary to deter
aggression and to defeat it should it occur. It makes clear that
doing this requires weapons as varied as the dangers confronting the United States. In all significant wars of the future,
nuclear weapons are likely to be employed. But if the United
States employs proper doctrine as well, the consequences need
not be disasterous to its survival. In Chapter 10 (The Strategy
of Ambiguity -- Sino-Soviet Strategic Thought) and Chapter 11
(The Soviet Union and the Atom), the nature of the Soviet
challenge in terms of ideology, diplomacy, and military policy is
analyzed. The development of a distinctive Soviet military
theory is outlined, particularly the trend towards acceptance of
the nuclear stalemate and Soviet vulnerabilities to war.

No. 191. Lambeth, Benjamin S.
How To Think About Soviet Military Doctrine.
Santa Monica, Calif.: The RAND Corporation (P-5939), February
1978, 22 p.

Soviet military doctrine is highly systematic, unambiguously
martial, and explicitly geared to a belief that should nuclear
deterrence fail, some recognizable form of victory is attainable
through the skillful exploitation of mass, initiative, and surprise.
This orientation has played an important role in guiding the
comprehensive Soviet military buildup of the past decade. It is
less clear, however, to what extent doctrine would govern actual
Soviet military behavior in a war. Soviet doctrine may provide a
useful intellectual ordering device for military planners, but it is
not binding on the Soviet political leadership. Given their
natural conservatism, the Soviet leaders would undoubtedly feel
strong compulsions toward caution and restraint in a major
superpower confrontation. Nonetheless, Soviet military doctrine
is an important indicator of Soviet leadership attitudes toward

3

26

the nature of modern war, the strategies and forces required to
deter it, and the broad objectives to be pursued should it occur.
(Paper presented at Harvard University, Program for Science
and International Affairs, February 1978.)

Reprinted as Chapter 4 in John Baylis and Gerald Segal (Eds.),
Soviet Strategy. (Monclair, N.J.: Allanfeld, Osmun and Co.,
1981), pp. 105-123.

No. 192. Lambeth, Benjamin S.
The Elements of Soviet Strategic Policy.
Santa Monica, Calif.: The RAND Corporation (P-6389), September
1979, 13 p.

An overview of the conceptual principles that inform the Soviet
approach to national security and underlie Soviet weapons
acquisition and force development. Although to some extent
Soviet strategic programs are influenced by the same sorts of
pressures and constraints that effect the defense decision-making
of all modern industrial countries, such factors as ideology and
doctrine play a major role in lending direction and purpose to
Soviet military program activities. As a result, Soviet strategic
policy has tended to be more consistant and goal-oriented than
that of the United States since the Soviet buildup began in the
mid-1960s. Its objective has been the accumulation of sufficient
forces and associated war-survival assets to provide a basis for
pursuing meaningful victory in the event of an unavoidable
deterrence failure. (Prepared for a conference of U.S. and PRC
Soviet specialists sponsored by Columbia University Research
Institute on International Change.)

No. 193. McConnell, James M.
"Shifts in Soviet Views on the Proper Focus of Military Develop-
ment."
World Politics, April 1985, pp. 317-343.

There is a widespread view in the West that Soviet strategic
doctrine has not changed much since the early 1960s, and still
concentrates on fighting and winning an all-out nuclear war.
This articles proposes a different thesis; that Soviet long-term
military development strategy has altered course on several
occasions. It presents evidence, in outlined chronological order,
of several changes from nuclear to conventional emphasis, where
it now remains. This is followed by an explanation of the Soviet
shifts in long-term military development, with emphasis on the
asymmetrical character of Soviet responses to Western initiatives.
Each side seems to have bet on strength against weakness, to
move into spheres into which the opponent has neglected to go,
or which he has vacated; each protagonist shifts from one end of
the scale of military options to the other as opportunities unfold

and advantages appear. It is thus no easy matter to find a way out of the essential asymmetry of the arms race.

No. 194. Petersen, Phillip A.
"The Soviet Conceptual Framework for the Application of Military Power."
Naval War College Review Vol. 34 No. 6 (May-June 1981), pp. 15-25.

Soviet military doctrine is a unified series of views and guides to action elaborated and adopted by the state. It is based upon military science, which also includes numerous hypotheses in its system of theories that are not selected as doctrine. The general theory of military science defines the interdependence and joint subordination of the relatively independent branches and disciplines within the military field. Military art, defined as the accepted body of thinking on the employment of forces in combat, is regarded by the Soviet military as the most important element of military science. It consists of strategy, operational art, and tactics. The conceptual framework created by the Soviet theory of military art is applicable to the waging of war regardless of whether the weapons of concern are primarily nuclear or conventional. In developing a conceptual framework that allows for the application of a range of means to a range of objectives, the Soviet military has institutionalized flexibility in force use. It has conceptually structured its planning to seek victory at the lowest possible cost. In doing so, it has made military power appear more useable, which enhances its deterrent value. Despite the predominant role of nuclear weapons in modern warfare, it has extended the functional value of military force through the continuing theoretical elaboration of its military doctrine.

No. 195. "The Soviet Doctrine of War."
Military Review Vol. 28 No. 9 (December 1948), pp. 79-82.
(Translated and digested from an article in Bellona, a Polish magazine published in Great Britain, No. 2, 1948).

This study is based mainly on references drawn from carefully examined material from Western and Eastern bloc professional and political sources, and to a lesser degree from published Soviet sources. The major features of the Soviet armed forces are their attachment to ground operations, mass concepts, and lag behind the armed forces of the Western nations. Soviet claims that the dispersion of Soviet industry will rob the atomic bomb of its significance would have a certain validity if it were not for the weakness of Soviet communications. Assuming that Soviet officials are aware of their military possibilities, that they are concealing their weaknesses, and that they are making a great effort to overcome their deficiencies, the conclusion is still that

Russia is and will be too weak for an armed conflict on a global scale.

No. 196. Van Cleave, William R.
"Soviet Doctrine and Strategy: A Developing American View."
In Lawrence L. Whetten (Ed.), The Future of Soviet Military Power.
New York: Crane, Russak and Co., 1976, pp. 41-71.

An enormous gap has appeared between the premises and expectations of dominant American strategic and arms control thought of the past decade, and the results obtained during these years. Observation of SALT and of Soviet strategic force planning have forced a reassessment of Soviet strategic concepts and objectives, and of basic U.S. strategic premises. Soviet literature on professional military doctrine is quite important in determining Soviet military doctrine, concepts and strategy. There are a number of inherent limitations to its usage, and although analyzing capabilities is not much more exact; still, it is possible to reach reasonable conclusions. At the strategic level, the Soviet Union is developing major counterforce capabilities; it also seems to have developed the basic elements of a true nuclear doctrine and strategy for theater warfare. It is conclusive that Soviet military capabilities are developing and becoming more flexible, and that Soviet operations and tactics are being studied, tested, and possibly refined in a variety of means and operations.

No. 197. Wolfe, Thomas W.
Soviet Strategy at the Crossroads.
Cambridge, Mass.: Harvard University Press, 1964, 342 p.

A study of contemporary Soviet thinking on problems of war and strategy in the nuclear age, particularly since the Cuban missile crisis of 1962. The new technological and political problems of the nuclear age affecting Soviet attitudes are discussed: 1) allocation of resources among competing sectors of the Soviet economy; 2) deterioration of the Sino-Soviet relationship; 3) Soviet awareness of the destructiveness of nuclear war; and 4) development of a military posture suitable to Soviet needs in the power contest with the United States. Two major decisions confronting Soviet leaders are examined: whether to abandon the present detente or whether to encourage the still-tentative habits of limited cooperation and communication with the West.

Also printed as RAND Memorandum RM-4085-PR (April 1964).

Reviewed by Raymond L. Garthoff, The Annals of the American Academy of Political and Social Science Vol. 359 (May 1965), pp. 181-182.

No. 198. Wolfe, Thomas W.
Soviet Military Theory: An Additional Source of Insight Into Its Development.
Santa Monica, Calif.: The RAND Corporation (P-3258), November 1965, 54 p.

A comparative examination of Soviet doctrine and strategy as presented in the 1960 and 1964 editions of On Military Science. The changing emphases in Soviet attitudes toward strategic warfare, the relationship between politics and military theory, and the principles of war are discussed.

B. DEVELOPMENT OF SOVIET STRATEGY

Overviews of Its Development

No. 199. Berman, Robert P.; and John C. Baker.
Soviet Strategic Forces: Requirements and Responses.
Washington D.C.: The Brookings Institution (Studies in Defense Policy), 1982, 171 p.

This study examines the strategic posture of the Soviet Union for signs of strengths and weaknesses in Soviet nuclear forces, and for indications of how Soviet leaders set defense priorities. The authors believe that strategic planning and missile development are closely related. As a guide to the evolution of Soviet strategic posture in the nuclear age, they trace the development of Soviet ballistic missiles since World War II. Their accounts of the design and development of Soviet weapons systems reveal how Soviet technical capacity has changed and what effect important political and military events have had on missile development. They warn that before 1985 Soviet leaders will have to make critical decisions that will govern weapon development until the turn of the century. The trends within the design bureaus and the disruptions in individual weapons programs that the authors have detected suggest what the USSR can reasonably be expected to do. The confines within which Soviet strategic planners must work are delineated in the appendices to this study, which describe the process of missile design and development, the design and operating characteristics of missiles, regional and intercontinental targeting assignments, the use of military reconnaissance satellites, and the strategic defense forces of the Soviet Union.

Reviewed by John Van Oudenaren, Political Science Quarterly Vol. 99 No. 2 (Summer 1984), pp. 393-394.

No. 200.   Erickson, John.
"Toward 1984:   Four Decades of Soviet Military Policy."
Air University Review Vol. 35 No. 2 (January-February 1984),
pp. 30-34.

A very plausible model of change and interaction in Soviet
military development can be derived by surveying the cycles of
the formulation of doctrine, development of corresponding armaments, and consequent diversification of command and control
mechanisms.   On the other hand, a scan of Soviet military
policies, programs, and postures over the past four years hints
that the insights of an actuary could be as useful as the skills
of the military analyst.   Ten year cycles intrude themselves,
each stamped with its own features yet interlocked: 1) 1945-53,
justifiable pride at victory but disfigured by the later Stalinist
immobilism; 2) 1953-63/64, nuclear introspection, a fundamental
tussle over doctrine, distorted by Khrushchev's own predilec-
tions; 3) 1964-74, satisfaction with the attainment of parity,
even to the point of winning a margin of advantage; and 4) 1974/
74-83, the "technocratization" of the command and search for
flexibility and sustainability, but consumed by a sense of fore-
boding in anticipation of an immense military technological competition with the United States.   After examination, these
cycles appear to be an illusion.   Looking backwards and forward,
one sees but one sustained cycle resting on a few tried and
tested strategic concepts embracing the fundamental Soviet quest
for military invulnerability, encompassing both offensive and
defensive designs.

No. 201.   Holloway, David.
The Soviet Union and the Arms Race.
New Haven, Conn.:   Yale University Press, 1983, 211 p.

This book examines the problem of what motivates Soviet military
policy by analyzing three elements of the Soviet military: its
role in the formation of the Soviet state, Soviet views on the
utility of military power in the nuclear age, and the economic
and political basis of the Soviet military.   The work shows how
the Stalin period ushered the Soviet Union into a major nuclear
arms race with the United States.   It then analyzes Soviet
thinking about nuclear weapons and nuclear war, Soviet arms
and arms control policy, and the Soviet use of military power as
an instrument of foreign policy.   Finally it discusses Soviet
military technology and the politics and economics of Soviet
defense.   It claims that Soviet leaders currently face difficult
decisions because their economic system, which has traditionally
been organized to protect the defense sector, has now become a
brake on the rest of the economy.   It urges Western governments to take account of the fact that the Soviet Union is at a
turning point, and to keep open the possibility of accommodation.

No. 202. Jones, Issac R.
Soviet Military Strategy.
Maxwell Air Force Base, Ala.: Air War College (Professional Study), 1974, 51 p.

A brief review of the Soviet military doctrinal changes that have occured since the Second World War, together with a discussion of the attendant technological transformation of the armed forces, serves as a background for addressing the current Soviet military strategy that evolved from these revolutionary changes. The discussion of the four main elements of Soviet military strategy represents a collection of contemporary views expressed by prominent Soviet military leaders on the subject.

No. 203. Jukes, Geoffrey.
The Development of Soviet Strategic Thinking Since 1945.
Canberra: Australian National University Press (Canberra Papers on Strategy and Defense No. 14), 1972, 45 p.

Soviet policies, like the policies of most other countries, are shaped by outside events as much as by internal happenings, and are sometimes affected by the conflicting aspirations of political and military leaders. This paper shows how Soviet strategic ideas have changed at various times, categorizing them into five periods. It demonstrates the flexibility of Soviet thinking and suggests ways in which Soviet strategy may develop. It provides a brief outline of the subject and illustrates some available sources.

No. 204. Jukes, Geoffrey.
"Soviet Strategy 1965-1990."
Chapter 4 in Robert O'Neill and D.M. Horner (Eds.), New Directions in Soviet Thinking.
London: George Allen and Unwin, 1981, pp. 60-74.

Soviet strategy since 1965 has retained a basic doctrinal framework which regards all types of war as lying on a continuum with small local wars at one end, and general nuclear war at the other. In political terms this framework appears to lack the distinct break which most Western thinkers make between nonnuclear and nuclear war, and therefore contains elements of irresponsibility. In practice this means that each type of war is seen as containing the elements of the next higher, so that troops must train for all types of war, including conventional operations within nuclear war. It also means that due to the lack of the "firebreak" concept, sub-nuclear wars are not to be undertaken lightly. The 1980s are likely to see little development in Soviet strategic thought as regards operations of strategic nuclear forces, armies and air forces, but will see some development in its naval aspect, especially in respect to shipborne aircraft and the amphibious forces. Although doctrinal changes will be minor, increased production and projection capacities will almost certainly lead to higher levels of activity outside the European and Chinese border areas.

No. 205. Lee, William T.; and Richard E. Staar.
Soviet Military Policy Since World War II.
Palo Alto, Calif.: Hoover Institution Press, 1986.

This book examines the thinking of the Soviet leadership as regards to the buildup of their armed forces: both the political and military leaders are committed to a warfighting nuclear doctrine and strategy in which victory is the final objective. They define the conditions for victory and assess capabilities of Soviet strategic forces to make prescribed contributions in a nuclear war. The net result is that the Soviet Union has progressed at great expense, although it must continue to do so before achieving all capabilities necessary to fight and win a nuclear war. The book presents correlations among three dimensions of Soviet military policy as it has evolved over the past forty years: military doctrine and strategy; weapons acquisition decisions and the quantitative and qualitative buildup of Soviet military forces; and trends among national priorities in terms of the growth of military outlays and its burden on the economy. While Soviet strategic offensive forces for the first time now can make their contribution to victory in a nuclear war, their strategic defenses still remain inadequate. The cost of adhering to this war-fighting strategy not only is the best single proof of Soviet political leaders' devotion to it but also is the single most important cause of the slowdown of the Soviet economy.

No. 206. Miller, Mark E.
Soviet Strategic Power and Doctrine: The Quest for Superiority.
Washington, D.C.: Advanced International Studies Institute, 1982, 298 p.

The purpose of this book is twofold: to provide a greater understanding of how and why the Soviet strategic force posture has evolved to its present form, and to enhance comprehension of the role and missions of Soviet strategic forces in peace and war. To mitigate the difficulties of determining Soviet intent, the book follows three premises: 1) that Soviet national style in military policy is the product of a political culture and historical experience profoundly alien to that of the United States; 2) Soviet strategic planning has been significantly influenced by the interaction of many factors, such as doctrine and strategy, technology, geography, U.S. strategy and capabilities, internal political and economic considerations, as well as the more subtle influence of Marxist-Leninist ideology and the Russian historical experience; and 3) that the most reliable approach for determining Soviet intentions and objectives is a comparison of words, deeds, and capabilities. The book is organized into three historical phases to demonstrate the patterns of Soviet strategic thought and the evolution of Soviet strategic systems: 1946-53, the pre-nuclear or Stalinist phase; 2) 1953-64, the transitional period; and 3) post-1964, the Brezhnev era of Soviet global superpower status.

Reviewed by Albert Boiter, "Soviet Military Doctrine," Washington Quarterly Vol. 5 No. 2 (Spring 1982), p. 218; Kenneth Whiting, Air University Review Vol. 3 No. 4, (May-June 1983), pp. 119-120.

No. 207. Monks, Alfred L.
"Evolution of Soviet Military Thinking."
Military Review Vol. 51 No. 3 (March 1971), pp. 78-93.

In January 1960, Nikita Khrushchev proclaimed a new military doctrine for the Soviet Union that subordinated the role of conventional forces to strategic missiles. This doctrine precipitated debate between "traditionalists" insisting that balanced conventional and nuclear forces were needed, and "modernists" maintaining that military goals can mainly be achieved by nuclear weapons. Khrushchev's ouster in 1964 intensified this debate, which from 1964-69 focused on: 1) the nature of a future war; 2) the organization and structure of the armed forces; 3) the concept of military power; and 4) the preconditions for victory. A third group, "centrists," tried to reconcile the debate; while a fourth, consisting mostly of political officers, tried to enhance the supremacy of the Communist Party in the armed forces. Increased defense spending in 1966 led to a reduction of interservice competition, showing that the problem of resource allocation was of central importance in providing the basis for the emergence, crystallization, and diminution of factionalism within the Soviet military establishment. A chart identifies important members of miltary factions.

No. 208. Monks, Alfred L.
Soviet Military Doctrine: 1960 to the Present.
New York: Irvington Publishers, Inc., 1984, 351 p.

The aims of this analysis are 1) to trace the evolution of Soviet military doctrine from 1918 to the present, 2) to describe changing Soviet perceptions of threat and show their influence on doctrine and policy, and 3) to determine the nature of the relationship between Soviet military doctrine and policy. Data for this analysis were gathered from various Russian-language newspapers, periodicals, and books. The "open literature" of the Soviet Union, these publications represent an important data source, since they are the primary mode by which the Soviet leadership communicates military information to people inside the country and to other nations. Finally, Western writings on

Soviet military strategy and doctrine were consulted. All publications included in this study are listed in the bibliography.

Initial Developments in Soviet Strategy

No. 209. Dinerstein, Herbert S.
"Soviet Strategic Ideas, January, 1960."
Soviet Survey, October-December 1960.

An analysis of a speech made by Khrushchev to the Supreme Soviet on January 14, 1960, and of two speeches by Malinovskii. One of the Malinovskii speeches was made in the Supreme Soviet on January 14, and the other was presented to a military group in Moscow on January 19. The main themes of these speeches are: 1) that the Soviet Union will continue to develop new weapons until a general disarmament agreement is reached and will continue to use nuclear blackmail for political purposes, 2) that the Soviet Union is now "unassailable" and hopes still to be the first to strike if war comes, and 3) that the danger of a third world war arises from the West German search for revenge.

Also published as RAND memorandum RM 2532, and RAND paper P-1925 (March 4, 1960), 32 p.

No. 210. Garthoff, Raymond L.
"The Death of Stalin and the Birth of Mutual Deterrence."
Survey Vol. 25 No. 2 (Spring 1980), pp. 10-16.

It has long been clear that Stalin failed to appreciate that possession of nuclear weapons by both the United States and the Soviet Union would lead to a strategic stalemate reflecting mutual deterrence. Past evidence that even before Stalin's death some of his key lieutenants in the Politburo had reached this conclusion and tried to establish a more realistic policy has not been noticed. In his last theoretical pronouncement Stalin attacked "some comrades" who dared suggest that "wars between capitalist countries have ceased to be inevitable." While the Soviet leaders who exposed this position after Stalin's death can easily be identified, it is not possible on present evidence to distinguish who had reached this conclusion before his demise. In addressing the development of Soviet political and military views on mutual deterrence and on strategic arms limitation, it may be useful to be aware of the early Soviet recognition of the non-inevitability and deterability of war in the nuclear age that began even before Stalin's death.

No. 211. Green, William C.
"The Early Formulation of Soviet Strategic Nuclear Doctrine."
Comparative Strategy Vol. 4 No. 4 (1984), pp. 369-386.

Western analysts, misled by Soviet polemics in the postwar
period, concluded that "Stalinist stagnation" prevented the
Soviet military from developing policies and doctrines to deal
with nuclear weapons. Reexamination of these formative years
shows that the Soviet military did important work on these issues
even prior to Stalin's death. It also sheds light on important
questions, such as how the Soviet military established consensus
on key points of nuclear weapons policy, the military's role
within the Soviet establishment in formulating basic principles
and assumptions, and the importance of long-range planning and
continuity in Soviet programs.

No. 212. Holloway, David.
"Research Note: Soviet Thermonuclear Development."
International Security Vol. 4 No. 3 (Winter 1979-80), pp.
192-197.

The object of this note is to make public a document which gives
more detailed information about Soviet nuclear weapons tests in
the 1950s. It raises a question about the place of the first
Soviet thermonuclear test device (Joe-4) in Soviet nuclear
weapons development. This device was not a true fusion weapon,
but a boosted fission weapon. The document makes it possible
to assess more accurately the progress of Soviet nuclear weapons
development in the 1950s, and to understand more clearly the
nature of Soviet-American strategic arms competition.

No. 213. Horelick, Arnold L.
"Deterrence" and Surprise Attack in Soviet Strategic Thought.
Santa Monica, Calif.: The RAND Corporation (RM-2618), July 1,
1960, 39 p.

A study showing the effect that current Soviet doctrine on
strategic surprise has on the Soviet attitude towards deterrence.
The relevant public statements of Soviet leaders are analyzed,
with particular emphasis on Khrushchev's January 14, 1960
speech to the Supreme Soviet on military affairs. The author
discusses the early post-Stalin Soviet debate on the reliability of
deterrence in the light of increased danger of surprise attack,
the conditions under which a prolonged state of mutual deterrence is acceptable to Khrushchev, and current Soviet efforts to
extract political advantage from the strategic equation by
asserting strategic superiority.

An earlier version was published as RAND Paper P-2016 (June
13, 1960). Also published in the Royal Canadian Air Staff
Journal.

No. 214. Jacobs, Walter Darnell.
"The Leninist Revival in Soviet Military Doctrine"
Military Review Vol. 38 No. 4 (July 1958), pp. 23-31.

Attempts by the Soviet military to liberate its thinking from the
restrictions of Stalin's "Permanently Operating Factors" have
accelerated the tendency of Soviet military publicists to reem-
phasize the writings of Lenin on war, armies, and military
science. In this connection, two collections of essays of
strikingly similar titles have recently been published in the
Soviet Union. One, issued in 1955 before the denigration of
Stalin, is entitled Marxism-Leninism on War, the Army, and
Military Science. The other book, published in 1956 after the
denigration of Stalin, is entitled Marxism-Leninism on War and
the Army. The 1955 work stresses the inevitability of war and
the increasing importance of the element of surprise. The 1956
book states that although "war is no longer fatalistically
inevitable," vigilance is necessary. Common to both is the contention that a new world war would not result in the destruction
of world civilization, but in the destruction of the imperialist
social system.

No. 215. Jacobs, Walter Darnell.
"Marshal Malinovskiy and Missiles."
Military Review Vol. 40 No. 3 (June 1960), pp. 14-20.

Marshal Rodion Malinovskiy succeeded Marshal Zhukov as Defense
Minister after Zhukov's removal for "bonapartism" -- attempting
to isolate the army from the Party. Malinovskiy has produced
almost no writings on military doctrine. Instead, he has simply
parroted the contemporary Soviet line on military affairs -- that
"limited war" is meaningless in clashes between first-rate
opponents. These wars can only be decided by the employment
of all arms, including nuclear rocket weapons, and by the
exertions of all sides of society.

No. 216. Jorgensen, K.
"The Rocket and Military Strategy."
Military Review Vol. 37 No. 4 (July 1957), pp. 101-103.

The USSR has already successfully tested a 1500 mile range
rocket. In a book entitled Thoughts Concerning Air Strategy,
which appeared in May 1955, by Marshal Pavel Zhigarev, Chief
of the Soviet Air Force, it is claimed that the strategic bomber
is obsolete. Its last sentence reads: "The present combat
airbases will become bomber graveyards in a future war." The
bomber fields which form the basis of NATO's strategy will
perhaps be useless in a very few years. The war-preventive
factor in peacetime -- or more retalitory action in war, can
therefore be seen to be a combination of bombing aviation and
rockets based far from the Soviet Union.

No. 217. Kramish, Arnold.
The Soviet Union and the Atom: The "Secret" Phase.
Santa Monica, Calif.: The RAND Corporation (RM-1896), April 11, 1957, 89 p.

The study discusses the virtual abandonment of Soviet atomic research during World War II and the renewal of this research in 1943. Although the project was maintained on a relatively small scale, the first Soviet chain-reacting device was achieved in 1947. With the test of their first atomic bomb more than two years away, however, the Soviet Union felt in 1947 that it could proceed confidently with the program.

No. 218. Kramish, Arnold.
The Soviet Union and the Atom: Toward Nuclear Maturity.
Santa Monica, Calif.: The RAND Corporation (RM-2163), April 25, 1958, 113 p.

Based on publicly available materials, this research memorandum describes the progress of the USSR atomic energy program: its organization and the nuclear research institutes serving as training centers, the new atomic communities built for research purposes, atomic and hydrogen bomb development, Soviet applications of nuclear explosions, the construction of reactors and reactor stations, the uses of radioisotope programs, the search for uranium and other rare materials, and the advanced state of nuclear accelerating machines. This investigation reveals that the Soviet Union is eager to venture into untried fields and is willing to give unprecedented financial support to to achieve scientific success.

No. 219. Ruggles, M.J.; and Arnold Kramish.
The Soviet Union and the Atom: The Early Years.
Santa Monica, Calif.: The RAND Corporation (RM-1711), April 2, 1956, 107 p.

This report is an attempt to evaluate the early progress of nuclear research in the Soviet Union until the time of the USSR's entry into World War II. The study indicates that, beginning in the 1920s and throughout the 1930s, Soviet achievements in atomic research, the caliber of Soviet scientists, and the direction of their inquiries were greatly advanced.

No. 220. Ruggles, M.J.; and Arnold Kramish.
Soviet Atomic Policy.
Santa Monica, Calif.: The RAND Corporation (P-853), May 23, 1956, 14 p.

This study shows the range and direction of Soviet nuclear research since the mid-1930s. The rapid strides of the Soviet

Union in military and non-military applications of atomic energy are discussed, together with related aspects of their foreign policy. It suggests that further research on Soviet atomic policy by the United States should prevent such technological and political surprises as those which occurred in the past.

A Time Magazine story of July 30, 1956 was based on this study.

Reactions to Marshal V.D. Sokolovskiy's "Military Strategy"

No. 221.   Abshire, David M.; and Robert D. Crane.
"Soviet Strategy in the 1960s: An Analysis of the Current Russian Debate Over Strategy."
Army Vol. 13 No. 7 (July 1963), pp. 20-21, 84, 86.

Soviet military leaders, and probably also party leaders, hoped that Sokolovskiy's Military Strategy would produce an acceptable consolidation of diverse views being hotly debated over strategy. The debate is between "radicals" who favor reliance on strategic weapons and on leapfrogging technology, and "traditionalists" who think in terms of mass armies and protracted nuclear war. The Sokolovskiy book represents a middle position, calling for the best of both. Whether the Soviet Union has the economic strength to support both courses is now being debated by both Soviet and free world economists.

No. 222.   Apel, Frank J.
The Sokolovsky Strategy: A Paradigm for Future Conflict or Soviet Propaganda?
Maxwell Air Force Base, Alabama: Air War College, 1972, 83 p.

Over the past decade, Soviet advances in military capability have placed the United States in a position of relative parity. Recent indications suggest that the USSR may, if it continues current trends in force acquisition and modernization, achieve clear superiority in the not too distant future. This study compares actual Russian military accomplishments over the last two years with the strategy of Marshal of the Soviet Union V.D. Sokolovsky to determine first, the strategy's authenticity, and secondly, its possible future application. The study concludes that the Sokolovsky strategy is valid and finds that the long range goal of Soviet planners is eventual world domination through nuclear blackmail.

No. 223.   Garthoff, Raymond L.
"A Manual of Soviet Strategy."
The Reporter, February 14, 1963, pp. 34-36.

Military Strategy, written by fifteen leading Soviet military theoreticians headed by Marshal Vasily Sokolovsky, is an authoritative look at current Soviet military thinking. It is a compromise of the views of the more radical or "modern" school with those of the conservative or traditional one. The "Khrushchev doctrine," with its stress on deterrence, has been modified to meet more fully the requirements seen by the military for waging nuclear war should one occur. The compounding of these divergent professional views has required both ready forces to meet the contingency of a relatively short and largely intercontinental war (envisioned by the "radicals") and forces to meet a protracted general war with extensive land theater campaigns (expected by the "conservative" majority). Since this is a compromise, and sice there will doubtless be recurring pressures for resource allocation, it is likely that future revisions will occur. But for the present the debate has evidently subsided.

Reprinted as a chapter in Howard Swearer and Richard Longaker (Eds.), Contemporary Communism: Theory and Practice (Belmont, Calif.: Wadsworth Printing Company, 1963); and as "'Military Strategy' in Perspective," Introduction to V.D. Sokolovsky (Ed.), Military Strategy: Soviet Doctrine and Concepts (New York: Frederick A. Praeger, Publisher, 1963).

No. 224.   Goure, Leon.
Notes on the Second Edition of Marshal V.D. Sokolovskii's "Military Strategy".
Santa Monica, Calif.:   The RAND Corporation (RM-3972-PR), February 1964, 107 p.

The second edition of Military Strategy, published in 1963, contains about 50 pages of new material and numerous changes in the original text. Some are intended to update the account of Western military postures, to take account of recent world events or to incorporate the information in speeches and publications of Soviet leaders. Others reflect developments in technology, improvements in military capability, or greater realism in considering the problems of war. Domestic and foreign criticism of the first edition has evidently led to a number of revisions. Finally, a few changes may be interpreted as the result of doctrinal developments. It is difficult to say how many of the revisions were made to influence Western opinion. The author compares selected passages from the two editions.

No. 225.   Green, Murray.
"Soviet Military Strategy."
Air Force Magazine Vol. 46 No. 3 (March 1963), pp. 38-42.

Marshal Sokolovskiy's Military Strategy was published in mid-1962. The work deserves serious attention in the West, for it is the first comprehensive Soviet treatment of the whole subject of doctrine and strategy and their relationship to larger state policy published since 1926. This collaborative effort also reveals some internal pulling and tugging inside the Defense Ministry to bring Soviet military strategy to reasonable terms with modern technology.

No. 226. Jacobs, Walter Darnell.
"Sokolovskiy's Strategy."
Military Review Vol. 43 No. 6 (July 1963), pp. 9-19.

Many readers have assumed that the version of Soviet strategic thinking presented to them by Western authors is accurate. After reading Marshal V.D. Sokolovskiy's Military Strategy (1962) they may be forced to change their opinions. Westerners who have been reading Soviet publications will find nothing new or startling. This book is a valuable compilation of existing Soviet views, presenting little that is original or imaginative. Its strategy includes the following: nuclear rocket strikes to destroy the military-economic potential of the enemy, disrupt his system of government and military control, and eliminate strategic nuclear forces and major troop units; military operation on land theaters to destroy the enemy forces; protection of the Soviet rear areas; and military operations in naval areas to destroy naval groupings. Sokolovskiy has stated the Soviet case for fighting and winning World War III.

No. 227. Kamoff-Nicolsky, G.
"Voennaya Strategiya: Its Validity in the Eighties."
Canadian Defense Quarterly Vol. 11 No. 2 (Autumn 1981).

Voennaya Strategiya (Military Strategy) was published in 1962 to outline Soviet strategy. The book was intended to resolve internal disputes over military doctrine in the Sovet Union, but neither inside nor outside the USSR has the book succeeded in resolving the basic issue of the Soviet use of nuclear weapons. The emphasis on a war-fighting strategy in Soviet Military Strategy was equated by Western specialists with aggressiveness, which contrasted to the then current U.S. doctrine of deterrence. What had actually happened was not a sudden onset of Soviet aggressiveness, but a decision by Khrushchev in 1960 not to fight long wars of attrition. Nuclear warfare was considered crucial to the strategy of a quick war, a war to be fought with the least possible damage to the USSR. Not all Soviet strategists have accepted the absolute dominance of nuclear weapons, and the debate continues in the USSR.

No. 228. McConnell, James M.
"The Irrelevance Today of Sokolovskiy's Book Military Strategy."
Defense Analysis Vol. 1 No. 4 (1985), pp. 243-254.

Three editions of an inclusive Soviet work on military strategy were published between 1962 and 1968 by a team of authors headed by Marshal V.D. Sokolovskiy. All three were exclusively preoccupied with a single Soviet option -- winning an all-out nuclear war. Over the past two decades, however, owing to changes in the conditions of warfare, Soviet strategy has found it necessary to restore virtually all the old principles and categories of the military art that had been rejected or modified by the Sokolovskiy team. This paper first discusses the changes registered for the military art by the Sokolovskiy team in the 1960s; then the Soviet treatment of strategic principles and categories in the 1970s and early 1980s that were implicitly at variance with the Sokolovskiy approach, and finally the explicit confirmation of Sokolovskiy's obsolesence in a book published in 1985 by General-Colonel M.A. Gareev, Deputy Chief of the General Staff.

No. 229. Muehleisen, Dolf E.
Changes in Soviet Military Strategy.
Menlo Part, Calif.: SRI International (Research Memorandum SED-RM-316) July 1974, 43 p.

In support of a broad study to define requirements and characteristics of a Soviet Indications and Early Warning Center as a resource to the national leadership of the Soviet Union, this study presents the results of an analysis of Soviet military strategy as focused in Military Strategy, edited by Marshal V.D. Sokolovskiy. Attention is focused on basic strategy, modern war considerations (particularly nuclear), concepts of leadership, total national involvement, global aspects, and command and control considerations, with particular consideration given to additions, deletions, and changes pertinent to the Soviet objectives among the three editions of the cited treatise.

No. 230. Odom, William E.
"Sokolovsky's Strategy Revisited."
Military Review Vol. 44 No. 10 (October 1964), pp. 49-53.

This article reviews a Soviet rebuttal to analysis and commentary by RAND specialists concerning Marshal Sokolovsky's Military Strategy. Two points are helpful in understanding the mainstream of the debate: 1) contrary to Western definitions of "military strategy," the book and rebuttal involve interpretations of Soviet policy rather than debate over theoretical principles; 2) to appreciate the strength of the Soviet authors' reply, it must be considered that they are embarrassed by the confusion and ambiguity in their own thought on the nature of nuclear war and the sagacity of Western commentators in discerning this. The actual rebuttal attacks four RAND conclusions: 1) that the consequences of the Soviet doctrine of preemption have not been fully thought out; 2) that attack on any Socialist country would

draw a first strike from the Soviet Union on the United States
(Soviet military writers state that "morally" this would be a
retalitory strike); 3) that the Soviet beliefs that a nuclear
conflict will instantly and automatically take the form of a
general war and that limited wars may escalate into general wars
are contradictory; and 4) the notion of a debate between "traditionalists" and "modernists."

No. 231. Verrier, Anthony.
"The Red Army's New Strategy."
The New Statesman, August 21, 1964, p. 238.

Most people assume that the United States and Soviet Union have
reached a tacit understanding; that their nuclear power is so
evenly matched that for either to embark on a European adven-
ture would be futile and costly. This new situation should be
ascribed at least in part to the recent reorganization of Soviet
missile and ground forces. Over the past five years Soviet
intermediate-range missiles have emerged as a powerful deterrent
force; concurrently the manned bomber lost favor as a retaliatory weapon and the Soviet ground forces have been reduced to
2 million men and 150 divisions. The orthodox Soviet strategic
assumptions, which rest on the inevitability of war and the value
of surprise if one is not to be surprised, are carefully rejected
by the Soviet military establishment in the new edition of Sokolovskiy's Military Strategy. The revolution in Soviet strategic
thought has been brought about by the nuclear weapons with
which it sought parity with the United States and security for
the homeland.

No. 232. Wolfe, Thomas W.
A First Reaction to the New Soviet Book 'Military Strategy'.
Santa Monica, Calif.: The RAND Corporation (RM-3495-PR),
February 1963, 134 p.

An analysis of the new Soviet book, Military Strategy. Its
significance is weighed against the background of certain known
developments of recent years: the military's resistance to
Khrushchev's strategic reforms of 1960; the dispute between
radical and traditionalist elements within the Soviet military
establishment; and the dialogue with the United States on the
strategic power balance. The author discerns signs of compromise among these conflicting viewpoints, which suggest to him
that the Soviet book reflects not a unified doctrine, but a
temporary balance of views in a continuing debate, whose later
phases are likely to bring further doctrinal modifications.

No. 233. Wolfe, Thomas W.
A Postscript on the Significance of the Book "Soviet Military
Strategy".

Santa Monica, Calif.: The RAND Corporation (RM-3730-PR), July 1963, 60 p.

Comments by one of the RAND translators of Sokolovskii's book. He believes that the book was meant primarily for Soviet internal information and also for propaganda. He feels that it marks not only the end of an internal debate on military policy, but a compromise of contending viewpoints. The instability of the compromise is suggested by the announcement of an impending revision of the book, by the continuing doctrinal disagreement within the Soviet bureaucracy, and by the various criticisms leveled at the book.

No. 234. Wolfe, Thomas W.
"Shifts in Soviet Strategic Thought."
Foreign Affairs Vol. 42 No. 2 (April 1964), pp. 475-486.

An analysis of the Soviet part in the recent strategic dialogue between the East and the West. The Sokolovskii book Military Strategy, its new edition out just fifteen months after the first, and the response in Red Star to the U.S. reception of the book indicate Soviet alertness to the strategic dialogue. Though Soviet perception is distorted by ideology, the image of the West in recent Soviet strategic discussions is beginning in some respects to take on more objective dimensions, notably in treating the United States as a strong but withal responsible adversary.

Also printed as The Soviet Voice in the East-West Strategic Dialogue (Santa Monica, Calif.: The RAND Corporation, P-2851, January 1964), 22 p.; and in Frank Barnett, William Mott, and John Neff (Eds.), Peace and War in the Modern Era: Premises, Myths, and Realities. (Garden City, N.Y.: Doubleday and Company, 1965), pp. 257-270.

Cuba: An Early Influence

No. 235. Crane, Robert Dickson.
"The Cuban Crisis: A Strategic Analysis of American and Soviet Policy."
Orbis Vol. 6 No. 4 (Winter 1963), pp. 528-563.

The United States faces a crucial and fundamental foreign policy decision during the next few years, for which it can choose one of three courses: 1) follow a conciliatory course designed to strengthen the hand of the "moderates" in the communist camp; 2) adopt a generally hard course to convince the "extremists" in the communist camp that conflict will result only in the loss of what it has already gained; or 3) develop and pursue a strategy of tension manipulation by initiatives designed to encourage the

144

"moderates" and discourage the "extremists." A policy of tension manipulation still leaves the United States with the necessity for choosing between general policies of firmness and conciliation. The background and result of the Cuban crisis will long serve as the best case study of the do's and don'ts in American foreign policy.

No. 236. Dinerstein, Herbert S.
Making of a Missile Crisis, October 1962.
Baltimore, Md.: The Johns Hopkins University Press, 1976.

This study depicts the abortive Cuban missile gambit as the culmination of a systemic Soviet foreign policy design against the U.S. and Latin America, whose origins ran back as far as the overthrow of the Arbenz regime in Guatemala in 1954. The principal thesis of the study is that the deepening Soviet involvement with Cuba and the parallel growth of Soviet interests in Latin America which began in the late 50s provided not only a lucrative opportunity but also the primary rationale for the buildup of Soviet weaponry in Cuba that resulted in the missile showdown of October 1962. This book illuminates the relationship between Moscow's Cuban policy and the ultimate Soviet missile decision, offers new insights into the timing of the decision, and speculates about possible Soviet internal infighting over strategies once the venture broke into confrontation.

Reviewed by Benjamin Lambeth, RAND Paper R-5700 (August 1976), 5 p.; James Carey, Military Affairs Vol. 41 No. 3 (October 1977), p. 162; Richard Gregor, Canadian Slavonic Papers Vol. 19 No. 3 (September 1977), pp. 385-386; H. Hanak Slavonic and East European Review Vol. 55 No. 4 (October 1977), pp. 567-568; Ronald Pope, Soviet Studies Vol. 29 No. 4 (October 1977), pp. 619-621; Elmo Zumwald, Slavic Review Vol. 36 No. 1 (March 1977), pp. 109-110.

No. 237. Horelick, Arnold L.
"The Cuban Missile Crisis: An Analysis of Soviet Calculation and Behavior."
World Politics Vol. 16 No. 3 (April 1964), pp. 363-389.

An analysis of Soviet political and strategic calculations and behavior in the Cuban missile crisis of October 1962. The analysis centers on: 1) Soviet objectives in deploying strategic weapons in Cuba; 2) the considerations that may have led the Soviet leaders to believe they could succeed; and 3) the reasons for their precipitate withdrawal of the weapons. Prime importance is attached to the role of the U.S.-Soviet strategic balance, both in determining the objectives pursued by the Soviet Union in Cuba, and in bringing about the crisis outcome.

Also printed as RAND paper RM-3779-PR (September 1963), 73 p.

No. 238. Pope, Ronald R.
Soviet Views on the Cuban Missile Crisis: Myth and Reality in Foreign Policy Analysis.
Washington, D.C.: University Press of America, 1982, 198 p.

A presentation and examination of the four major Soviet commentaries on the Cuban missile crisis: Khrushchev's complete correspondence with Kennedy; his Supreme Soviet speech of December 1962; the relevant material from both volumes of Khrushchev Remembers; and a two part article by Anatolii Gromyko, the only major Soviet academic analysis of the crisis. In particular, this work addresses the question of to what extent the Soviets may actually believe their implied claim that they did not miscalculate in placing their missiles in Cuba. It combines discussions, documents, annotations, and a concluding analysis.

Debates Prior to SALT

No. 239. Clemens, Walter C., Jr.
"The Soviet Militia in the Missile Age."
Orbis Vol. 8 No. 1 (Spring 1964), pp. 84-105.

There are objective factors which could lead the Soviet government to reestablish a territorial militia like that which existed in the Soviet Union from 1922 to 1939, parallel with the regular army. This step is supported by the "modernist" faction in the Soviet military, which holds that nuclear weaponry implies a reduced role for other arms; and opposed by the "traditionalist" faction, which argues for adding nuclear capabilities to existing forces rather than replacing them. Six functions are described in which a territorial army could augment or replace existing forces. In addition, a territorial army would probably strengthen Moscow's strategic and bargaining posture in disarmament negotiations, and give it a military advantage should agreement on force reductions be reached.

No. 240. Crane, Robert Dickson (Ed.).
Soviet Nuclear Strategy: A Critical Appraisal.
Washington, D.C.: Center for Strategic Studies, Georgetown University, 1963, 82 p.

This analysis of Soviet nuclear weapons policy is based on discussions held during the spring of 1963 to bring together some of the diverse views of American specialists on developments in Soviet strategic thinking before and after the Cuban Missile Crisis. The 18 participants addressed themselves to specific issues and questions illustrated by quotations provided from recent Soviet writings on nuclear war and strategy. Material is also included, such as the discussion on the internal strategy debate in the Soviet Union, which will be useful to those employed in the study of Soviet strategy.

No. 241. Deriabin, Peter (Ed.).
The Penkovsky Papers.
New York: Doubleday and Company, 1965, 320 p.

This book purports to be a translation of notes written by Col. Oleg Penkovsky, a Soviet military intelligence officer who spied for the United States, that were smuggled out of the Soviet Union shortly before his arrest in October 1962. In 1978 a high-ranking CIA official revealed in congressional testimony that the book was actually prepared by the CIA from Penkovsky's reports after his arrest and presumed execution. The book covers a wide variety of Soviet politico-military topics, including many details on the new Soviet nuclear strategy that was developed between 1960 and 1962.

Reviewed by Hugo Dewar, "Spies Unlimited," Problems of Communism Vol. 15 No. 4 (July-August 1966), pp. 54-57.

No. 242. Kolkowicz, Roman.
Soviet Strategic Debate: An Important Recent Addendum.
Santa Monica, Calif.: The RAND Corporation (P-2936), July 1964, 38 p.

An analysis of an article by Col. I Korotkov on the development of Soviet military theory in the postwar years. A translation of the article is appended.

No. 243. Kolkowicz, Roman.
The Red "Hawks" on the Rationality of Nuclear War.
Santa Monica, Calif.: The RAND Corporation (RM-4899-PR), March 1966, 71 p.

A consideration of the latest phase in relations between the military and the Communist Party in the Soviet Union. Under Khrushchev and his successors, the rejection of nuclear war as a political weapon has prevailed. A military spokesman, LtCol. E. Rybkin, however, has attacked these views as defeatist and politically dangerous. His opinions, in turn, have been indirectly countered in the Polish press by Professor J.J. Wiatr. This paper discusses the arguments for both attitudes, and gives observations and conclusions based on them. Both Rybkin's and Wiatr's articles are appended.

No. 244. Kolkowicz, Roman.
"Strategic Parity and Beyond: Soviet Perspectives."
World Politics Vol. 23 No. 3 (April 1971), pp. 431-451.

This study examines 1) political and strategic styles and preferences of several key Soviet leaders; 2) the dynamics of interaction between Soviet military doctrines and capabilities and
those of the United States; and 3) adversary perception, i.e.,
some generally accepted views about the nature of the United
States as an adversary held by several Soviet elites. These
contributing factors have had an overwhelming impact on Soviet
strategic thinking and on the ordering of Soviet resources,
forces, and postures in the past two decades. Conservative
attitudes and pressures in the Soviet Union and the United
States have raised and reinforced their respective threat-
assessment levels and have provided the dynamics for the arms
race and for the corollary strategic doctrines and policies.
Given the "action-reaction" strategic relations between the superpowers and the internal "mad momentum" of nuclear technology,
it becomes difficult for political leaders to halt the institutional
pressures for military arms programs. In a broader sense, this
analysis suggests the failure of certain beliefs about the relationship between modern technology and the traditional political
processes. It has become clear that the teleology of the nuclear
arms race points to madness and oblivion; that political leadership fails to control this military power for discernable political
purposes. The analysis also suggests that modern war technology is an autonomous, transnational, trans-ideological phenomenon that creates and imposes its own imperatives on the fabric
of politics.

No. 245. Long, J.F.L.
"Shifts in Russia's Strategic Posture."
Royal Air Force Quarterly Vol. 6 No. 4 (Winter 1966), pp.
297-302.

The top Soviet military leadership does not appear to have come
up with a coherent military doctrine. This may reflect the
existence of "hawk" and "dove" factions inside the Politburo.
An interesting reflection of the pressures the political leaders
are probably under can be seen in a recent interview by Marshal
Sokolovskiy and General-Major Cherednichenko. They present a
vigorous case for bringing Soviet military potential up to that of
the United States and its NATO allies. Their point is that there
can be no meaningful discussion at the General Staff level of the
shape of a war-winning strategy or the appropriate degree of
readiness unless the shortcomings of the current strategic planning system are eliminated. It must be expected that a coherent
doctrine will emerge, but for the moment, the signs are of
adjustment. One of these is the steady upgrading of Soviet
naval power.

No. 246. McGuire, Frank C.
"Soviets Revert to ICBM Emphasis."
Missiles and Rockets, December 2, 1963.

One American commentator concluded that the absence of the usual references to combined arms and conventional forces in Marshal Krylov's pronouncement (of November 17, 1963 in Izvestiya) presents "an obvious retreat from the compromise (combined arms) strategy and a return to Premier Khrushchev's strategy, which calls for the diversion of investment funds for the lagging agricultural sector of the economy, and not from ICBM production, ICBM defense, or spaceflight, but instead from conventional military strength." [Abstract from Onaczewicz and Crane, p. 177.]

No. 247. Wolfe, Thomas W.
Soviet Strategic Thought in Transition.
Santa Monica, Calif.: The RAND Corporation (P-2906), May 1964, 21 p.

A discussion of the transition in Soviet strategic posture and the underlying problems necessitating it. During the decade since the death of Stalin, Soviet leadership has attempted to adapt military doctrine and strategy to new problems arising out of the changing technological and political environment of the modern world. The cumulative effect of these problems has become increasingly evident in the development of Soviet defense policy and posture during the past two years.

Reprinted as Chapter 3 in Eleanor Dulles and Robert Crane (Eds.), Detente: Cold War Strategies in Transition (New York: Frederick A. Praeger, Publisher, 1965), pp. 63-76.

No. 248. Wolfe, Thomas W.
"Some New Developments in the Soviet Military Debate."
Orbis Vol. 8 No. 3 (Fall 1964), pp. 550-562.

Over the past few years, the primacy of strategic missile forces has become a tenet of Soviet military doctrine. It would now appear, judging from recently published Soviet military discussions, that a countertrend has begun -- representing a reaction in some quarters against the new orthodoxy embodying such Khrushchevian strategic notions as the absolute primacy of nuclear missile weapons. In part, this reaction may represent merely a continuation of the modernist-traditionalist debate. Some military writers from both schools have now begun to suggest that such ideas have been carried too far, threatening to create a new orthodoxy that could cripple the creative development of Soviet military theory and of other forces, particularly aviation.

Pages 556 to 562 also printed as Some Recent Signs of Reaction Against the Prevailing Soviet Doctrinal Emphasis on Missiles (Santa Monica, Calif.: The RAND Corporation, P-2929, June 1964), 11 p.

No. 249.   Wolfe, Thomas W.
Note on the Naming of a Successor to Marshal Biriuzov.
Santa Monica, Calif.:   The RAND Corporation (P-3025), December 1964, 23 p.

A discussion of certain aspects of the appointment of Marshal M.V. Zakharov to the post of Chief of the Soviet General Staff, succeeding Marshal S.S. Biriuzov who died shortly after Khrushchev's ouster in mid-October 1964.   The Paper: 1) reviews Zakharov's previous tenure as Chief of the General Staff, 1960 to 1963; and 2) discusses the implications of his reappointment for the military policy line contemplated by the new Soviet leadership.

Current Debates

No. 250.   Hasegawa, Tsuyoshi.
"Soviets on Nuclear-War-Fighting."
Problems of Communism Vol. 35 No. 4 (July-August 1986), pp. 86-79.

By the early 1980s, the top Soviet political leadership had incorporated "mutual assured destruction" into Soviet military doctrine.   But the Soviet high command, and notably Nikolay Ogarkov, were reluctant to accept this concept, which postulates that in a nuclear war neither the attacker nor the defender can emerge victorious.   Marshal Ogarkov was relieved of his position as chief of the General Staff when he continued to insist that a defender could withstand a nuclear first strike and defeat an aggressor after retaliating with a second strike.   It is by no means clear that Ogarkov's dismissal means an end to military opposition or that the military has now incorporated mutual assured destruction into Soviet war-fighting strategy.

No. 251.   Herspring, Dale R.
"Marshal Akhromeyev and the Future of the Soviet Armed Forces."
Survival Vol. 28 No. 6 (November-December 1986), pp. 524-535.

Marshal Sergei Akhromeyev succeeded Marshal Ogarkov as Chief of the General Staff of the Soviet Union in 1984, for reasons that remain the subject of considerable debate.   It is rumored that Akhromeyev was an Ogarkov protegee, which suggests that the armed forces will continue to follow the lines followed under Ogarkov's tenure.   Unlike Ogarkov, Akhromeyev has avoided comment on political issues, such as military involvement in national security decision making, although he may have misgivings about Gorbachev's arms control and budgetary policies.   In practical terms this means that Gorbachev could be

faced with indirect resistance from senior military personnel on
budget issues, and that they will continue to argue for greater
reliance on modern technology, particularly for conventional war,
since a condition of nuclear parity exists. Akhromeyev's less
controversial approach could make him more effective in dealing
with senior political officials than the more aggressive Ogarkov.

No. 252. Odom, William E.
"Soviet Force Posture: Dilemmas and Directions."
Problems of Communism Vol. 34 No. 4 (July-August 1985), pp.
1-14.

The Soviet General Staff is engaged in its third revision of force
development policy since the Russian Civil War. The current
need for change in Soviet military doctrine and force structure
is occasioned by new technologies, including micro-circuitry and
directed energy systems. Yet the success of this latest Soviet
military modernization effort will depend more than past such
efforts on the nature of the West's arms control and trade
policies, as well as on NATO's own force development policy.

No. 253. Strode, Dan L.; and Rebecca V. Strode.
"Diplomacy and Defense in Soviet National Security Policy."
International Security Vol. 8 No. 2 (Fall 1983), pp. 91-116.

Soviet military doctrine has traditionally held that a nuclear war
would be a continuation of politics, and that despite the scale of
destruction, socialism would emerge victorious. Starting in the
early 1970s, however, articles began to appear in the Soviet
press which implicitly challenged the prevailing view, and by
1981 this challenge was being explicitly expressed by the top
political leadership. But there is substantial evidence of continuity in Soviet strategic thought, both in statements by Soviet
military leaders and in the direction and magnitude of Soviet
weapons procurement. Given the pattern of recent Soviet
military exercises, the new Brezhnev/Ustinov declaratory policy
must also be irrelevant to the Defense Ministry's approach to
force structuring and nuclear weapon utilization. Many Western
analysts reconcile this incongruity by suggesting that the Soviet
Union is engaged in a "disinformation" campaign designed to
mislead Western public opinion while its real policy remains
unchanged. But a more plausible explanation is that there is an
element of conflict in the formulation of military doctrine between
"diplomacist" and "unilateralist" factions.

No. 254. Weiss, Peter.
"Room at the Top for Ogarkov Again."
International Defense Review Vol. 18 No. 10 (October 1985), pp.
1559-1560.

Marshal Ogarkov's dismissal was an indication that the Party leadership was cutting the military down to size and bringing it to heel again. However, it would be wrong to regard this as a demotion, since he now heads a separate Western Supreme Command, which controls the 95 Soviet divisions facing NATO as well as the 54 divisions from the Warsaw Pact countries. This supposedly new command structure dates back to World War II, when strategic operations were prepared and directed from Stavka. Since the decision to "go nuclear" is of paramount significance at any level, any engagement of strategic nuclear targets would come under the immediate direction of the appropriate commander-in-chief/Stavka plenipotentiary. Gorbachev has apparently been unable to do without the outstanding military talents of Ogarkov. This strong-willed, talented senior officer, of proven capability, will bear close watching in the future.

C. MUTUAL PERCEPTIONS OF NUCLEAR WEAPONS POLICY

Soviet Strategic Culture

No. 255. Gray, Colin S.
"The Most Dangerous Decade: Historic Mission, Legitimacy, and Dynamics of the Soviet Empire in the 1980s."
Orbis Vol. 25 No. 1 (Spring 1981), pp. 13-28.

The 1980s will be uniquely dangerous to the United States, not so much because of the strength of the Soviet Union but because of its weakness. This contention rests on an appraisal of all the influences that work upon the character of the foreign policy of a superpower. The Soviet Union shows the fragility of a true empire, and hence any Soviet leaders must seek to improve the quality of their control over "the world outside." The Soviet propensity to view "nuclear war as an instrument of policy" should be understood as: "to go first in the last resort." The Soviet Union has not sought "strategic superiority" in the narrow military terms of the West, but instead has sought and achieved a reversal in the "correlation of forces," a term that encompasses political, economic, technological, and psychological dimensions. The dangers to the West flow from the mutual miscalculation that the clash of Soviet and American national style invites. Irresponsible Western defense policies have permitted the Soviet Union to achieve a measure of "useful advantage" at virtually all levels of combat. In sum, war may occur in the 1980s because of the combination of a short-term Soviet military optimism and the medium to long-term pessimism specified above.

No. 256. Katzenbach, Edward L.
"Russian Military Development."
Current History Vol. 39 No. 231 (November 1960), pp. 262-266.

U.S. strategists have frequently forgotten that the Russians do not necessarily think like Americans. For example, Western enthusiasts of graduated deterrence and of limited nuclear war failed to note that both demanded Soviet cooperation, yet the Soviet military has apparently developed weapons and theory around high explosives and megatons, without a thought for limited nuclear warfare. One of the many things which makes it difficult for the U.S. military to understand the Soviet Union is that there is a serious lag in Soviet strategic thinking, several years behind that of the United States. While the Soviet Union is now thinking of preemptive nuclear war, the United States has already moved on to the concept of stable deterrence. One hopes to interest the Soviet Union in this concept, especially since it can be argued that the use of military force, except in local situations, is a thing of the past. This being the case, the future of warfare is more likely to be political and economic in the broader sense that it is to be military.

No. 257. Rowney, Edward L.
"The Soviets Are Still Russians."
In Kenneth M. Currie and Gregory Varhall (Eds.), The Soviet Union: What Lies Ahead?
Washington, D.C.: Government Printing Office (Studies in Communist Affairs Vol.6), 1985, pp. 148-153.

General Rowney, writing from his experience as the U.S. Military Representative to SALT II, argues that the United States must face certain facts when negotiating arms control with the Soviet Union. Mutually beneficial treaties only result when the United States and the Soviet Union share a common objective, and the two superpowers do not share a common approach to arms control negotiations. He maintains that the absence of a common cultural heritage and a common objective has blunted U.S. attempts to achieve a mutually advantageous treaty with the USSR.

No. 258. Simes, Dimitri K.
"The Military and Militarism in Soviet Society."
International Security Vol. 6 No. 3 (Winter 1981-82), pp. 123-143.

Russian history provides grounds for strikingly different interpretations of the Soviet military phenomenon. A fairly benign view is articulated by George Kennan, who believes that Soviet preoccupation with force reflects a fundamental sense of insecurity. He reminds us of the numerous invasions, occupations, and devastations that Russia has had to suffer. Richard Pipes argues that a country does not become the largest state in the world by repelling foreign invasions. He sees militancy -- a commitment to violence and coercion -- as central to Soviet Communism. A third perspective is provided by a Soviet historian, P.A. Zayonchkovskiy. He shows that 19th century Russia had to counter serious war preparations from its adversaries, especially Germany, but that imperial absolutism was "not strictly defensive in nature." Very few things can be taken for granted in history; the self-perpetuation of Russian/Soviet militarism is not among them. The forthcoming leadership succession in the Soviet Union may bring important changes in the objectives and methods of Russian leaders. But to overcome the "militaristic way" would be so difficult that the only prudent assumption on the part of Western policymakers is that Russian militarism will outlive the Brezhnev rule, remaining an important factor in shaping the policies of the Soviet regime.

No. 259. Snyder, Jack.
Soviet Strategic Culture: Implications for LNOs.
Santa Monica, Calif.: The RAND Corporation (R-2154-AF), September 1977, 40 p.

This study identifies several factors -- historical, institutional, and political -- that have given rise to a uniquely Soviet approach to strategic thought. American doctrines of limited nuclear war and intrawar deterrence are examined in light of this Soviet doctrinal tradition. Such doctrines conflict with deeply-rooted Soviet beliefs; hence, Soviet decision-makers may not abide by American notions of mutual restraint in the choice of targets and weapons. Three caveats are stressed, however. First, evidence on Soviet strategic doctrine is ambiguous. Second, even deeply-rooted doctrinal beliefs may change, albeit slowly, in response to technical or other environmental changes. Third, doctrinal preference is not the only important factor that might affect Soviet behavior in a nuclear crisis. Situational temptations and constraints may carry independent weight.

No. 260. Strode, Rebecca V.
"Soviet Strategic Style."
Comparative Strategy Vol. 3 No. 4 (1982), pp. 319-339.

For historical, economic, geopolitical, and sociopolitical reasons, the Soviet Union has developed a distinctive approach to national security, one which is characterized by militarism, conservatism, and an emphasis on mass. These factors affect the USSR's strategy, force posture, and manpower policies, and reflect both the strengths and weaknesses of the Soviet political system. On the one hand, they provide a unity of purpose to Soviet strategy that is often lacking in American strategic debate. This very unity of purpose, however, may degenerate into a narrow view

of means that limits the flexibility of the Soviet Armed Forces in
adapting to a fundamentally changed situation.

Soviet Perceptions of U.S. Nuclear Strategy

No. 261. Brown, Dallas C., Jr.
"Origins of the Cold War: The Soviet View."
Chapter 3 in Graham D. Vernon (Ed.), Soviet Perceptions of War
and Peace.
Washington, D.C.: National Defense University Press, 1981, pp.
27-50.

Soviet views on the origins of the Cold War are deeply rooted in
historical experience as well as Marxist-Leninist ideology. For
the Soviet Union, the conflict began in 1917 and has not ended.
The experiences of the interwar period and World War II confirmed their views concerning fundamental Western hostility.
The foreign policy objectives of the Soviet Union in Europe at
the end of World War II were somewhat more limited than often
presumed in the West. Yet, increased tensions were almost
unavoidable because of the diametrically opposed interests of the
Soviet Union and the United States concerning political arrangements in Eastern Europe and other areas. Further, the paranoia
of Stalin, who ruled the Soviet Union with absolute power during
those critical years, made the period of heightened tensions
essentially inevitable.

No. 262. Clemens, Walter C., Jr.
"Kto Kovo? The Present Danger as Seen from Moscow."
Worldview Vol. 20 No. 9 (September 1977), pp. 4-9.

Kto Kovo?, according to Lenin, is the fundamental question of
politics. "Who's going to do in whom?" One side or the other
could win -- not both, a zero-sum conception of politics. The
zero sum conception also exists in the United States -- it is a
prominent factor in the ongoing debate about Soviet strategic
objectives and capabilities, for instance, in statements by the
Committee on the Present Danger. Soviet policy is an ongoing
struggle between fear of foreign incursions and hope for time to
buildup Russia's political, economic, and military resources. The
Kremlin's anxieties have helped goad its arms buildup but has
also reinforced its interest in arms control. One beneficial
influence of SALT has been to give Dr. Georgi Arbatov, head of
the Institute for the Study of the USA and Canada and personal
advisor to Brezhnev, a role like that of Marshal Shulman,
Columbia University Professor and primary advisor on Soviet
Affairs to Cyrus Vance -- both men explain to domestic
audiences why the other superpower acts so unreasonably, while

advising elites on the other side to behave with more restraint.
What the Soviets now rationalize as a temporary expedient of
cooperation could over time become a strategy. Meanwhile,
Westerners will have to endure Soviet assertions regarding the
"inevitable collapse of capitalism and the victory of socialism on
world scale." Russians, in turn, may have to put up with the
cyclical hyperbole of U.S. electioneering, alarms of present
dangerists, and captive nations resolutions.

No. 263. Foster, Gregory D.
"Soviet Perceptions of U.S. Strategic Activities: A Realtime
Retrospection."
In Kenneth M. Currie and Gregory Varhall (Eds.), The Soviet
Union: What Lies Ahead?
Washington, D.C.: Government Printing Office (Studies in Com-
munist Affairs Vol. 6), 1985, pp. 670-692.

This essay is concerned with Soviet perceptions of U.S. strategic
developments. It asserts that U.S. policy has shown an insen-
sitivity to Soviet perceptions; the result has been inconsistent,
mixed, or even contradictory signals to Moscow. The United
States must understand the impact of its words and actions upon
the Soviet Union. The failure to do this will place the United
States at a considerable disadvantage in the global balance of
power.

No. 264. Goure, Leon.
"The U.S. 'Countervailing Strategy' in Soviet Perception."
Strategic Review Vol. 9 No. 4 (Fall 1981), pp. 51-64.

The "countervailing strategy" publicized by the Carter Administration's Presidential Directive 59, and apparently still being
adhered to by the Reagan Administration, represents an effort to
emphasize the nuclear warfighting aspects of the U.S. strategic
doctrine and posture. It has been recognized -- and, indeed,
anticipated -- as such by Soviet analysts. But beyond the
Soviet propaganda onslaughts there seems to be genuine puzzle-
ment about the intentions behind the strategy and particularly
about the warfighting scenarios envisaged for it. If it is sup-
posed to influence Soviet perceptions, moreover, the strategy
suffers from credibility weaknesses: notably the slowness in the
U.S. procurement of requisite weapons systems, the implausibil-
ity (in Soviet eyes) of the concept of "victory denial," and the
asymmetrical vulnerabilities of U.S. and Soviet societies to
nuclear war.

No. 265. Goure, Leon.
"Nuclear Winter in Soviet Mirrors."
Strategic Review Vol. 13 No. 3 (Summer 1985), pp. 22-38.

The hypothesis advanced by some Western scientists concerning long-term, devasting climatic effects of nuclear war -- "nuclear winter" -- has elicited positive echoes from the scientific community in the Soviet Union, or at least from those Soviet scientists who have become regular participants in the various international forums addressed to provide ostensibly independent confirmation of the findings of their Western counterparts concerning the nuclear winter phenomenon. Yet, an analysis of those presentations, and of the "models" adduced by the Soviet scientists, shows a basic and persistant reliance on Western data and scenarios, notwithstanding repeated entreaties by their Western colleagues for inputs presumably available from Soviet weapons tests and other relevant experience. There are also revealing differences in the ways the Soviet government has tailored the nuclear winter theme for consumption at home and abroad. Even taking into account the obvious constraints bearing upon Soviet scientists within their system, the evidence thus far strongly supports the conclusion that the issue is being used by the Soviet Union primarily for political and propaganda purposes.

No. 266. Guertner, Gary L.
"Strategic Vulnerability of a Multinational State: Deterring the Soviet Union."
Political Science Quarterly Vol. 96 No. 2 (Summer 1981), pp. 209-223.

This article examines the geopolitical, economic, ethnographic, and historical factors that influence the calculus of Soviet strategic planning. Its central thesis is that Soviet sensitivity to these problems, and particularly to the loyalty of the non-Russian nationalities, introduces an element of doubt in Soviet strategy sufficient to strengthen the credibility of U.S. strategic forces at levels below the current SALT II ceilings, and without further U.S. development of counterforce or limited nuclear options. Soviet strategic analysts are attentive to the full continuum of possibilities ranging from politics to war. To conclude that an emphasis on warfighting constitutes a rejection of deterrence is to engage in a very selective reading of Soviet doctrine; the ability to deny victory to the enemy strengthens deterrence but does not preempt its importance in Soviet doctrine. American policymakers and academics fail to take into account the effects of their discussions of Soviet vulnerabilities. The Soviets' heightened perception of U.S. hostility could easily lead to an escalation of the arms race.

Also published in Kenneth M. Currie and Gregory Varhill (Eds.), The Soviet Union: What Lies Ahead? (Washington, D.C.: Government Printing Office, Studies in Communist Affairs Vol. 6, 1985), pp. 378-394.

No. 267. Holloway, David.
"Soviet Scientists Attack Schlesinger."
The New Scientists Vol. 64 No. 926 (November 5, 1974), p. 707.

Reports on an article published in the journal of the Institute
for Study of the USA and Canada of the Soviet Academy of
Sciences SShA (No. 11, 1974, p. 10) by two institute staffers
specializing in strategic affairs, M.A. Milstein and L.S. Semeiko.
This article contends that the Schlesinger doctrine is an attempt
to restore to U.S. strategic power the political utility it lost as a
result of the growth of Soviet military strength. But this
attempt is useless, for "unleashing a missile-nuclear exchange
and keeping it within safe limits is a myth." Holloway concludes
that the new policy is even more dangerous than its Western
critics have argued, for if the Soviet Union believes a limited
strategic war to be impossible, such a U.S. action would be
treated as the first move in a general nuclear war.

No. 268. Horelick, Arnold L.
"The Strategic Mind-Set of the Soviet Military: An Essay-
Review."
Problems of Communism Vol. 26 No. 2 (March-April 1977), pp.
80-85.

A review of translations of The Armed Forces of the Soviet State
(1975) by A.A. Grechko and Soviet Military Strategy by V.D.
Sokolovskiy. The utility of Soviet military literature for understanding the strategic purpose of the USSR is critically assessed. Comparison of successive editions of the books under
review offer the specialist an opportunity to explore in minute
detail changes in authoritative Soviet military views on the broad
range of subjects. For general readers the volumes are recommended primarily for the insights they offer into the strategic
mind-set of the Soviet marshals -- basic and remarkably stable
attitudes toward nuclear war that appear to be fundamental
elements in the belief system of the Soviet military. The author
concludes that differences between Soviet and American outlooks
are less likely the consequence of a temporary "lag" in Soviet
strategic sophistication than of profound differences between the
political cultures of the two societies.

Also printed as RAND Paper P-5813 (February 1977), 12 p.

No. 269. Jackson, William D.
"Soviet Images of the U.S. as Nuclear Adversary, 1969-1979."
World Politics Vol. 33 No. 4 (July 1981), pp. 614-638.

Images of the United States as nuclear adversary presented in
official Soviet commentary provide useful clues in the analyses of
Soviet strategic policy. Hard, high-threat images stressing the
continuing danger of nuclear war are functionally associated with

conservative policies emphasizing the need for efforts to improve war-fighting capabilities. Less militant adversary images appear associated with more moderate defense policies. In the 1970s, sharp divergences in adversary images appeared in official Soviet commentaries, indicative of disagreement within the Soviet Union on the defense policy implications of SALT. The policy implications of shifts in adversary images and the location of the political leadership in terms of conflicting moderate and conservative images are examined for the period 1969-1979.

No. 270. Lee, William T.
"Soviet Perceptions of the Threat and Soviet Military Capabilities."
Chapter 5 in Graham D. Vernon (Ed.), Soviet Perceptions of War and Peace.
Washington, D.C.: National Defense University Press, 1981, pp. 67-96.

In attempting to look at Soviet military capabilities from the Soviet point of view, it is useful to examine Soviet perceptions of the threat posed by the United States and its allies to the Soviet Union and the "socialist camp," and Soviet views of the nature of a war between the two superpower coalitions, its political objectives, and how the Soviets would wage such a war. Given the missions assigned to the Soviet armed forces in the event of a nuclear war between the two superpower coalitions, the capabilities of Soviet forces to perform these missions may be evaluated. Inasmuch as the relationship between missions and capabilities is a dynamic one, it is useful to explore how the Soviets may view the long-term trends in this relationship and the effect thereof on the trends in the military "correlation of forces" between the two superpowers.

No. 271. Lockwood, Jonathan S.
The Soviet View of U.S. Strategic Deterrence: Implications for Decision-Making.
New Brunswick, N.J.: Transaction Books, 1983, 202 p.

Soviet perspectives of U.S. strategic doctrine have influenced their use of military power in foreign policy. This book discusses the implications of this perception for arms control and disarmament. It is based on Soviet sources: newspapers, radio broadcasts, and books. Soviet analysts show a marked tendency to project their own notions of nuclear strategy onto U.S. doctrine and intentions. They have no incentive to engage in arms control on a serious basis, because they perceive that they have forced changes in U.S. strategic doctrine resulting from the need to accommodate the growth of Soviet strategic superiority. Soviet commentators and writers make use of "declaratory deterrence" statements in a thus far successful effort to misinform the United States about their intent. The book concludes

with suggestions as to how the United States might best for-
mulate a doctrine designed to deter the Soviet Union to the
greatest extent possible by taking their perceptions into account,
along with the realities of the U.S. position in the nuclear age.

Reviewed by Roman Kolkowicz, Political-Science Quarterly Vol. 99
No. 1 (Spring 1984), pp. 184-186.

No. 272.   Papp, Daniel S.
"Soviet Perceptions of the Strategic Balance."
Air University Review Vol. 32 No. 2 (January-February 1981),
pp. 2-17.

There is considerable disagreement among analysts of Soviet
affairs over what the reality of Soviet perception of the strategic
balance actually is.   Despite different attitudes expressed by
Soviet leaders and in the Soviet media, those sources of data
which provide most of the information about Soviet perceptions of
the strategic balance -- Soviet military writings, statements by
senior political and military leaders, and strategic force procurement and deployment --contain within their internal contradictions
a considerable degree of consistancy.   This article examines
three areas of Soviet perceptions of the strategic balance: force
capabilities, threat assessment, and employment doctrine -- in an
effort to delimit both contradictions and consistencies.   From this
examination it can be concluded that: 1) Soviet leaders believe
current nuclear forces are approximately equal but do not believe
this situation will necessarily persist in the long-term; 2) Soviet
leaders believe the "American threat" is increasing; 3) Soviet
leaders do not equate surviving a nuclear war with victory and
have no consensus over whether such a war could be survived;
4) there is an on-going Soviet debate over MAD; 5) the Soviet
Union has adopted publicly a comprehensive targeting posture,
although other targeting postures also exist; 6) Soviet leaders
accept the concept of deterrence;   and 7) Soviet leaders are
cognizant of the political utility of nuclear weapons and believe
parity aids the Soviet Union.

No. 273.   Richelson, Jeffrey T.
"Soviet Responses to MX."
Political Science Quarterly Vol. 96 No. 3 (Fall 1981), pp.
401-410.

This article examines the options available to the Soviet Union in
responding to the MX.   One can expect Soviet planners to be
influenced by two major objectives: to guarantee the survivability of their own ICBMs, and to maintain the ability to threaten
U.S. ICBMs.   It is assumed that the Soviet leadership is inclined
to continue observing the limits established by SALT II, at least
until it decides whether an acceptable SALT II agreement can be
reached.   It is also assumed that the Soviet Union sees the

Reagan election victory as sharply increasing the chances of either deep reductions in ICBM limits or a complete breakdown of SALT. Finally, it is assumed that MX is to be deployed in a land-based shell game protected mode.

No. 274. Scott, William F.
"Soviet Military Doctrine and Strategy: Realities and Misunder-standings."
Strategic Review Vol. 3 No. 3 (Summer 1975), pp. 57-66.

Current Soviet military doctrine, adopted by the Party in the late 1950s, "requires that the Armed Forces, the country, and the whole Soviet people be prepared for the eventuality of a nuclear-rocket war." This doctrinal decision required a new strategy, which was made known to the West in August 1962, through the publication of Marshal Sokolovskiy's Military Strategy. Further explanations of Soviet military doctrine and strategy have been presented since that time in hundreds of Soviet books, pamphlets, and articles. Subsequent events, such as the Cuban Missile Crisis, the Nuclear Test-Ban Treaty, and SALT negotiations have not altered their basic provisions. Development, production, and deployment of Soviet weapons systems have been in accordance with stated military objectives and principles. Despite the clarity with which Soviet military doctrine and strategy have been stated, most Western analysts throughout the 1960s misinterpreted or ignored their basic thrust. While seeking to find internal dissention among the Soviet political-military leadership, Western analysts have failed, as a group, to inform the public about the fundamental tenets of military doctrine and strategy upon which Soviet military-political policies are based.

No. 275. Scott, William F.; and Harriet Fast Scott.
"Soviet Perceptions of U.S. Military Strategies and Forces."
Chapter 6 in Graham Vernon (Ed.), Soviet Perceptions of War and Peace.
Washington, D.C.: National Defense University Press, 1981, pp. 97-112.

Since the early 1960s the Soviet people have been told that the United States is preparing for a surprise unlimited [neogranich-ennoye] nuclear strike against the Soviet Union and other socialist nations. In the late 1960s this assertion was revised to admit the possibility that the United States might begin war with conventional weapons only, then proceed to the limited use of nuclear weapons, followed by escalation to world nuclear war. The United States is portrayed as having "unleashed" an arms race, and as possessing forces and weapons systems beyond those needed for its defense. Many Soviet writings about U.S. military strategies and forces appear simply as propaganda, serving to justify Soviet actions, the buildup of Soviet forces, and the heavy defense burden of the Soviet people. Still, the top Soviet leadership, supposedly with access to factual information about the West, appears to hold the same distorted views as those reflected in the Soviet news media. If these represent actual views, there is danger that the Soviet Union might begin a war through misunderstanding and miscalculation of the capabilities of U.S. forces and the intentions of NATO's leaders.

No. 276. Shulsky, Abram N.
Soviet Perceptions of the U.S.-U.S.S.R. Rivalry.
Alexandria, Va.: Center for Naval Analyses (P-1046), March 1976, 11 p.

The work on which this presentation is based was done in response to a request for studies of the Soviet perception of the strategic-arms race. First some methodological questions are presented and then a general description of some of the important issues is discussed.

U.S. Perceptions of Soviet Nuclear Strategy

No. 277. Buchan, Glenn C.
"The Anti-MAD Mythology."
Bulletin of the Atomic Scientists Vol. 37 No. 4 (April 1981), pp. 13-17.

A major myth put forth by MAD critics is that "the Soviets do not accept MAD, therefore, neither should we." Even this premise is dubious, being based on a somewhat selective interpretation of Soviet open writings on nuclear war, their historical experience, and their weapons program. Statements in accord with MAD by the Soviet leadership and prominent Soviet political analysts such as Georgy Arbatov are dismissed as propaganda. Inferring Soviet grand designs and philosophies from the details of their weapons programs has the same problem. But the most important objection to this notion is that it is irrelevant. MAD is a reality, since in a general nuclear war the Soviet Union would risk incalculable damage.

With a response by Colin Gray, "Chacun a son gout," Bulletin of the Atomic Scientists Vol. 37 No. 6 (June-July 1981), p. 65.

No. 278. Cohen, Samuel T.; and Joseph D. Douglass, Jr.
"Selective Targeting and Soviet Deception."
Armed Forces Journal, September 1983, pp. 95-101.

Deterrence requires shaping Soviet assessments about the risks of war -- assessments they will make using their own models, not American ones. But does the United States really know enough about the actual targets to realistically implement a selective targeting strategy? While American planners are beginning to recognize Soviet doctrine, they have yet to accept one of its central tenets --the importance of surprise and the need to employ secrecy, cover, and deception to mislead the enemy.

No. 279. Douglass, Joseph D., Jr.
"Soviet Disinformation."
Strategic Review Vol. 9 No. 1 (Winter 1981), pp. 16-25.

On the shadowy U.S.-Soviet battleground of intelligence and reciprocal strategic analysis, the Soviet Union has been able to magnify the advantages of systemic secrecy with a sustained campaign of disinformation. Indeed, according to U.S. intelligence testimony, disinformation has been elevated by the Soviet Union into a major instrument of policy. Yet the documented cases tell only the tip of the story and of the treacherous terrain of fact and fiction in which any conclusive analysis of Soviet strategic intentions must operate. There is urgent need of a concerted attack on the problem -- all the more so in anticipation of a burst of disinformation activities that is likely to attend a new leadership succession in the Kremlin.

No. 280. Douglass, Joseph D., Jr.
"Strategic Planning and Nuclear Insecurity."
Orbis Vol. 27 No. 3 (Fall 1983), pp. 667-694.

It is essential that U.S. strategy not be divorced from the realities of U.S. capabilities, which was the failing of PD 59. In addition, a realistic acceptance of Soviet strategy is needed. This not only includes acceptance of its central surprise, decisive, first-strike approach; but also the fact that the Soviet Union is working hard to acquire the capabilities to implement it. An effective U.S. strategy, however, cannot be developed in the absence of national-level interest and direction, sound military strategy, and the continuity of long-range strategic planning.

No. 281. Dyson, Freeman.
"On Russians and Their View of Nuclear Strategy."
Chapter 7 in Charles W. Kegley, Jr. and Eugene R. Wittkopf (Eds.), The Nuclear Reader: Strategy, Weapons, War.
New York: St. Martin's Press, 1985, pp. 95-99.

The American experts who study the Soviet armed forces and analyze the Soviet literature devoted to military questions have reached diverse conclusions concerning Soviet strategy. Some say that Soviet intentions are predominantly defensive, others that they are aggressive. The two experts on whom this analysis is based are George Kennan and Richard Pipes. Their views are

sharply divergent -- Kennan has a reputation for diplomatic
moderation, Pipes for belligerence. Yet while they differ in the
implications they draw about Soviet strategy, their accounts of
its contents are similar. The confidence of the Russian people
in their ability to survive the worst we can do to them is a
stabilizing influence, not a threat to U.S. security. It is futile
to expect to convert the Soviet military leaders to the U.S. way
of thinking, but it is also unnecessary. The two nations only
need to understand that it is possible to think differently and to
respect each other's points of view.

No. 282.   Ermath, Fritz W.
"Contrasts in American and Soviet Strategic Thought."
International Security Vol. 2 No. 2 (Fall 1978), pp. 138-155.

The essence of U.S. "strategic doctrine" is to deter nuclear war
through the credible threat of catastrophic damage to the enemy
should deterrence fail. Soviet strategic doctrine stipulated that
the Soviet Union must survive as a nation and in some politically
and militarily meaningful way, defeat the main enemy should
deterrence fail. The most influential factor inhibiting lucid
comparison of U.S. and Soviet strategic thinking has been the
uncritical assumption that they are very similar, or at least
converging over time. A more thorough appreciation of the
differences in U.S. and Soviet thinking must be developed. It
is not useful to have three familiar schools of thought on Soviet
doctrine arguing past each other: one saying, "Whatever they
say, they think as we do"; the second insisting, "Whatever they
say, it does not matter"; and the third contending, "They think
what they say, and are therefore out for superiority." Instead,
comparative strategy should address systematically a series of
questions that reveal the complications, qualifications, and
contradictions that affect the assymmetrical strategic doctrines.
The failure of U.S. strategic thought to address these issues
has had a number of dangerous consequences for the U.S.-
Soviet strategic relationships.

Also printed as a RAND paper (P-6120), May 1978; as Chapter 3
in Derek Leebaert (Ed.), Soviet Military Thinking (London:
George Allen and Unwin, 1981), pp. 50-72; and as Chapter 22 in
P. Edward Haley et al. (Eds.), Nuclear Strategy, Arms Control,
and the Future (Boulder, Colo.: Westview Press, 1985), pp.
159-165.

No. 283.   Freedman, Lawrence.
U.S. Intelligence and the Soviet Strategic Threat.
Boulder, Colo.: Westview Press, 1977.

This study begins by looking at the estimating process in the
United States for Soviet strategic arms. It then discusses some
of the key intelligence debates of the 1940s and 1950s to illus-

trate some of the arguments developed on the relationship
between the organization of the intelligence community and the
character of its product, to demonstrate the impact of improved
means of intelligence collection on the estimating process, and to
set the stage for a detailed study of the "Minuteman vulnerability" issue as it developed through the 1960s and 1970s. As a
case study this issue has a number of advantages. As it was
featured in strategic analysis from the 1950s to the present, the
relationship between threats and policy over a long period can
be explored. This enables an examination of how the changing
strategic and policy environment affected that relationship. It
provides a slightly different persective for the analysis of U.S.
strategic arms policy, which has tended to be dominated by
studies of particular weapons programs. Finally, it allows a
detailed assessment of the performance of the U.S. intelligence
community in the face of the major strategic arms build-up of the
Soviet Union which began in 1965 and has been progressing ever
since.

Reviewed by Walter C. Clemens, Slavic Review Vol. 38 No. 4
(December 1979), p. 685; Keith Dunn, Parameters Vol. 8 No. 3
(September 1978), pp. 97-98; Economist Vol. 256 No. 7011
(January 14, 1978), pp. 106-108; Bernard Nording, Review of
Politics Vol. 40 No. 4 (October 1978), pp. 553-558; Harry
Ranson, International Affairs Vol. 54 No. 3 (July 1978), pp.
461-462; Richard Ullman, Survival Vol. 20 No. 6 (November-
December 1978), pp. 275-276; Russell F. Weigley, Annals of the
American Academy of Political Science No. 440 (November 1978),
pp. 170-171; RUSI Journal Vol. 123 (June 1978), p. 84; Naval
War College Review Vol. 32 (February 1979), pp. 107-108.

No. 284. Hanson, Donald W.
"Is Soviet Strategic Doctrine Superior?"
International Security Vol. 7 No. 3 (Winter 1982-83), pp. 61-83.

There is a new argument in the current strategic debate: that
the American defense community has erred in having seriously
underestimated the merits of Soviet strategic thinking. Among
American analysts there has long been a current of opinion that
Soviet doctrine would converge with American ideas. Today one
finds the idea expressed that the better course for U.S.
strategic thought is "reverse convergence" with Soviet doctrine.
There are both merits and defects in this thesis, but taken as a
whole, it involves strategic advice which ought not to be
accepted. It is one thing to insist that deterrence can fail and
in that case nuclear weapons might have to be used. It is
another to claim that because the need for a viable employment
doctrine exists, a strategy for victory and survival can be
found.

No. 285. Hart, Douglas M. "The Hermeneutics of Soviet Military Doctrine."
Washington Quarterly Vol. 7 No. 2 (Spring 1984), pp. 77-88.

Hermeneuts were members of the early Church who interpreted the worship service for congregations that did not understand Latin or Greek. This essay examines the impact of the hermeneutics of Soviet military doctrine upon the formulation of U.S. defense and arms control policy. Policymakers require the services of hermeneuts for interpretation of Soviet military doctrine because the typical decision-maker does not understand Russian, has no time to read the fraction of material that gets translated, and lacks the expertise to discern trends and watersheds in the stylized, ideology-laden literature of Soviet military theory. In order to determine the impact of the hermeneutics of Soviet military doctrine, it is necessary to examine in detail the different interpretations currently vying for attention. These include primitivism, convergence, neoclausewitzianism, talmudism, imperialism, and eclecticism. As long as decision makers face an artificial choice posed by analysts who adhere to unilateral interpretations of Soviet military thought, policymakers have no reason to consider arguments other than whether or not an interpretation supports a preestablished policy goal. If analysis of Soviet military doctrine is to become a useful tool for policymaking, all-inclusive, single-factor, interpretive models must be eschewed in favor of less ambitious mechanisms that focus on specific aspects of Soviet military thought.

No. 286. Jackson, William D.
"Cold War Demonology."
Bulletin of the Atomic Scientists Vol. 38 No. 8 (October 1982), pp. 52-54.

This article contends that the Reagan administration's belief that the Soviet Union is solely responsible for the arms race is distorted. It discusses the distortions surrounding both the SALT debate and the claim that the SALT process led the United States to neglect its strategic forces almost totally during the 1970s. The latter half of the 1970s was simply a pause in the enhancement of U.S. strategic power since the operational U.S. strategic arsenal changed very little during this time. Progress in arms control requires that both the United States and the Soviet Union deal with the dynamics of arms competition more objectively and avoid distortion of the record on arms control negotiations.

No. 287. Jacobson, C.G.
"The Soviet Military Reappraised."
Current History Vol. 80 No. 468 (October 1981), pp. 305-308, 336-338.

The Reagan administration has adopted an extreme position on strategic weapons and arms control, even though many of the military and military-political arguments on which it rests are open to challenge. It can be presumed that the reason is psychological -- to check the self-inflicted damage arising from the myth of Soviet strategic invulnerability. This myth was spread both by the Soviet propaganda apparatus and by American opinion makers serving their own domestic political purposes. The new administration believes a major show of machismo and determination is necessary not on military grounds, but to counter false assumption about American strength. However, there are two elements to a development that will undercut both the administration's hopes and fears. One is the international skepticism that greets Soviet and American ideological pretentions; the second is the trend toward military anarchy spurred by the emergence of sophisticated weaponry which is inexpensive and easy to operate, squeezing out superpower options.

No. 288. Jones, David R.
"Nuclear War and Soviet Policy."
International Perspectives, November-December 1982, pp. 17-20.

The Reagan Administration bases its belief that U.S. forces must be strengthened on assumptions that the West is inferior to the Soviet Union in strategic nuclear weaponry and that Soviet military thought considers warfare a rational means for attaining political goals. The validity of the second argument is examined in this article by discussing the foundations of Soviet military doctrine and current Soviet defense policies. It concludes that Soviet leaders seem sincere in their fears about thermonuclear warfare, and in their intention to use nuclear weapons only as a response to an enemy's first strike.

No. 289. Jones, W.M.
Escalation Space and Assumptions about Enemy Motives: Elements in Warning Assessment.
Santa Monica, Calif.: The RAND Corporation (N-1269-AF), January 1980, 29 p.

Strategic warning may be viewed as contingently predicting an imminent, significant escalation of a confrontation. Warning of an imminent Soviet strategic nuclear attack is one of a large set of possible escalations, although of unique consequence. Confrontations and conflicts may be characterized as a series of escalations and de-escalations by one or both sides, involving some six factors that cover the participants, the locale, the degree of superpower involvements, the types of weapons in use, and the targets of the military violence. By locating these variables on each of these ladders at every juncture in a confrontation, the warning analyst can identify the various steps open to the enemy. To assist him in deciding which possibilities warrant his close attention, he must make some basic assumptions about enemy decision-making determinants. The making of such assumptions is inevitable; they should be explicit.

No. 290. Kaiser, Robert G.; and Walter Pincus.
"The Doomsday Debate: 'Shall We Attack America?'"
Parameters Vol. 9 No. 4 (December 1979), pp. 79-85.

Looking five years into the future, this short story imagines a Soviet Union at the point of greatest theoretical advantage over the United States in nuclear forces. Brezhnev's "peace" faction in the Politburo has been defeated, and the new General Secretary believes the time has come for a showdown with the imperialists. A team of Soviet experts is ordered to prepare a plan to exploit the "window of vulnerability" the new leader has read about in the American press. After exploring all the options, they conclude there is no useful way the Soviet Union can exploit its nuclear arsenal.

Reprinted from the Washington Post, August 12, 1979, p. B1.

No. 291. Lambeth, Benjamin S.
The State of Western Research on Soviet Military Strategy and Policy.
Santa Monica, Calif.: The RAND Corporation (N-2230-AF), October 1984, 65 p.

This report traces the evolution of Western research on Soviet strategic policy since its beginnings in the 1950s, reviews the ongoing debate over major issues regarding the Soviet "threat," discusses some important rules of evidence and interpretation as they apply to Soviet military research, and suggests new directions the field might profitably take in the years ahead. It is specifically concerned with Soviet military doctrine and its bearing on Soviet force planning and behavior.

No. 292. Monks, Alfred L.; and Kenyon N. Griffin.
"Soviet Strategic Claims, 1964-1970."
Orbis Vol. 16 No. 2 (Summer 1972), pp. 520-544.

The purpose of this article is to analyze specific functions of Soviet strategic claims for the period 1964-1970 in an effort to clarify their ambiguity in meaning and function. Data for this analysis were collected from various Russian-language sources to shed light on the following questions: 1) the relationship between Soviet strategic claims and actual capabilities, 2) whether Soviet claims serve as a means of influencing domestic political debates in the United States; and 3) the differences

168

between claims by top-echelon Soviet military officers and their subordinates which might suggest that the former constituted a significant pressure group. For each claim the information was broken down into six variables: 1) nature of the claim, 2) assertiveness of the claim, 3) strategic state claimed by the Soviets, 4) date of the claim, 5) rank of the official making the claim, and 6) Party Central Committee membership. This breakdown enabled the data to be analyzed in various relationships, providing a basis for addressing the research questions.

No. 293. Murray, J.E.
An Approach to Long-Range Forecasting.
Santa Monica, Calif.: The RAND Corporation (N-1609-01A), January 1981, 23 p.

An introduction to a method for making long-range (10-20 years) forecasts of Soviet strategic weapons developments. As the end product of a heuristic reasoning process, the methodology has a "requirements" orientation, based on clues from Soviet military writings, Soviet technology, and Soviet acquisition practices. Progressing through a sequence of four central inquiries, the methodology examines various Soviet mission priorities, weapons deficiencies, and weapon options to forecast Soviet weapon choices. These four inquiries are supported by five background inquiries into Soviet military concepts, Soviet perceptions of threat, current Soviet weapon capabilities, Soviet advanced weapons technology, and available Soviet resources. After describing the overall methodology, this note discusses each of the nine inquiries and presents the author's viewpoint on their boundaries and emphasis.

No. 294. Nunn, Jack H.
The Soviet First Strike Threat: The U.S. Perspective.
New York: Praeger Publishers, 1982, 292 p.

Since the end of World War II, U.S. national security planning has been dominated by concern over the threat of a Soviet nuclear disarming first strike. This threat is defined as the possibility that a surprise attack, a first strike by the Soviet Union, would so devastate U.S. military strength that the United States could not reply to the attack. This implies not only an attack against U.S. forces which physically disarms the country, but also a host of contingencies in which the United States, while not physically disarmed, would still be unable to reply effectively to an attack. The emphasis on this threat in U.S. military planning and arms control debates raises questions about its dominant role in U.S. national security planning. As a result, it is appropriate to examine the development of the U.S. fear of a Soviet disarming first strike and to explore the beliefs that form the basis for judgements on this threat.

No. 295. Petersen, Phillip A.
"American Perceptions of Soviet Military Power."
Parameters Vol. 7 No. 4 (1977), pp. 71-82.

Before the United States can analyze Soviet behavior and act accordingly to influence it, there must emerge a consensus of beliefs and values, a determination of why the United States should support them, and a clear articulation of them. Currently a great debate is occurring over the issue of what is motivating the great buildup of Soviet military power. The turmoil is forcing national security decision-makers to make their important images and beliefs explict, to try to discover the crucial elements that underlie their policy preferences, and to consider what evidence would tend to confirm or deny their preferences. Such activities can only lead to the minimizing of dangerous misperceptions.

No. 296. Possony, Stefan T.
"U.S. Intelligence at the Crossroads."
Orbis Vol. 9 No. 3 (Fall 1965), pp. 587-610.

The majority of U.S. experts on communism are best described as "menshevik" in their intellectual makeup; not necessarily wrong or mischievous, but given to ambivalent estimations of communism, confident that henceforth the Soviet Union will be governed by moderate and progressive rulers. The attraction of menshevik optimism is demonstrated by Soviet Strategy at the Crossroads, a recent book by Thomas Wolfe. His thesis is that Soviet strategy has reached a crossroads where the Kremlin will be forced to make basic and painful decisions, and he presents evidence that there are debates between Soviet military leaders over the types of war to prepare for and to avoid. Hence the celebrated debate -- if it does have doctrinal relevance and assuming that the Soviet deception machinery did not fake part of it -- deals with the entirely secondary question of how much ground force is necessary in addition to the strategic systems. On the main intercontinental theater of conflict, the arms the Soviet Union has been procuring are precisely those that will be needed to defeat the United States, provided that greater quantities and better quality are available. The Soviet Union may never achieve a nuclear war-winning capacity, but if the United States adheres to its theory that a technological "plateau" has been reached, this ominous date might advance.

Comment by Thomas W. Wolfe, pp. 611-612.

No. 297. Prados, John.
The Soviet Estimate: U.S. Intelligence Analysis and Russian Military Strength.
New York: The Dial Press, 1982, 367 p.

The growth of Soviet military power has been one of the most significant and disturbing trends of postwar history. In at least one area -- the strategic nuclear forces that directly threaten the United States -- the Soviets have made such progress that it is now disputed whether conditions reflect "parity" with the United States or even actual Soviet nuclear superiority....In the 1960s periodic and explicit statements by Defense Secretary Robert MacNamara described Soviet nuclear forces and programs in considerable detail, based on national intelligence estimates. Today, however, numerous commentators tell us that much of that information was in error, that intelligence "systematically underestimated" both the pace and scope of Soviet strategic force developments. This book assesses whether the national intelligence estimates were indeed wrong, and if so, whether it was due to the CIA's being mistaken, duped, or manipulated.

Reviewed by Michael Mikhalka, Survival Vol. 25 No. 5 (September-October 1983), pp. 239-240.

No. 298. Simes, Dimitri K.
"The Anti-Soviet Brigade."
Foreign Policy No. 37 (Winter 1979-80), pp. 28-42.

Concern about the Soviet threat is growing in the United States. Many Americans feel that the West has been short-changed in detente. But the pro-detente consensus of the early 1970s was not based on an increase in Soviet accommodation with the West, but on the public mood in a United States tired of the war in Vietnam and distrustful of the morality, will, and judgment of its leadership. Recovery from this period is both natural and encouraging, but in the process the Soviet Union is being made the scapegoat for America's own weaknesses. For the New Right coalition, the Soviet Union must be punished for refusing to accommodate the United States in its time of trouble. But anti-Soviet policies are inherently unsustainable, since a policy based on false images of reality cannot be perpetuated. According to recent opinion polls, the American public is more capable of appreciating and accepting a complex, multi-dimensional policy toward the Soviet Union than is the U.S. political elite. It is up to presidential leadership to turn this public sophistication into a new foreign policy consensus.

No. 299. Stevens, Jennie A.; and Henry S. Marsh.
"Surprise and Deception in Soviet Military Thought."
Military Review Vol. 62 Nos. 6 and 7 (June and July 1982). Part I, pp. 2-11; Part II, pp. 24-35.

The concepts of surprise and deception [vnezapnost' and maskirovka] have become increasingly more important to the Soviet military as it strives to meet the growing threat which it perceives from NATO. This article addresses several salient questions regarding the Soviet application of surprise and deception in contemporary warfare. Based on Soviet writings, the synergism between the two concepts is explored, with commentary on the specific prerequisites required for their effective application. Both surprise and deception are examined at their three levels of military application -- strategic, operational, and tactical -- to clarify the Soviet view on how these concepts may be efficiently and selectively applied to meet a variety of battlefield requirements. Part I concentrates on surprise; Part II on the Soviet use of deception.

No. 300. Stoehrmann, Kenneth C.
"Perceptual Differences in Thinking the Unthinkable: World War III."
In Kenneth M. Currie and Gregory Varhall (Ed.), The Soviet Union: What Lies Ahead?
Washington, D.C.: Government Printing Office (Studies in Communist Affairs Vol. 6), 1985, pp. 730-751.

This paper focuses on the different perceptions of future war held by the likely participants and the probable impact of those perceptions upon policies and actions keyed to preventing such a war. Understanding these divergent perceptions is crucial to understanding the actions of the nations involved. Examining three different actors -- the United States, the Soviet Union, and NATO -- through the use of a perceptual scheme based on intensity and escalation scales, the paper shows how the actions may well be related to perceptions of a future war. A better understanding by each actor of the others' perceptions may produce a synergistic effect of preventing war from occuring.

No. 301. Talbott, Strobe.
"The Dilemma of Nuclear Doctrine."
Time Vol. 118 No. 22 (November 30, 1981),pp. 60-61.

Declaratory nuclear doctrine is an official statement from superpowers defining when they would use nuclear weapons. America's declaratory nuclear doctrine is an auxiliary to military deterrence. For the Soviet Union, however, it is an auxiliary to diplomacy and propaganda. These basic differences in declaratory nuclear doctrine have permitted the Soviet Union to seem peaceful and the United States to seem bellicose. The new American attitude has come close to frightening U.S. allies and strengthening the Soviet Union's cause.

No. 302. Walt, Stephen M.
Interpreting Soviet Military Statements: Methodological Analysis.
Alexandria, Va.: Center for Naval Analyses (CNA 81-0260.10), 5 December 1983, 108 p.

The Soviet military press is a potentially rich source of information about the beliefs and strategic intentions of the Soviet leaders. Unfortunately, the range of different interpretations that has emerged from the analytic community reflects more disagreement than consensus. The central premise of this paper is that one of the main reasons for the failure of efforts to resolve such differences is the lack of an explicit set of procedures to use in making inferences about Soviet beliefs from the statements available in the Soviet press. In short, the debate over Soviet military doctrine remains confused and dysfunctional, and scholars do not even agree on why they disagree. To develop a methodological consensus, a model of the inferential process must be developed that is sufficiently general and comprehensive to permit the various assumptions, pieces of evidence, guesses, and conclusions made by different analysts to be exposed and compared. This paper is a first step towards developing such a model, for by revealing the sources of disagreement among a number of prominent interpretations of published Soviet statements, it will indicate what additional types of evidence might be used to resolve interpretative disputes.

4

Soviet Strategic Defense

A. ACTIVE DEFENSE

No. 303. Goure, Daniel.
"Strategic Offense and Defense: Enhancing the Effectiveness of
U.S. Strategic Forces."
Annals of the Academy of Political and Social Science Vol. 457
(September 1981), pp. 28-45.

The United States is faced with a series of imminent strategic
force posture decisions. Complicating resolution of force planning issues are growing concerns about the adequacy of current
U.S. strategic doctrine and persistent disagreements over alternative strategic policies. The most promising solution to the
ICBM vulnerability problem appears to be a combination of rebas-
ing and active defense. Active defense against ballistic missiles
is a technically plausible option in the 1980s. The increased
viability of strategic defenses and their improving cost-
effectiveness calls into question existing strategic doctrine with
its emphasis on offensive systems and deterrence via threat of
retaliation. A potential answer to the problem of an uncertain
strategic vision may be movement toward a more balanced offense-
defense posture or even to a "defense-heavy" strategic posture
and corresponding strategy based on assured survival.

No. 304. Goure, Daniel.
"The Strategic Competition and SDI."
In Zbigniew Brzezinski et al. (Eds.), Promise or Peril: The
Strategic Defense Initiative.
Washington, D.C.: Ethics and Public Policy Center, 1986, pp.
227-236.

The basic reason for the Soviet Union's negative reaction to SDI
is the belief that it may be successful in altering the strategic
balance and would deny Moscow what it sees as the necessary
margin of political and strategic superiority. SDI critics assert
that offensives are always less expensive, and therefore more

174

useful, than defenses. Even if that were the case, with U.S. defenses the Soviet military mission would become exceedingly complex and difficult to achieve. The Soviet Union will have to begin making decisions about future war-fighting strategies without knowing what the eventual U.S. strategic defense will look like. Seen through Soviet eyes, SDI is quite different from what Americans -- both critics and proponents -- make it out to be. For the Soviet Union there is no absolutizing of offense or defense; they have always expected defenses to play a major role in limiting damage to their homeland.

No. 305. Goure, Daniel.
"Soviet Counters to SDI."
NATO's Sixteen Nations Vol. 31 No. 2 (April 1986), pp. 34-37.

At present, with SDI in its initial stage, strategic planners must make careful calculations of possibilities, but with still largely untried or unknown technologies. The Soviet leadership will soon have to commit itself to major policy decisions on strategic forces which, in any case, will divert resources either from present military modernization plans or from the civil sector. Their commitment to a powerful land-based strategic missile force now poses them monumental problems. Yet it can hardly be expected that the Soviet Union will allow its hard-won advantage in ballistic missile striking power to be negated by U.S. strategic defenses. There are a number of counter-strategies available to Moscow. The most obvious is to limit or defeat the SDI politically. The others are likely to be increasingly costly and difficult to develop. They include proliferation of missiles and warheads, attempting to suppress or destroy the defenses, circumventing the defenses, deceiving the defenses by employing decoys and masking agents, or altering the total force posture to deemphasize ballistic missiles to the benefit of air-breathing systems.

No. 306. Goure, Daniel; and Gordon H. McCormick.
"Soviet Strategic Defense: The Neglected Dimension of the U.S. Soviet Balance."
Orbis Vol. 24 No. 1 (Spring 1980), pp. 103-128.

This article examines Soviet perspectives and capabilities in the area of strategic defense. It does so by first delineating the place of defense in Soviet nuclear strategy. This is followed by an assessment of the prevailing static balance in defensive deployments and by a discussion of the dynamic interaction between Soviet damage-limiting capabilities and U.S. offensive forces. Finally, it briefly examines the implication of defense asymmetries for U.S. strategic policy. Strategic defense can be an effective substitute for offensive superiority. A well-configured defense promises to enhance Soviet uncertainty about probable success in war, and thus will help deter Soviet action in times of crisis.

No. 307. Hahn, Walter F.; and Alvin J. Cottrell.
"Ballistic Missile Defense and Soviet Strategy."
Orbis Vol. 9 No. 2 (Summer 1965), pp. 316-337.

Examining ABM development from Moscow's vantage point gives clues to long-range Soviet intentions and action, deducing them from a broad sweep of Soviet strategic options, limitations, and expectations. This can be done by: 1) gauging Soviet intentions with regard to an ABM development within the context of Soviet strategic nuclear policy; 2) assessing the various ways in which the Soviet Union would hope to exploit an ABM capability; and 3) projecting likely Soviet reactions to a U.S. deployment. The Soviet leaders appear to have deferred an ABM procurement decision in favor of continued reseach and development, a decision that was probably reinforced by uncertainty as the best way to exploit an ABM capability. However, the most logical Soviet response to a highly effective ABM deployment by the United States would be an acceleration of the broad Soviet strategic development effort, offensive as well as defensive.

No. 308. Harris, William R.
"Arms Control Treaties: How Do They Restrain Soviet Strategic Defense Programs?"
Orbis Vol. 29 No. 4 (Winter 1986), pp. 701-708.

Five presidential reports to the Congress from 1983 to 1985 confirm that the Soviet Union has defeated the essential purposes of some, but not all, restraints on both offensive and defensive arms. The Soviet record of arms control compliance is unusually poor in connection with the ABM Treaty. This was so before President Reagan announced the Strategic Defense Initiative, and it remains so even while the Soviet Union has taken selective initiatives to improve their compliance with other arms control agreements. The ABM Treaty has not been an effective restraint, because it has not been accompanied by robust development of strategic defenses on the U.S. side and because its violation has not resulted in responses that give incentives for treaty compliance. Whether future arms control programs actually restrain Soviet behavior in the future may depend more on the competative posture of the United States than on its legal obligations.

No. 309. Krebs, Thomas.
"Can the Soviets Counter SDI?"
Washington, D.C.: The Heritage Foundation (Backgrounder No. 454), September 17, 1985.

Opponents of SDI argue that it almost surely will be foiled by three types of Soviet countermeasures: 1) destroying the U.S. missile defense; 2) protection of Soviet weapons from U.S. defenses; and 3) proliferation of offensive weapons to saturate any U.S. defense. But it seems unlikely that the Soviet Union would vigorously develop and deploy such countermeasures or gain any significant advantage if they did. All of these create problems for Soviet military planners. They are costly, and some countermeasures undermine others. For example, shielding boosters increases their weight, requiring them to carry fewer warheads. Three other factors are far more likely to disrupt American plans for strategic defense. Soviet BMD programs could guarantee Soviet strategic superiority and could even give Moscow enough power of intimidation to stop U.S. BMD deployment. Their new emphasis on bombers and cruise missiles has put the Soviet Union in a position to adopt a strategy that no longer relies on ballistic missiles. Finally, Soviet propaganda efforts in Europe and the United States will generate political opposition to the U.S. SDI program; a low-cost, low-risk effort.

Reprinted as Chapter 23 in Zbigniew Brzezinski et al. (Eds.), Promise or Peril: The Strategic Defense Initiative. Washington, D.C.: The Ethics and Public Policy Center, 1986, pp. 249-263.

No. 310. Lord, Carnes.
"Taking Soviet Defenses Seriously."
Washington Quarterly Vol. 9 No. 4 (Fall 1986), pp. 83-99.

A number of relatively recent developments suggest the desirability of a comprehensive reassessment of the Soviet strategic defense posture and its implications for the United States. Any analysis of Soviet thinking on the question of strategic defense must begin with a consideration of basic Soviet attitudes towards the defense as a form of warfare. The dialectical relationship of offense and defense is particularly apparent in Soviet thinking about the role of strategic offensive forces. Soviet doctrine has consistently emphasized the primacy of a damage-limiting, counter-force mission for Soviet nuclear weapons. There is strong circumstantial evidence that the ABM Treaty of 1972, far from dampening Soviet interest in Soviet BMD, has been seen by the Soviet Union as an opportunity to reach parity with the United States in conventional BMD technology and technological surprise in the development of exotic BMD. The deployment of new U.S. offensive systems might or might not provide the impetus for a fundamental Soviet rethinking of the role of BMD. It is certain that the future of U.S. forces can no longer be sensibly debated without reference with the Soviet Union's ability and commitment to prevent those forces from executing their mission.

No. 311. Meyer, Stephen M.
"Soviet Military Programmes and the 'New High Ground'."
Survival Vol. 25 No. 5 (September-October 1983), pp. 204-215.

The enormous magnitude and scope of the Soviet military effort
in space appears to be accelerating, leaving the United States
behind. This paper directly addresses three questions: what
military missions can the USSR perform in and from space; how
important Soviet space capabilities are to key military missions;
and how vulnerable Soviet space capabilities are to disruption.
This provides a foundation for discussion of a fourth question:
what the Soviet Union can do, unilaterally and through arms
control, to enhance the capability and survivability of her space
system. There are eight concluding observations: the Soviet
Union may outspend the United States 2-to-1 in space, but
probably gets little extra in return; the high Soviet launch rate
suggests a resilience that could be useful during crises or war;
the large number of Soviet satellites make them fairly insensitive
to ASAT attack; Soviet investments in space seem oriented to
peacetime and crisis management planning, not wartime battle
management; Soviet military planners would prefer that neither
side had their space assets intact rather than that both sides
preserved them; therefore the United States will not be able to
deter a Soviet ASAT attack by posing an analogous threat;
Soviet ASAT is a low priority military program; and while the
Soviet Union will probably be the first to orbit a laser weapon-
bearing satellite, it will have little initial military value and will
require at least a decade of incremental improvements before it is
capable of even a basic military mission.

No. 312. Meyer, Stephen M.
"Soviet Strategic Programmes and the U.S. SDI."
Survival Vol. 27 No. 6 (November-December 1985), pp. 274-292.

This examination of the likely Soviet view of the U.S. SDI
program suggests that there are underlying biases that cut in
several directions. Most of the elements considered here, except
the state of the Soviet economy, bias a Soviet decision towards
some response to SDI. Many elements, such as deterrence and
damage-limitation requirements, and military-economic decisions,
bias a Soviet decision towards an off-setting response -- implying
a mid- to far-term time horizon. There are, however, some
powerful stimuli for a near-term emulating response. It is most
probable that the Soviet response to the SDI challenge will
contain both off-setting and emulating components. Hard confirmation of Soviet intention to emulate the SDI, in the form of
testing and prototype weapons, would not appear for many
years. The Soviet Union views the SDI as an effort to undermine the past twenty years of Soviet military policy and planning. Therefore, strategic offensive forces will continue to
dominate Soviet military policy. By pursuing arms control, the
Soviet leaders could hope to satisfy the different biases in their

decision-making process by holding off new military programs
while negotiating to prevent a U.S. "Star Wars" system from
emerging. There is a "schizophrenic" quality to the Soviet
leadership's view of SDI: it is seen as a major challenge, even
though they possess a range of responses that may significantly
weaken it. For the Soviet Union, the SDI is symbolic of a
fundamental challenge between social systems, calling into contention the political, economic and industrial, scientific and
technological, and military potentials of the superpowers.

No. 313. Odom, William E.
"The Implications of Active Defense of NATO for Soviet Military
Strategy."
Chapter 5 in Dan Quayle et al. (Eds.), Strategic Defense and
the Western Alliance.
Washington, D.C.: Center for Strategic and International Studies
Significant Issues Series Vol 8 No. 6 (1986), pp. 49-56.

Ballistic missile defense in Europe could cause a significant
theater nuclear force (TNF) sizing problem for the Soviet Union,
and would also have disturbing implications for Soviet theater
operations. In summary, it would cost the Soviet Union two or
three times the TNF it has currently, and perhaps more. That
is not a trivial add-on to the force structure. It also would
raise serious doubts as to whether the high-speed offensive
could be conducted without losing synchronizations and bogging
down. Third, it puts a high premium on reconnaissance. This
combination of elements shows the value of active defense toward
the protection of the NATO alliance.

No. 314. Rivkin, David B., Jr.
"What Does Moscow Think?"
Foreign Policy No. 59 (Summer 1985), pp. 85-105.

The Soviet Union's strong opposition to the Strategic Defense
Inititative has lead many Western critics of the SDI to conclude
that it will provoke a Soviet buildup in offensive strategic
weapons and undermine any hope of progress in arms control
talks. A closer reading of Soviet statements on strategic
defense suggests, however, that Moscow might eventually co-
operate with the United States in moving away from a regime of
nuclear deterrence based on the threat of mutual suicide. In
fact, the magnitude and pace of Moscow's own strategic defense
programs suggest that the decision on what to do about strategic
defense will not be that of the United States alone. While
conceivable in principle, this transition would require a careful
and well executed U.S. policy. Even if the United States
pursues a sensible SDI program in the years ahead, there is no
assurance that the Soviet Union would eventually agree to co-
operate in a defensive transition. However, given its pessimistic

assessment of the prospects of its present policy, the Soviet Union's cooperation is a possibility that should be encouraged.

No. 315. Rivkin, David B., Jr.; and Manfred R. Hamm.
In Strategic Defense, Moscow is Far Ahead.
Washington, D.C.: The Heritage Foundation (Backgrounder No. 409), February 2, 1986.

Even if a transition from an offense to defense-dominant strategic environment would be sought by Moscow, given existing offensive and defensive assymetries, it would be difficult to implement without U.S.-Soviet arms control understandings. This offers some hope for eventual Soviet moderation. As such, the Reagan Strategic Defense Initiative offers the best opportunity to stabilize U.S.-Soviet competition and remove the threat to civilian populations of nuclear war. It is ironic that those most vocal in warning of the horror of a "nuclear holocaust" and "nuclear winter" are those who refuse to consider that SDI offers the best way of escaping what they say they most fear. SDI has much to comment it. Moscow, after all, is moving inexorably towards deploying a sizable ABM system. Were the United States to delay developing its own strategic defenses, it is very unlikely that the Soviet nuclear buildup or nuclear defense deployments would be slowed. What would happen, almost certainly, is that the credibility of the U.S. deterrent would be eroded further, thus increasing the danger of war. Reagan's SDI, on the other hand, offers the prospect of strengthening deterrence, limiting civilian casualties should conflict occur, and deep mutual arms reductions.

No. 316. Ruehle, Hans.
"Gorbachev's 'Star Wars'."
NATO Review Vol. 33 No. 4 (August 1985), pp. 26-31.

This article outlines Soviet research and development in missile defense since the 1950s. Soviet deployments of missile defense seemed to have been abandoned by the time of the 1972 ABM Treaty, and some military thinkers saw the treaty as a sign of convergence of Western and Soviet strategy. However, the Soviet Union apparently signed the treaty only because it feared that the United States would gain the lead in missile defense. Because of the SALT ABM Treaty, American research into missile defense came virtually to a halt; yet the Soviet Union continued its programs. Over the past twenty years numerous defensive installations have popped up in the Soviet Union that seem to have little cohesion. In the closed system of the Soviet Union it is relatively easy to deploy the elements of weapons systems in such a way that each seems of little significance, but when brought together represent a qualitative advance. The present debate on strategic defense focuses on the American SDI, yet for the foreseeable future the United States will be producing only documents while the Soviet Union is already building actual systems.

Reprinted as Chapter 22 in Zbigniew Brzezinski et al. (Eds.), Promise or Peril: The Strategic Defense Initiative. Washington, D.C.: The Ethics and Public Policy Center, 1986, pp. 237-248.

No. 317. Scott, William F.
"Troops of National Air Defense."
Air Force Magazine (Soviet Aerospace Almanac No. 4) Vol. 61
No. 3 (March 1978), pp. 56-66.

Proponents of Mutual Assured Destruction (MAD) believe that the Anti-Ballistic Missile Treaty of 1972 between the United States and the Soviet Union served to codify the concept. But there is no evidence that the Soviet leadership accepted MAD in 1972 or has accepted it since then. Recent Soviet publications on air defense emphasize Soviet intentions for aerospace defense and war survival. Even in this era of SALT, Soviet military doctrine still "requires that the Armed Forces, the country, the whole Soviet people, be prepared for the eventuality of a nuclear war." The concept of MAD is not a consideration in the Politburo's military planning.

No. 318. Scott, William F.
"The Soviets and Strategic Defense."
Air Force Magazine (Soviet Aerospace Almanac No. 12) Vol. 69
No. 3 (March 1986), pp. 40-45.

Only three senior military promotions were announced in the Soviet press in 1985, the year Mikhail Gorbachev took over the leadership. Of the three, only Anatoliy U. Konstantinov, Commander of the Moscow Air Defense District and promoted to Marshal of Aviation, occupied a major position within the Soviet Ministry of Defense. In such a sparse year, why Konstantinov? Soviet propagandists, seeking to enlist support against the U.S. Strategic Defense Initiative, seldom acknowledge that the Soviet Union not only has an analogous program, but also has deployed defenses, for which Konstantinov has responsibility. A review of the Soviet program shows continuity of developing systems, consistancy with publicly articulated Soviet military doctrine, and considerable successes.

No. 319. Soviet Military Space Doctrine.
Washington, D.C.: Defense Intelligence Agency (DDB-1400-16-84), 1 August 1984, 36 p.

This report seeks to define Soviet military space doctrine. An examination of Soviet views on their general military doctrine reveals that this doctrine demands the inclusion of a strategy for

using Soviet space-based military capabilities. The key elements
of Soviet military doctrine are the overwhelming offensive
application of superior military force to further Soviet interests
and the combined arms approach to combat operations. Both of
these elements are equally essential for Soviet military space
doctrine. Western analyses of the Soviet space program provide
convincing evidence of Moscow's intention to acquire military
superiority in outer space. Soviet military space capabilities
illuminate Soviet objectives in space much more effectively than
their statements do. These analyses permit the following determination of Soviet Military Space Doctrine: The Soviet Armed
Forces shall be provided with all resources necessary to attain
and maintain military superiority in outer space sufficient both to
deny the use of outer space to other states and to assure
maximum space-based military support for Soviet offensive and
defensive combat operations on land, at sea, in the air, and in
outer space.

No. 320. Soviet Strategic Defense Programs.
Washington, D.C.: U.S. Department of Defense and Department
of State, October 1985, 27 p.

The Strategic Defense Inititative has been the subject of much
discussion within the United States and allied countries since its
inception. There has been comparatively little public discussion,
however, about the trend in Soviet defensive as well as offensive
forces which provides the essential backdrop to the SDI.
Indeed, the Soviet Union has intentionally tried to mislead the
public about its strategic defense activities. Soviet efforts in
most phases of strategic defense have long been far more extensive than those of the United States. The USSR has major
passive defense programs, designed to protect important assets
from attack. It also has extensive active defense systems, which
utilize weapons systems to protect national territory, military
forces, or key assets. Soviet developments in the area of active
defenses fall into three major categories: air defense; ballistic
missile defense based on current technologies; and research and
development on advanced defenses against ballistic missiles.
This publication sets forth Soviet defensive programs, and
provides a summary of key Soviet offensive force developments
in the annex, since they are critical to an understanding of the
impact of Soviet strategic defense programs. Soviet offensive
forces are designed to be able to limit severely U.S. and allied
capability to retaliate against attack. Soviet defensive systems
in turn are designed to prevent those retaliatory forces which
did survive an attack from destroying Soviet targets.

No. 321. Stevens, Sayre.
"The Soviet BMD Program."
Chapter Five in Ashton B. Carter and David N. Schwartz (Eds.),

Ballistic Missile Defense.
Washington, D.C.: The Brookings Institution, 1984, pp. 182-220.

The significant disparity in the momentum of strategic defense
activities between the United States and the Soviet Union apparently gives the latter nation a number of opportunities for
improving its strategic position. But all of these opportunities
have costs and may generate negative reaction. Consideration of
all factors apt to influence a Soviet decision to abandon the ABM
Treaty reveals few powerful incentives for them to do so in the
near term. While Soviet technology is closer to application, it is
only at the level of technology available to the United States ten
years ago, and the United States has clear superiority in high
technology particularly important to advanced BMD systems.
Treaty abandonment also would threaten a vigorous Soviet propaganda effort to weaken NATO, and place major additional costs
on the strained Soviet economy. Finally, the current treaty
favors the Soviet Union by leaving it virtually alone in the
pursuit of effective BMD. While military pressures for Soviet
BMD deployment do not seem overwhelming in the near term,
U.S. initiative might trigger a Soviet deployment response. If
this were to occur, Soviet and U.S. priorities in the choice of
targets to be defended would differ, the Soviet Union opting for
defense of high-value clusters of targets, while the United
States would protect its retalitory forces. Ballistic missile
defense is fundamentally unsettling to the strategic balance, but
even more so in the context of our current uncertainties.

No. 322. Stevens, Sayre.
"The Soviet Factor in SDI."
Orbis Vol. 29 No. 4 (Winter 1986), pp. 689-702.

An intriguing feature of the Strategic Defense Initiative is that
it has apparently produced a role reversal between the United
States and the Soviet Union on the matter of strategic defense.
For a variety of reasons, the United States has traditionally
found reasons to avoid investing in defenses, while the Soviet
Union has given them great priorities. This article discusses
some possible reasons for the shift in this attitude brought about
by the SDI, and concludes with a discussion of three implications
of this peculiar role-reversal. One is that the level of public
and international debate will exacerbate the problems of accom-
modating the SDI to the current arms control regime. A second
is that if U.S. enthusiasm for SDI dies for political reasons and
the program is discarded or scaled-back, Soviet work on defense
will have been energized to the disadvantage of the United
States. The final implication is that the United States has
committed itself to SDI. It must seek to understand where the
SDI might lead and what its longer-term promises and dangers
are. It cannot simply turn off the SDI and pretend it did not
exist.

No. 323. Strode, Rebecca; Robert Jastrow, William Scott, Robert
Hotz, and Douglas Graham.
"The Soviet Response to U.S. Strategic Defense."
In W. Bruce Weinrod, Assessing Strategic Defense: Six Round-
table Discussions.
Washington, D.C.: The Heritage Foundation (The Heritage Lec-
tures No. 38), 1985, pp. 37-64.

The fundamental point made by this panel was that the Soviet
Union is already developing strategic defenses. Any Soviet
"response," therefore, would be merely a continuation of present
policies. Nonetheless, the prospect or actual deployment of a
U.S. strategic defense system would be a major development.
The Soviet Union might react by continuing to take actions which
violate the spirit if not the letter of the ABM Treaty; seeking to
force the United States to withdraw from the Treaty first, thereby reaping a propaganda advantage by blaming it for "undermining arms control," developing countermeasures for the SDI,
or seeking to cause a unilateral U.S. halt in the SDI through a
propaganda offensive for the "demilitarization" of space.

No. 324. Thomas, John R.
"The Role of Missile Defense in Soviet Strategy."
Military Review Vol. 44 No. 5 (May 1964), pp. 46-58.

Several considerations are involved in answering the question of
why the Soviet Union has promoted ABM development and deployment after expressing strong misgivings and in the face of
increasing U.S. missile capabilities. The most important is that
overriding political and strategic requirements have fueled Soviet
ABM activity regardless of the obstacles involved. The foreign
policy of the Soviet Union requires an effective ABM capability
to enhance the image of its military power, which is needed to
advance Soviet interests without the dangerous use of force.
The Soviet Union's strategy also allots a major role to ABMs in
the event that Soviet foreign policy misfires and war ensues. In
such a conflict, the Soviet Union's objective is to exploit its ABM
capabilities politically regardless of how low its military worth
might be rated. This suggests that the West's efforts should be
focused on avoiding the validation of Soviet ABM claims, so that
the Soviet Union will have difficulty in politically exploiting its
ABM capability.

Reprinted as "The Role of Missile Defense in Soviet Strategy and
Foreign Policy," in John Erickson et al. (Eds.), The Military-
Technical Revolution (New York: Frederick A. Praeger, Pub-
lisher, 1966), pp. 187-218.

No. 325. Yost, David S.
"Soviet Ballistic Missile Defense and NATO."
Orbis Vol. 29 No. 2 (Summer 1985), pp. 281-292.

By contrast to the U.S. Strategic Defense Initiative (SDI),
Soviet ballistic missile defense has been relatively neglected by
Europeans. This is unfortunate, because it promotes misleading
impressions about the strategic context of the SDI, and obscures
the fundamental political-military challenges that Soviet BMD
could pose. These include the growing Soviet potential for
"breakout" or "creepout" from the 1972 ABM Treaty restraints,
and the interaction of offense and defense in Soviet military
doctrine. Soviet BMD has four major implications for alliance
security: 1) the credibility of NATO's strategy of "flexible
response" could be reduced; 2) Soviet prospects for victory in
conventional operations could be improved; 3) potential Soviet
control over the escalation process could be enhanced; and 4) the
credibility of the British and French nuclear deterrents could be
lowered.

No. 326. Yost, David S.
"Soviet Ballistic Missile Defense and the Atlantic Alliance."
Chapter 7 in Dan Quayle, Robert E. Hunter, and C. Elliot
Farmer (Eds.), Strategic Defense and the Western Alliance.
Washington, D.C.: Center for Strategic and International Studies
Significant Issues Series Vol. 8 No. 6, 1986, pp. 70-85.

Soviet ballistic missile defense capabilities and activities have
received little notice because public attention has been focused
on the U.S. Strategic Defense Initiative (SDI). In European
political circles, the SDI frequently has been portrayed as a
threat to arms control and strategic stability, and as the start of
an accelerated arms race with wasteful and potentially dangerous
consequences. The article seeks to balance this assessment of
the SDI's strategic context by including Soviet ABM capabilities
and activities, potential explanations of Soviet BMD efforts, and
the implications of Soviet BMD for the security of the Atlantic
Alliance.

B. CIVIL DEFENSE

No. 327. Aspin, Les.
"Soviet Civil Defense: Myth and Reality."
Arms Control Today Vol. 6 No. 9 (September 1976), pp. 1-4.

Claims about the great extent and effectiveness of Soviet civil
defense abound, but most are exaggerated or unsupported.
Three indicators are frequently cited as evidence of the Soviet
civil defense program: 1) the dispersal of Soviet population and
industry; 2) annual civil defense expenditures of one billion
dollars; and 3) the potential for limiting casualties in a nuclear
conflict by crisis evacuation of urban populations. The Soviet
Union does put a higher priority on defensive measures than the

United States, and has undertaken more elaborate measures to protect certain war-related industries and its national leaders. But the U.S. nuclear deterrent is hardly in jeopardy -- the enormous gap between Soviet rhetoric about civil defense efforts and its actual capabilities should not be overlooked.

No. 328. Bladley, Stephen C.
The New Soviet Civil Defense Program: A Warning for America.
Maxwell Air Force Base, Ala.: Air War College (Professional Study No. 4288), 1971, 10 p.

A brief history of the Soviet Civil Defense effort is followed by a detailed description and analysis of significant changes noted during the past ten years. Some of these new emphases are interpreted by the author as warnings to America and are listed in the concluding section.

No. 329. Goure, Leon.
Soviet Civil Defense.
Santa Monica, Calif.: The RAND Corporation (P-1887), March 14, 1960, 21 p.

A description of the Soviet civil-defense program, based on the many Soviet publications issued in connection with the program. Such aspects of the program are discussed as its background, basic Soviet civil-defense theory, organization, training, means of protection, shelter habitability, evacuation, pre-attack measures, and postattack operations. While Soviet citizens are relatively apathetic toward civil defense, it is likely that in time of crisis they would respond to their training. They know that the Soviet authorities are prepared to enforce obedience and to punish ruthlessly any unauthorized or panic-inspired behavior. Presented before the Conference on Civil Defense, held at the National Academy of Sciences, Washington, D.C., February 11-12, 1960, and published in the proceedings of the Conference.

No. 330. Goure, Leon.
Civil Defense Training in Russia.
Santa Monica, Calif.: The RAND Corporation (P-2340), June 8, 1961, 15 p.

A discussion of Soviet efforts, especially since 1955, to develop a large civil defense organization and train the majority of its population in civil defense. Such aspects are considered as organization and registration, training objectives and programs, training procedures and techniques, control over population, and the present status of civil defense training.

Reprinted in Air Force Magazine Vol. 44 No. 9 (August 1961), pp. 38-41.

No. 331. Goure, Leon.
Soviet Civil Defense.
Santa Monica, Calif.: The RAND Corporation (P-2415), August
22, 1961, 25 pp.

An attempt to ascertain the nature of the Soviet civil defense
doctrine, the character and scope of the Soviet program, and
the extent of its implementation. Some of the limitations and
assumptions of the Soviet civil defense program are also suggested. Evidence indicates that the Soviet authorities are
serious about civil defense and that they have been trying over
a period of years to develop (within the limits of available
financial, technical, and material resources) a significant civil
defense capability.

Also published in Civil Defense-1961, Hearings before a Subcommittee of the Committee on Government Operations, House of
Representatives, 87th Congress, 1st Session, August 1, 2, 3, 4,
7, 8, and 9, 1961. Presented before the Military Operations
Subcommittee.

No. 332. Goure, Leon.
"Soviet Views on the Role of Civil Defense."
Current History, November 1961.

A discussion of the reasons why Soviet leaders believe their civil
defense program is an integral part of the Soviet defense posture, contributing directly to the country's readiness for war.
Their postwar civil defense program has been in effect over the
past ten years and has been expanded and accelerated since
1955. Its purpose is not only to ensure the physical survival of
a substantial element of the population, but also to preserve
civilian morale and provide for the rapid recuperation of the
country from attack. In the event of a war, it becomes essential
to ensure the survival of the administrative control and the
industrial forces that may be expected to influence the further
course of the war and possibly even to determine its outcome.

Also published as RAND paper P-2425 (August 28, 1961), 17 p.

No. 333. Goure, Leon.
The Resolution of the Soviet Controversy Over Civil Defense.
Santa Monica, Calif.: The RAND Corporation (RM-3223-PR),
June 1962, 29 p.

A discussion of some recent developments in the Soviet civil
defense program. The differences between foreign and domestic
Soviet propaganda on civil defense are shown. A debate among
the Soviet leaders on the value of civil defense is also described, a debate that was resolved at the May 1962 Congress of
DOSAAF (the civil volunteer organization). Recent vigorous

endorsement of DOSAAF by Party and press may be one indication of impending changes in Soviet domestic and foreign policies.

No. 334. Goure, Leon.
Civil Defense in the Soviet Union.
Berkeley, Calif.: University of California Press, 1962, 207 p.

A description of the doctrine and actual program of Soviet civil
defense, and an attempt to relate both doctrine and program to
underlying Soviet attitudes and beliefs concerning international
conflict and the nature of possible future wars. The available
evidence regarding the Soviet civil defense program is viewed in
the context of Russia's political and administrative systems and
decision-making process. Covered in detail are the organization
of Soviet civil defense, the compulsory national training program,
means for protection against chemical, bacteriological, and radio-
logical warfare, types and availability of shelters, warning
systems and evacuations, pre-attack measures, and plans for
post-attack operations and recovery.

Reviewed by Raymond Garthoff, The Russian Review Vol. 21 No.
3 (July 1962), pp. 291-292.

No. 335. Goure, Leon.
The Role of Civil Defense in Soviet Strategy.
Santa Monica, Calif.: The RAND Corporation (RM-3703-PR),
June 1963, 34 p.

A description of the Soviet military's views on the importance of
civil defense in a future war. These views derive from an image
of war in which the opponent's will to resist and economic
capacity to continue the struggle are primary targets for attack.
The importance of such targets increases in the event of a
protracted war, whose occurrence is regarded by the Soviets as
sufficiently likely to justify considerable investment in a civil
defense program designed to permit the Soviet Union to survive
and to seek to win strategic nuclear superiority in the course of
the war.

No. 336. Goure, Leon.
Recent Developments in the Soviet Civil Defense Program.
Santa Monica, Calif.: The RAND Corporation (P-2752), June
1963, 26 p.

A survey of recent Soviet activities in civil defense. The information comes mainly from open Soviet publications and from the
author's personal observations in 1960. The program is far from
complete and suffers from a variety of shortcomings. In the
author's opinion, however, the available evidence shows that the
Soviet Union is engaged in an extensive civil defense program,

which it believes to be worth further effort and continued investment.

No. 337. Goure, Leon.
Soviet Emergency Planning.
Santa Monica, Calif.:   The RAND Corporation (P-4042), Febru-
ary 1969, 14 p.

A review of the Soviet civil defense system, prepared for publication in NATO--Fifteen Nations. Considerable effort and investment apparently have been expended in the longstanding Soviet
civil defense program in progressive recognition of the character
of strategic weapons and their effects. However, no information
has been published on the program's scope. Relying heavily on
early warning of an attack (several days), the present system
gives priority to the survival of population elements essential to
the preservation of the political organization and of military and
economic potential. Soviet officials claim a high degree of effectiveness for the systems, but continue to call for improvements.
The Eastern European Communist states have similar civil defense
operations, and their staff leaders are trained in Soviet schools;
but these countries' investments and capabilities are not uniform.

No. 338. Goure, Leon.
Soviet Civil Defense Revisited, 1966-1969.
Santa Monica, Calif.:   The RAND Corporation (RM-6113-PR),
November 1969, 111 p.

Initiated in the 1950s and upgraded in 1961, the Soviet civil
defense program has increased in scope and intensity since 1966.
The system is considered vital to the maintenance of crucial
military, industrial, and political capabilities in the event of a
nuclear attack. Because of economic contraints, special shelters
have been built only for those workers engaged in critical
national services. The remainder of the population will be
protected mainly by means of evacuation and dispersal to pre-
selected safety zones. Because the program relies heavily on
several days warning of attack and is primarily concerned with
protecting certain population elements, the Soviet leaders might
be very sensitive to economic damage strikes against their cities.
This seems to be borne out by their increasing concern with
recovery operations for industries, utilities, and transportation
facilities. In any case, this survey leaves no doubt that Soviet
leaders are continuing to invest heavily in civil defense.

No. 339. Goure, Leon.
Soviet Civil Defense, 1969-70.
Coral Gables, Fla.:   University of Miami (Center for Advanced
International Studies), 1972.

This report describes developments in the Soviet civil defense program and related activities at the turn of the decade. It deals with current Soviet views on nuclear war and the role of civil defense in ensuring victory and the survival of the Soviet state; and recent Soviet efforts to improve the long-standing program for the protection of the population and economy from attacks with nuclear, chemical, and biological weapons, and for maintaining critical production and popular morale.

Reviewed by Eugene D. Betit, Military Review Vol. 55 No. 1 (January 1975), pp. 105-106.

No. 340. Goure, Leon.
Shelters in Soviet War Survival Strategy.
Coral Gables, Fla.: University of Miami (Center for Advanced International Studies), 1974.

This report assesses and describes the Soviet shelter categories, their equipment and habitability, Soviet expedient shelters and fallout covers, and indication of the availability of ready shelter space, as well as their cost. The study is based entirely on open sources.

No. 341. Goure, Leon.
War Survival in Soviet Strategy: USSR Civil Defense.
University of Miami: Center for Advanced International Studies, 1976, 218 p.

This study analyzes the great attention and large resources the Soviet Union has devoted to developing a comprehensive war survival capability, and focuses on the accelerated and expanded scope of the Soviet civil defense program to raise the "combat readiness" of the USSR sharply. The program includes measures for the protection of the population by means of shelter construction and pre-attack urban evacuation; for the preservation of the regime's control system and the economy by industrial dispersal and hardening; and the preparation of the population to withstand the shock of a nuclear war by compulsory civil defense training, exercises, and political-psychological indoctrination. The aim of the program is to alter the strategic balance in favor of the Soviet Union, to degrade seriously the reality and credibility of the U.S. "assured destruction" deterrence posture, and to ensure the survival of the USSR and the Soviet system in case a nuclear war actually occurs.

Reviewed by Lord Chalfont "Why Russia May Think She Can Win a Nuclear War," The London Times August 2, 1976, p. 7; Raymond Garthoff, Slavic Review Vol. 36 No. 2 (June 1977), pp. 318-319; Jeff Chin, Russian Review Vol. 36 No. 3 (July 1977), pp. 374-374; James Kerr, Military Review Vol. 57 No. 3 (March

1977), pp. 101-102; Erich Pruck, Osteuropa Vol. 28 No. 5 (May 1977), p. 454.

No. 342. Goure, Leon.
Civil Defense in Soviet Strategic Perceptions.
Washington, D.C.: Advanced International Studies Institute (DNA 5174F), 1 January 1980, 214 p.

This study examines and analyzes possible Soviet views on the strategic significance and utility of civil defense for deterrence, war-fighting, and crisis management. Specifically, it describes and assesses Soviet views on the need and requirements for and the role of civil defense in the Soviet defense posture, policies and strategy; and on its contribution to war fighting, war outcome, and recovery. It analyzes the Soviet targeting doctrine and its relationship to civil defense priorities, measures for assuring system, national and economic survival, and essential support for the armed forces. The study also examines possible methods for Soviet exploitation of its civil defense capabilities for crisis mangement.

No. 343. Green, William C.
Civil Defense and the Strategic Balance.
Claremont, Calif.: Public Research Syndicated Article No. 125 (February 4, 1981), 5 p.

The Soviet Union is far better prepared than the United States to defend its population against nuclear attacks, this preparation partially reflecting the Soviet view that it is possible to survive a nuclear war while defeating the enemy. The Soviet civil defense program, also provides the government with a means of controlling the Soviet population, and it increases Soviet strategic leverage in crisis situations.

No. 344. Hubbell, John G.
"Soviet Civil Defense: The Grim Reality."
Reader's Digest Vol. 112 No. 670 (February 1978), pp. 77-80.

The Soviet Union has added a major civil-defense component to its military posture. In 1972 the United States and Soviet Union signed the ABM treaty, agreeing not to deploy weapons that could effectively defend against the other's nuclear missiles. But the Soviet Union, with its continuing and increasingly elaborate civil-defense program has in effect been circumventing the intent of the treaty. Had the Soviet Union not gone ahead with civil defense, the U.S. deterrent force would still be effective. However, the Soviet Union is now able to shelter or disperse most of its people. This means that its losses could be roughly half the 20 million lost in the Second World War; about four percent of its population. Without the advantage that civil

defense gives them, Soviet leaders would be much less likely to
challenge the United States in areas of vital interest.

No. 345. Kaplan, Fred M.
"The Soviet Civil Defense Myth."
Bulletin of the Atomic Scientists, Part I (March 1978), pp.
14-20; Part II (April 1978), pp. 41-58.

The upshot of the Soviet civil defense program, according to
many U.S. analysts, is that in the face of a retaliatory strike by
the United States, all but 2 to 10 percent of the Soviet population could be protected as well a a significant portion of its
industrial base. In all its phases, however -- from the training
program to the evacuation and sheltering, to the assumed nature
of the U.S. attack, to the post-attack recovery estimates -- the
basic analysis, common to virtually all studies expressing concern
over Soviet civil defense, suffers from unrealistic assumptions,
leaps of faith, violations of logic, and a superficial understanding
of the dynamics of a national economy. It appears from available
evidence that the Soviet civil defense program would be inadequate in the face of a nuclear attack; that Soviet intentions are
probably other than aggressive, and that the United States
currently has more than sufficient capacity to nullify whatever
passive-defense measures may have been taken by the Soviet
Union.

With a reponse by Leon Goure, "Another Interpretation," Bulletin
of the Atomic Scientists, April 1978, pp. 48-51.

No. 346. Kaplan, Fred M.
"Soviet Civil Defense: Some Myths in the Western Debate."
Survival Vol. 20 No. 3 (May-June 1978), pp. 113-120.

Several U.S. defense analysts believe that the Soviet Union's
civil defense program is so comprehensive that it significantly
alters the strategic balance. The components of Soviet civil
defense that are assumed or described in many of these analyses
include: a massive evacuation and sheltering plan; nation-wide
industrial protection and dispersion; a well-trained public; huge
budgetary resources; and preparations for post-attack rescue
and recovery missions. This paper questions the existence of
each of these components. Whatever the motivation behind
Soviet civil defense, it is clear that the Soviet economy is conducive to comprehensive protection, that the Civil Defense Chief
himself doubts the program's effectiveness, that the program
itself is quite unimpressive, and that even if it improved the
United States could easily counter any Soviet efforts.

Condensed in Military Review Vol. 59 No. 3 (March 1979), pp.
57-64.

192

No. 347. Soviet Civil Defense -- Post-Strike Repair and Restoration.
Coral Gables, Fla.: University of Miami Center for Advanced International Studies (ASDIRS 4262), 1973, 49 p.

This report analyzes, on the basis of Soviet source material, Soviet civil defense doctrine, organization, and plans and activities pertaining to post-strike emergency repair and restoration operations. It is noted that Soviet doctrine places great emphasis on measures to assure the viability of essential industrial facilities, utilities, services and transportation in wartime as vital to the war effort and for the attainment of victory. Measures to limit damage from an attack include industrial dispersal, relatively simple hardening, stockpiling of raw materials and parts, as well as the preparation of large civil defense forces to conduct rescue, repair and restoration work in areas damaged by a nuclear strike.

No. 348. Staudenmaier, William O.
"Civil Defense in Soviet and American Strategy."
Military Review Vol. 58 No. 10 (October 1978), pp. 2-14.

This article examines the differing American and Soviet theories of nuclear war and civil defense, and outlines their civil defense programs. U.S. policy has been based on the doctrine of mutual assured destruction, which maintains that nuclear war is unwinnable; the USSR, on the other hand, has always thought nuclear warfare was a viable policy option. The U.S. civil defense effort has therefore been meager compared with that of the Soviet Union, which believes that limiting the effects of a nuclear war would enhance its winnability. The difference in commitment to civil defense is significant, because even if civil defense is not effective, the Soviet Union may think itself at a strategic advantage. Therefore, in a crisis, execution of the USSR's civil defense plan could force concessions from the United States.

No. 349. Thompson, Andrew C.
Civil Defense in the Soviet Union.
Maxwell Air Force Base, Ala.: Air Command and Staff College (Research Study No. 1945-71), 98 p.

The purpose of civil defense is to protect the population and economy. Civil defense can also help precipitate war. This could occur when an aggressive nation believes itself secure and asserts itself in pursuit of its national interest. This study analyzes civil defense in the Soviet Union and concludes that the Soviet Union has a credible civil defense. The study also concludes that because of the security provided, and coupled with Soviet strategic arms, the possibility of conflict is increasing. Because of this, the United States must exercise great caution in formulating and conducting foreign policy.

No. 350. Weinstein, John M.
"Soviet Civil Defense and the U.S. Deterrent."
Parameters Vol. 12 No. 3 (March 1982), pp. 70-83.

This article advances four major points: 1) the Soviet Union's
force structure and strategic doctrine do not eschew deterrence;
2) the Soviet Union is likely to continue to subscribe to the goal
of stable deterrence in the future, even if it pursues this goal
through different means than those employed by the United
States; 3) the Soviet Union's civil defense program cannot make
a significant contribution to that country's warfighting or war
survival capabilities, and therefore does not have a destabilizing
effect on the strategic balance; and 4) America's deterrent
remains potent and adequate to deter the Soviet Union. Several
conclusions are suggested by these points: 1) something as
inconsequential as the Soviet civil defense program should not
color U.S. thinking, since it is in the best interests of the
United States to pursue arms control with the Soviet Union; 2)
the United States should not attempt to duplicate the Soviet civil
defense program, since not only is it technically and economically
unfeasible, but it is incompatible with a democratic society; and
3) the United States should continue to modernize its nuclear
and conventional forces to maintain the credibility of deterrence.

No. 351. Wolfe, Thad A.
"Soviet-United States Civil Defense: Tipping the Strategic Scale?"
Air University Review Vol. 30 No. 3 (March-April 1979), pp.
40-55.

The United States considers civil defense to be an "insurance
policy," whereas to the Soviet Union it is a "factor of great
strategic importance." One can gain some insight into these
diverse perceptions by examining U.S. and Soviet national
security objectives, policies, and strategies. Will the present
actual or perceived civil defense imbalance erode the U.S.
assured destruction capability? Soviet leaders believe their
passive measures would be a decisive factor in a postwar
balance, and hence, that nuclear war is a viable political element
enhancing the overall correlation of forces. But measures can
be taken to offset the potential advantage the Soviet Union hopes
to gain without major alteration to U.S. programs or strategy.

5

Theater and Tactical Nuclear Weapons Policy

A. SOVIET THEATER INTERESTS AND POLICIES

No. 352. Close, Robert.
"Soviet Strategy, the Atlantic, and the Defense of the West."
Atlantic Community Quarterly Vol. 18 No. 4 (Winter 1980-81),
pp. 403-412.

The defense of NATO, admittedly a worrisome topic, should be
considered in a global strategic context. The elements of this
consist of: 1) a worrying international situation, due to massive
growth of the Soviet arsenal and its expansionist policies; 2) A
fundamental change in the strategic environment, since nuclear
parity makes less credible the American promise of automatic
nuclear mobilization in support of Europe; 3) the U.S. decision
for rapid reinforcement of Europe in the event of a conflict,
showing that U.S. resolve is still present; and 4) a growing
awareness of public opinion about the problems arising over
restoring a balance in forces. This essay examines successively
four areas key to the balance of forces: strategic nuclear,
Eurostrategic, and conventional forces, as well as the subversive
element. NATO is in a paradoxical position of having forces
sometimes weaker than they were in the context of the earlier
strategy of massive retaliation, when their role was confined to
that of an alarm bell.

No. 353. Donnelly, Christopher N.
Heirs of Clausewitz -- Change and Continuity in the Soviet
War Machine.
London: Institute for European Defense and Strategic Studies,
1986, 40 p.

The Soviet Union is considered a superpower not because of its
economic strength or ideological potency, but because of its
impressive military power. Military power is therefore the area
in which the USSR is least likely to make real concessions. The
greatest danger for the West is not war as such, but rather the

threat of war and that the West could succumb to that threat and be gradually Sovietized without ever a shot being fired. The current widespread changes in the organization, tactics, and training of the Soviet armed forces indicate that, in a future military conflict, overwhelming emphasis would be placed on speed and surprise and the maintenance of a very high rate of advance, so as to precipitate the collapse of NATO's defenses. It is therefore serious that there are several gaps in NATO's defenses. NATO's policy of allocating each national corps a slice of the frontier to defend, the lack of an enforced standard doctrine to integrate the activities of the various NATO corps, and the fact that SACEUR would be bound by political decisions taken at the national level all combine to make a degree of surprise possible.

No. 354. Erickson, John.
"Soviet Military Posture and Policy in Europe."
In Richard Pipes (Ed.), Soviet Strategy in Europe.
New York: Crane, Russak, and Company, 1976, pp. 169-209.

Even allowing for over-insurance, for the inevitable professional military inflation of NATO's capabilities, and for the need to maintain a high military investment in Eastern Europe -- indeed, allowing for almost any conceivable rationale -- the expansion of Soviet military capability in Europe seems to defy the strictly rational. The improvement in Soviet political relations with Western Europe seems to have eliminated the need for any growth in coercive capability. The present Soviet position, then, implies two threats. The first is not of this force being used but of its simple existence -- an overweening military presence, the high visibility of military force, and the persuasion of Eastern Europe that conformity is the only permissible stance. The second is the changing capability of the Warsaw Pact forces, especially their demonstrable capacity for a rapid turnover to high-speed military operations to obtain limited political objectives. The NATO strategy of relying on available warning time -- 23 days of political and military warning -- seems gravely at risk. While the Soviet leadership may place an obsessive reliance on military force, Western Europe has increasingly chosen to ignore the military factor.

No. 355. Evangelista, Matthew A.
"Stalin's Postwar Army Reappraised."
International Security Vol. 7 No. 3 (Winter 1982-83), pp. 110-138.

This article attempts to refute the common perception of an overwhelming Soviet conventional threat to Western Europe during the early postwar period by assessing the military capabilities of Stalin's army for launching a successful invasion. It focuses on the period 1947-48, which coincides with the end

of Soviet demobilization and the beginning of discussions in the
West leading to the formation of the North Atlantic Treaty Organization in 1949. It now seems that the Soviet military threat was
greatly exaggerated during this period; the notion of an over-
whelmingly large Soviet army facing only token Western forces
was inaccurate. Given the extent to which powerfully formed
impressions can persist, it seems plausible that Western views of
Soviet military power in Europe today can be traced to the
misconceptions of the early postwar period. And whatever the
truth about the balance today, the evidence now available shows
that in the late 1940s the "Red Juggernaut" was anything but.

No. 356. Garthoff, Raymond L.
"Brezhnev's Opening: The TNF Tangle."
Foreign Policy No. 41 (Winter 1980-81), pp. 82-94.

Soviet proposals for arms limitation that would affect the deployment of long-range U.S. nuclear weapons systems in Europe may
be far more serious than most Western observers have allowed.
In October 1979, Soviet President Brezhnev first declared Soviet
willingness to reduce the number of medium-range nuclear
delivery means deployed in Western areas of the Soviet Union,
provided that no additional such systems were deployed in
Western Europe. He also insisted that a theater nuclear balance
already exists and that Soviet deployment of new LRTNF systems
has not increased total force levels. This claim is valid, and
Western failure to acknowledge this has contributed to the difficulties of weighting the balance of considerations and perceptions of the two sides. Yet only in this way can a basis be
laid for possible negotiation and agreement that could serve
allied security interests at a lower cost and with less tension
than unlimited competition.

No. 357. Goure, Leon.
Soviet Limited War Doctrine.
Santa Monica, Calif.: The RAND Corporation (P-2744), May
1963, 15 p.

An examination of Soviet views on limited war. Since by
definition the Soviet Union is not aggressive, it is said to stand
in no need of a limited war doctrine. Limited war is thus
ignored in Soviet military doctrine. Despite habitual Soviet
denials of the possibility of keeping limited wars from expanding,
however, Soviet military writers and even Khrushchev have
given some recognition to the likelihood of their occurrence.
The Soviet decision to engage in a limited war and the scale of
that war will depend less on any doctrine than of Soviet assessment of risks, gains and losses involved, and on the actions and
policies of the opponent.

No. 358. Jones, Christopher D.
"Equality and Equal Security in Europe."
Orbis Vol. 26 No. 3 (Fall 1982), pp. 637-664.

The Soviet Union has imposed an offensive doctrine and force
structure on the Warsaw Pact, to be supported by the Soviet
theater nuclear force (TNF). This strategy has a double objective: it impresses NATO and keeps NATO from interfering in
Eastern Europe, and it keeps the Warsaw Pact countries from
setting up national defense forces that could be used against the
USSR. Thus, an attack on Western Europe is not the real
mission of the Soviet TNF; keeping NATO in check and the
Warsaw pact in line is. This aspect of the Soviet TNF is also
indicated by the basing, even of short-range weapons, inside
the USSR, where theater-level counterattacks would result in a
strategic exchange. The structure of the Soviet TNF is not as
threatening as is usually believed and is actually roughly equal
to the NATO TNF.

No. 359. Kolkowicz, Roman.
"On Limited War: Soviet Approaches."
Chapter 5 in Robert O'Neill and D.M. Horner (Eds.), New Direc-
tions in Strategic Thinking.
London: George Allen and Unwin, 1981, pp. 75-88.

Trends in the development of thinking about limited war in the
United States and Soviet Union appear puzzling and contradictory. Yet on close examination they yield plausible explanations: a strategically inferior Soviet Union could not risk the
danger of confronting a strategically superior United States in a
local, limited, or theater war that might escalate rapidly into a
nuclear strategic confrontation. In order to forestall such a
possibility, the Soviet Union had to reject Western notions of
controlled war. In the 1970s and 1980s the Soviet Union has
obtained strategic nuclear parity and at the same time has begun
to accept the idea of controlled, limited war. Its foreign and
military strategies have become harmonious and congruent. The
inherent Soviet drive to expand its influence in the Third World
has been matched by a capability to do so. In the past the
Soviet Union has practiced confrontation avoidance whenever a
direct clash with the other superpower seemed unavoidable, but
in the 1980s this situation will have changed drastically.

No. 360. Thomas, John R.
"Limited Nuclear War in Soviet Strategic Thinking."
Orbis Vol. 10 No. 1 (Spring 1966), pp. 184-212.

Soviet writers seriously question whether any conflict involving a
direct conflict between U.S. and Soviet forces can be prevented
from escalating into general war; the use of nuclear weapons
would only reinforce the certainty of this. They would prefer

limitations, but are pessimistic that events would develop in a way permitting limitations to operate. The Western notion that the escalation might resemble a neat military ladder on which the warring sides could go up or down appears irrelevant in Soviet eyes. The difficulties would be compounded if the Soviet Union believed that the rules of limitation and escalation control were designed to prevent them from exploiting Western vulnerabilites in the event of a European conflict.

No. 361. Vigor, Peter H.
"Soviet Military Developments -- 1976."
Strategic Review Vol. 5 No. 2 (Spring 1977), pp. 74-82.

An understanding of the political currents in Soviet affairs in recent years is essential to an assessment of the significance of Soviet military developments in 1976. The most important developments, militarily and politically, were the MPLA victory in Angola, the continued build-up of all types of ships of the Soviet Navy, and the increasing strength and improvement of equipment of Soviet forces in East Germany. Notable too were Soviet efforts to improve relations with China, continued civil defense preparations, lack of progress in reaching SALT II and MBFR agreements, and interference with verification of arms control compliance. These developments in 1976 all indicate deliberate, steady advances in the politico-military capability of the USSR, consistent with Soviet political ambitions, which threaten the security of the Free World.

No. 362. Wolfe, Thomas W.
Soviet Commentary on the French "Force de Frappe".
Santa Monica, Calif.: The RAND Corporation (RM-4359-ISA), January 1965, 38 p.

A survey of the general trend of Soviet reactions to the French Force de Frappe. Principal themes and their treatment by Soviet commentators are examined.

No. 363. Wolfe, Thomas W.
The Soviet Union and the Sino-Soviet Dispute.
Santa Monica, Calif.: The RAND Corporation (P-3203), August 1965, 63 p.

A study, divided into five categories of issues arising from the Sino-Soviet dispute: 1) problems of intra-Bloc unity and leadership; 2) policy toward emerging nations; 3) issues relating to the question of war in the nuclear age; 4) differing approaches to Southeast Asia; and 5) problems of Sino-Soviet military relationships.

No. 364. Wolfe, Thomas W.
The Evolving Nature of the Warsaw Pact.
Santa Monica, Calif.: The RAND Corporation (RM-4835-PR), 1966, 54 p.

An examination of the changes that have taken place in the Warsaw Pact alliance since 1960. The author finds that the first years of the alliance merely institutionalized existing arrangements in East Europe (i.e., the six East Europe countries as a Soviet defensive zone against the West). This function remains; since 1961, however, the Soviets have also expected the six countries to contribute armed forces to military operations. This has meant a more thorough integration of East European forces into Soviet operational plans. The apparent result is a two-way pull; 1) toward increasing interdependence, and 2) toward asserting separate national interests, and, on the part of East Europe, insisting on a greater role in the decision-making process. The political reasons for the changes in the alliance, and their implication for future Soviet policy, are discussed in detail. An annotated bibliography on the history of the Warsaw Pact is provided.

No. 365. Wolfe, Thomas W.
Soviet Military Power and European Security.
Santa Monica, Calif.: The RAND Corporation (P-3429), August 1966, 53 p.

An analysis of the military dimensions of Soviet policy toward an evolving Europe. Stalin's military policies in the early postwar years, development of Soviet military posture up to Stalin's death, and the problems and reforms of the Khrushchev era are reviewed. There has been no essential repudiation of Khrushchev's policies under the Brezhnev-Kosygin regime. Although the Warsaw Pact is evolving into an alliance that can no longer be considered merely the compliant instrument of Soviet policy, its dissolution is not indicated and its military potential is greater than when the Soviet Union assumed the military responsibility for its members. Until the issues which underlie the division of Europe are brought closer to political settlement, Europe's security will require collaborative measures by the West to ensure that the threat of Soviet military power remains immobilized.

No. 366. Wolfe, Thomas W.
Soviet Power and Europe.
Baltimore, Md.: Johns Hopkins Press, 1970, 534 p.

A study of postwar Soviet policies toward Europe, focusing on the interaction of political and military factors. It examines the increasing influence on foreign policy of internal tensions within the Soviet Union and Eastern Europe, the interplay of Moscow's

European policy with her global interests and strategic rivalry with the U.S., and the effects of disruptions within the Communist world, especially the Sino-Soviet border crisis. The development of Soviet power politics in Europe during the regimes of Stalin and Khrushchev is detailed, and the first five years of the Brezhnev-Khrushchev regime are assessed. The author argues that the invasion of Czechoslovakia represents a serious failure of Soviet policy. It demonstrates that the Soviet Union could not tolerate even minimal liberalization and that its control of Eastern Europe depends not on diplomacy and mutual interest, but on military strength.

No. 367. Wolfe, Thomas W.
The Soviet Union's Strategic and Military Stakes in the GDR.
Santa Monica, Calif.: The RAND Corporation (P-4549), January 1971, 19 p.

Comments on the postwar Soviet military position in Europe, particularly concerning the German Democratic Republic. This paper suggests strategic factors that may contribute to changes in Soviet thinking on the need for stationing of sizeable theater force elements in East Germany: 1) the USSR appears anxious in the aftermath of the Czechoslovak episode to work out new pan-European security agreements; 2) the cost of maintaining a military standoff in Europe could be lowered by mutual troop reductions, an attractive consideration for the USSR leaders when investment resources are being sought for the current Five Year Plan; 3) mutual reduction of Soviet and U.S. forces in Europe would be advantageous for the USSR, both because of its geographic proximity and because withdrawal of U.S. forces would mean depriving NATO of the most important factor now holding it together. Kremlin leaders must now decide whether "European division equals Soviet security" is still the best Soviet policy.

No. 368. Wolfe, Thomas W.
Role of the Warsaw Pact in Soviet Policy.
Santa Monica, Calif.: The RAND Corporation (P-4973), March 1973, 19 p.

Explores prospects for major changes in Soviet policy on the Warsaw Pact. The Pact enables the Soviets to impose their will on Eastern Europe in the name of "proletarian internationalism" and "fraternal solidarity." It also provides bases for 25 to 30 Soviet divisions, tactical air and missiles, plus joint force exercises and equipment standardization. Motives that may account for the present detente phase of Soviet policy include: 1) desire for more Western credits, technology, and management know how; 2) to obtain "legal" recognition of the territorial and political division of Europe and Soviet supremacy in East Europe; 3) to loosen U.S. ties with NATO; 4) to influence Western force;

and 5) to free military resources to threaten China. It remains to be seen how the Soviet leaders evaluate their competitive position with and without the Warsaw Pact alliance. For presentation at an Inter-University Research Colloquium at the Institute for Sino-Soviet Studies, George Washington University.

No. 369. Wolfe, Thomas W.
"Soviet Military Capabilities and Intentions in Europe."
In Richard Pipes (Ed.), Soviet Strategy in Europe.
New York: Crane, Russak and Company, 1976, pp. 129-167.

This paper reviews various quantitative and qualitative factors that must be taken into account in appraising Soviet-bloc military capabilities and intentions versus NATO. In addition to purely military considerations, detente and the MFR negotiations are among the important variables that may influence the way each side perceives and elects to deal with its security problems in Europe. The paper suggests that the most reasonable measurement of Soviet capabilities today lies somewhere between the older prudential view that Soviet theater forces could overrun Europe in a matter of days, and what might be called the newer revisionist view that Soviet capabilities have been greatly overrated. Regarding Soviet military intentions, which are contingent upon many premeditated circumstances, it is far less likely that the Soviets will launch a premeditated invasion of NATO Europe than that they will rely, as in the past, upon military power to sustain political influence in Western Europe and to ensure their hegemonial control over Eastern Europe.

Also printed as RAND Paper (P-5188), March 1974, 45 p.

B.   SOVIET THEATER NUCLEAR WEAPONS POLICY

No. 370. Barber, Ransom E.
"The Conventional Wisdom on Soviet Strategy: Is It Conventional?"
National War College Forum No. 17 (Summer 1973), pp. 21-30.

Conventional wisdom on the military strategy and associated force design of the Soviet Union suggests that it has rejected the proposition that a war between major powers could long remain conventional or that the nuclear battle could be limited. According to this view, the Soviet Union has created a large, balanced force that is primarily structured for a wide variety of missions on the nuclear battlefield. With this thinking goes the conclusion that Soviet forces are not capable of conducting a sustained conventional campaign because Soviet force planners will respond to a first use by NATO of nuclear weapons with a massive and theater-wide strike. Thus the picture of a massive Soviet armed force poised to execute a strategy of instant nuclear response is sharply engraved by what the Soviet military advertises as their warfighting approach. Accepting these notions at face value can be dangerously misleading. A combined analysis of Soviet pronouncements and military capabilities makes the point that the Soviet Union has built a military machine that can conduct a wide variety of operations other than the advertised lightning-quick, all-destructive nuclear battle.

No. 371. Barber, Ransom E.
"The Myth of the Soviet Nuclear War Strategy."
Army Vol. 25 No. 6 (June 1975), pp. 10-17.

Major military powers tend to describe their strategy in two different ways, for internal and external consumption. The long-standing Soviet axiom that a big-power war could only be nuclear might be examined in that light, since the Soviet force structure suggests other options.

No. 372. Brown, Dallas C.
"Conventional Warfare in Europe -- The Soviet View."
Military Review Vol. 55 No. 2 (February 1975), pp. 58-71.

Soviet views on the possibility of conventional warfare in a new European conflict are a subject of controversy among Western strategic theorists: do the Soviet leaders consider nuclear war to be "inevitable" in the event of a conflict between the two alliances? As the strategic nuclear balance shifted in the 1960s, the Soviet Union began to reason that NATO might be prevented from using nuclear weapons. As a result, they modified their policies to prepare for the possiblity of nuclear conflict. They remain uncertain over the duration of conventional operations before NATO uses nuclear weapons to avoid defeat. It is almost certain, however, that the Soviet military would fight with conventional weapons as long as NATO would, or unless unexpected reverses threatened the survival of the Soviet state.

Response by Graham D. Vernon, Military Review Vol. 55 No. 8 (August 1975), pp. 2, 11.

No. 373. Cimbala, Stephen J.
"Soviet 'Blitzkrieg' in Europe: The Abiding Nuclear Dimension."
Strategic Review Vol. 14 No. 3 (Summer 1986), pp. 67-76.

Western military analysts have increasingly focused on the likeli-hood of a Soviet "conventional-only" option of waging a "blitz-krieg" offensive against NATO in the event of war in Europe. Clearly Soviet planners would prefer such an option to the risks entailed in a resort to nuclear weapons. Yet, in embracing the option, the Soviets would have to make a series of extremely fragile assumptions regarding the progression of the battle and NATO responses. Moreover, a close study of Soviet operational art and tactics, along with the historical record of Soviet warfighting, indicates preferred modes of operation substantially different from the classical blitzkrieg model. In all, a conventional war in Europe on any appreciable scale will be a war capable of quickly turning nuclear.

No. 374. Deane, Michael J.; Ilana Kass, and Andrew G. Porth. "The Soviet Command Structure in Transformation." Strategic Review Vol. 12 No. 2 (Spring 1984), pp. 55-70.

The Soviet command structure is being streamlined for the sake of a more rapid transition to wartime operations and optimal exploitation of advanced weaponry. The principal innovations include heightened day-to-day operational functions for the Supreme High Command under the top authority of the Defense Council, the creation in peacetime of theaters of military operations (TVDs), and the establishment of a separate and unifed command structure for strategic nuclear forces. These significant realignments, which apparently represent the culmination of a long-standing effort, carry immense implications for Western force structures, deployment plans, and strategic warning capabilities.

No. 375. Douglass, Joseph D., Jr. The Soviet Theater Nuclear Offensive. Washington, D.C.: Government Printing Office (Studies in Communist Affairs Vol. 1), 1976, 127 p.

This study analyzes the Soviet open-source military literature as it applies to war in Europe. The nature of the Soviet threat may be changing in such a way as to bring into question many planning factors and assumptions that have been closely associated with the need for 7,000 weapons and their role in NATO/U.S. strategic planning. The major objective of this study is to lay out the Soviet image of theater nuclear war and assess the prospects for limiting such a conflict. More specifically, it is to provide insight into the following types of questions: what is their view of what a theater nuclear war might look like; how do their concepts and doctrine for theater nuclear war appear to be designed; what appear to be their inherent weaknesses, limitations, and flexibility; and, most importantly, what changes appear to be developing? The analysis is pointed toward uncovering doctrine, attitudes, and goals -- not achievements or capabilities; it yields nine general conclusions. But what actually would happen in any given situation is highly scenario-dependent, and considerable care must be exercised in transitioning from general conclusions to any specific situational analysis.

Reviewed by Joseph E. Thach, Jr., Strategic Review Vol. 5 No. 2 (Spring 1977), pp. 95-96.

No. 376. Douglass, Joseph D., Jr.
"Soviet Nuclear Strategy in Europe: A Selective Targeting Doctrine?"
Strategic Review Vol. 5 No. 4 (Fall 1977), pp. 19-31.

Heretofore unavailable evidence shows that Soviet nuclear strategy in Europe may be oriented more toward selective targeting and damage limiting -- and toward the objective of capturing Western Europe largely intact -- than toward deterrence, retaliation, and massive destruction. If valid, this strategy has profound implications for NATO. It counters the dominant image of massive damage that has inhibited NATO tactical nuclear doctrine and force planning more generally. It weakens the notion that the Soviet Union may be "self-deterred" from engaging in aggression in Europe, and it casts a possibly different light on the buildup of Soviet war-fighting capabilities, both conventional and nuclear, in Europe.

No. 377. Douglass, Joseph D., Jr.
"The Theater Nuclear Threat."
Parameters Vol. 12 No. 4 (December 1982), pp. 71-81.

This article traces the history of Soviet planning for nuclear war in Europe since the mid-1950s. It outlines the principles that form the basis of Soviet nuclear strategy: nuclear weapons are strategically important; surprise is the key to achieving a successful first strike; the offensive is the key to winning a war; and all forces and equipment must be used throughout the theater. It includes a scenario of what a Soviet-initiated theater nuclear war might be like, and focuses on several aspects of Soviet strategy for the main attack that are usually overlooked in Western studies on theater nuclear war, including the possible use of chemical weapons, the nuclear strike itself, and Soviet preparations for offsetting the effects of NATO's nuclear weapons.

No. 378. Douglass, Joseph D., Jr.
"The Theater Nuclear Threat."
Defense Science 2001+, December 1983, pp. 23-37.

Since the mid-1950s, the Soviet Union has been preparing seriously for war in Europe. As Soviet strategy has evolved, four basic principles have received special emphasis: 1) the strategic importance of nuclear weapons; 2) the need to achieve surprise; 3) the importance of the offensive; and 4) to concentrate efforts at the decisive time and place, and to attack throughout the depth of the theater. This is a decisive and

short-war-oriented strategy, but one that recognizes the prospect of extended conflict. One should expect this pattern to
continue, with detailed attention placed on the effective use of
new technologies such as high-accuracy delivery systems, highly
effective chemical and biological weapons, computers, and elec-
tronics.

No. 379. Douglass, Joseph D., Jr.; and Amoretta M. Hoeber.
"The Nuclear Warfighting Dimension of the Soviet Threat to
Europe."
Journal of Social and Political Studies Vol. 3 No. 2 (Summer
1978), pp. 107-146.

Under current logic, the main objective of NATO is the avoidance
of conflict. All it needs in capability, in this view, is enough to
"deter," to raise the specter of nuclear war and to communicate
the linkage between Soviet aggression and strategic war. This
of itself will insure that the Soviet Union will appreciate the
risks to itself and the absence of benefits that would attend any
aggression towards NATO Europe. But there are persistent
inconsistencies between the Soviet interest in preserving an
occupiable, exploitable Europe and presumed limitations in Soviet
capabilities. These inconsistencies are explored in this article
through a reexamination of Soviet political objectives, military
doctrine, and capabilities as they relate to Europe since the late
1950s. The common perceptions may be based on only part of
the avilable data and may reflect a serious shortcoming in Western
understanding of Soviet objectives, forces, and doctrine.

No. 380. Douglass, Joseph D., Jr.; and Amoretta M. Hoeber.
Conventional War and Escalation: The Soviet View.
New York: National Strategy Information Center, 1981, 63 p.

In recent years a number of Western analysts have supported
the notion that the Soviets, having come to agree with the West
that nuclear war is impossible, are undergoing a shift away from
nuclear and toward conventional doctrine and strategy. This
study reviews a large body of evidence from the Soviet military
literature of the 1960s and 1970s, and concludes that no such
shift can be identified either in Soviet military writings or in
their force improvements. The Soviets assume that major war in
nearly all cases will either begin with nuclear strikes or become
nuclear as the conflict progresses. Within the context of this
tenet of Soviet thinking, the Soviet approach to conventional
capabilities and operation and the relationship of conventional
conflict to nuclear war is analyzed. The major topics addressed
in this monograph include: Soviet interests in conventional
capabilities (in particular, sub-unit operations), the advantages
which might be derived from a conventional phase (most of which
are oriented toward better achievement of an effective, surprise
nuclear strike), the characteristics of a conventional phase, and

the factors that bear on the timing of the transition to nuclear operations.

Reviewed by Laura Hutchinson, Friday Review of Defense Literature (82-6), February 12, 1982, pp. 3-4.

No. 381. Erickson, John.
"Soviet Military Capabilities in Europe."
RUSI Journal Vol. 120 No. 1 (March 1975), pp. 65-69.

Recent improvements within Soviet (and non-Soviet Warsaw Pact) forces in the European theater amount to more than mere tinkering with organization and weapons. Soviet doctrine continues to emphasize the rapid seizure of the initiative from the "defensive," and high speed penetration into the whole depth of the theater. While this does imply a "short war in a nuclear environment," one of the noticeable features over the past year or so has been increased Soviet interest in the possiblity of substantial non-nuclear operations even in the initial stage of a major engagement, for which reason the "attack norms" of a nuclear blitzkrieg have been scaled down to meet the conditions of a conventional phase.

No. 382. Erickson, John.
"Soviet Theater-Warfare Capability: Doctrines, Deployments, and Capabilities."
In Lawrence Whetten (Ed.), The Future of Soviet Military Power. New York: Crane, Russak, and Co., 1976, pp. 117-156.

Since the end of World War II, the Soviet Union has maintained a theater posture of relative superiority. Both conventional and nuclear capabilities have been modernized recently, and suggest that the Soviet military's concepts of operations envision a blitzkrieg-type assault against the West, using massed armored strike divisions along several main thrusts. The Soviet military does not have a Western-style concept of the incremental use of force, or even of escalation. Maximum power is to be employed to achieve victory, with high confidence, whereas the nuclear option is to be used at any level or time required. These improvements have resulted in the strongest, most versatile theater-force structure the Soviet Union has yet constructed. The high quality of the weapons and equipment leaves the training and morale of the fighting man the chief question in the proficiency of this posture. Since World War II, Soviet units have been used only for policing operations within their own security zone. Soviet troops train with chemical and nuclear weapons to a far greater extent than do their Western counterparts. But these simulated exercises are only games, and the differences between them and a nuclear environment are almost impossible to comprehend.

No. 383.   Erickson, John.
"The Ground Forces in Soviet Military Policy."
Strategic Review Vol. 6 No. 1 (Winter 1978), pp. 64-79.

The Soviet Ground Forces not only have survived the
vicissitudes of Stalin's postwar reorganization and Khrushchev's
"new look," but they have prospered as an integral component of
the Soviet military system, an essential element in the formation
of Soviet strategy and of the Warsaw Pact system, and a vitally
important organizational and political influence within the Soviet
system as a whole.   Each of the five major stages in the Soviet
Army's postwar evolution has been linked to a reappraisal of
Soviet strategic policy.   Although the Soviet ground order of
battle has remained stable since 1969, the combat power of the
Army has been substantially enhanced.   If anything, the
prominence of the Ground Forces grows sharper in the context
of a more independent Soviet "theater option" and the quest for
a "sustained combat capability" for all operational contingencies,
nuclear and non-nuclear.

No. 384.   FitzGerald, Mary C.
"Marshal Ogarkov on the Modern Theater Operation."
Naval War College Review Vol. 39 No. 4 (Autumn 1986), pp.
6-25.

In his writings, Marshal N.V. Ogarkov has consistently
contrasted the stability of conventional conflict with the innate
instability of nuclear warfare.   Yet some Western analysts persist
in depicting him as the last of the nuclear war-wagers, and pit
him against a more "conciliatory" politico-military leadership.
Ogarkov has long been the prophet of the "third revolution" in
Soviet military affairs, which involves changes in Soviet doctrine
generated by emerging technologies and new, nonnuclear
weapons.   He has downgraded the military utility of nuclear
weapons in the face of Mutual Assured Destruction and
described limited nuclear options as impossible in practice.   In
1977, with Ogarkov's elevation to Chief of the General Staff, the
Soviet Union designated an independent conventional war option
as its long-term military development goal.   Other Soviet writers
also provided evidence of the conventional option, especially in
their perceptions of the Western threat, and specifically of the
Air-Land Battle and "Rogers Plan."   By their own admission,
Soviet military science is being adapted to operational concepts
based on large-scale incorporation of smart, non-nuclear
weapons.   At the same time, Western analysts are documenting
more and more changes in Soviet strategy, operational art, force
structure, and weapons modernization that point clearly to a
conventional high-tech option.

No. 385.   Gormley, Dennis M.
"Understanding Soviet Motivations for Deploying Long-Range

Theater Nuclear Forces."
Military Review Vol. 61 No. 9 (September 1981), pp. 20-34.

Recent Soviet deployment of the SS-20 mobile missile and Backfire bomber represents a new intermediate range perspective. The Soviet Union began to install large numbers of medium and intermediate range ballistic missiles and aircraft in 1959. But the new Soviet regional nuclear systems come at a time when the real or perceived loss of U.S. strategic superiority has shifted attention to regional disparities. This article explores and identifies Soviet motivations for deploying long-range theater nuclear forces, and highlights differing Soviet and U.S. conceptions and definitions of doctrine, strategy, and theater warfare planning. Understanding important asymmetries in U.S. and Soviet approaches to theater nuclear forces provides a sound foundation for negotiating arms control or reduction, as well as for devising force planning options in response to any regional nuclear disparity.

No. 386. Gormley, Dennis M.
"A New Dimension to Soviet Theater Strategy."
Orbis Vol. 29 No. 3 (Fall 1985), pp. 539-570.

New Soviet short-range missiles (SS-21, SS-22, and SS-23), tied to an offensive strategy emphasizing the pre-emptive employment of massive numbers of high-performance aircraft, presage emerging Soviet nuclear and non-nuclear attack options that will turn shortcomings in NATO's defenses into dangerous deficiencies. Soviet views about theater warfare contingencies include three major courses of conflict: 1) massive nuclear strikes to the full depth of the theaters of military operations; 2) an escalating conflict in which a short period of conventional operations precedes an increasingly more widespread use of nuclear weapons; and 3) a conventional-only conflict. As a result of the improvements in the quality and quantity of new weapons, the Soviet military instituted a number of institutional and organizational changes that helped to improve operational concepts to capitalize on the new conventional capabilities and reshape the Soviet armed forces to enable them to execute these improved concepts. The new short and medium range missiles play an important role, especially because of the increasingly unstable set of NATO vulnerabilities. There is bitter irony in the Soviet coupling of conventional missiles to an offensive war strategy: while the threshold between conventional and nuclear war is seemingly raised, the vital threshold between war and peace may be lowered.

No. 387. Gormley, Dennis M.; and Douglas M. Hart.
"Soviet Views on Escalation."
Washington Quarterly Vol. 7 No. 4 (Fall 1984), pp. 71-84.

Soviet views of escalation appear to have changed significantly from 1960 to the present. Moreover, the Soviet Union appears quite sensitive to notions of limited means and ends in modern warfare. Because of the importance of this issue to the current debate on NATO strategy, this paper has a dual purpose: first, it surveys the evolution of Soviet views on escalation from 1960 to the present, relating changes in views to growth in military capabilities; second, it examines contemporary Soviet escalation incentives and disincentives in the framework of evolving Western defense strategy. Several factors are essential to any evaluation of Soviet declaratory policy on escalation. First, Soviet military writings convey serious attention to a strict set of military and political preconditions surrounding the decision to escalate to nuclear warfare. Second, Soviet authorities have asserted that nuclear weapons have become an increasingly inexpedient tool of policy, while the Soviet military has developed ever more robust and flexible conventional warfighting forces.

No. 388. Hansen, James H.
"Countering NATO's New Weapons: Soviet Concepts for War in Europe."
International Defense Review Vol. 17 No. 11 (November 1984), pp. 1617-1624.

This article surveys the Soviet design for combat in the mid-1980s from the viewpoint of a Soviet military planner. In a three sided approach, the Soviet military detects new Western weapons in early stages of development and identifies means of "negating" those which pose the greatest threat. It would counter the US/NATO forces in an engagement with all available forces at its disposal, attempting to do so at the very start of operations. The four sections of this article analyze how the Soviet Union would conduct an integrated campaign against: 1) NATO's nuclear forces; 2) aviation units; 3) ground based weapons; and 4) early warning and intelligence means. Soviet military doctrine is based on a calculation of political, economic, scientific-technical, and military forces. Therefore, it adapts continuously to perceived shifts in the correlation of forces between the United States and the Soviet Union, between NATO and the Warsaw Pact, and to the activities of the enemies of the Soviet Union.

No. 389. Hines, John G.; and Phillip A. Petersen.
"Changing the Soviet System of Control: Focus on Theater Warfare."
International Defense Review Vol. 19 No. 3 (March 1986), pp. 281-292.

The Soviet military's wartime control of forces is developed around three types of "strategic military action" that it must execute: "strikes by strategic nuclear forces" against the enemy in adjacent theaters and on distant continents; strategic operations "to repulse the enemy's aerospace attack" and to defend the homeland from nuclear strikes; and offensive and defensive strategic theater operations around the periphery of the Soviet homeland. Soviet thinking about the relative importance of these various types of strategic military action has changed from the early 1960s scenario of a global nuclear exchange followed by theater nuclear strikes and mopping up by ground and air forces to today's dominant scenario of war in continental theaters peripheral to the Soviet Union involving advanced conventional and possibly some nuclear weapons. This shift in forces has led Soviet military scientists to make a major reexamination of the command system for wartime control of forces. The identities, boundaries, and associated command structures of forces in various "Theaters of Strategic Military Action" and strategic directions described in this article reflect how the Soviet military thinks about organization and control of war around the Soviet periphery.

No. 390.   Hines, John G.; Phillip A. Petersen, and Notra Trulock III.
"Soviet Military Theory From 1945-2000: Implications for NATO."
Washington Quarterly Vol. 9 No. 4 (Fall 1986), pp. 117-137.

Evidence has been accumulating to indicate that the Soviet military believes the objective requirements for yet another "revolutionary turn" in military affairs have been created. While they are cautiously optimistic that Soviet military science will once again meet this challenge, the Soviet leaders also recognize that its military-technical implications may lead the East-West military competition in directions unfavorable to the Soviet Union. This essay describes Soviet views concerning the changing role of nuclear and conventional weapons in future war, the Soviet assessment of alternative options and courses of action open to meet their absolute requirement to stay abreast of these developments, and the implications of them for peace and security. Soviet planning is based on the assumption that NATO will possess sizable, survivable nuclear forces at both the tactical and strategic levels able to destroy large elements of Soviet maneuver groups and command and control. The clear Soviet determination to avoid initiation of nuclear use implies that the Soviet Union is unlikely to begin military operations in the absence of confidence on the part of Soviet military planners that success is achievable at the non-nuclear level. The strength of NATO's conventional defense might become the determinant of whether the Soviet Union would remain deterred.

No. 391.   Howell, Phillip D.
"Divergent Doctrines Snarl Nuclear Face-Off: 'Unthinkable Weapon' Integral Part of Soviet Battle Philosophy."
Army Vol. 31 No. 12 (December 1981), pp. 18-23.

In the past fifteen years, the Soviet Union has modified its doctrine of nuclear war-fighting from a limited nuclear war scenario to that of a full theater nuclear war doctrine. Soviet military planners emphasize the value of the first strike, preemption, seizing the theater nuclear initiative, and integration of the theater conventional and nuclear force structure into a theater nuclear war-fighting force. NATO's policy for the use of nuclear force in a theater is one of flexible response through the use of tactical nuclear weapons after the NATO ground forces have failed to halt a conventional attack. The intent of the "first use" policy is deterrence of a Warsaw Pact conventional ground force attack rather than a nuclear war-fighting doctrine. The tremendous improvement in the quality and quantity of Soviet theater missiles and frontal aviation makes the possibility of a disarming Soviet counterforce strike very dangerous.

No. 392. Hyland, William G.
"Soviet Theater Forces and Arms Control Policy."
Survival Vol. 23 No. 5 (September-October 1981), pp. 194-199.

The level of Soviet theater nuclear forces (TNFs) in Europe has remained remarkably constant since the late 1950s. There was a slight drop in the 1960s but it was not until the mid-1970s that a significant change occurred. This change was more one of quality than quantity and occurred with the deployment of the SS-20 during the SALT II negotiations. The SS-20 gives the USSR important advantages by allowing the Soviet Union to decide on the level of escalation during a war in Europe. The SS-20 is a powerful counterforce weapon in any context, and, in view of the consistent size of the Soviet TNF, is probably part of a long-standing targeting policy in operational support of theater forces.

No. 393. Kennedy, Robert.
"Soviet Theater Nuclear Forces: Implications for NATO Defenses."
Orbis Vol. 25 No. 2 (Summer 1981), pp. 331-350.

This article contrasts Soviet and U.S. strategy in Europe, and contends that the advent of strategic nuclear parity and the Soviet theater nuclear buildup have altered the political equation on the continent. The USSR and its Warsaw Pact allies are prepared to wage combined arms warfare using all types of weapons (conventional, nuclear, and chemical), while the United States and its NATO allies continue to focus on conventional forces and the planning for a conventional conflict. Three broad actions should be taken by NATO to redress the current imbalance: a shift in emphasis from conventional to conventional/nuclear/chemical warfare; a shift from short-range to long-range Eurostrategic systems; and a modernization of battlefield nuclear capabilities.

Also published in Kenneth M. Currie and Gregory Varhall (Eds.), The Soviet Union: What Lies Ahead? Washington, D.C.: Government Printing Office (Studies in Communist Affairs Vol. 6), 1985, pp. 395-414.

No. 394. Meyer, Stephen M.
Soviet Theatre Nuclear Forces, Part I: "Development of Doctrine and Objectives," 51 p.; Part II: "Capabilities and Implications," 63 p.
London: The International Institute for Strategic Studies (Adelphi Papers Nos. 187 and 188), Winter 1983-84.

These papers examine the historical evolution of Soviet theater nuclear force (TNF) planning and posture from the end of World War II to the present. Particular emphasis is placed on evaluating Soviet TNF capabilities in the context of Soviet force planning and employment concepts as enunciated by the Soviet leadership. They examine issues such as: the extent to which Soviet TNF has been capable of carrying out the tasks and missions set out by Soviet military planners, the variance in this relationship over time, changes in TNF planning and capabilities, and the implications of these changes. In Part II the Soviet TNF capabilities and their implications for NATO military planning are examined. Here, the changing background of Soviet military doctrine and strategy provides the framework for analyzing the evolving Soviet TNF posture.

No. 395. Petersen, Phillip A.; and John G. Hines.
"Military Power in Soviet Strategy Against NATO."
RUSI Journal Vol. 128 No. 4 (December 1983), pp. 50-57.

The strong Soviet preference for conventional victory in Europe is based, among other considerations, on the simple assessment that while such a war would result in death and destruction in East and West Europe, it is much less likely than is nuclear war to lead to massive destruction in the Soviet Union. Paradoxically, Soviet military power is central to Soviet hopes for achievement of peace as they define it; just as large, survivable nuclear forces at tactical, theater, and global levels are required to support the Soviet preference to limit any war to the use of conventional weapons alone. In the event of a major war, the Soviet Union would seek to win it at the conventional level through a combination of surprise, speed, political pressure, and superiority at every level of conflict intensity. Superior military power is the basis for Soviet hope of victory without war, and superior tactical, theater, and global nuclear capability is central to Soviet hope to dominate nuclear escalation and, if possible, achieve victory with conventional weapons alone should war occur.

No. 396. Record, Jeffrey.
Sizing Up the Red Army.
Washington, D.C.: The Brookings Institution, 1975, 51 p.

The sheer size of the Soviet Army is its most salient characteristic, and one of the most revealing signs of the nation's contemporary military orientation. The army's size became an issue
during the Khrushchev era when modernists argued that nuclear
weapons, rather than masses of men, would be decisive in any
conflict. In the past decade, while developing their nuclear
capability, the Russians have reemphasized ground forces and
their conventional use. Moreover, these forces are structured
for rapid mobilization and swift deployment, and are more heavily
armored and mechanized than their NATO counterparts. All this
bespeaks the Soviet preparation to wage war of the sort they
believe is most likely: a short, intense conflict initiated (perhaps)
by a preemptive strike and characterized by their own massive,
rapid offensive designed to overwhelm the enemy. This orientation has its costs. For one thing, it leaves the Russians unprepared for the prolongation of a conflict beyond the period
envisioned in their current plans. Furthermore, the narrowing
of the focus to warfare in the European theater entails a corresponding neglect of the means to wage war elsewhere -- however
effective Soviet troops might be. In writing this assessment of
the Soviet Army, the author has relied on recent doctrinal
literature emerging from Soviet military sources. His analysis
leads him to recommend restructuring U.S. forces to make them
more effective against the strengthened Soviet forces, and he
warns against the recent proposals for reduction in NATO combat
forces.

No. 397. Reinhardt, G.C.
"Atomic Weapons and Warfare."
Chapter 37 in B.H. Liddell Hart (Ed.), The Red Army.
New York: Harcourt, Brace and Company, 1956, pp. 420-438.

How are Soviet armed forces responding to the stimulus of the
atom? The over-publicized surprise attack with nuclear weapons
against a powerful opponent is too great a gamble for cold-eyed
men whose fundamental ideology tells them that time is on their
side. Comprehensive instructions published (1954 and 1955) in
the Soviet press advise soldiers, civilians, and leaders of junior
rank not merely how to survive atomic explosions, but primarily
stress "how they can carry out their missions" under nuclear
attack. The fundamental idea beneath these "instructions" is to
indicate a belief in the invulnerable power of Communist armies
when subjected to atomic attack. In spite of this false facade,
however, conclusions that Communist armies will be unprepared
to employ and exploit tactical atomic weapons would be as rash
as the assumption that the Communist air forces cannot deliver
strategic nuclear strikes.

No. 398.   Saunders, Richard M.
"The Soviet Buildup: Why Does the Threat Grow?"
Military Review Vol. 60 No. 4 (April 1980), pp. 61-71.

While the buildup of Soviet conventional forces in Europe is widely recognized, few understand the reasons for the improvements.   This article argues that it is the result of political, doctrinal, and economic factors originating from the Soviet world view.   These factors have significant implications for both the professional soldier and national policy-makers whenever the capabilities of the Warsaw Pact and NATO are compared.

No. 399.   Scott, William F.
"The Themes of Soviet Strategy."
Air Force Magazine (Soviet Aerospace Almanac No. 10)   Vol.   67 No. 3 (March 1984), pp. 68-73.

Over the past two decades the dominant themes in Soviet military writings on doctrine and strategy have revolved primarily around nuclear missiles of the various services.   NATO military journals, and also the popular press, have described a new Soviet military strategy based on the employment of operational maneuver groups (OMGs), which would seize Europe using conventional weapons before NATO's leaders could determine whether to employ their own nuclear weapons.   Is this scenario realistic?   It is possible that at some future time the Soviet leadership might consider that a demoralized NATO, weakened by internal unrest, might fall quickly to Soviet attack using only conventional weapons.   For the present, however, there is little decrease in the attention of Soviet military leaders in planning or preparing for the possibility of a nuclear war.   In fact, for reasons that are not yet clear, Soviet military writings for the past two years have stressed the tactical use of nuclear weapons.

No. 400.   Vernon, Graham D.
"Soviet Options for War in Europe: Nuclear or Conventional?"
Strategic Review Vol. 7 No. 1 (Winter 1979), pp. 56-66.

There is a conviction in NATO that a Warsaw Pact attack in Europe would unfold without the use of nuclear weapons and that the Soviet Union would prefer a war in Europe to remain conventional.   Some factors would seem to favor that proposition, notably: the Soviets' belief in their ability to wage a successful conventional war; the risks of nuclear escalation to a strategic exchange; Moscow's likely desire to minimize destruction of potential assets in Western Europe; and Soviet confidence in their capability to preempt a possible resort by NATO to nuclear weapons, combined with their possible assessment of the unwieldiness of NATO nuclear release procedures.   Yet, countervailing against these factors are Soviet doctrine advocating the advantages of a surprise nuclear first strike, NATO avowals of intent to use nuclear weapons rather than accept defeat, the strengthened means of discriminating nuclear strikes, time factors favoring the Soviet Union in a short nuclear war, and NATO's vulnerabilities to nuclear attack. On balance, the weight of evidence supports the probability that the Soviets would open a war with a theater-wide nuclear strike and thus challenges the scenarios on which the NATO defense is predicated.

No. 401. Vigor, Peter H.; and Chris N. Donnelly. "The Soviet Threat to Europe." RUSI Journal Vol. 120 No. 1 (March 1975), pp. 69-75.

European security planning does not require a decision as to whether the chief reason for the stationing of large Soviet forces in Central Europe and the creation by the Soviet Union of the Warsaw Pact armies is essentially offensive or defensive. It is sufficient to realize that, whether a war between East and West in Europe were to be born of an offensive or defensive Soviet politico-military policy, or was merely the unhappy offspring of an East-West misunderstanding, the result would be that the Warsaw Pact forces would immediately embark on the offensive and aim to defeat the NATO forces on the field of battle in a short, sharp, decisive campaign. If any should doubt this, they have only to look at Soviet equipment and the reports of Soviet exercises to see that such a war is indeed the only war that the Pact forces are equipped and trained to fight, in addition to Soviet insistence that this is so, which is expressed in their military books and journals. If it is true that current Soviet military doctrine preaches the necessity of fighting a short war, as the kind of war that the Soviet Union is most likely to win in the context of hostilities in Europe, then the significance of the northern and southern flanks of NATO becomes of secondary importance.

No. 402. Vincent, R.J. Military Power and Political Influence: The Soviet Union and Eastern Europe. London: The International Institute for Strategic Studies (Adelphi Paper No. 119), Autumn 1975, 29 p.

Detente between East and West, in particular its European aspect, gives the subject of the political effect of Soviet military power in Europe its current interest. The great powers are unable to use their nuclear weapons, because to do so would be to invite their own destruction. But nuclear weapons do preserve a balance through deterrence, and though they may not be used, their use may be threatened. This paper examines first the Soviet Union, supposedly exercising influence by dint of military power, and then some of the states supposedly influenced by it. This is done, first, by looking at the possible circumstances in Europe in which the presence of Soviet military power might be decisive or make a difference to European politics, and secondly, by investigating the influence Soviet military power has on the domestic and foreign policies of Western European states, independent of the particular will of the Soviet Union on a particular occasion. While the actual extent of influence gained by Soviet military power is difficult to assess precisely, there is clearly a relationship between military power in being and political impact on its environment. And in the Soviet view, detente is regarded as a swing of the balance of forces in the favor of the Soviet Union. It is a state of affairs dependent upon Soviet strength.

No. 403. Wolfe, Thomas W.
Trends in Soviet Thinking on Theater Warfare, Conventional Operations, and Limited War.
Santa Monica, Calif.: The RAND Corporation (RM-4305-PR), December 1964, 119 p.

Discussions of problems in Soviet military thinking and planning during recent years which have arisen from the relationship between strategic and theater warfare and the forces they require: 1) the size of the armed forces; 2) special problems of theater warfare, conventional warfare in a theater, and limited warfare (including the use of tactical nuclear weapons); 3) limiting third-power conflicts in Europe (e.g., Cyprus); 4) national liberation wars, in light of Chinese criticism and the Southeast Asia situation; 5) limited war and the debate over war as an instrument of policy; and 6) improving Soviet local war capabilities (e.g., amphibious forces, the Marines).

Reprinted as "Trends in Soviet Thinking on Theater Warfare and Limited War," in John Erickson et al. (Eds.), The Military-Technical Revolution (New York: Frederick A. Praeger, Publisher, 1966), pp. 52-79.

No. 404. Wolfe, Thomas W.
The Soviet Quest for More Globally Mobile Military Powers.
Santa Monica, Calif.: The RAND Corporation (RM-5554-PR), December 1967, 28 p.

An analysis of the Soviet Union's efforts to improve the mobility of its traditionally continental military power. This study, prompted by rising interest in the question of what the Soviet leaders intend to do with a growing capability for intervention in different regions of the world, assesses the accomplishments and present ability of the Soviets to challenge the West in the domain of globally mobile military power. The Soviet Union took its first steps toward this goal under Khrushchev: military aid to the countries of the Third World, development of long-range transport aircraft, a tactical interest in amphibious and airborne landing, and a steady rise in merchant shipping. Brezhnev and Kosygin have continued these developments. Efforts toward mobility are overshadowed by a desire to strengthen the Soviet strategic posture, but the two taken together bring the military force into better line with the Soviet Union's growing obligations and commitments. The military balance of power continues to favor the United States, but the disparity is lessening.

Reprinted as "Russia's Forces Go Mobile," Interplay of European/ American Affairs Vol. 1 (March 1968), pp. 28, 33-37.

No. 405. XXX.
"The Adaptation of Soviet Ground Forces to Nuclear War."
Military Review Vol. 46 No. 9 (September 1966), pp. 11-17.

Current Soviet military doctrine is based on a type of "blitz war" in which the use of nuclear weapons is considered normal. Envisioned in this doctrine is a massive initial nuclear strike by strategic missiles. This would be followed by an immediate exploitation by large armored and mechanized forces combined with airborne raids by paratroops. The objectives of this doctrine are to achieve a rapid and complete defeat of the enemy, the destruction of remaining enemy potential, the removal of all opportunity for further resistance, and to occupy the enemy territory with a view toward installing a government favorable to communism. Some Western commentators claim to have detected indications in Soviet publications that there is a change in Soviet thinking leading to a doctrine envisioning more conventional forms of war. Their observations are based on some very subjective interpretations of some offical text or declaration in which the omission of certain words or parts of words is considered significant. It is highly probable that in a conflict in Europe the Soviet army will apply the dynamic principles of the current military doctrine taught and accepted in the military quarters of the USSR.

Translation of "Adaptation des Forces Terrestres Sovietiques a une Guerre Nucleaire," Revue de Defense Nationale (Paris), February 1965, p. 16.

C.   SOVIET TACTICAL NUCLEAR WEAPONS POLICY

No. 406. Baxter, William P.
"Survival, Fighting-on Stressed in Red Nuclear Defense Doctrine."
Army Vol. 31 No. 7 (July 1981), pp. 59-61.

The effects of enemy tactical nuclear weapons are routinely taken into account in Soviet Army training and doctrine. However, the recovery guidelines emphasize equipment and unit integrity over care of casualties. This set of priorities creates potential morale problems, suggesting that as the duration of a tactical nuclear war increases, the quality of Soviet forces might decline. To avoid this the Soviet Army plans to exploit surprise, deception, preemption, and a numerical advantage on the battle-field.

No. 407. Baxter, William P.
Soviet Airland Battle Tactics.
Novato, Calif.: Presidio Press, 1986, 269 p.

This book is focused on the understanding of Soviet military theory. Comparisions in theory as well as in practice with the Western world are inevitable. For instance, Lenin held that war is a continuation of politics and that peace is a temporary, unstable armistice between two wars. In the Western view, war is a temporary, unstable condition interrupting peace. This assessment is followed by a practical examination of the modern Soviet military, including a study of the Russian soldier, the organization of command, the use of weapons, views on offense versus defense, and the Soviet art of military prognosis and prediction.

Reviewed by Wayne A. Kilkett, "How the Soviet Army Views Itself," Armed Forces Journal, January 1987, p. 67.

No. 408. Betit, Eugene.
"Soviet Tactical Doctrine and Capabilities and NATO's Strategic Defense."
Strategic Review Vol. 4 No. 4 (Fall 1976), pp. 95-107.

In an era of essential strategic force equivalence, the balance of conventional forces between the Warsaw Pact and NATO attains heightened importance. Yet as inflation and increased personnel costs eat into Western procurement budgets the trends appear to favor the Warsaw Pact. Following Soviet precepts, the Warsaw Pact appears to have prepared for an entirely different type of war than NATO planners seemed to envision. Their massed armor formations are designed for a blitzkrieg, using steamroller tactics to overwhelm the technologcially superior West in a matter of days. NATO, on the other hand, projects long lead times to effect mobilization and convert its factories for a protracted war effort. NATO tactics are basically linear -- envisioning a cohesive defense of the European plain, which stretches some 870 miles from the Baltic Sea to the Alps. Soviet doctrine calls for a series of lightning armor thrusts followed by motorized rifle troops to liquidate strong points and seize cities. Their campaign seems to call for a roll-up of NATO defenses and arrival at the Channel ports in 10-14 days -- before NATO's inherently greater strength could be mobilized. Unless NATO makes the effort to pose a credible counterpoint to Warsaw Pact forces already in being, the gradual erosion of the political balance will continue.

No. 409.   Clark, Richard W., Jr.
Soviet Views on Tactical Nuclear Weapons.
Oberammergau, West Germany: U.S. Army Institute of Advanced Russian Studies, 1 April 1962, 43 p.

The Soviet Union rebukes the West for its use of tactical nuclear weapons in a limited situation, yet almost every edition of Soviet military publications contains references to the application of tactical nuclear weapons.   This apparent paradox actually reflects the Soviet discounting of the possibility of limitation of atomic weapons, but not the use of them.   In other words, any use of atomic weapons by the West in a limited "local" war inevitably would result in a general world war, but the use of limited yield or tactical nuclear weapons can be envisioned in conjunction with other weapons in such a war. This study examines the conditions under which tactical nuclear weapons could be used, the Soviet concept of their use, the preparations being made to ready the Soviet army for their use, and the problems which are being encountered in this field by the Soviet Union.

No. 410.   Cohen, S.T.; and W.C. Lyons.
"A Comparison of U.S.-Allied and Soviet Tactical Nuclear Force Capabilities and Politics."
Orbis Vol. 19 No. 1 (Spring 1975), pp. 72-92.

After more than two decades of tactical nuclear weapon (TNW) development and deployment the actual utility of these weapons and their associated forces remains, to Western strategists, the most poorly understood component of our military defense.   They were first developed and used as military devices for mass destruction -- an image that has persisted up to the present time.   As a consquence, their use in a limited theater in support of a conventional field army has seemed almost contradictory. What has been missing in the TNW debate throughout the years (not only in congressional hearings, but in most of the U.S. professional literature as well) is an accounting of precisely what the Soviet Union has been doing in the field of tactical nuclear weapons development, deployment, and doctrine.   Moreover, insufficient attention has been given to comparing Soviet capabilities and doctrines with those of the West.

No. 411.   Despres, J.H.; L. Dzirkals, and B. Whaley.
Timely Lessons of History: The Manchurian Model for Soviet Strategy.
Santa Monica, Calif.:   The RAND Corporation (R-1825-NA), July 1976, 84 p.

The Soviet invasion of Manchuria was the last large-scale combat operation of World War II. Soviet analyses of the Manchurian campaign reveal an important strain of modern Soviet military thought, suggesting that published studies of the campaign may have been deliberately used in the 1960s and early 1970s to promote a model of modern, combined arms operations that has significant implications for Soviet strategy, military development, and foreign policy. To make the illusions, ideals, and interests of Soviet authorities more accessible, this report describes and appraises the peculiarities of their perceptions and evaluations of the campaign. It focuses on distilling the contents of certain Soviet military publications, and on identifying the strategic concerns, institutional preoccupations, and political initiatives that were most closely associated with Soviet military interest in the Manchurian model.

No. 412. Dick, C.J.
"Soviet Operational Manoeuver Groups: A Closer Look."
International Defense Review Vol. 16 No. 6 (1983), pp. 769-776.

Soviet strategy has moved away from being nuclear-dominated toward accepting the possiblity of a purely conventional operation, or at least a conventional phase, with later escalation to the use of theater nuclear forces (but not strategic weapons). This new strategic flexibility makes it desirable to be, in turn, more flexible operationally, and to find an operational formula more attuned to achieving rapid victory during the conventional phase of a war. There have been significant improvements in the technical capabilities of weapon systems and other equipment becoming available to Soviet formations. In the Soviet view, it is necessary to find an operational form not only to exploit these improved Soviet technical capabilities but also to deny the enemy the exploitation of his improved capabilities. These two considerations have led to the restructuring of the Group of Soviet Forces, Germany, and to the introduction of the Operational Maneuver Group (OMG) concept.

No. 413. Dick, C.J.
"Catching NATO Unawares: Soviet Army Surprise and Deception Techniques."
International Defense Review Vol. 19 No. 1 (January 1986), pp. 21-26.

The Warsaw Pact is markedly weaker than NATO in almost every measure of military potential except for deployed military strength. The Soviet leadership knows well that in 1941 the Germans came within measurable distance of destroying Soviet Communism, and that a strategic nuclear exchange would make the last war look like a skirmish. It does not, however, seem to conclude from this that a war against NATO cannot be won. It has concluded instead that a war with NATO must be won very

quickly -- before NATO can either complete its defensive preparations or agree on the use of nuclear weapons. The Soviet
military identifies five essentials for a quick victory: surprise, a
heavy blow, a rapid advance, simultaneous attacks throughout
the enemy's depth, and air superiority. It stresses that the
element of surprise has long been the most important principle of
military art. Two steps NATO might take are the deployment of
field fortifications and accepting, for planning purposes, that it
will be the victim of strategic surprise should war come.

No. 414. Donnelly, Christopher N.
"The 'March' in Soviet Tactical Doctrine."
RUSI Journal Vol. 119 No. 3 (September 1974), pp. 77-79.

Soviet tactical doctrine is basically offensive, and Soviet
commanders believe that only offensive action, pushed to the
limit, waged at great speed with deep penetration, will give them
an assured victory in the event of war in Europe. It necessarily involves exposed flanks and no continuous front line as
such. The movement of ground troops to contact and into battle
therefore requires the most careful organization, so that the
troops can be led into action without a check and be able to
react to the emergencies of battle. The Soviet army terms this
drill "the march." The aim is to deploy into action without a
check, and to feed successive echelons into the combat as the
leading ones are used up or come to a standstill. There are two
cases: a long approach march from the rear areas will take into
account the varying speeds of vehicles; in a tactical march the
order of battle will be in mixed battle groups of all arms ready
to go into action without any regrouping.

No. 415. Donnelly, Christopher N.
"Tactical Problems Facing the Soviet Army: Recent Debates in
the Soviet Military Press."
International Defense Review Vol. 11 No. 9 (September 1978),
pp. 1405-1412.

This decade has seen a gradual shift of emphasis in the Soviet
military press from a study of the nuclear battlefield to a study
of conventional operations, albeit with the proviso that, in any
major conventional conflict, weapons of mass destruction might be
used at any moment. It must have rapidly become clear to the
Soviet General Staff that both the tactics and equipment of their
army were not adequate for the task of winning a conventional
war quickly. The discussions in the Soviet military poress have
centered on two areas of concern. The first relates to actual
tactical practice and the ability to remain viable in the face of
enemy action; the second relates to the ability of the officer, in
particular his ability to cope with tactical problems and display
initiative.

No. 416.   Donnelly, Christopher N.
"The Soviet Operational Maneuver Group: A New Challenge for NATO."
<u>International Defense Review</u> Vol. 15 No. 9 (September 1982), pp. 1177-1186.

New research shows that the Soviet Union has recently changed its strategy in Europe so as to defeat NATO's active defense concept on the Central Front.   On Day One of an offensive, each attacking army of the Group of Soviet Forces in Germany will launch one or more division-sized Operational Maneuver Group (OMGs) at very high speed into the rear of NATO's main defensive belt.   They will each be launched, probably on two axes, to punch through at the points of greatest success of their parent army's main force attacks. Each army OMG will be a heavily armored, highly maneuverable and self-contained formation, with organic mechanized infantry, SP artillery, SAM, helicopter, engineer, and technical support units. They will also receive massive fixed-wing air support.   The primary role of the army-level OMGs is to speed the advance of the army main forces.   Their tasks will be either to seize major objectives on the main axis behind the NATO defenses, preventing reinforcement or retreat, or to act as raiding groups in the depth of the defenses. They will at all times be under the control of the Front (army group) commander, and act according to his operational plan.   If they are successful, he may follow through on Day Two of the offensive with a much larger, Front-level OMG (army-sized), in an attempt to bring about a very rapid strategic conclusion before NATO commanders can obtain nuclear release.

No. 417.   Dzirkals, Lilia.
<u>"Lightning War" in Manchuria: Soviet Military Analysis of the 1945 Far East Campaign</u>.
Santa Monica, Calif.:   The RAND Corporation (P-5589), January 1976, 116 p.

Presents the initial result of a survey of Soviet military literature on the short but decisive campaign that the Soviet Union waged against Japanese forces in Manchuria in August 1945.   These works examine in great detail the experience of planning, staging, and conducting the campaign.   The analyses identify lessons for combat in the Far East and for the theory of modern military operations.   Specifically, they view this campaign as an instructive example of successful lightning war.   The paper is intended as a guide to the material.   It is organized according to the elements in the campaign effort, ranging from plan conceptualization to missions of individual forces.   An extensive bibliography is appended as well as a listing of the major commanders of the Soviet forces in the campaign.

No. 418. Erickson, John.
"Trends in the Soviet Combined Arms Concept."
Strategic Review Vol. 5 No. 1 (Winter 1977), pp. 38-53.

Although the Soviet military leaders appear confident that the
central strategic relationship between the United States and the
Soviet Union is generally favorable to them, they show a
nervousness rooted in long-standing and traditional Soviet shortcomings. One area of concern, expressed by General Kulikov,
is that of tactical efficiency in combined-arms operations. In
order to close the growing gap between theory and practice,
Kulikov stresses the need for a further strengthening of the
Soviet armed forces and the rigorous analysis of future forms of
conflict. The main task is to devise new methods of conducting
conventional military operations to exploit modern weapons and
equipment to the fullest; to increase maneuverability and enhance
surprise; improve reconnaissance, electronic warfare, and
camouflage techniques; to maximize use of specialist and support
facilities; and to improve command, control, and communications
procedures. The strengths and weaknesses of Soviet combat
forces as the Soviet military leaders perceive them are revealed
in an analysis of the changes in the mix of combat functions, in
troop control, in training, and in tactics. Soviet preoccupations
include the "short war" question, routes and density of the
assaulting force, the role of maneuver, allocation of air effort,
suppressive artillery fire, resources for the meeting engagement,
the role of deep penetration, sub-unit performance, and the
competence of junior and non-commissioned officers.

No. 419. Erickson, John.
"Soviet Combined Arms Operations: An Evalution."
Armor, May-June 1980, pp. 16-21.

In the event of either a general nuclear war or operations
directed against any area of the Eurasian land mass, speed is
absolutely vital, and with it, tempo, the flexibility and agility of
action which can build up advantages. Both the tank troops and
motorized rifle forces of the Soviet ground forces have no
illusions regarding these requirements. The problem is how to
overcome NATO's defenses, in particular the antitank defense,
which if not suppressed by nuclear weapons are quite formidable. The Soviet commander has a number of options relative to
NATO's defenses: 1) the nuclear option; 2) the artillery option;
3) tactical air; 4) ATGMs; and 5) small arms/tank gun support.
This brings up the question of tactical handling, a question
extensively debated in Soviet military articles. Other constraints
upon Soviet combined arms performance include the complexity of
managing the interaction process [vzaimodeistvie]. But in both
of the major Soviet variants -- the breakthrough and the meeting
engagement -- the combined arms mode is deemed indispensable.

No. 420. Hart, Douglas M.; and Dennis M. Gormley.
"The Evolution of Soviet Interest in Atomic Artillery."
RUSI Journal Vol. 128 No. 2 (June 1983), pp. 25-34.

Conventional artillery has remained a major ground force weapon
in the Soviet Army, but the case of nuclear-capable artillery is
far more problematic. Significant time passed between American
development and deployment of artillery fired atomic projectiles
(AFAPs) and Soviet deployment of similar weapons. Nevertheless, Soviet primary military sources indicate a somewhat
complicated development and acquisition process, not a simple lag
of one or two decades between mirror-image deployments. This
unique Soviet response has produced a distinctly different system
of control and organization, as well as substantially fewer numbers of AFAPs, when compared to NATO, deployed against a
specific and closely defined set of NATO targets.

No. 421. Heymant, Irving.
"The Challenge of the Soviet Army."
Military Review Vol. 40 No. 5 (August 1960), pp. 49-55.

The Soviet army is now designed for fast, wide-ranging combat
on either a nuclear or non-nuclear battlefield. The Soviet
military has concluded that nuclear weapons permit surprise to
effect the outcome of the war decisively, particularly in the
opening stages. They carefully differentiate between a preemptive attack and a preventive war. Their conclusions on the
influence of nuclear weapons on warfare have resulted in recent
reorganizations of their army and changes in tactical doctrine.
According to their publications, the Soviets do not intend to use
nuclear weapons except in retaliation. However, it would be
reasonable to expect them to use nuclear weapons against any
situation which could not be handled effectively by non-nuclear
means.

No. 422. Hines, John G.; and Phillip A. Petersen.
"The Soviet Conventional Offensive in Europe."
Military Review Vol. 64 No. 4 (April 1984), pp. 2-28.

The Soviet military clearly believes that nuclear weapons will
have a decisive impact on any future war. However, this
attitude is based on the notion that the existence of nuclear
weapons shapes how a war must be fought regardless of whether
such weapons are used. Since the mid-1960s the Soviet Union
has considered the capability to fight with or without nuclear
weapons to be vital to its well-being, and has refined military
strategy and force structure accordingly. Recent developments
indicate, however, that it would prefer to fight a war in Europe
without resorting to nuclear weapons.

No. 423. Hoeffding, Oleg.
Troop Movements in Soviet Tactical Doctrine.
Santa Monica, Calif.: The RAND Corporation (R-878-PR),
November 1971, 40 p.

An annotated chapter, entitled "Troop Movements," from V.G.
Reznichenko's Tactics (Moscow, Voeyenizdat, 1966), a Soviet
textbook. The chapter covers the doctrine of Soviet troop
movement under their own power, by rail or water, and by air.
Major points include the following: 1) the Soviets have a causal
and non-committal approach to movement of troops by air. (This
aspect of doctrine is probably obsolete by now with the Soviet
acquisition of a major troop airlift capability.); 2) There is an
unqualified expectation that troop movements in the European
theater will proceed under conditions of tactical nuclear warfare,
and confidence that orderly movements will be feasible under
such conditions; 3) Soviet doctrine expects enemy efforts toward
mobility interdiction by air; 4) Soviet troops moving under their
own power appear to be capable of laying and using rough
"column tracks" to overcome demolition of regular roads or to
increase the capacity of inadequate road networks in offensive
operations.

No. 424. Meehan, John F., III.
"Soviet Maneuvers, Summer 1971."
Military Review Vol. 52 No. 4 (April 1972), pp. 14-21.

In the Soviet Union, division-size maneuvers are commonplace
among those units based in European Russia as opposed to those
deployed in Eastern Europe and on the Chinese border. An
analysis of last summer's activities provides a good example of a
typical summer training program in the Soviet Union. In 1971,
there were no large scale maneuvers; the absence of such "show-
case" maneuvers provides an opportunity to view the Soviet
summer schedule as it is normally conducted. The Soviet
military leaders are concerned with the lack of combat experience
in their units, but successfully compensate for this by a rigorous
training program. In the past several years, the Soviet Union
has not only substantially improved its strategic offensive and
defensive capabilities but has made comparable increases in the
tactical capability to conduct conventional warfare. Realistic and
demanding training exercises maintain Soviet forces in this state
of high readiness.

No. 425. Mets, David R.
"The Origin of Soviet Air Theory and Doctrine."
Military Review Vol. 55 No. 8 (August 1975), pp. 36-48.

The literature which does exist on Soviet air power gives little
attention to the theoretical side of the subject. There were
several impressive theoretical, organizational, technological, and

personnel aspects to Russian and Soviet air power before the Second World War and even the Revolution. The recent SALT negotiations have made us aware that Soviet military theory and organization are very different from what they were in 1945. Yet there is also a strong element of continuity, and understanding can be advanced by studying the pre-nuclear history of Russian military aviation.

No. 426. Miller, Martin J.
"Soviet Nuclear Tactics."
Ordinance (May-June 1970), pp. 624-627.

The Soviet Union is well prepared to fight a land nuclear war. Its army is completely equipped with nuclear weapons and delivery systems down to the divisional level, and the once dominant role of conventional artillery has largely been replaced with rocket artillery armed with nuclear weapons. It contemplates employing nuclear weapons to support all types of ground operations, and constantly stresses the importance of large operations carried out in the early days of a modern war. It believes that tactical nuclear weapons will be most effective when employed en masse and in support of the main attack forces. Tactical nuclear weapons, for it, are not just quantitatively but also qualitatively superior to conventional weapons because of their psychological effects. Unlike U.S. doctrine, the Soviet army does not stress pinpoint accuracy and strict target selection but rather mass barrages intended to smash paths through enemy formations and rear areas for the ground units to exploit. There is little indication that it has seriously considered concepts such as controlled nuclear response. Unlike official NATO strategy, the Soviet military makes no distinction between tactical and strategic nuclear war, contending that any use of nuclear weapons will lead to all-out nuclear war. The Soviet theory of a spontaneous global war is intended to reinforce the credibility of Soviet massive retaliation and to discourage the United States and its allies from setting up guidelines for limiting nuclear war. Overall, the Soviet army is geared to fight a nuclear war, but it also has the capability to fight in a conventional manner.

No. 427. Petersen, Phillip A.
The Soviet Conventional Offensive in Europe.
Washington, D.C.: Defense Intelligence Agency (DDB-2622-4-83), May 1983, 52 p.

Since the mid-1960s the Soviet military has perceived the need to be able to fight with or without nuclear weapons, and since then they have been refining their military strategy and adjusting their force structure to fight and win at all levels of conflict. In the Soviet view, defeating NATO without using nuclear weapons would depend almost entirely on the speed of the initial Soviet conventional offensive. Soviet forces would strive to fragment NATO's forward defense quickly and occupy key political and economic centers in an effort to convince the NATO allies that continued resistance or nuclear escalation would be futile. It should be noted that the Soviet military continues to plan for the contingency that NATO would resort to the use of its surviving nuclear weapons. Accordingly, it places great emphasis on the transition from conventional to nuclear warfare to conclude a campaign successfully. By pursuing the capability to fight and win a conventional war in Europe under "protection" of more survivable theater nuclear weapons, the Soviet Union is expanding its options in a direction that would limit NATO's options.

No. 428. Rose, John P.
"The Battlefield Threat: Soviet Concepts, Doctrine, and Strategy.
Air Defense, July-September 1978, pp. 24-29.

The purpose of this article is to examine the continuing trend in Soviet military literature, doctrine, training, and equipment toward combat in a nuclear environment. What appears to be the basic Soviet approach to war, especially in Europe, is that nuclear weapons would be used and that the nation best prepared for their use would win. Soviet doctrinal literature focuses around this approach; Soviet military organization and equipment are able to fight and survive in a nuclear environment; the Soviet Union has developed, tested, and deployed a variety of nuclear capable weapons systems, and it advocates an offensive strategy through which they can be used. Soviet writers on military affairs appear, generally, to see nuclear weapons and nuclear armed forces as central to all phases of Soviet military power.

No. 429. Scott, William F.
"Changes in Tactical Concepts Within the Soviet Forces."
In Lawrence Whetten (Ed.), The Future of Soviet Military Power.
New York: Crane, Russak, and Co., 1976.

This essay examines Soviet tactical concepts; the organization and structure of the Soviet Armed Forces, including officer recruitment, training, and education; and tactical lessons learned from limited wars. It concludes that when construction troops, railway engineers, logistical support units, border security forces, and so on are included, the total manpower figures for the Soviet Armed Forces should be increased by at least one million over the present official U.S. total. It also examines the Soviet military school system and concludes that the actual size of the trained reserves is substantially higher than officially estimated, and that troop training has been demonstrated as highly proficient. This should be attributed to the elaborate reservist organization and its complex training and equipment maintainance responsibilities. Soviet military education has been a long-neglected subject. This article estimates that there are at least 141 highly specialized military schools in the USSR. They grant the equivalent of university degrees and have entrance requirements similar to those of the U.S. service academies. The chief difference is that the Soviet military produces specialized officers for selected career fields; for example, engineers, artillery, and so on. Furthermore, normal universities have reserve officer training programs for all physically qualified male students, adding to the number and cadre of the reserve formations. On balance there is solid evidence that the United States has miscalculated the total strength of the in-being and deployable manpower of the Soviet Armed Forces. These conclusions should not be regarded as alarmist views that the Soviets are suddenly twelve or even eight feet tall, but as indications of deficiencies in past research and as a suggestion for future work.

No. 430. Stockell, Charles.
"Soviet Military Strategy: The Army View."
In Michael MccGwire (Ed.), Soviet Naval Developments: Capability and Context.
New York: Praeger Publishers, 1973, pp. 82-92.

The last 10 years have seen a revolution in Soviet affairs; the dramatic change in its military capabilities. Soviet strategy and national goals have basically changed very little since 1917 except to adjust to new demands, new weaponry, and new threats to Soviet aspirations. On the other hand, tactics and organization have undergone major modifications. Primarily, the threat, rather than the use, of Soviet military power gives meaning to political moves and international economic initiatives. The West can, in the coming years, expect to see the Soviet Union, with its increased confidence and sense of security due to its improved military situation, move more boldy into world politics and seek a more dominant role in international affairs. The major means in this projection of political power will continue to be the Soviet armed forces.

Reprinted in Military Review Vol. 53 No. 10 (October 1973), pp. 72-81.

No. 431. Trapans, A.
Logistics in Recent Soviet Military Writings.
Santa Monica, Calif.: The RAND Corporation (RM-5062-PR), August 1966, 38 p.

The increasing emphasis on logistics in Soviet military publications is analyzed in terms of two specific problems: the scope of logistic activities during a nuclear conflict, and alternative means of transport for resources. Soviet military periodicals published between 1964 and 1966 reflect the impact of logistical ideas expressed in Sokolovskii's <u>Military Strategy</u>, and a new emphasis on the logistics of nuclear war. Military economists and logisticians now stress the peacetime accumulation of stocks and forces for wartime use. On the question of transport, the viability of railroads is under debate. Large tactical pipelines, to be laid immediately after advancing troops, are considered as second only to motor transport of fuel. Consideration is also being given to the air delivery of fuel to missile forces, using cargo aircraft, helicopter, and airdrop.

No. 432. "USSR: Atomic Tactics."
<u>Military Review</u> Vol. 35 No. 10 (January 1956), pp. 73-74.

From a study of proposed defensive tactics, it appears the Soviet Army is not deeply concerned about the prospect of large troop losses from atomic radiation. It appears prepared to sacrifice large numbers of troops in line with the "human sea" tactics of World War II. The Soviet army has begun training its troops in the use of atomic means and is studying the views of its probable enemies on atomic tactics. From this, Soviet policies are being worked out in theory and practice.

No. 433. Van Cleave, William R.; and S.T. Cohen.
<u>Tactical Nuclear Weapons</u>: An Examination of the Issues.
New York: Crane, Russak, and Company, Inc., 1978, 119 p.

Spurred by concern and reawakened interest in improving NATO's tactical nuclear capabilities, the NATO Nuclear Planning Group recently initiated studies of the military and political implications of advanced technologies relative to improved tactical warheads, target acquisition, precision guidance, and communications. The policy direction behind these studies was cast in the mold of NATO's basic policy of "flexible response." However, very substantial changes in the U.S.-NATO-Soviet-Warsaw Pact nuclear balance have taken place since the flexible response doctrine was formulated. This book reexamines the policy issues surrounding tactical nuclear weapons and warfare in Europe under three headings: the political, the military, and the technical. In each case, a comparative critique is drawn of the Western and the Soviet or Warsaw Pact approach. In addition, conceptual problems such as escalation and the distinction between nuclear and non-nuclear conflict, and tactical and strategic nuclear war are analyzed. Finally suggestions are given for improving the ability of the United States and NATO to cope with the threat of theater or tactical nuclear warfare.

Reviewed by Kevin Lynch, "Carteritis: Rx," <u>National Review</u>, August 22, 1980, pp. 1030-1031; Wolfgang Heisenberg, <u>Survival</u>, September-October 1979, pp. 238-239; Dan Caldwell, <u>Annals of</u>

the American Academy of Political and Social Science, May 1979, pp. 149-150; Philip W. Dyer, Political Science Quarterly, Spring 1979, pp. 146-147.

No. 434. Vigor, Peter H.
"The Soviet Armed Forces on Exercise."
Bulletin of the Institute for the Study of the USSR Vol. 18 No. 10 (October 1971), pp. 5-22.

This article is devoted to the Soviet army exercises "Dnieper" (1967) and "Dvina" (1970) and to the intriguing circumstances that surround them. In neither case were any Western representatives invited. The formidable colossus of Soviet publicity and propaganda was aimed at the Soviet Union and representatives of the countries of the "socialist camp". The maneuvers were basically battles between two sets of conventional ground forces, with nuclear weapons playing only a subsidiary role in "Dvina," and not employed in "Dnieper." Both exercises featured a tremendous tank battle, termed a "meeting engagement" [vstrechnye boi], as well as airborne landings and river crossings. From this it can be seen that the Soviet Union is adopting the essence of the Western doctrine of "flexible response." However, the publicity surrounding these two maneuvers should not be taken to mean that no exercises of importance were held in other years, and the fact that their tactics and strategy were almost indistinguishable should not lead to supposition that the Soviet armed forces are not capable under different circumstances.

No. 435. Vigor, Peter H.
The Soviet Blitzkrieg Theory.
New York: St. Martin's Press, 1983, 218 p.

In the West, the idea of blitzkrieg has become almost synonomous with bad strategy. The Soviet military, on the other hand, has long realized and respected its possibilities, if it is properly conducted. It believes that a major war is winnable, if it can be won quickly with conventional weapons. They have concentrated on examining the causes of both Hitler's victories and his defeats, and on scrutinizing the strategic principles which might allow them to succeed where Hitler failed.

Comment by John E. Tashjean, "Could the Soviets Carry Off a Blitzkrieg in Europe?", Armor Vol. 94 No. 4 (July-August 1986), pp. 50-52.

Reviewed by Laurent F. Carrel, Survival Vol. 29 No. 4 (July-August 1984), pp. 189-190.

No. 436. Vigor, Peter H.; and Christopher N. Donnelly.
"The Manchurian Campaign and Its Relevance to Modern History."
Comparative Strategy Vol. 2 No. 2 (1980), pp. 159-178.

From studying the Soviet campaign in Manchuria we can derive
several principles of Soviet military strategy that are still
relevant today: 1) the importance of diplomacy in deciding the
outcome of war; 2) the primacy of the offensive; and 3) the
desirability of achieving strategic surprise. Nevertheless,
although principles of Soviet military art have changed little
since 1945, the means by which these principles would be put
into practice at the tactical level have changed. The increase in
the destructive power of conventional weaponry, combined with
the development of precision-guided munitions, has increased the
relative effectiveness of the defense. Although the Soviet Army
is making impressive efforts to deal with the problems that
confront it, there is a question as to whether these can be
successful in the absence of radical changes in its organization
and command structure.

No. 437. Williams, E.S.
"Soviet Military Thought and the Principles of War."
Royal Air Forces Quarterly Vol. 15 (Spring 1975), pp. 17-22.

The ten "Principles of War," distilled by Major General J.F.C.
Fuller in 1920, are still very much alive in Western military
thought. Soviet military thought has roots not only in Marxism-
Leninism, but also in the bourgeois military thought existing at
the time of the Revolution that was summarized by Fuller. A
recent Soviet military work, The Officer's Handbook, contains a
section entitled "The Principles of Soviet Military Structure," in
which the older accepted principles are visible in oblique
reference behind the Marxist verbiage.

D. SOVIET NAVAL NUCLEAR WEAPONS POLICY

No. 438. Ackley, Richard T.
"No Bastions for the Bear: Round 2."
U.S. Naval Institute Proceedings Vol. 111 No. 4 (April 1985),
pp. 42-47.

In his 1984 prize-winning essay, David B. Rivkin, Jr. argued
that a fifteen-carrier battle group, 600 ship navy is required to
support a U.S. forward strategy in response to a revolutionary
change in Soviet naval posture. This is the positioning of
Soviet nuclear-powered ballistic missile submarines (SSBNs) in
bastions to target the United States from the safety of well-
defined home waters or under the polar ice cap. This essary
will reassess the SSBN threat and suggest how it might be met

now and in the future. The proposed solution is central to the use of U.S. nuclear-powered fast attack submarines (SSNs) operating under and near the polar ice cap. The SSN can penetrate Soviet SSBN bastions at will.

No. 439. Dismukes, Bradford.
Roles and Missions of Soviet Naval General Purpose Forces in Wartime: Pro-SSBN Operations?
Alexandria, VA.: Center for Naval Analyses (PP 130), August 1974, 19 p.

This paper deals with the relationship between general purpose force levels and capabilities and the nuclear ballistic missile submarine (SSBN) security issue from the viewpoint of Soviet naval policy. It re-examines the body of available evidence by asking two questions which thus far have been given scant attention: what kind of threat to its own SSBNs does the Soviet Navy perceive in Western ASW systems? What has been their reaction, if any, to this potential threat?

No. 440. Herrick, Robert W.
Gorshkov Makes the Case for Further Great Expansion of Soviet Navy: Current Series of Articles in "Morskoi Sbornik" by Fleet Admiral Sergey Gorshkov, Commander in Chief, Soviet Navy.
Alexandria, Va.: Center for Naval Analyses (M 1012), October 19, 1972.

This paper contains a preliminary analysis of a series of articles written for Morskoi Sbornik (Naval Digest) by Fleet Admiral Sergey Gorshkov, Commander in Chief of the Soviet Navy. It points out that while Gorshkov's professed aim is to foster unity within the Soviet Navy as to its proper role under existing circumstances, his real objective is to justify vast naval construction. Using historical examples to convey its proper role in the defense of the Soviet Union, Gorshkov interprets every occurrence in both Tsarist and Soviet history to demonstrate that the USSR has an urgent need to get about building the much larger navy he holds as necessary for defense against the Western States and furtherance of the USSR's expanding maritime interests. This analysis proceeds on the assumption that Gorshkov's interest is not that of an historian and that he is not interested in writing an objective history, but that he is concerned with the further development of the Soviet Navy and is using military policy and strategy.

Reprinted as "The Gorshkov Interpretation of Russian Naval History," Chapter 23 in Michael MccGwire (Ed.), Soviet Naval Development: Capability and Context. New York: Praeger Publishers, 1973, pp. 306-323.

No. 441. Herrick, Robert W.
The USSR's "Blue Belt of Defense" Concept: A Unified Military
Plan for Defense Against Seaborne Nuclear Attack by Strike
Carriers and Polaris/Poseidon SSBNs.
Alexandria, Va.: Center for Naval Analyses (PP 111), May 1973,
11 p.

In a speech made at the 23rd Communist Party Congress on April
1, 1966, Soviet Defense Minister Marshal Malinovsky made an
unamplified reference to a new Soviet military concept which
neither he nor any other Soviet leader or publicist has ever
again referred to in the public media: "We stand tranquilly and
confidently in the defense of the peaceful work of our people,
the more so now when the creation of the Blue Belt of Defense
has been completed for our State." This statement generated a
wave of journalistic speculation as to the nature of the Blue Belt
system and the Soviet forces involved. Examining various media
statements and other open source comments, the paper concludes
that the Soviet system is not purely naval. Although the Blue
Belt is solely concerned with the sea-borne nuclear threat from
the strike carriers and missile submarines of the United States
and other NATO states, the defense against this threat is a
mission shared jointly with other service branches.

Reprinted as Chapter 9 in Paul Murphey (Ed.), Naval Power in
Soviet Policy (Washington, D.C.: Government Printing Office,
Studies in Communist Affairs Vol. 2, 1978), pp. 169-178.

No. 442. Herrick, Robert W.
"Roles and Missions of the Soviet Navy: Historical Evolution,
Current Priorities, and Future Prospects."
In James L. George (Ed.), The Soviet and Other Communist
Navies: The View From the Mid-1980s.
Annapolis, Md.: Naval Institute Press, 1986, pp. 39-61.

This paper describes broad politico-military perspectives and
other developments through the eyes of the leaders of the Soviet
Navy. From this vantage the Soviet leaders react to U.S.
initiatives today as they did to those of Germany and other
European adversaries before 1945. But they also engage in
initiatives of their own, bringing a Soviet cast to tactical and
technical innovation. This emphasis on the service-level perspective naturally focuses attention on potential internal bureaucratic
determinants of Soviet naval policy. Thus, throughout its
history the Soviet Navy has been in a more or less continuous
process of defining and redefining its identity and purposes in
the face of at best grudging tolerance on the part of the bureau-
cratically dominant ground forces.

No. 443. Herrick, Robert W.; James M. McConnell, and Michael
K. MccGwire.

Admiral Gorshkov on the Soviet Navy in War and Peace.
Alexandria, Va.: The Center for Naval Analyses (M 1015), 1973.

In February 1972 the Soviet Navy's monthly journal, the Naval
Digest, began the publication of a series of eleven articles by
Admiral of the Fleet Sergey Gorshkov, Commander in Chief of
the Soviet Navy. The general title of the series was "Navies in
War and Peace." The series of three working papers is devoted
largely to a summary presentation and an analysis of the
rationale presented by Gorshkov for building an even larger
Soviet Navy.

No. 444. Kassing, David.
Changes in Soviet Naval Forces.
Alexandria, Va.: Center for Naval Analyses (PP 183), November
1976, 33 p.

In a recent book, Seapower of the State, Admiral Gorshkov
suggests some of the ideas that underlie the transformation of
the Soviet navy under his command. Though the book considers
all aspects of seapower, it concentrates on the history and
development of the Soviet navy and concludes with a lengthy
discussion of "problems in the art of naval warfare." The
accuracy of what Gorshkov says about the missions and
capabilities cannot be determined without examining whether what
he says is consistent with the development of Soviet forces and
operations.

No. 445. Kime, Steve F.
"A Soviet Navy for the Nuclear Age."
Parameters Vol. 10 No. 3 (March 1980), pp. 58-70.

Although naval power has never played a primary role in the
Soviet scheme of nationhood, the Soviet navy has managed to
flourish. How the navy of a traditionally continental military
power arrived at a position where it commands a significant
portion of a large defense budget is the subject of this essay.
Admiral Sergei Gorshkov has been able to justify his programs.
A great deal of latitude for political use of Soviet naval power,
extending into denial and interposition roles vis-a-vis the U.S.
Navy, is a new fact of life in the nuclear age. So is a large
range of strategic offensive and defensive missions. The
prospects for future American security depend as much upon
U.S. naval developments, however, as on the future composition
of the Soviet Navy. There is no more reason for the United
States to accept parity or less on the world's oceans than there
is for the Soviet Union to accept U.S. conventional domination on
the European continent.

Reprinted as an introductory essay to Myron Smith (Ed.),
The Soviet Navy, 1941-1978: A Guide to Sources in English

(Santa Barbara, Calif.: American Bibliographic Center -- Clio
Press, 1980), pp. 1-15.

No. 446. MccGwire, Michael.
"Contingency Plans for World War."
In James L. George (Ed.), The Soviet and Other Communist
Navies: The View from the Mid-1980s.
Annapolis, Md.: Naval Institute Press, 1986, pp. 61-81.

Contemporary Soviet naval developments derive largely from
decisions reached in two periods. The first decision period,
1967-1968, was the direct consequence of a change in military
doctrine on the likely character of a future world war. This
was that such a war might not be nuclear and would not necessarily involve an intercontinental nuclear exchange. This doctrinal change resulted in a fundamental restructuring of Soviet
force requirements and operational concepts. In 1976-1977 the
effects of this restructuring were reviewed, and significant
adjustments to earlier decisions regarding naval policy were
made. This account of Soviet naval development considers, in
turn, these two decision periods, their objectives and related
strategic concepts, and their implications.

No. 447. McConnell, James M.
Military-Political Tasks of the Soviet Navy in War and Peace.
Alexandria, Va.: Center for Naval Analyses (PP 148), February
1976, 61 p.

Over the course of 1972-1973 the monthly journal of the Soviet
Navy, the Naval Digest, published a series of eleven articles by
its Commander in Chief, Fleet Admiral of the Soviet Union S.G.
Gorshkov. For Gorshkov this was an unprecedented effort and
it is understandable that the series should have aroused attention
in the West. Unfortunately, Western analysts have not been able
to come to a meeting of the minds either on the intent of the
articles or on the question of whether Gorshkov was lobbying or
speaking authoritatively -- and this too is understandable, since
he does not make it easy for us to interpret him. The author
takes the position that Gorshkov is probably speaking authoritatively; that his work represents, not a doctrinal statement as
such, but what the Soviet military refers to as a "concrete
expression of doctrine," i.e., a work rationalizing particular
tenets of military doctrine that apply to the Navy.

Reprinted in John Hardt and Herman Franssen (Eds.), Soviet
Oceans Development, for the Senate Commerce Committee (Washington, D.C.: Government Printing Office, October 1976), pp.
183-209.

No. 448. McConnell, James M.
"The Gorshkov Articles, The New Gorshkov Book, and Their
Relation to Policy."
Chapter 29 in Michael MccGwire and James McDonnell (Eds.),
Soviet Naval Influence: Domestic and Foreign Dimensions.
New York: Praeger Publishers, 1977, pp. 565-620.

The debate among Western analysts, now over three years old,
is about a series of articles Admiral Gorshkov published under
the title of "Navies in War and Peace," in his Navy's monthly
journal, Naval Digest, over the course of 1972-73. This paper
was originally intended to sum up "the state of the debate"
dealing with the arguments of all the participants. This plan
was changed by the publication, in February of this year, of a
book by Gorshkov, entitled Seapower of the State. The theme is
the same as the series, and much of the data is only repetition,
but here and there a point that is only alluded to in the series
(i.e., command of the sea) is expanded into an entire section,
and even when the book only supplements the series, it often
firms up what could previously only be inferred.

Also printed as a Center for Naval Analyses Paper (PP 159),
July 1976, 93 p.

No. 449. McConnell, James M.
Strategy and Missions of the Soviet Navy in the Year 2000.
Alexandria, Va.: Center for Naval Analyses (PP 206), November
1977, 48 p.

This paper deals briefly with some features of Russian naval
development that have persisted over time, as well as some that
have shown changes and fluctuations, especially those revealing
regularities even in the process of change. It then discusses at
greater length trends in our own period, since the 1950s,
drawing on evidence from allocations, capabilities, operations,
and especially stated intentions. In the final section, strategy
and missions for the year 2000 are projected, bearing in mind
past and current trends, pointing out areas when history is a
very uncertain guide, and paying attention to requirements and
limitations imposed from the political side, as well as purely
naval requirements and the state of the art and technological
potential for satisfying these requirements. Presented at a
conference on Problems of Sea Power as We Approach the 21st
Century, sponsored by the American Enterprise Institute for
Public Policy Research, October 6, 1977.

Also published in James L. George (Ed.), Problems of Seapower
as We Approach the Twenty-First Century (Washington, D.C.:
American Enterprise Institute, 1978), pp. 39-68, with commentary
and discussion by Frank Uhlig, Jr., Hershel Kanter, and John
Moore, pp. 69-95.

No. 450. McConnell, James M.
Possible Counterforce Roles for the Typhoon.
Alexandria, Va.: Center for Naval Analyses (PP-347), March
1982, 24 p.

A recent (August 1981) article by Vice-Admiral K. Stalbo, one of
the most eminent Soviet naval spokesmen, merits interest for
revealing what appears to be a new role for the Soviet Navy's
ballistic-missile submarines (SSBNs). This is a significant
statement by Stalbo, all the more credible for being esoterically
expressed. It strongly implies, given the modalities of Soviet
discourse, that their SSBNs have a strategic counterforce role
over and above that assigned them in the past. In this paper
the 1960s and 1970s backgrounds necessary for a proper understanding of Stalbo's August 1981 statement itself, together with
its implications and the requirements for further research in
other fields are analyzed.

No. 451. McConnell, James M.
"New Soviet Methods for Antisubmarine Warfare?"
Naval War College Review Vol. 38 No. 4 (July-August 1985), pp.
16-27.

In the summer of 1982 there was an apparent shift in Soviet
views on the future potential for combating submarines. Using
alleged U.S. views as an almost certain surrogate for their own,
they indicated that a "technological breakthrough" in ASW --
possibly non-acoustic and space-based -- was imminent. If the
Soviet Union is on the verge of a long-range detection capability,
it might revive the concept, abandoned in the 1970s, of using a
submarine-launched ballistic missile system for hitting mobile
targets at sea. There are a number of factors in favor of a
sea-strike solution. One is inter-service politics -- the Soviet
Navy appears to have successfully secured for itself the prepon-
derent role of hitting naval targets. Second, sea-based strikes
provide the option of disassociating Soviet territory from a
possible nuclear engagement at sea.

No. 452. McConnell, James M.
"The Soviet Naval Mission Structure: Past, Present, and
Future."
In James L. George (Ed.), The Soviet and Other Communist
Navies: The View from the Mid-1980s.
Annapolis, Md.: Naval Institute Press, 1986, pp. 37-60.

This paper traces the shifts that have taken place in the mission
priorities of the Soviet Navy and suggests possible lines of
evolution in the future. They can be understood only in the
context of the general Soviet military orientation, since in the
USSR there is no naval policy or doctrine, only naval aspects of
a single military policy or doctrine. The navy, owing to its

properties of mobility and survivability, has played a crucial role in several of the USSR's limited military options. Military doctrine is sychronized with the five-year plans to carry out policies agreed upon earlier. In 1976-1977 the Soviet Union changed its long-range military-political priorities to make conventional forces the sword and nuclear forces its shield. Doctrinal implementation came in the 1981-1985 five-year plan. The shift to protracted, conventional war has increased the importance of two navy missions -- interdicting sea lines of communication and supporting the ground troops on maritime axes. Their importance relative to nuclear options designed to inhibit Western escalation, however, has not changed.

No. 453. Parker, T. Wood.
"Theater Nuclear Warfare and the U.S. Navy."
Naval War College Review Vol. 35 No. 1 (January-February 1982), pp. 3-16.

Tactical nuclear warfare at sea is more likely than Western analysts wish to believe. Their hope that political and moral inhibitions prevent the superpowers from crossing the nuclear threshhold is a poor deterrent against escalation. The United States Navy must accept the possibility of having to fight a nuclear war at sea and must, therefore, prepare to win it.

No. 454. Petersen, Charles C.
Soviet Tactics for Warfare at Sea.
Alexandria, Va.: Center for Naval Analyses (PP 367), November 1982, 64 p.

This paper focuses primarily on the development of Soviet views on anti-surface warfare (ASUW). The period with which this analysis deals begins in the early 1960s, when Soviet theorists first began to weigh the implications of their Navy's acquisition of nuclear-missile weapons on its tactics. Only a thorough understanding of the issues raised in this debate will enable us to assess the meaning and impact of Soviet tactical writings today.

No. 455. Rivkin, David B., Jr.
"No Bastions for the Bear: Prize Essay 1984."
U.S. Naval Institute Proceedings Vol. 110 No. 4 (April 1984), pp. 36-43.

As the Soviet Union places more of its nuclear assets in submarines, guaranteeing the survival of their SSBNs becomes a high-priority goal. The Soviet military seems intent on turning waters adjacent to the Soviet landmass into bastions where its submarines would be protected by the Soviet Navy and by land-based air. But if war erupts, the United States can permit no such sanctuaries. Wherever the bear is, there the U.S. Navy must be prepared to conduct offensive naval operations.

Responses by F.J. Glaeser and W.J. Ruhe, June 1984, pp. 14-15; R.H. Smith, July 1984, pp. 14-20; L.E. Lacoutre, August 1984, p. 101; R.O. Welander and J.D. Williams, September 1984, p. 164; J.A. Marcely, October 1984, pp. 172-178; L. Brooks, November 1984, pp. 97-100; C.H. Builder, January 1985, p. 129; P.G. Johnson, May 1985, pp. 14-17; James Tritten, July 1985, p. 112. Also see Richard T. Ackley, "No Bastion for the Bear: Round 2," U.S. Naval Institute Proceedings Vol. 111 No. 4 (April 1985), pp. 42-47.

No. 456. Shulsky, Abram N.
Admiral Gorshkov on Naval Arms Limitations: KTO KOGO?
Alexandria, Va.: Center for Naval Analyses (M 1024), January 1974, 20 p.

In his series "Navies in War and Peace," Admiral Gorshkov presents a generally pessimistic view of the naval arms limitation agreements of the period between the two world wars. He notes that they did not achieve their stated purpose of naval arms limitation, and that "from the mid-1930s a new unrestrained and in no way regulated naval arms race began." He borders on sarcasm in his description of the successive naval conferences as "the war of the diplomats for supremacy at sea."

Printed as Chapter 14 in Paul Murphey (Ed.), Naval Power in Soviet Policy (Washington, D.C.: Government Printing Office, Studies in Communist Affairs Vol. 2, 1978), pp. 247-258.

No. 457. Smith, Clyde A. "The Meaning and Significance of the Gorshkov Articles."
Naval War College Review Vol. 26 No. 5 (March-April 1974), pp. 18-37.

The Gorshkov articles represent a "window" into the planning offices of the Soviet Navy. Admiral Gorshkov speaks from a background of vast experience and from a position of authority. He presents a clear message that the Soviet Navy is no mere transitory phenomenon on the world's maritime stage.

No. 458. Tritten, James John.
Soviet Naval Forces and Nuclear Weapons: Weapons, Employment, and Policy.
Boulder, Colo.: Westview Press, 1986.

The use of the Soviet Navy for political gain in peacetime has been the subject of extensive previous analysis. In that analysis, the primacy of the nuclear war mission is acknowledged but rarely subjected to exhaustive scrutiny. The conclusions of previous studies on the employment of the Soviet Navy in a nuclear war have been primarily based upon opinion backed up by modest content and hardware analysis. The objective of this work is to challenge these previous studies and either validate them or suggest alternate possibilities. To do so, two major techniques were employed. The first was formal content analysis of the speeches, articles, books, etc., of the head of the Soviet Navy, Admiral S.G. Gorshkov, and individuals who served as Minister of Defense or head of the Politburo. Themes relating to the aims of war and means of influencing its outcome were tracked from 1964 through 1983. These themes included both manifest and latent messages, and formed the basis for the stated declaratory policy for the strategic employment of the Soviet Navy in a nuclear war with the United States involving strikes on homeland territory. The second methodology employed was general hardware analysis, supplemented by analysis of exercises and deployment behavior. The mobilization case, the existing case (Bolt from the Blue with forces on routine patrol), and a mid-range surge case were quantified and subjected to sensitivity and contingency analyses. Study findings compare declaratory policy with capability and demonstrate matches and mismatches. Conclusions and implications address Soviet political military doctrine, Soviet military strategy, and various implications for Western doctrine, strategy, and arms control. As a whole, the study addresses the worth of taking the extra steps in such an exhaustive method of studying the Soviet Navy and whether or not the major benefit -- reduced uncertainty over findings -- is worth the effort.

No. 459. Tritten, James John.
"(Non)Nuclear Warfare."
U.S. Naval Institute Proceedings Vol. 113 No. 2 (February 1987), pp. 64-70.

In addition to considering the unique problems of maritime nuclear war, navies need to examine thoroughly the relationship of non-nuclear warfare to nuclear operations and deterrence. Failure to understand these relationships might lead to planning for nuclear and conventional operations with totally separate staffs and differing approaches, resulting in incongruous war plans and tactics. Non-nuclear and nuclear warfare are related and even symbiotic. This relationship encompasses the areas of warfighting, intra-war deterrence, and the use of conventional naval forces for crisis response. During a war, non-nuclear forces will probably be used to degrade or enhance the employment of nuclear weapons. The possibility of nuclear weapons being used against conventional forces and vice versa should be planned for.

No. 460. Vigor, Peter H.
"Admiral Gorshkov's Views on Seapower."
RUSI Journal for Defense Studies Vol. 119 No. 1 (March 1974),
pp. 53-60.

In February 1972 the Commander-in-Chief of the Soviet Navy,
Admiral S.G. Gorshkov, published in Morskoi sbornik (Naval
Digest) the first article of what was to be a fairly extensive
series under the general title of "Navies in War and Peace." As
it subsequently transpired, there were eleven articles in the
series, the last of which appeared in Morskoi sbornik in February 1973. Since Morskoi sbornik is the best-known Soviet naval
journal and is published under the auspices of the Soviet
Ministry of Defense, the fact that it was featuring a whole series
of well-argued articles by no less a person than the Commander-
in-Chief of the Soviet Navy naturally lent them an unusual
degree of interest and importance. The overwhelming impression
on the readers is of supreme value for any country having a
strong fleet.

No. 461. Vigor, Peter H.
"Strategy and Policy in Soviet Naval Warfare."
Strategic Review Vol. 2 No. 2 (Spring 1974), pp. 68-75.

Soviet policy makes military strategy the handmaiden of politics.
It regards the "most fundamental objectives" as the unconditional
surrender of the enemy and conversion of his economy and
society to a Marxist system. This would be the aim of nuclear
war in which Soviet ballistic missile submarines would pulverize
the enemy's industry and cities to destroy his will to resist, and
attack submarines would sever his sea lines of communication. A
conventional war might be a limited war in which a territorial
advantage would be seized, with success or failure not bearing
on Soviet vital interests. In this instance, the Navy would
support the operation with local seaborne security operations but
without extending operations to more distant elements of enemy
strength.

No. 462. Weinland, Robert G.
An Analysis of Admiral Gorshkov's "Navies in War and Peace".
Alexandria, Va.: Center for Naval Analyses (PP 131), July 1974.

The first objective of this paper is to describe the publication of
"Navies in War and Peace" and summarize the arguments
advanced there by Admiral Gorshkov. The second objective is
to examine potential links between the publication of his
statement and the domestic and international contexts in which it
appeared. The third objective is to present some summary
judgements on the meaning and importance of "Navies in War and
Peace."

Summarized as "Admiral Gorshkov's Navies in War and Peace, Part IV, by Robert Weinland, Robert Herrick, Michael MccGwire, and James McConnell in Survival Vol. 17 No. 2 (March-April 1975), pp. 54-63; and reprinted in abridged form as Chapter 29 in Michael MccGwire et al. (Eds.), Soviet Naval Policy: Objectives and Contraints (New York: Praeger Publishers, 1974), pp. 547-572.

No. 463. Welander, R.O.; J.J. Herzog, and F.D. Kennedy, Jr. The Soviet Navy Declaratory Doctrine for Theatre Nuclear Warfare. McLean, VA.: The BDM Corporation (DNA 4434T), 30 September 1977, 56 p.

This topical report presents an analysis of unclassified Soviet writings on the Soviet military and naval doctrines for nuclear warfare. Based on this analysis, a postulation of Soviet Navy Doctrine for Theater Nuclear Warfare is presented.

No. 464. Woolridge, E.T., Jr. "The Gorshkov Papers: Soviet Naval Doctrine for the Nuclear Age." Orbis Vol. 13 No. 4 (Winter 1975), pp. 1153-1175.

In 1972, Admiral Gorshkov, Commander-in-Chief of the Soviet Navy, initiated a series of eleven articles entitled "Navies in War and Peace," in Morskoi Sbornik, the Soviet naval digest. Publication of articles dealing with doctrine, strategy, naval science, or military art by a flag officer of the Soviet Navy is commonplace in the USSR. This series, however, has evoked considerable interest and speculation in Western Europe and the United States because it extended over a period of thirteen months and amounted to over 50,000 words. Of equal significance is the manner in which Gorshkov expounds on Soviet naval operational and strategic concepts, force compositions, missions, the influence of Marxist-Leninist precepts on the conduct of modern war at sea, and the utility of naval presence in peacetime as a political instrument. The depth of the study and the fact that the treatise was published under the name of the Commander-in-Chief have caused it to be compared to A. Svechin's Strategy, published in 1926, and the three editions of Marshal V.D. Sokolovskiy's Military Strategy, published from 1962 to 1968.

6

Some Related Issues

A. DEFENSE DECISION-MAKING

No. 465. Alexander, Arthur J.
Modeling Soviet Defense Decision-making.
Santa Monica, Calif.: The RAND Corporation (P-6560), December 1980, 20 p.

This report provides a summary of a model of decision-making in Soviet defense to clarify issues and identify points of disagreements and misunderstanding by Western analysts. This paper is organized around problems observed in some of the literature on Soviet defense decision-making and in informal statements and comments on the subject. These problems include inappropriate and confused imputations of influences, effects, and relationships in the flow of the decision process. Two levels of the decision-making process -- high-level and low-level -- and their patterns of behavior are examined. The high-level process is composed of the Politburo, Central Committee Secretariat, and Presidium of the Council of Ministers. The low-level includes the production ministries, Defense Ministry, and Party organizations below the Central Committee. The report suggests that the progress made in understanding Soviet defense decision-making can help unify the several existing models used to explain not only Soviet decision-making but decision-making in general.

No. 466. Alexander, Arthur J.
"Research in Soviet Defense Production."
NATO's Fifteen Nations Vol. 26 No. 5 (October-November 1981), pp. 52-64.

The Soviet Union has made great technological advances in military equipment and armament in the last twenty years. This article discusses several tendencies of Soviet weapons design, including simplicity in equipment; common use of subsystems, components, and parts; incremental growth; and limited performance and mission capabilities. It presents examples of these

tendencies and describes exceptions to them. In addition, the
article explains how the sources of Soviet weapons design come
from the organization and structure of military research and
development and from military doctrine, and illustrates how the
USSR selects weapons on the basis of necessity.

No. 467. Alexander, Arthur J.
Patterns of Organizational Influence in Soviet Military Procurement.
Santa Monica, Calif.: The RAND Corporation (N-1327-AF), April
1982, 13 p.

Although political choices have established the thrust of present
Soviet weapons procurement policies, these choices and their
implementation are conditioned by decision-making procedures
and organizational relationships. The military maintains a near-
monopoly of information and expertise on military affairs. This
monopoly, coupled with a generation of alternative policies in
military and civilian sectors that is conservative and incremental,
requires that non-incremental change be stimulated by intervention from the political leaders. But, in order to preserve its
stability, the collective leadership of the past 15 years is also
conservative and incremental. We can therefore expect continuation of present trends until major change is broadly
supported by the leadership.

No. 468. Erickson, John.
"Towards a New 'Soviet High Command': 'Rejuvenation' Renewed
(1959-1969)."
RUSI Journal, September 1969.

Looking at the age distribution within the senior command group
of the Soviet armed forces for the years 1945 and 1965 one notes
that both sets of figures are highly skewed. In 1945 this was
the youngest command group in the world; in 1965 it was the
oldest. It seems a plausible explanation that the present political
leadership prefers a comparable age group in its senior military
men, and is prepared to run the gamut of the generation gap to
get it. There is some logic in this position as it ensures
continuity and a certain stablity in party-military relations. On
the other hand, the technological requirements of the new Soviet
armed forces have forced rejuvenation upon the command even
though the process has been uneven. It may be assumed that
the "mobility" at the military district level will be maintained, and
that some features already clearly observable will continue: the
appearance of new men, with key posts as "stepping stone"
promotions.

Condensed as "Rejuvenating the Soviet High Command," Military
Review Vol. 50 No. 7 (July 1970), pp. 83-94.

No. 469. Erickson, John.
Soviet Military Power.
London: Royal United Services Institute for Defense Studies,
1971, 112 p.

This study follows a simple progression, asking a few questions
in turn -- in what terms did the Soviet leadership and command
see the position in and after 1965, who implemented these policies
and how has this "command group" evolved, how has the weapons
build-up proceeded and with what objectives, what is embodied
in Soviet combat training programs and, finally, what interests
are being served? How does this assortment of policies, men,
weapons techniques, training programs, and commitments all fit
together? These questions are addressed by in-depth examination of Soviet and East European materials. They indicate
that the Soviet military effort, while it may be impelled by
certain ideas and governed by a variety of motives, is nevertheless the work of a particular command group. "Doctrine"
does not exist in the abstract and some of the more significant
changes have not been dissected by Soviet military theoreticians;
it is necessary, therefore, to pass from considering revisions in
doctrine to outlining the reshaping of the command in the post-
Khrushchev period, for these are the men who put the "doctrine"
into practice.

Reprinted by the United States Strategic Institute (USSI Report
73-1), 1973, 127 p.

No. 470. Erickson, John.
"Soviet Command and Control."
Military Review Vol. 52 No. 1 (January 1972), pp. 41-50.

Condensed from Chapter 4 of Soviet Military Power by John
Erickson. In the Soviet view, there are three stages to the
revolution in military affairs -- the advent of nuclear weapons,
the appearance of the missile, and the application of automation
to the problems of command and control. The first two stages
have had a great impact on the Soviet military establishment; the
third promises to be equally significant. In fact, it is the
logical outcome of applying stages one and two in order to exploit
fully the potentialities of the new weapons. The implications of
the new weapons have forced the Soviet Command to reappraise
the nature of its establishment and to consider how it might best
work under these especially arduous conditions -- hence, the
first investigations into the psychology of the military collective
and the study of the importance of the subunit. Similarly, the
advent of automation in the area of troop control has caused
both military professionals and party authorities to think about
the nature of command.

No. 471. Erickson, John.
"The Soviet Military Press, 1978."
Strategic Review Vol. 7 No. 3 (Summer 1979), pp. 83-96.

If one theme dominated Soviet military literature in 1978, it was command and control [upravlenie voiskami]. A quite sophisticated approach was adopted: if modes of "command and control" have been amplified, adapted, and changed, do traditional definitions of "battle/combat" still hold? A review of the eleven most important Soviet military journals reflects a current preoccupation with command and control within the senior levels of the Soviet command, and their formal and official encouragement of a "debate" over the subject by younger officers. These "debates" will certainly not result in any great upheaval in tactical/operational methods, but they invalidate notions of utter and unbending rigidity in Soviet military circles. If there has been a shift, it is away from tactical theory as such and into the practicalities of tactical handling and tactical experiment.

No. 472. Frost, Howard.
"Soviet Party-Military Relations in Strategic Decisionmaking."
In Kenneth M. Currie and Gregory Varhall (Eds.), The Soviet Union: What Lies Ahead?
Washington, D.C.: Government Printing Office (Studies in Communist Affairs Vol. 6), 1985, pp. 58-74.

According to conventional wisdom, relations between the Communist Party of the Soviet Union and the Soviet Armed Forces are tense because they are two distinct bodies in competition with each other; their conflicts can and do impair the formulation of military policy. Recent analyses, however, have focused on elements of cooperation between the groups, with the conclusion that military policy is more a product of coordination than competition between them. The analysis presented in this paper concludes that, while tensions do exist between the Soviet political and military leaders, they do not impair significantly their cooperation in the formulation of military strategic policy.

No. 473. Gallagher, Matthew P.; and Karl F. Spielmann, Jr.
Soviet Decision-making for Defense: A Critique of U.S. Perspectives on the Arms Race.
New York: Praeger Publishers, 1972, 102 p.

The predictability of Soviet defense decision-making depends upon whether the Soviet leaders share U.S. perceptions of the strategic situation and whether they operate according to the dictates it seems to impose. These questions require a careful look at what American strategic concepts imply about the Soviet decision-making process, and an even more careful look at how the Soviet Union decides military policy issues in practice. This

book attempts to show what can and cannot be said about the
Soviet decision-making process on the basis of the evidence.
The purpose is to establish the parameters for the more speculative efforts that may be required to fill out a working model of
the Soviet decision-making system. It exploits the scholarship
that has accumulated on Soviet studies over the past decade and
applies it to the problem of interpreting Soviet military policy
decisions.

No. 474. Garthoff, Douglass F.
"The Soviet Military and Arms Control."
Survival Vol. 19 No. 6 (November-December 1977), pp. 242-250.

In the face of continuing Soviet secrecy about its political
process and defense matters, it is impossible for Western observers to reach clear-cut conclusions about the role of the Soviet
military in arms control. While the military does not necessarily
think about arms control as a unified group, its voice on arms
control is coordinated, probably within the General Staff. There
are no examples of the Soviet military initiating a significant
arms control measure; the political leadership initiates such
policies and the military often at least begins by opposing them.
Early Soviet proposals set the precedent of seeking to counter
Western strength by means other than simply building arms.
The military's active role in SALT probably contributed significantly to the lack of friction in its participation in SALT and the
agreements that have been reached. Presumably, differences
over particular policies -- though rarely, if ever, political conflict -- result from the more conservative stance of the Soviet
military over arms control, as opposed to the political leadership.
But although the Soviet military feels that arms control threatens
some aspects of its professional interest, arms control does not
seem to have eroded the military's mission or essential place in
Soviet society and policy. In addition, arms control can reduce
the uncertainties in Soviet military planners, and funds not
spent on some weapons as a result of an arms control prohibition
may be used for other military purposes. Over the longer term,
the Soviet military's direct participation in negotiating agreements may alter its attitudes towards the value of arms control,
and even toward the adversary.

No. 475. Garthoff, Raymond L.
The Soviet High Command and and General Staff.
Santa Monica, California: The RAND Corporation (P-684), May
27, 1955, 18 p.

A paper on the organization of the armed forces under the
Soviet Ministry of Defense. The General Staff, the Stavka, the
military districts and groups of forces, and the political controls
in the Soviet armed forces are described.

Also published as a chapter in Basil H. Liddell Hart (Ed.), The Red Army (New York: Harcourt, Brace, and Co, 1956).

No. 476. Garthoff, Raymond L.
"SALT and the Soviet Military."
Problems of Communism Vol. 24 No. 1 (January 1975), pp. 21-37.

In November 1969 the USSR and the United States commenced formal talks on the limitation of strategic arms. These talks, commonly known as SALT, led in May 1972 to a treaty between the two powers restricting the deployment of antiballistic missile systems and to an interim agreement on the limitation of strategic offensive arms. During the subsequent phases of the negotitions, popularly called SALT II, the exchanges have focused on further reductions on strategic offensive weapons systems. General Secretary Leonid Brezhnev and President Gerald Ford reached agreement at Vladivostok in November 1974 on the basis for negotiating, during 1975, a 10-year limitation agreement covering such offensive arms. The talks themselves have been private, and the diplomatic record remains closed. But the following record presents observations and reflections on one important aspect of SALT by a direct participant in the negotiations for more than three years, written from his personal perspective.

Response by Lewis A. Frank, and reply by Garthoff, Problems of Communism Vol. 24 No. 2 (September-October 1975), p. 88.

Reprinted as "The Soviet Military and SALT," Chapter 6 in John Baylis and Gerald Segal (Eds.), Soviet Strategy (Monclair, N.J.: Allanheld, Osmun, and Company, 1981), pp. 154-184.

No. 477. Ghebhardt, Alexander O.; and William Schneider, Jr.
"The Soviet High Command: Recent Changes and Policy Implications."
Military Review Vol. 53 No. 5 (May 1973), pp. 3-14.

Since World War II there have been three major shakeups of the Soviet High Command. The first, in 1946, occured when Stalin discarded most of the wartime leadership to ensure the postwar reliability and loyalty of the armed forces. The second, in 1957, was the direct result of Marshal Zhukov's ouster as Defense Minister. Limited changes were made in the Soviet High Command in 1967 following the death of Defense Minister Marshal Malinovsky. These changes were a precursor of major changes which took place in 1972.

No. 478. Ghebhardt, Alexander O.; and William Schneider, Jr.
"The Soviet Air Force High Command."

Air University Review Vol. 24 No. 4 (May-June 1973), pp. 75-83.

The organizational structure of the Soviet Air Force is a useful vehicle for an understanding of the fundamental military concepts and doctrine that support the raison d'etre of the military organization. This is especially true of Soviet armed forces because of their acute general awareness of the necessity that organizational form follows doctrinal underpinnings. The Soviet armed forces in general and Air Force in particular have departed radically from the Western form of military organization to meet their specific and unique requirements. All branches of the Soviet armed forces are subordinate to a single Minister of Defense, a key element of the post-Stalin reorganization of the Soviet armed forces in 1953.

No. 479. Glagolev, Igor S.
"The Soviet Decision-Making Process in Arms-Control Negotiations."
Orbis Vol. 21 No. 4 (Winter 1978), pp. 767-776.

The terms of the SALT agreements both reflect the real correlation of forces in the international arena and induce changes in that correlation. Since Soviet decisions in arms control and strategic force planning -- along with decisions of a completely different character in the United States -- played a decisive role in the shift, it is useful to examine the characteristics of such Soviet decision-making: 1) the process is continuous, with hundreds of persons participating as new and more effective weapons systems are periodically tested and deployed; 2) the vast majority of the Soviet population is not informed by the government about the deployment of weapons systems, nor does it participate in the decision-making process; 3) the sale of strategic and conventional armament in the USSR is limited by the capacity of the Soviet economy, not the exhortations of foreign diplomats; 4) the number of participants in discussions of strategic problems is restricted, as are the number of documents prepared; and 5) problems concerning the limitation of strategic arms are viewed in the USSR as military questions, not as problems of disarmament. On the whole, the entire decision-making process with respect to the Soviet position on SALT gives preponderant expression to the interests and objectives of the military-industrial complex.

No. 480. Goure, Daniel.
"C^3 and the New Soviet Nuclear Forces."
Signal Vol. 41 No. 4 (December 1986), pp. 86-89.

Over the past six years, the Soviet military press has made frequent references to the "strategic nuclear forces." Some analysts have concluded that these references mean that the

Soviet Union has organized its strategic nuclear forces into a single unified command resembling the U.S. Strategic Air Command but also including submarines carrying ballistic missiles. Others believe that these references do not reflect a change of organizational affiliation but one of strategy. Either conclusion would have profound implications for understanding the organization and command and control (C^2) of those branches of the Soviet armed forces concerned with the mission of conducting strategic strikes, the way the Soviet military views strategic nuclear war, and the relationship between nuclear and non-nuclear warfare in Soviet military strategy.

No. 481. Hart, Douglas M.
"Soviet Approaches to Crisis Management: The Military Dimension."
Survival Vol. 26 No. 5 (September-October 1984), pp. 200-234.

This paper explores the military steps which the Warsaw Pact could be expected to take in the course of an East-West crisis in central Europe, based on an assessment of Soviet doctrinal, force level, and exercise trends, as well as actual Soviet military behavior during the 1973 Yom Kippur War. Discussion of crisis scenarios is followed by examination of military activity which could be used to reinforce diplomatic signals, and actions that Soviet military planners would probably consider necessary to support the Soviet leadership should the decision be made at some point that war is inevitable. It concludes with some general observations on Soviet notions of instability, escalation, and crisis management.

No. 482. Hemsley, J.
"Command Technology: Voennaya Sistemotekhnika. An Algorithmic Approach to Decision-making."
RUSI Journal Vol. 125 No. 3 (September 1980), pp. 58-64.

Many Western analysts fail to approach and define their investigations into Soviet military thinking and practice from a Russian viewpoint; nowhere is this weakness more apparent than in the area of command and control. The current phase of the Soviet "revolution in military affairs" has seen considerable debate revolve around the role and introduction of military cybernetics, with discussion focusing on the scale and degree to which automation should be required. The advent of nuclear battlefield tactics, with their consequential impact on operational doctrine, imparted an added importance to the subjects. Detailed investigation of work by V. Druzhinin and D. Kontorov entitled Idea, Algorithm, Decision (Moscow: Voenizdat, 1972) gives insight into the views of a vocal and influential section of the Soviet military convinced that the integration of automation equipment into the command and staff organization was the only solution to the problem of decision-making under these conditions. One important reason for examining this book is that it appears in all Soviet military instructional institutions and forms part of the required reading for officers and cadets. Another is that it shows the Soviet technical, methodological, and philosophical approach to command and control at a time when the Soviet military is uncertain of its potential performance under conditions of general war.

No. 483. Hemsley, John.
Soviet Troop Control: The Role of Command Technology in the Soviet Military System.
Oxford: Brassey's Publishers Limited, 1982, 276 p.

Advances in automated command and control systems have generated a new area of military science, that of battlefield cybernetics. Like their Western counterparts, Soviet military commanders have closely investigated its relevance to operational tempo, structure and logistics, information evaluation and man-machine matching, as well as the pronounced consequences for leadership, initiative and training. No Western work until now has examined the impact of command technology [voyennaya sistemotekhnika] on orthodox command and control theory [upravleniye voyskami]. This work focuses upon Soviet modeling and quantification methods.

No. 484. Holloway, David.
"Strategic Concepts and Soviet Policy."
Survival Vol. 13 No. 11 (November 1971), pp. 364-369.

The discussion, between the United States and the Soviet Union, of certain fundamental issues of strategy and arms control would contribute to a mutual understanding through which specific agreements could be reached. This article examines Soviet military-strategic thinking in the light of these issues, and considers its role in Soviet policy-making, particularly the decision to take part in SALT. The complexity of the relationship between concepts and policy makes it imperative to take into account the relationships between the various institutions involved in the making of strategic policy. Present Soviet policy seems to be the result of a compromise reached in 1968 to pursue SALT, and at the same time continue to deploy strategic armaments. The study of Soviet policy must go beyond the analysis of concepts to that of immensely complex political and bureaucratic processes.

No. 485. Holloway, David.
"Decision-Making in Soviet Defense Policies."
In Prospects of Soviet Power in the 1980s, Part II.
London: International Institute for Strategic Studies (Adelphi Paper No. 152), Summer 1979, pp. 24-31.

This article examines the structure of the Soviet policy-making process, the pressures and influences that come into play, and the way in which Soviet security concerns are formulated. It asks whether knowledge of the decision-making process makes it possible to determine which Western policies might influence Soviet decisions in the direction of restraint, cooperation, and arms control. The formal structure of the defense decision-making process is not very different from that which existed under Stalin, but the informal process has changed in important ways. The Brezhnev Politburo is more responsive to the different elements in the Party-state bureaucracy; wherever a policy is controversial, the effort is made to assuage doubts with compensating measures. Some general predictions can be made about Soviet defense policymaking in the 1980s: 1) Party leadership will remain dominant, but military influences will remain strong; 2) Major shifts in policy are unlikely as long as the present leadership is in charge; 3) if the Soviet Union faces serious economic problems in the 1980s, a strong pressure for a shift of resources away from the military will arise within the Party-State bureaucracy; and 4) the possibility that the West could influence Soviet defense policy is remote.

No. 486.   Jacobsen, C.G.
Soviet Strategy -- Soviet Foreign Policy: Military Considerations Affecting Soviet Policy Making.
Glasgow: Robert Maclehose and Co., Ltd. (The University Press), 1972, 269 p. (Second edition, 1974.)

This book, in considering the role of the military as a pressure group affecting Soviet foreign policy, contends that although the armed forces constitute one of the policy-effecting instruments at the disposition of the political leadership, the armed forces establishment is integrated into this political leadership to an extent which entails considerable influence on the choice of instruments. In support of this thesis, it addresses recent Soviet naval developments, increases in the Soviet defense budget, and the noticeable presence within the party system of military professionals. Its conclusion is that while the Soviet Party will not permit a challenge from the military to its societal role, the pressures in the international arena of the 1970s will require it to tolerate a greater degree of flexibility in regard to the military's position and influence.

No. 487.   Kolkowicz, Roman.
"The Military and Soviet Foreign Policy."
Journal of Strategic Studies Vol. 4 No. 4 (December 1981), pp. 337-355.

The foreign policy of the Soviet Union serves to promote its security and the power of the Communist Party, expand Soviet influence outside the country, and support and promote inter-

national communism in support of Soviet national interests.
A prime characteristic of Soviet foreign policy is its close
relationship to and dependence on military capabilities -- it
appears to be a function of military "reach" and scope. The
Soviet military is assuming increasing institutional and political
power and influence in the Soviet Union. If this persists, the
Party leadership will find itself progressively more dependent
upon the military, the military's style and preferences will
become more pervasive in national policy, and the Party and
military leadership will institutionize this changed relationship.
The Soviet military has a vast arsenal based in a war-
preparedness indoctrinated society. Its growth is apparently
uninfluenced by theories, policies, and fantasies of detente,
deterrence, and arms control. The Soviet military seems in
search of a goal that would go beyond the static balances and
inertias of deterrence.

No. 488.   Lambeth, Benjamin S.
Arms Control and Defense Planning in Soviet Strategic Policy.
Santa Monica, Calif.:   The RAND Corporation (P-6644), July
1981, 20 p.

A perspective on how Soviet arms control strategies should be
understood, with emphasis on the important differences between
the Soviet approach and that pursued by the United States.
The paper examines the role assigned to arms control in the
overall Soviet concept of national security, reviews specific
examples suggested by the apparent linkage between Soviet ICBM
modernization programs and SALT negotiating positions, and
highlights those features of the Soviet SALT policymaking
context that most clearly illustrate the close integration of arms
control and force planning in Soviet defense deliberations.

No. 489.   Lambeth, Benjamin S.
Risk and Uncertainty in Soviet Deliberations About War.
Santa Monica, Calif.:   The RAND Corporation (R-2687-AF),
October 1981, 28 p.

Surveys the elements of risk, uncertainty, and unpredictability
that might moderate Soviet behavior and undermine the
confidence with which Soviet decision-makers would consider
entering into a major military engagement with the United States.
Although the report does not question the substantial threat
implications of Soviet force improvements that have been under
way in recent years, it does describe certain realities of Soviet
style and leadership concern about possible Soviet military
inadequacies that make the more ominous features of Soviet
doctrine and force development appear somewhat less alarming.
The analysis is based on a combination of evidence suggested by
past Soviet crisis behavior, information offered in Soviet
literature concerning the management and training of troops, and

inferences from known or suspected Soviet political practices, organizational characteristics, and operational concerns.

Reviewed by Jon Englund, The Friday Review of Defense Literature (82-1), January 8, 1982.

Reprinted in abridged form as "Uncertainties for the Soviet War Planner," International Security Vol. 7 No. 3 (Winter 1982-83), pp. 139-166.

No. 490. Mahoney, Shane E.
"Posture and Purpose of the Soviet Military."
Problems of Communism Vol. 28 No. 1 (January-February 1979), pp. 55-58.

Essay-review of Soviet Armed Forces Review Annual, David R. Jones (Ed.); The Future of Soviet Military Power, Lawrence L. Whetten (Ed.); Political Control of the Soviet Armed Forces, Michael G. Deane; and The Military in Contemporary Soviet Politics: An Institutional Analysis, by Edward L. Warner (Ed.). After noting that few Western observers, including the authors of these works, disagree that the Soviet Union is engaged in a large military buildup, the essay goes on to point out that the purposes behind it are unclear and in dispute. It contrasts the view of Erickson and the contributors to the Whetten volume, that there is a high correlation between Soviet military doctrine and the developing force posture, with that of Deane and Warner, who see the emerging Soviet military posture as less related to doctrine than to trade-offs between competing groups or institutional forces within Soviet society.

No. 491. McDonnell, John.
"The Organization of Soviet Military Defense and Military Planning."
Chapter 3 in Michael MccGwire and John McDonnell (Eds.), Soviet Naval Influences: Domestic and Foreign Dimensions.
New York: Praeger Publishers, 1977, pp. 61-106.

In detailing the institutional framework of Soviet defense/military policy making, this work provides a comprehensive history from 1918. It includes a discussion of military councils, and of the organization of the Ministry of Defense and the five branches of service. It stresses the Soviet version of civilian control of the armed forces (i.e., political officials constituting "defense leadership" as constrasted with the professional "military leadership." It also seeks to establish a relationship, over the past two decades, between Central Committee plenums and the resolution of military policy. Three occasions are described when attendance at Central Committee plenums appears to have been temporarily expanded to include the entire military leadership, on occasions when key military decisions were "ratified."

No. 492. Olmstead, Freeman B.
The Soviet Ministry of Defense: Some Aspects of Its Professional
Behavior and Its Possible Reaction to United States Policy
Initiatives.
Maxwell Air Force Base, Ala.: Air Command and Staff College
(Research Study No. 1460-71), 1971, 65 p.

Recent studies of the Soviet military establishment have highlighted periodic differences of opinion between Soviet military
and political leaders. These differences have been described in
historical, situational, and ideological terms. The study suggests
the existence of functional military imperatives within the Ministry
of Defense, which would explain Soviet military behavior in the
cited debates. The study concludes that these purely military
motives could continue to be at variance with the international
objectives of the Communist Party of the Soviet Union. It recom-
mends that consideration of Soviet military motivational and be-
havioral patterns be included in the U.S. policy process.

No. 493. Pappageorge, John G.
"The Development of Soviet Military Policy."
Military Review Vol. 52 No. 7 (July 1972), pp. 36-43.

Once again there seems to be a correlation between U.S. and
Soviet military development. If the Soviets are, in fact, still
following along in our footsteps, then they need to follow closely
the military developments that accrue from the Nixon doctrine to
see what direction their own evolution will take. On the other
hand, we should watch carefully Soviet military developments --
particularly military budget outlays -- to get an indication of
their recent foreign policy decisions reached in secret at the last
Communist Party Congress.

No. 494. Porter, Richard E.
Soviet Military Decision-making: A Framework for Analysis.
Santa Monica, Calif.: The RAND Corporation (N-1515-AF),
June 1980, 39 p.

This note explores Soviet decision-making on behalf of those with
a special interest in the long-term directions of Soviet military
policy. Consequently, it approaches the topic from a different
perspective and introduces a methodology derived from an
analysis of cognitive processes. Using this methodology, it then
identifies a structured decision-making process based on some
novel insights about Soviet decision-making and the special
political-military relationships that accompany it.

Also published in Kenneth M. Currie and Gregory Varhall
(Eds.), The Soviet Union: What Lies Ahead? (Washington,
D.C.: Government Printing Office, 1985), pp. 6-20.

No. 495. Rehm, Allan S.
An Assessment of Military Operations Research in the USSR.
Alexandria, Va.: Center for Naval Analyses (AD 770116), September 1973, 19 p.

This paper has four sections followed by conclusions and an assessment. The first section concerns the historical development of operations research in the USSR and related areas along with some comments on the political background in which this occurred. The second section discusses open Soviet military literature in general, and is intended to point out both its abundance, and how it shows that they follow our own open literature very closely. The third section looks briefly at each of the several Soviet books on military operations research with some comparisons with our own literature. The final section looks at what can be discerned from the literature taken as a whole with regards to personalities, organization, and trends.

No. 496. Scott, Harriet Fast.
"The Soviet High Command."
Air Force Magazine (Soviet Aerospace Almanac No. 3) Vol. 60 No. 3 (March 1977), pp. 52-56.

Much is written in the United States about deterrent concepts, arms control, and other related concepts. The utility of these concepts is directly related to understanding of probable Soviet reactions. This requires detailed knowledge of Soviet decision-making bodies, as well as of military command and control (C^2). Studying the Soviet high command is one key to this understanding. It consists of three bodies: the Council of Defense, the Main Military Council, and the General Staff. Attached to them are other such agencies as the Military-Industrial Commission and the General Staff's Scientific-Technical Committee. The Soviet high command represents one of the most experienced bodies of political-military leadership the world has ever seen. It knits military and political leadership into a seamless fabric. The differences between U.S. and Soviet military organization at the top level, and the implications of Soviet centralization of authority, need to be understood by U.S. policymakers.

No. 497. Scott, Harriet Fast; and William F. Scott.
The Soviet Control Structure: Capabilities for Wartime Survival.
New York: Crane, Russak and Company, Inc., 1983, 146 p.

A nation's leadership must be able to maintain effective control over its people and economy in the event of war. The procurement and mobilization measures required for successful military operations demand stringent control mechanisms. The possible use of nuclear weapons would place unprecedented strains on political and military leaders as well as on society as a whole. How does the Soviet leadership view this subject, and what do such views mean about Soviet politico-military intentions? This book is an analysis of the total Soviet Party-military control organization, starting with the agencies of the Communist Party and government, and extending down through the KGB, MVD, Armed Forces, and Civil Defense establishment. The examination of the multi-faceted and overlapping elements of the Soviet control structure, including trade unions, "volunteer" groups, and legislative devices such as martial law, is based on Soviet sources. It traces the historical roots of Soviet control measures and discusses Soviet civil defense preparations, command and control responsibilities, and the psychological indoctrination of the population for the possibility of conflict in a nuclear environment.

No. 498. Spielmann, Karl F.
Analyzing Soviet Strategic Arms Decisions.
Boulder, Colo.: Westview Press, 1978, 184 p.

The importance to Western policymakers of determining the significance of Soviet strategic arms decisions is matched by the difficulty of doing so. The high stakes involved and, in many cases, the inadequacy of evidence can all too easily lead to generalizations that rest more on passionate conviction than on accepted principles of scholarly inquiry. This book examines three approaches that might be pursued in juxtaposition in examining individual Soviet strategic arms decisions. The first two basically reflect two broad schools of thought on the Soviet-U.S. strategic arms relationship. They stress, alternatively, responsiveness to the international threat and internal bureaucratic and organizational processes as shapers of strategic arms programs. The third approach represents a middle ground that heretofore has not been emphasized. These three approaches are outlined without extensive elaboration to give an initial indication of the usefulness of juxtaposing discrete sets of analytic assumptions in addressing the whys and wherefores of a particular Soviet strategic arms decision. The concluding chapter demonstrates how a multiple-approach analysis might be begun in the case of the first Soviet ICBM, and gives suggestions for undertaking further analytic tasks of this sort.

Also printed as Institute for Defense Analyses Paper P-1256, April 1977.

Reviewed by Raymond L. Garthoff, Slavic Review Vol. 39 No. 4 (December 1980), p. 694.

No. 499. Warner, Edward L.
The Military in Contemporary Soviet Politics: An Institutional Analysis.
New York: Praeger Publishers, 1979, 314 p.

Aspects of the Soviet military establishment, including its organizational structure, weaponry, military doctrine, and apparent
role in formulating Soviet domestic and foreign policy, have been
extensively and intensively studied in the West. This study
attempts to develop a comprehensive framework for the orderly
integration of these concerns, and to demonstrate its utility
through specific applications to a number of Soviet military
policy issues. The framework is derived from two different
bodies of scholarly activity: the interest group and bureaucratic
politics schools of policy analysis. The issues examined in this
study show that the Soviet military establishment is an active
participant in Soviet politics. The Ministry of Defense expresses
and promotes a series of basic viewpoints and policy preferences,
and its efforts to advance these interests are enhanced by the
Soviet defense policy-making arrangements. The framework
established in this book allows the development of process-
oriented explanations or predictions of policy outcomes, although
data deficiences make informed speculation about the domestic
political display associated with these issues the best that can be
managed.

Reviewed by Shane Mahoney, "Posture and Purpose of the Soviet
Military," Problems of Communism Vol. 28 No. 1 (January-
February 1979), pp. 55-58; Timothy J. Colton, Soviet Studies
Vol. 31 No. 2 (April 1979), pp. 293-295.

No. 500. Whitton, Tommy J.
"Soviet Strategic Wartime Leadership."
In Kenneth M. Currie and Gregory Varhall (Eds.), The Soviet
Union: What Lies Ahead?
Washington, D.C.: Government Printing Office (Studies in Com-
munist Affairs Vol. 6), 1985, pp. 706-729.

This paper explores the question of how the Soviet Union would
control its military forces in the event of war. It examines the
World War II role of the State Defense Committee (GKO) and the
Supreme High Command (Stavka) and their control of the troops
in the field through the General Staff and intermediate commands.
If war should occur, a portion of the present Party Politburo
would consitute the new GKO and the current Defense Council
would become the Stavka. The Soviet leadership likely would
also create High Commands in theaters where major military
operations were being conducted.

No. 501. Wolfe, Thomas W.
Role of the Soviet Military in Decisionmaking and Soviet Politics.
Santa Monica, Calif.: The RAND Corporation (P-2767), July
1963, 19 p.

A look at the role of the military in Soviet policy formation on
the national, strategic, and internal levels, in light of recent

developments, especially the publication of Sokolovskiy's Military Strategy. The paper evaluates Soviet reviews of Sokolovskiy's book and subsequent articles and pamphlets relative to Party-military relations.

No. 502. Wolfe, Thomas W.
Comments on Lomov's "Soviet Military Doctrine".
Santa Monica, Calif.: The RAND Corporation (P-2816), October 1963, 17 p.

Comments on the May 1963 brochure by Colonel-General Professor N.A. Lomov. In an earlier article, Lomov had ascribed the formulation of military doctrine almost wholly to the military establishment; in this later one, he appears to give more recognition to the primacy of political leadership in military matters.

No. 503. Wolfe, Thomas W.
The Soviet Military Scene: Institutional and Defense Policy Considerations.
Santa Monica, Calif.: The RAND Corporation (RM-4913-PR), June 1966, 195 p.

Since Khrushchev's fall, the growing importance of professional expertise and the return to collective leadership have tended indirectly to strengthen the influence of military professionals on Soviet defense policy. The Party, however, is clearly determined to prevent the military from intruding into essentially political affairs. In any case, the military elite does not seem to want formal political power. Despite a heightened sense of group identity among the military, there are tensions between the technical experts of the armed forces and the more conservative, traditional type of officers. The political leadership has seemed uncertain and divided over the allocation of resources to economic and defense requirements. By the spring of 1966, military claims seemed to have an edge over stated economic goals. (Marshal Rotmistrov speaks for a group that would upgrade the ground-air theater forces.) The ambitious Soviet program of military research and development suggests a quest for qualitative excellence and new systems rather than a determination to alter radically the present strategic power balance. In spite of the present atmosphere of detente between the superpowers, it cannot be assumed that the Soviet Union is now ready to underwrite international instability and orderly change in concert with the United States.

No. 504. Wolfe, Thomas W.
Evolution of Soviet Military Policy.
Santa Monica, Calif.: The RAND Corporation (P-3773), February 1968, 40 p.

An analysis of Soviet military policy under the Brezhnev-Kosygin regime. Soviet efforts in the strategic field have been toward buildup of the strategic delivery forces and the strengthening of strategic defenses, including the initiation of ABM deployment. The regime also has attempted to improve the mobility of Soviet conventional or general-purpose forces, a process which has involved transforming the Soviet navy from its traditional role of a mere adjunct to Soviet land power into an instrument for global support of Soviet interests. Political-military relations, an area of recurrent tension during the 50 years of Soviet history, have taken on new significance in view of the special problems created by the nuclear age. These problems fall into three categories: 1) maintaining political control over the armed forces in times of crisis; 2) meshing industrial-military planning; and 3) balancing military influence on Soviet policy formulation against the need of political authorities to rely increasingly on the professional expertise of the military leadership.

Reprinted as Chapter 6 in John Strong (Ed.), The Soviet Union Under Brezhnev and Kosygin: The Transition Years (New York: Van Nostrand, Reinhold and Company, 1971), pp. 75-92.

No. 505. Wolfe, Thomas W.
Soviet Interests in SALT: Political, Economic, Bureaucratic, and Strategic Contributions and Impediments to Arms Control.
Santa Monica, Calif.: The RAND Corporation (P-4702), September 1971, 41 p.

Soviet participation in SALT will be affected by both international and domestic factors. The whole pattern of international politics is changing from bipolar confrontation to multipolar alignments. Moreover, Soviet foreign and military policy is tending toward globalism, and the Soviet state is now exhibiting a great power dynamism -- an energy and enthusiasm for playing the role of a great power in world affairs. Although economic pressures have helped to bring the Soviet Union to SALT talks, economic considerations have not been the prime determinant of Soviet strategic policy in the past, nor are they likely to be in the future. Soviet strategic policies are also influenced by several institutional and bureaucratic interest groups, including the foreign affairs intelligentsia, the scientific intelligentsia, the military, and the "military-industrial" complex. Soviet leaders will have to choose the strategic posture that will most effectively support their political and economic objectives: parity or superiority.

Reprinted in William R. Kintner and Robert Pfaltzgraff (Eds.), SALT: Implications for Arms Control in the 1970's (University of Pittsburg Press, 1973), pp. 21-54.

No. 506. Wolfe, Thomas W.
The Military Dimension in the Making of Soviet Foreign and Defense Policy.
Santa Monica, Calif.: The RAND Corporation (P-6024), October 1977, 44 p.

This paper discusses how military considerations enter into the making of Soviet foreign and security policy and how the substance of Soviet policy may be affected thereby. It reviews basic assumptions generally applied to analyzing the Soviet decision-making process and structure and operation of the decision-making bureaucracy, as well as the nature of Soviet civil-military relations. It notes that there is a division of labor between political and military, with the political leadership tending to leave the professional details of security planning to the military and reserving to itself the right of final decision, especially on issues involving large resources of war and peace. It concludes that growth and modernization of Soviet military power can be expected to continue and the Soviets, while not indifferent to negotiated limits on arms programs, are unlikely to accept a SALT agreement that would call for dismantling substantial portions of the military machine they are still in the process of building.

No. 507. Wolfe, Thomas W.
"The Soviet General Staff."
Problems of Communism Vol. 28 No. 1 (January-February 1978), pp. 51-54.

This essay-review uses two recent works, John Erickson's Road to Stalingrad (New York: Harper and Row, 1975) and Marshal of the Soviet Union V.G. Kulikov's Academy of the General Staff (Moscow: Voyenizdat, 1976) as points of departure for a discussion of the structure, function, and role of the Soviet General Staff. It begins by outlining the role played by the General Staff in preparing for the Second World War, including its purge by Stalin in 1937-38. Much attention is given to the General Staff's key role in the war, including the 1960s "Front-Center" debate between retired operational commanders and General Staff officers. It concludes with a brief discussion of the role of the General Staff in both the evolution of Soviet military theory and the practical management of Soviet military power.

B. DEFENSE ECONOMICS AND SYSTEMS ACQUISITIONS

No. 508. Alexander, Arthur J.
The Process of Soviet Weapons Design.
Santa Monica, Calif.: The RAND Corporation (P-6137), March 1978, 37 p.

Traces how Soviet institutions, constraints, incentives, and values influence the process of Soviet weapons design. Differences between U.S. and Soviet military capabilities do not arise from differences in resources, but from the processes and choices that determine how those resources are employed. Design of Soviet weapons can be summarized by their outstanding features: simplicity in equipment; common use of subsystems, components and parts; incremental growth; and limited performance and missions capabilities. On the whole Soviet weapons technology is less advanced than comparable U.S. weapons technology, yet there is considerable evidence that these shortcomings often do not result in lesser military value. Incremental change has become the hallmark of Soviet weapons acquisitions. This strategy has advantages that are valuable in the Soviet context, and can be expected to continue into the future. Presented at Technology Trends Colloquium, U.S. Naval Academy, March 1978.

No. 509. Alexander, Arthur J.
Soviet Science and Weapons Acquistion.
Santa Monica, Calif.: The RAND Corporation (R-2942-NAS), August 1982, 42 p.

This report describes Soviet weapons acquisition and its ties to Soviet science; it then discusses the logic of restricting the transfer of scientific information, which is categorized into several classes. The report specifically discusses organizations in Soviet weapons R&D and science, the Soviet weapons acquistion process, characteristics of Soviet weapons design, science ties to the Soviet military, types of linkages between science and the military, the nature of scientific support, and the logic of controlling scientific information transfer.

No. 510. Alexander, A.J.; A.S. Becker, and W.E. Hoehn, Jr.
The Significance of Divergent U.S.-USSR Military Expenditure.
Santa Monica, Calif.: The RAND Corporation (N-1000-AF), February 1979, 57 p.

Due to steady increases in Soviet military expenditure over the last 15 years, plus sharp decreases in U.S. outlays in the 1970s, the size of Soviet military programs has exceeded that of the United States for several years. The margin has been widening and is forecast to persist. The disparity in many mission outlay areas is impressively large: a three-to-one advantage to the Soviet Union in Strategic Forces; about 75 percent more than the U.S. for General Purpose Forces; and near parity with the U.S. in Support Forces. In military investment the Soviet margin has been 50 to 80 percent above the U.S. These disparities constitute an additional indicator that the U.S. needs military effort. However, the so-called "defense spending gap" cannot indicate the U.S. effort required. The latter depends on the mix of military capabilities necessary to meet peacetime crisis and long-term competition criteria.

No. 511. Becker, Abraham S.
Soviet Military Outlays Since 1955.
Santa Monica, Calif.: The RAND Corporation (RM-3886-PR), July 1964, 199 p.

A survey and elaboration of open-source information on the growth of total Soviet military outlays since 1955. As the first detailed view of what is and is not known about Soviet military outlays, the study may also contribute to the discussion on budgetary disarmament. The starting point of the analysis is the explicit Soviet budget allocation to "defense." After concluding that additional military outlays, over and above this defense appropriation, must be presumed to exist, the rest of the Memorandum is devoted to the estimation of concealed expenditures and the evaluation of these estimates.

No. 512. Becker, Abraham S.
Soviet Growth, Resource Allocation, and Military Outlays.
Santa Monica, Calif.: The RAND Corporation (P-4135), June 1969, 10 p.

This statement before a Congressional subcommittee addressed the Soviet Union's economic capability to accomplish its military objectives. The peacetime growth rate of aggregate output has been notably rapid, but is seems unlikely that it can be raised much above the level achieved in recent years. Nor should the possibility of a decline be ruled out, if attempts at patchwork repairs to the economic mechanism prove unsuccessful. But the USSR is rich in physical and human resources, and muddling through may still carry it a long way. The ceiling has apparently been reached on the rate of investment attainable under the present arrangement, and relative stability also characterizes the shares of the major sectors of consumption and defense. This does not mean that the Soviet Union will not be able to maintain its strong and growing military machine. Given growth increments at least as large as those obtained in recent years, it should be able to continue building up the forces to help meet national objectives.

No. 513. Becker, Abraham S.
CIA Estimates of Soviet Military Expenditure.
Santa Monica, Calif.: The RAND Corporation (P-6534), August 1980, 18 p.

Focuses on the public debate over the size and growth of Soviet military expenditure and the estimates of these indicators made by the CIA. The subject is surrounded by controversy because of Soviet secrecy, the CIA's reluctance to disclose sources and methods, technical complexities, and the political sensitivities of the results, which have an important casual bearing on U.S. military outlays. In this context, the paper makes a number of judgements on the validity of the CIA estimates and major current concerns. Statement prepared for hearings before the Sub-committee on Oversight of the House Permanent Select Committee on Intelligence, 3 September 1980.

No. 514. Becker, Abraham S.
Guns, Butter, and Tools: Tradeoffs in Soviet Resource Allocation.
Santa Monica, Calif.: The RAND Corporation (P-6816), October 1982, 17 p.

An "overview" of three papers in the area of Soviet military economics. One of the three papers is concerned with the tradeoffs between defense and GNP or consumption. The second focuses on tradeoffs between military and nonmilitary uses of machinery production, while the third is directed to Soviet leadership choices between defense and investment. It appears that cutting back on military expenditure growth is not a panacea for the Soviet economic dilemma in the short run. Yet the military budget does impose a burden on the economy and the leadership may not be able to ignore that reality indefinitely. Nevertheless, the case for skepticism with respect to the likelihood of a change in Soviet resource allocation policy still seems strong, as sharp decreases in the military budget would threaten the cherished beliefs and fundamental interests of the most powerful groups in the society. If their opposition is to be overcome, it will probably require a much bleaker economic picture than is presently visible, and a new set of leaders in the Kremlin.

No. 515. Becker, Abraham S.
Sitting on Bayonets? The Soviet Defense Burden and Moscow's Economic Dilemma.
Santa Monica, Calif.: The RAND Corporation (P-6908), September 1983, 35 p.

This paper discusses three issues: the level of Soviet military expenditure and the size of the resulting burden on the economy; current Soviet resource allocation policy dilemmas and the role of the military-economic system in their generation and possible future resolution; and the implications of the inter-connections between defense spending and overall resource allocation for future growth of the military budget. The paper concludes that on political as well as economic grounds the best bet on future development is that the Kremlin will continue to be reluctant to embark on an intensive arms race requiring major acceleration of defense spending. However, economic difficulties would not prevent a vigorous Kremlin response to perceived intensification of the external threat to Soviet security.

Reprinted as Chapter 8 in Roman Kolkowicz and Ellen Mickiewicz (Eds.), The Soviet Calculus of Nuclear War (Lexington, Mass.: Lexington Books, 1986), pp. 171-204.

No. 516. Checinski, Michael.
"The Soviet War-Economic Doctrine in the Years of Military-Technological Challenge (1946-1983): An Overview."
Crossroads No. 12 (1984), pp. 23-51.

The war-economic doctrine and resultant policies are the most stable factors of all major decisions of the Soviet leaders in the sectors of both economy and defense. It follows that for Western policymakers concerned with estimating Soviet military capabilities and Soviet long-range military-political aims, an analysis of the Soviet war-economic doctrine and policy could become a primary source of information. For a number of reasons the war-economic aspects of the Soviet defense policy have usually been neglected in Western assessments. This article attempts to fill some gaps in the present knowledge in this field.

No. 517. Deane, Michael J.; and Mark E. Miller.
"Science and Technology in Soviet Military Planning."
Strategic Review Vol. 5 No. 3 (Summer 1977), pp. 77-86.

The Soviet Union's emphasis on military development as a key factor in the correlation of forces places great importance on the relationship of science and technology to the economy. Soviet leaders appear convinced that a strong link between military-related production and scientific-technical innovation will provide the Soviet armed forces with the most advanced weaponry and equipment. Scientific research establishments, especially in military areas, are encouraged to exhibit the innovativeness, flexibility, and foresight necessary to respond to the demands of fluctuating trends in military developments to ensure that Soviet weaponry remains unsurpassed. Fearing a weapons breakthrough by the United States, the Soviet Union seeks to conclude an agreement banning new weapons systems while pursuing further qualitative improvement of its own weapons and equipment. Stressing the importance of technological initiative, Soviet war-winning doctrine mandates achieving and maintaining strategic superiority.

No. 518. Field, Brian.
"Soviet Military Expenditure Estimates: Meaning and Measurement."
NATO Review Vol. 34 No. 4 (August 1986), pp. 28-31.

Too often, an unwarrented precision and accuracy is attributed to estimates of Soviet military expenditures. This article reviews the way in which different estimates are built up and what they purport to measure. The great utility of expenditure estimates is that they combine dissimilar items into summary measures. In spite of many differences of detail, independent Western analyses using the building block approach do show essential agreement concerning overall magnitudes and longer term trends in Soviet military activities.

No. 519. Garthoff, Raymond L.
Recent Trends in Soviet Military Policy.
Santa Monica, California: The RAND Corporation (P-726), August 30, 1955, 10 p.

This paper provides a discussion of the Soviet Union's attempt to ease international tension by recently reducing its armed forces. It suggests that the primary Soviet objective is designed to reallocate manpower resources, shift an overly strong sector of national power to the understrength economic sector, balance the armed forces between the Soviet bloc and NATO, and demonstrate the "new look" in Soviet strategic thinking.

Published in Combat Forces Journal, October 1955.

No. 520. Gordon, Michael R.
"Rubles for Defense -- Are the Soviets Really Outspending the Pentagon?"
National Journal Vol. 13 No. 15 (April 11, 1981), pp. 601-604.

Estimates of Soviet and American defense spending over the last ten years vary widely, but there is no doubt that the Soviet Union greatly increased its forces during the 1970s. Assessing Soviet defense spending is important to American strategic decision-making, and it serves as a guide to future Soviet military capabilities. The CIA method of calculating Soviet defense expenditures overestimates Soviet procurement and manpower costs. Soviet military spending may be as high as fifteen percent -- this places a severe strain on the Soviet economy.

No. 521. Holloway, David.
"Technological Change and Military Procurement."
Chapter 5 in Michael MccGwire and John McDonnell (Eds.),
Soviet Naval Influence: Domestic and Foreign Dimensions.
New York: Praeger Publishers, 1977, pp. 123-131.

This essay describes a society suffering from insufficient developmental facilities, reluctance of factories to innovate and endanger plan fulfillment, administrative barriers between the research and development system and the industrial producer, and an intruding economic planning system. Yet technological progress seems to be more rapid in the defense sector than in civilian industry. This is because the defense sector is able to achieve a "consumer sovereignty" rare elsewhere in the Soviet Union, because of pressure on its behalf from the political leadership of the country. A postulated procurement process for the Soviet Navy is sketched out in this work. It develops the thesis that the Navy is in the forefront of exploring new scientific techniques and approaches. However, most of the scientific research is actually conducted outside the defense sector.

No. 522. Holzman, Franklyn D.
Financial Checks on Soviet Defense Expenditures.
Lexington, Mass.: Lexington Books, 1975, 103 p.

This study was undertaken in the hope that it would contribute to the achievement of peace by facilitating a reduction in Soviet and American military expenditures. The USSR has several times proposed before the United Nations that the major powers agree to reduce their military expenditures by ten or fifteen percent. This book examines this type of proposal, particularly to try to deal with some of the obvious obstacles to its adoption by the U.S. government. It attempts the following: to clarify the problems involved in financial verification of reductions in military expenditures in light of the paucity of data provided by the USSR; to spell out the kinds of data that might be required for verification; and, if possible, to devise verification techniques that would be sufficiently unintrusive to be acceptable to the USSR as well as other major nations.

No. 523. Holzman, Franklyn D.
"Are the Soviets Really Outspending the U.S. on Defense?"
International Security Vol. 4 No. 4 (Spring 1980), pp. 86-104.

This article has two purposes. The first is to expose several sources of bias in CIA comparisons of U.S. and Soviet military expenditures which in every case exaggerate Soviet defense expenditures. In addition, the implications of these flawed estimates for the national security debate are critical and should be brought to light. Two obvious sources of bias are the failures to take account of the higher quality of U.S. military personnel and equipment. Further suspicion of bias stems from the fact that "index number effects" are smaller than those usually experienced in U.S.-Soviet comparisons. The CIA might claim that it cannot make precise estimates of some of these factors, but in that event they should make either imprecise estimates or none at all. For the errors of estimate which result do not cancel each other out -- they reinforce each other so that a totally false picture of Soviet strength emerges. Second,

there are undoubtedly Soviet counterparts to the CIA that cal-
culate U.S. defense expenditures in rubles. They are also
likely to possess asymmetric loss functions that would lead them
to overstate U.S. military outlays, so that each nation might
escalate spending continually under the impression it was behind.
This is a plausible explanation for the continuous rise over the
past decade in Soviet defense spending.

No. 524.   Hopkins, M.M.; M.P. Kennedy, and M.F. Lawrence.
The Tradeoff Between Consumption and Military Expenditures
for the Soviet Union During the 1980s.
Santa Monica, Calif.: The RAND Corporation (R-2927-NA),
November 1982, 111 p.

This study develops a relatively new approach to the modeling of
the Soviet economy that uses optimal control theory. The resulting Hopkins-Kennedy optimal control model is used to address
the primary research question of the study: What will be the
tradeoff between Soviet consumption and defense spending during
the 1980s? Section II is devoted to the model. Its strength is
indicated by a number of historical scenarios in Section III in
which the model makes predictions which can be checked against
what actually occurs. Section IV examines the implications of
an alternative view of Soviet economic history, put forth by
Rosefielde and Lee. Section V examines demographic change, in
terms of both growth of the labor force and its ethnic composition. The impact of differing rates of productivity growth and a
scenario in which poor weather continues into the next decade
are studied in Section VI. Section VII describes the impact of
the increasing cost of energy. Foreign trade, which is likely to
play a central role in the Soviet economy in the next decade, is
examined in detail in Section VIII. Section IX compares a best
case and a worse case scenario.

No. 525.   Hopkins, M.M.; and M.P. Kennedy.
Comparisons and Implications of Alternative Views of the Soviet
Economy.
Santa Monica, Calif.: The RAND Corporation (R-3075-NA), March
1984, 77 p.

This report uses the Hopkins-Kennedy optimal control model of
the Soviet Union to explore the implications of and make
comparisons between three "worlds" (views) that hold differing
assumptions concerning the nature of the Soviet economy. These
are the "Birman world," the "CIA world," and the "Rosefielde-
Lee world." A secondary object is to investigate a large number
of scenarios concerning foreign trade so as to improve understanding of this important aspect of the Soviet economy.

No. 526. Jacobs, Walter Darnell.
"Soviet Strategic Effectiveness."
Journal of International Affairs Vol. 26 No. 1 (1972), pp.60-71.

Recent statistics indicate that the Soviet Union now has the initiative in weapons technology over the United States. It now has a mixed military establishment capable of supporting all foreign policy goals and of neutralizing or overcoming American counter-capabilities. While Soviet planners probably never set a specific date for attaining strategic superiority, neither did U.S. planners actually intend to accept strategic inferiority. Both reacted to objective conditions within their political frameworks with the almost inevitable result of American slippage in the Soviet drive for superiority. Soviet planners, working under political leadership, have developed these forces, slowly at first but now rapidly, while American planners, working more within the parameters of public opinion, have observed a decline in U.S. power to the point that one can foresee American security endangered. In any current comparison, it is clear that the Soviet military-industrial complex has been more efficient than its American counterpart. Both military-industrial complexes have their problems, and will continue to have them, but the prognosis for the Soviet military-industrial complex is good while that for the American complex is uncertain.

No. 527. Lee, William T.
"The 'Politico-Military-Industrial Complex' of the USSR."
Journal of International Affairs Vol. 26 No. 1 (1972), pp. 73-86.

In reviewing the Soviet counterpart of the U.S. "military-industrial complex," it is useful to distinguish four aspects: the institutional structure devoted to the organization of weapons development and production; the characteristics and quantities of the weapons systems actually fielded; the principle tenets of Sovit military doctrine; and the budget trends and economic consequences of military programs. The Soviet military-industrial complex appears to be a thriving and productive concern, and according to current Soviet planning will receive a steady substantial increase in its budget through 1975. Only a SALT agreement would appear to be a threat to the military's claim to some ten percent of Soviet GNP for at least several more years.

No. 528. Lee, William T.
"Soviet Defense Spending: Planned Growth, 1976-1980."
Strategic Review Vol. 5 No. 1 (Winter 1977), pp. 74-79.

Soviet defense spending is a subject of uncertainty and controversy. Although the CIA recently doubled its estimates, the new estimates continue to understate both the magnitude and rate of growth of Soviet defense expenditures. Yet reasonable approximations of current Soviet spending and future plans can

272

be derived from routinely published data. Planned growth can
be estimated both from data on national income shares and from
planned outlays for procurement. Estimates of actual expenditures can be inferred from performance data routinely published about eighteen months after the fact, and can be checked
by an independent budget analysis. The continued growth of
Soviet defense expenditures both absolutely and as a share of
GNP for nearly twenty years, and the projected growth for the
next five, reflect Soviet priorities. Soviet defense spending
policies evidently are based on a broad, stable consensus within
the Soviet power elite. Soviet leaders have been increasingly
explicit about the contribution of their growing military power to
the success of their policy of "peaceful coexistence." Soviet
defense expenditures are consistent with their stated objective of
achieving qualitiative and quantitative superiority over the
military forces of the United States and its allies.

No. 529. Lee, William T.
Estimation of Soviet Defense Expenditures, 1955-75: An Uncon-
ventional Approach.
New York: Praeger Publishers, 1977, 358 p.

This study has five principle objectives: 1) to evaluate the
alternative methodologies currently used to estimate Soviet
national security expenditures (NSE); 2) provide an alternative
estimate of Soviet NSE; 3) demonstrate the sensitivity of the
direct-costing approach to its underlying assumptions and explore
the possibility of reconciling the results with Soviet data; 4)
provide some preliminary comparisons of trends in the magnitude
and structure of U.S. and Soviet NSE; and 5) outline the policy
implications of alternative measures of Soviet NSE. The study
outlines and analyzes the alternative methods of determining
Soviet NSE (CIA, SRI, and the unconventional method developed
in this study). It describes the data base of each and presents
and documents estimates of national security durables, operations
and maintenance, military research development test and evaluation, and space. It compares the results with the findings of
the CIA and SRI approaches in the context of the Soviet State
budgets, national income, and GNP. Finally, it offers a partial
analysis of the impact of NSE on the Soviet economy.

No. 530. Lee, William T.
Soviet Defense Expenditures in an Era of SALT.
Washington, D.C.: United States Strategic Institute (USSI Report
79-1), 1979, 31 p.

The ability to estimate the extent of Soviet military expenditures
is an element of national intelligence essential to the security of
the West. Moreover, if arms control treaties are to be nego-
tiated in a meaningful manner, it is essential to have reasonably
precise estimates the Soviet Union is likely to undertake. CIA

estimates were accepted without question until 1976, when they were acknowledged to be grossly in error and doubled. This report submits that the revised CIA estimates are, once again, underrating Soviet military expenditures by nearly a factor of two.

Reviewed by Donald M. Snow, Air University Review Vol. 32 No. 6 (September-October 1981), p. 125.

No. 531. Lee, William T.
"The Shift in Soviet National Priorities to Military Forces, 1985." Annals, American Academy of Political Science No. 457 (September 1981), pp. 46-66.

This article traces the shift in Soviet national economic priorities from civilian uses, primarily consumption, to support of the Soviet military establishment since the late 1950s. It treats certain methodological issues involved in international comparisons, outlines the methodology used to estimate Soviet defense expenditures from published Soviet economic data, and compares the results with the CIA's estimates before and after the CIA was forced to double its estimates by new information which confirmed the author's estimates. A brief list of some of the major weapons systems whose development, procurement, and operations have driven the shift in Soviet national priorities from civilian to military uses is provided. The article concludes with the prospects for further increases in the military burden on the Soviet economy in the 1980s.

No. 532. Leitenberg, Millar.
"The Counterpart of Defense Industry Conversion in the United States: The USSR Economy, Defense Industry, and Military Expenditure."
Journal of Peace Research Vol. 16 No. 3 (1979), pp. 263-277.

This article describes the difficulty of estimating Soviet defense spending. It discusses recent efforts to gauge Soviet military expenditures by measuring opportunity costs in terms of capital and industrial imports.

No. 533. Maddock, R.T.
"Some Economic Contraints on Defense Spending in the Soviet Union."
RUSI Journal Vol. 124 No. 3 (September 1979), pp. 38-43.

This article considers some of the constraints that defense spending imposes on the Soviet economy. As with other economies, tradeoffs of input factors and technologies exist among various sectors. The Soviet Union is believed to spend as much in real terms on defense as does the United States, although the Soviet

burden is nearly twice that of the U.S. burden in terms of GNP.
In an age of declining economic growth and increasing consumer
demands, sustaining the Soviet defense burden is becoming
difficult. While the Soviet leadership's resolve to bear this
burden is unlikely to change, the Soviet economy's condition is
likely to worsen.

No. 534. Michaud, Norbert.
"An Epigog for an Increasing Soviet Defense Share, 1965-1979."
In Kenneth M. Currie and Gregory Varhall (Eds.), The Soviet
Union: What Lies Ahead?
Washington, D.C.: Government Printing Office (Studies in Com-
munst Affairs Vol. 6), 1985, pp. 434-451.

What percentage of Soviet industrial output is represented by
the Soviet military machine? This paper argues that the rapid
growth in the defense machinery sector of the Soviet economy
has far exceeded the growth of Soviet industry as a whole or of
the entire economy. The Soviet defense industry likely constitutes fourteen to sixteen percent of the total Soviet industrial
output. Increased defense procurement underlies the growth in
the Soviet machine industries.

No. 535. Rosefielde, Steven.
False Science: Underestimating the Soviet Arms Buildup, An
Appraisal of the CIA's Direct Costing Effort, 1960-80.
New Brunswick, N.J.: Transaction Books, 1982, 321 p.

Most Western assessments of the Soviet military threat depend
on the accuracy of the CIA's direct cost estimates of Soviet arms
expenditures. These estimates not only measure the cost of
Soviet defense programs, they also provide essential information
on the real rate of Soviet procurement growth, serving in this
way as an indicator of the aggregate annual improvement in the
quantity and quality of Soviet weaponry. Confidence in the
reliability of the CIA's direct cost estimates and by extension
perception of the real dimension of the Soviet military threat was
very high. This confidence reflected the agency's own appraisal
of the quality of its work, a judgment broadly supported in the
foreign policy community. New information obtained from covert
sources in 1975 has shattered this comforting illusion. The
agency was forced to revise its estimates of Soviet procurement
for 1970 from 5.5 to 18.5 billion rubles, and its estimate for total
defense spending from 25 to 50 billion rubles. The new information raises serious doubts about the merit of the CIA's direct
costing effort for the entire period from 1960 to 1980. Was the
discrepancy between the agency's estimates for 1970 and the true
values fortuitous, or did it reflect fundamental deficiencies
inherent in direct costing? If fundamental deficiencies existed,
were they artifacts of the methodology or were they attributable

to other factors such as inadequate data, inept calculation, or
discretionary manipulation? This book attempts to assess these
important issues on the factual and analytic levels, both to judge
the merit of the CIA's direct costing effort and to determine the
probable magnitude of the Soviet military threat.

No. 536. Rosefielde, Steven.
"Economic Foundations of Soviet National Security Strategy."
Orbis Vol. 30 No. 2 (Summer 1986), pp. 317-330.

This article demonstrates that Soviet force developments
challenge Western beliefs and explains why the properties of the
Soviet economic system might encourage its military planners to
embrace a strategy of "compellence" -- coercive military action or
threat that compells an adversary to acquiesce, because it is
inferior in the theater and unwilling to escalate. It further
shows that although Soviet economic deficiencies ultimately might
prevent the Soviet leadership from achieving compellent aims, the
prevailing sectoral productivity structure of the economy
enhances the appeal of compellant strategies, despite the
undeniable benefits afforded by arms control, arms reduction,
and deterrence. Soviet adoption of a compellent strategy, or
even a more ambitious pursuit of assured escalation dominence,
depends principally on three external factors: arms control,
foreign military preparedness, and technology. Assured
escalation dominence, which would leave the Soviet Union free to
fight a conventional war in Europe, could be attained through
one-sided disarmament agreements that degraded American
ballistic missile counter-strike capabilities, through the self-
inflicted erosion of Western strategic nuclear forces, and through
the failure to develop and deploy advanced defensive counter-
systems.

No. 537. Rupp, Rainer W.
"Assessing Soviet Military Expenditure: A Complex and Contro-
versial Task."
NATO Review Vol. 29 No. 5 (October 1981), pp. 23-28.

This article discusses the controversy over Soviet defense
spending estimates and the problems posed by the estimating
procedures used, particularly by the CIA. The CIA began to
produce its estimates of Soviet military spending in response to
skepticism about Soviet expenditure annoucements. Criticism of
CIA estimates by individuals and groups who produce estimates
of their own has resulted in a widely diverse array of figures.
Accurate estimates are hindered by Soviet secrecy and the
technical complexities of the process. The CIA's direct costing
method identifies and estimates costs of the individual elements
of Soviet military expenditure. A more realistic comparison of
U.S. and Soviet defense expenditures would require comparing
Soviet and U.S. spending in both rubles and dollars, and thus

avoiding the "index number" problem of the CIA's approach. This problem results in subjectivity of the estimates because it assumes Soviet equipment is bought at U.S. prices. There are also problems, however, with ruble costing of U.S. systems. NATO has produced a report containing the collective estimates of NATO members' intelligence services. This report emphasizes the interplay between the Soviet military and civilian economic sectors and the economic implications of the Soviet military buildup. However, Western intelligence estimates should focus on the scale of Soviet military capabilities rather than on attempts to deduce Soviet military spending.

No. 538. Rush, Myron.
"Guns Over Growth in Soviet Policy."
International Security Vol. 7 No. 3 (Winter 1982-83), pp. 167-179.

The top priority given to Soviet armed forces in budgets during the Brezhnev period cannot rightly be attributed to long-standing feelings of insecurity. It also is not a response to new military dangers or a tribute exacted by professional soliders from Soviet politicians. The arms buildup appears to have resulted from a reevaluation by the Brezhnev leadership of the place of military means in the attainment of Soviet objectives. Brezhnev knew that favoring defense at the expense of invest-ment since 1976 would worsen the economic problems anticipated in the decade ahead. He has purchased a position of limited military superiority for the next several years that will be difficult to maintain thereafter. It is reasonable to conclude that he did so in the expectation of achieving international gains that would alleviate the strategic consequences of the economic slow-down. This indicates that the Soviet leadership has resolved to practice a bolder form of "strategic opportunism."

No. 539. Spielmann, Karl F. "Defense Industrialists in the USSR."
Problems of Communism Vol. 25 No. 5 (September-October 1976), pp. 52-69.

The Soviet defense industrialists appear to have a stake in the regime's decisions on two key elements of Soviet detente policy toward the West --SALT and the effort to secure Western tech-nology -- which seem not only to be considerable but also dis-tinguishable in broad terms from those of other concerned parties in the USSR. It is difficult to establish that the defense industrialists have been able to extert a direct impact on Soviet defense and foreign policy decisions. But an increased compre-hension of the workings of the Soviet defense economic sector could illuminate some of the opportunities and dangers which make a detente relationship with the USSR something other than a simple either-or-proposition for the West.

No. 540. Strode, Rebecca.
"The Soviet Armed Forces: Adaptation to Resource Scarcity."
Washington Quarterly Vol. 9 No. 2 (Spring 1986), pp. 55-69.

In order to pursue its disparate economic objectives in the face of slow economic growth, the Soviet government had to make difficult choices between military and civilian claimants on resources. During the period 1965 to 1976, Soviet defense spending grew at an average rate of four to five percent per year. During the years 1977 to 1982, however, the growth in defense outlays declined to only about two percent per year, and procurement was flat. Evidence suggests this was the result of a deliberate policy decision to tie the rate of growth of defense spending to the growth of the economy as a whole. This slow-down created competition for scarce resources, and had important effects on political-military relations. Debates occurred both among the top political and military leadership, and between the services, over spending. The resource issue undermined the status of the military, and the consensus for arms control. The new Gorbachev leadership's emphasis on technological innovation may lead to an increase in military spending.

No. 541. Wolf, Charles Jr.; K.C. Yeh, E.D. Brunner, A. Gurwitz, and M.F. Lawrence.
The Costs of the Soviet Empire.
Santa Monica, Calif.: The RAND Corporation (R-3073/1-NA), September 1983, 66 p.

This study develops and applies a comprehensive framework for estimating all of the economic costs incurred by the Soviet Union in acquiring, maintaining, and expanding its empire. The bulk of the study is devoted to estimating the total and component costs of the Soviet empire (CSE) for the period from 1971 through 1980. The principal components include implicit trade subsidies; export credits; military aid deliveries; economic aid deliveries; incremental costs of Soviet military operations in Afghanistan; and costs of Soviet covert and related activities that can be reasonably imputed to the empire, rather than to maintenance of the Soviet system at home. These costs are expressed in current and constant dollars and rubles; and scaled in relation to Soviet GNP and military spending. After considering total costs and their changes over the 1970s, the cost of each component is examined separately. Finally, the question of whether CSE will be higher or lower in the 1980s than in the 1970s is considered, as well as several policy issues relating to the burden imposed by CSE on the Soviet economy, the relative size of comparable U.S. costs, and the desirability and feasibility of U.S. policies for raising CSE.

No. 542. Wolfe, Thomas W.
Impact of Economic and Technological Issues on the Soviet

278

Approach to SALT.
Santa Monica, Calif.:   The RAND Corporation (P-4368), June
1970, 36 p.

Draft of a paper presented on 20 May 1970 to the Armed
Services Subcommittee on Strategic Arms Limitations Talks of the
Committee on Armed Services, U.S. Senate. An examination of
the performance of the Soviet economy under the present
collective leadership emphasizes three sets of requirements
competing for priority: 1) consumer needs; 2) military and
defense industry claims; and 3) overall economic growth. It is
conjectured that economic pressures have helped propel the
USSR into the SALT talks; evidence of the uneven performance
of Soviet economy has multiplied since the latter part of 1969. A
number of interrelated questions are discussed with regard to
foreign and defense policy in the USSR, including the technological dilemma and its implications, the motivation behind the
Soviet strategic buildup during the past 5 years, and the issues
of "militance and caution" concerning future Soviet behavior.

C.   IDEOLOGY AND POLITICAL CONTROL OF THE ARMED
      FORCES

No. 543. Alsop, Joseph.
"Concern Stirred by Seeming Rise of Soviet Military Over
Civilians."
Washington Post, January 10, 1969.

A recent article in Communist of the Armed Forces, the journal
of the political directorate of the Soviet defense ministry,
appears to claim that "military affairs" are of too great
importance to be completely subjected to civilian party control.
This fits with a report by the former head of the political
directorate in the Czech defense ministry, General Jan Sejna,
that the Soviet Politburo wished to replace Marshal Rodion
Malinovskiy, who had died of cancer, as defense minister by
Dmitri Ustinov. He is a civilian party leader charged with Soviet
defense production. The senior marshals forced the naming of
one of their own, Marshal Andrei Grechko. Military services
able to name their own defense ministers cannot be fully
controlled, which is worrying.

No. 544. Barry, James A.
"Military Training of Soviet Youth."
Military Review Vol. 53 No. 2 (February 1973), pp. 92-103.

On 1 January 1968, a new Soviet law on universal military
service became effective. Among its provisions were a lowering
of the draft age from 19 to 18 years, a change in the criteria

for draft deferments and, most important, a decrease in the term of service for conscripts. Official explanations stressed "the substantial increase in the general education and technical level of young people" as the major factor in this decision. It seems more likely that the military was under pressure from the bureaucracy to release more trained manpower for the civilian economy although the desire to build up a large reserve for possible protracted conflict with China may have had some bearing on the decision. Another possibility is that the Soviet leadership was seeking to allay its growing doubts about the ideological purity of Soviet youth by subjecting greater numbers of young people to army-sponsored indoctrination.

No. 545. Beumer, Robert S.
"The Soviet Draft: Cornerstone of USSR Nuclear Strategy." Military Intelligence Vol. 5 No. 4 (October-December 1979), pp. 38-44.

In this article, the issue of Soviet compulsory military service is explored for: 1) its ability to provide massive numbers of trained personnel necessary for any confrontation between the superpowers; 2) costs accrued by Soviet society as a result of compulsory military service; 3) training and ability of a draft army in a technologically sophisticated environment; and 4) societal attitudes toward the draft army. One overall conclusion can be drawn: Soviet conscription is not intended to deter war, but rather to use military might to advance Soviet political goals, pressure Western powers, or in the ultimate expression of national will, to fight and win any war, including nuclear war.

No. 546. Caron, Gerald C., Jr.
"Soviet Civil-Military Relations: Conflict and Collaboration Among Comrades."
Naval War College Review Vol. 24 No. 4 (December 1971), pp. 65-91.

The concept of continuing institutional conflict between the Communist Party and the armed forces can lead to entirely inaccurate conclusions about the relations between the civilian leaders and career military officers in the U.S.S.R. The top figures in both groups are all political professionals, and most of the so-called conflicts -- both of historic and contemporary genre -- transcend normal institutional lines. Although the peculiar Soviet version of the classic Great Russian politico-military model is characterized by an inherent potential for discord, it also includes unique provisions for perpetuating the present political system and for sustaining the thrust of the country's national and strategic objectives.

No. 547. Colton, Timothy J.
"Civil-Military Relations in Soviet Politics."
Current History Vol. 67 No. 398 (October 1974), pp. 160-163,
181-182.

The military establishment's place in the Soviet political system
remains remarkably stable. The Soviet military remains a status
quo group under firm civilian control. Western reports of
greatly increased military influence in Moscow are without basis.
A useful device for conceptualizing the Soviet army's participation in politics is to think of it in terms of two dimensions of
participation: scope of issues, and means employed. In theory,
scope can range from purely professional issues bearing directly
on the military establishment's function to progressively more
general issues having less and less relation to the military's
professional function. The means an army uses can range from
the provision of expert advice to the use of political bargaining,
to the employment of force. Barring unforeseen developments,
the Soviet military establishment is unlikely to pose any major
challenge to existing political arrangements.

No. 548. Colton, Timothy.
Commissars, Commanders, and Civilian Authority.
Cambridge, Mass.: Harvard University Press, 1979.

Most Western scholars have posited a basic dichotomy of interests
between the Soviet army and the Communist Party. They view
the two institutions as conflict-prone, with civilian supremacy
depending primarily upon the Party's control of officers through
its organs within the military establishment, a thesis that is
challenged in this book. It argues that the military Party organs
have come to possess few of the attributes on an effective
controlling device, and that the commisars and their heirs have
operated as allies rather than adversaries of the military commanders. In explaining the extraordinary stability in army-
Party relations in terms of overlapping interests rather than
controlling mechanisms, the book offers a major case study and a
new model of Soviet political-military relations.

Reviewed by Joseph Thach, Jr., Naval War College Review
Vol. 33 No. 4 (July-August 1980), pp. 112-114.

No. 549. Deane, Michael J.
"The Main Political Administration as a Factor in Communist Party
Control Over the Military in the Soviet Union."
Armed Forces and Society Vol. 3 No. 2 (February 1977), pp.
295-324.

In assessing the complex linkage between the Communist Party of
the Soviet Union and the professional military apparatus of the
Soviet armed forces, examination must focus on the Main Political

Administration (MPA) as an important variable in the party's attempts to exert control. Three broad issues are involved in this assessment: 1) the organizational capability of the MPA to implement control over the professional military; 2) the interests of the MPA in influencing the party-professional military relationship; and 3) the areas in which the MPA is eager to exert its influence and authority. Examination of these issues shows that the interests of the MPA are not codeterminous with those of any other institutional group, and that the MPA is itself not homogeneous. However, the MPA is likely to move, over considerable internal opposition, in the direction of being an instrument and spokesman for military professionalism.

No. 550. Deane, Michael J.
Political Control of the Soviet Armed Forces.
New York: Crane, Russak and Company, 1977, 297 p.

The Kremlinological and conflict schools attempt to demonstrate the existence of ongoing power struggles, especially at the higher levels of government. The purpose of this book is to examine the debate on political-military affairs among Soviet leaders and spokesmen, and to evaluate the effect of these conflicts on the political control of the Soviet military. It is concerned with the interaction among the Party, the professional military, and the Main Political Administration (MPA) of the Soviet Army and Navy. Divisions within and among these three interest groups, particularly as they have developed during the Brezhnev era, are examined in detail. The volume attempts to demonstrate that the professional military has an independent voice in Soviet decision making, usually separate from and often in conflict with the current party line. It also examines the MPA as an independent interest group, as opposed to its traditional image as an appendage of the Party. Two methods of analysis are employed: 1) policy and content analysis of Soviet and non-Soviet sources; and 2) scrutiny of the careers of major political and military leaders, especially members of MPA elites who are responsible for political control of the military. Open Soviet sources have been employed as the main basis for the analysis.

Reviewed by Yaroslav Bilinsky, Annals of the American Academy of Political Science No. 436 (March 1978), pp. 165-166; Dale Herspring, Slavic Review Vol. 37 (March 1978), pp. 134-135; Eugene Betit, Military Review Vol. 58 No. 8 (August 1978), pp. 93-94; Shane Mahoney "Posture and Purpose of the Soviet Military," Problems of Communism Vol. 28 No.1 (January-February 1979), pp. 55-58.

No. 551. Dukes, William C.
"Psychological Conditioning of the Soviet Soldier."
Military Review Vol. 54 No. 12 (December 1974), pp. 69-78.

Preparing the soldiers psychologically for battle is neither new nor unique to the Soviet Army. The tremendous emphasis which is currently being placed on psychological training by the Soviet military leadership, however, is unique. This emphasis stems from the Soviet view of modern nuclear warfare.

No. 552. Ermath, Fritz.
"Soviet Military Politics."
Military Review Vol. 48 No. 1 (January 1968), pp. 32-36.

Under Brezhnev and Kosygin, the military establishment has healed many of the inner divisions over policy issues which resulted from Khrushchev's assault on the traditional forces. It stands united in support of a diversified and large military effort. But the Party resisted tentative attempts by the Soviet military to enlarge its sphere of institutional control over military policy with comparative ease. The political leadership could probably move against military interests with considerable vigor if it chose to do so. To describe Soviet interest groups in terms simply of party, government, military, and policies is an unenlightening abstraction. Purposeful party leadership can split these rather vague and broad institutions badly. The party can be expected to attempt to repoliticize the control apparatus of the Armed Forces. On a broad front it is faced with the deepening irrelevance of its self-image of the "leader of all aspects of Soviet life." Tensions will be aggravated between the Party and other institutions, including the military, where pluralizing forces are at work.

Condensed from the conclusions of a research paper presented at a seminar in Soviet politics at the London School of Economics: Soviet Military Politics Under Brezhnev and Khrushchev (Munich: Radio Free Europe, 16 May 1967).

No. 553. Ferri, Albert Jr.
Selections from the Soviet Military Press, 1968-71.
Menlo Park, Calif.: Stanford Research Institution (SRI Project 8474, Technical Note SSC-TN-8974-70), 1973, 142 p.

This study presents major ideas in Soviet force planning, without the usual Marxist-Leninist propaganda. In certain cases, however, where there is a need to understand the political side of force planning and use, this material is presented in the article.

No. 554. Garthoff, Raymond L.
The Role of the Military in Recent Soviet Politics.
Santa Monica, California: The RAND Corporation (RM-1638), March 1, 1956, 89 p.

A study of the role of military issues and the part played by the senior military leaders in Soviet political developments since the death of Stalin in 1953. In particular, the policy differences between Malenkov and his supporters on one hand and the Khrushchev faction on the other are emphasized. See revised version P-937.

No. 555. Garthoff, Raymond L.
"The Role of the Military in Post-Stalin Politics."
Russian Review Vol. 16 No. 2 (April 1957), pp. 15-24.

A discussion of the effects of Stalin's death on the role of the military. Certain events in the USSR since 1953 have increased the political status of the military leaders. However, if in the future the political leaders conflict over issues which directly affect military requirements, the military may be forced to become an active contestant for power. A revised version of RM-1638.

Also published as RAND Paper P-937 (September 12, 1956), 22 p.

No. 556. Goure, Leon.
The Military Indoctrination of Soviet Youth.
New York: National Strategy Information Center (Strategy Papers No. 16), 1973. 75 p.

Explores and analyzes current Soviet efforts to instill in the youth nationalism, militarism, and a readiness for war on a scale unprecedented in peace time, even in the Soviet Union, and which are leading to an increasing militarization of the entire Soviet educational system. Suggests that the military-patriotic indoctrination program should be viewed not only as an important and far-reaching development in Soviet education, but also as likely to have significant influence on future Soviet relations with the rest of the world and on the evolution of the Soviet system.

Reviewed by Eugene D. Betit, Military Review Vol. 55 No. 1 (January 1975), pp. 105-106.

No. 557. Heinlein, Joseph J.
"The Main Political Administration in Today's Soviet Forces."
Mlitary Review Vol. 53 No. 11 (November 1973), pp. 55-64.

From the time of its introduction into the Soviet Army by Trotsky in 1918, the political commissar system has had the overriding mission of ensuring the subordination of the military to the political leadership of the Communist Party of the Soviet Union (CPSU). The need for such an organization was clearly apparent in 1918. The Soviet leadership has evidently been satisfied with its effectiveness since that time even though the particular circumstances giving cause for concern over military deference to political authority have varied considerably over the years. The argument advanced here is that the CPSU believes that the political control system in the Soviet Armed Forces has considerable utility beyond its traditional role and remains viable today under conditions which are vastly different from those of the Stalin era. What follows herein is an elaboration of the "revolution in military affairs" as viewed from what Erickson calls "the political side of the Soviet military house."

No. 558. Herspring, Dale R.
"The CPSU and the Military."
Problems of Communism Vol. 25 No. 2 (March-April 1976), pp. 71-75.

This essay-review provides a short description of two recent works on the Soviet military as a preface to a broader discussion of current views on Communist political-military relations, based on what English-language information is available. The two books are A.Y. Khmel (Ed.), Education of the Soviet Soldier: Party-Political Work in the Soviet Armed Forces (Moscow: Progess Press, 1972); and Herbert Goldhammer, The Soviet Soldier: Soviet Military Management at the Troop Level (New York: Crane, Russak & Co., 1975). The focal point of these works on Soviet political-military relations is the role of the political officer in the Soviet military. Is it characterized by conflict, or does its support of many functions that executive and staff officers perform in the West lead to cooperation and a sense of identification with the military?

No. 559. Herspring, Dale R.
"The Soviet Military in the Aftermath of the 27th Party Congress."
Orbis Vol. 30 No. 2 (Summer 1986), pp. 297-316.

With the removal of Marshal Ogarkov in 1984 as Soviet Chief of Staff, the Soviet armed forces were deprived of their most influential spokesman, and in consequence their influence appears to have decreased. The new Defense Minister, Marshal Sergei Sokolov, appears to be a lightweight with little to say on issues of importance to the Soviet military, such as strategy and doctrine. At the 27th Party Congress he was not elevated to voting status in the Politburo, as might have been expected from precedent. The significance of this lessening of military influence is heightened by the fact that the new General Secretary, Mikhail Gorbachev, lacks close ties to senior officers and does not praise the military as much as his predecessors. This suggests that although he is in control of the armed forces, the senior officers are probably dissatisfied with his policies. Some observations that can be made include: the recent spate of high-level military personnel changes does not appear to have undercut the Soviet military; Marshal Ogarkov should not be dismissed as an important force in the Soviet leadership; senior military officers have adopted a lower profile; they probably feel that additional unilateral Soviet steps in arms control could weaken Soviet security; they are also concerned about the defense budget; Soviet military doctrine is developing along lines set during Ogarkov's tenure; the technical side of Soviet military doctrine is reserved for Soviet military officers to develop; the appearance of civilian strategists could undercut the military; and the debate between senior military and Party officials appears to be continuing, with the Party having the upper hand.

No. 560. Hickox, Joseph E.
Party-Political Work in the Soviet Armed Forces.
Maxwell Air Force Base, Ala.: Air Command and Staff College (Research Study), 1974, 101 p.

The Communist Party has developed a vast and well-organized network of political organs and organizations throughout the Soviet Armed Forces. This study examines the role of the Party in the military, including its structure, functions, and objectives as defined by the Central Committee. Evidence is presented that focuses attention upon the political organs as possessing the real power and authority to direct and control Party-political work. Although many military professionals voice their resentment over constant Party control, the conclusion was reached that the Soviet military establishment is unquestionably loyal to its country and the Communist party.

No. 561. Jones, Christopher D.
"The 'Revolution in Military Affairs' and Party-Military Relations, 1965-70."
Survey Vol. 20 No. 1 (Winter 1974), pp. 83-100.

The "revolution in military affairs" -- the strategic adaptation necessitated by the technology of intercontinental missiles with nuclear warheads -- has precipitated a revision of Soviet strategic doctrine and has had considerable impact on Party-military relations. The Party will lose its legitimacy in the military sphere if it cannot prove that it is necessary to the development of Soviet military power. To preempt this possibility the Party has placed renewed emphasis on the role of the "moral-political factor" in military affairs. Despite shortcomings, the Soviet military control system, headed by the MPA, has achieved some measure of success in utilizing the moral-political factor. The Party is certainly aware of the shortcomings of the central system, but does not consider them costly enough to spend more human and material resources to improve the MPAs results.

No. 562. Kolkowicz, Roman.
Conflicts in Soviet Party-Military Relations: 1962-1963.
Santa Monica, Calif.: The RAND Corporation (RM-3760-PR),
August 1963, 50 p.

An analysis of certain conflicts between the Soviet Communist
party leadership and some sectors of the Soviet army. The
basic conflicts are: 1) divergent views of the protagonists on
strategic-doctrinal formulas announced by Khrushchev in January
1960; and 2) opposition by the military to intensified political
controls attempted by the party during the past year.

No. 563. Kolkowicz, Roman.
A General and the Apparatchiks.
Santa Monica, Calif.: The RAND Corporation (P-3298), January
1966, 8 p.

This paper illustrates the manner in which the Soviet Communist
Party controls the military. It presents the case of General-
Major Rogatyuk, whose professional and private conduct brought
him into conflict with the Party. The story, published in the
Soviet Union as a warning to other recalcitrant officers, tells
how Rogatyuk was tried for "uncommunist" behavior in a ritual
designed to humiliate him and extol the Party.

No. 564. Kolkowicz, Roman.
Soviet Party-Military Relations: Contained Conflict.
Santa Monica, Calif.: The RAND Corporation (P-3371), May 1966,
48 p.

This paper is an analysis of the conflict-prone relations between
the Communist Party and the military in the Soviet Union. The
Party's attitude is the result of a delicate balance between the
desire for hegemony in the state and the need to maintain a
strong military-political posture in the world. The clash
develops primarily because of the military's wish to retain its
identity and autonomy in the face of the ruling elite. Although
the paper traces this clash of interests back to the revolutionary
era, it concentrates on the post-Stalin period, when the more
moderate social and political climate, plus the growing complexities of warfare, increased the inherent power of the military.
The Party's methods of controlling the military, from socio-
economic privileges to intimidation, are described, as well as the
techniques the military has adopted for its own defense.

No. 565. Kolkowicz, Roman.
The Impact of Modern Technology on the Soviet Officer Corps.
Santa Monica, Calif.: The RAND Corporation (P-3380), June
1966, 24 p.

This paper provides a discussion of the changes of function and attitude among Soviet officers. The conflicts between the new technocrats and the conventional officers within the military, between the attitudes of the two groups toward strategic doctrine, and between the technically expert officers and the politically powerful members of the Party are examined. Possible developments resulting from the eventual resolution of the conflict are suggested.

No. 566. Kolkowicz, Roman.
Political Controls in the Red Army: Professional Autonomy Versus Political Integration.
Santa Monica, Calif.: The RAND Corporation (P-3402), July 1966, 31 p.

This paper gives a description of the network of Party organs, committees, cells, denunciation sessions, propaganda, and other means by which the Communist Party of the Soviet Union controls its armed forces. Unlike most other military establishments, the Red Army operates under a system of overlapping, competative authority sources. Commanders are subject to the criticism and direction of civilian Party functionaries, political "assistants," and subordinates of all ranks. Officers and soldiers are required to study Marxism-Leninist doctrines, and are encouraged to participate in Party-sponsored activies. Officers are kept guessing about their status, which is subject to political assessment. The consequent problems of morale and efficiency are recognized by Party leaders, who accept them as the price of detailed control over the military.

No. 567. Kolkowicz, Roman.
The Soviet Military and the Communist Party.
Princeton, N.J.: Princeton University Press, 1967, 445 p.

An analysis of the conflict of ideas and interests between the two dominant institutions in the Soviet Union -- the Communist Party and the military establishment -- and its implications for future Soviet policy. Under Stalin, the Party, through an elaborate system of control and indoctrination, dominated the military. The power struggle that followed Stalin's death weakened the control mechanisms and strengthened the military's position. During the past twelve years, the officer corps has been progressively transformed from a group of relatively expendable commanders into a group of technocrats who are becoming increasingly indispensible to the maintenance of highly complex weapons systems. If the Soviet military assumes the more active role in Soviet politics that it is now in a position to take, it will probably emphasize defense needs at the expense of social planning. The military is likely to reappraise policies geared to detente and may well modify or abandon them.

288

Also printed as The Soviet Army and the Communist Party:
Institutions in Conflict (Santa Monica, Calif.: The RAND
Corporation, R-446-PR, August 1966).

No. 568. Kolkowicz, Roman.
"Interest Groups in Soviet Politics: The Case of the Military."
Comparative Politics Vol. 2 No. 3 (April 1970), pp. 445-472.

The Soviet military is imbued with many characteristics usually
associated with an "interest group." Another aspect of the
Soviet military's role in the Soviet state derives from the per-
petual tension in its relationship with the Party leadership.
While the military presents a monolithic facade externally, it is
far from being a homogenous community. When its basic interests
are threatened, however, members tend to unify and offer a
concerted response to their challenges.

No. 569. Kolkowicz, Roman.
"Strategic Elites and Politics of Superpower."
Journal of International Relations Vol 26 No. 1 (1972), pp.
40-59.

The essential thesis of this essay is that there are two kinds of
dynamics in superpower politics within the nuclear context: one
derives from the unrelenting march of technology and weaponry,
the second from the vacillating efforts to seize and dominate that
process for policy purposes. The dynamics of international
politics, strategic doctrines, and war in the nuclear context
imply a certain kind of "logic." According to this logic the
demands of technology, its range of inevitable consequences, and
the pressures it exerts on "rational" policy makers all cut
across national, systemic, and ideological boundaries. The roles
of strategic elites in the discovery and systematization of the
various aspects of nuclear technology have been impressive.
They discerned the dangers in superpower relations, labored for
the formulation of rules for superpower politics, challenged
earlier, pernicious attitudes to war, and educated policymakers
how to think in the nuclear context. The Soviet system seems
to contain stronger institutional and political "filters" to encourage an upward flow of technological and strategic ideas. At the
same time, though, it selectively screens out elitist pressures on
policy, and thereby retains a stronger political dominance over
technological imputs.

No. 570. Mackintosh, J. Malcolm.
Recent Developments in Political Instruction in the Soviet Army.
Oxford: St. Antony's Papers on Soviet Affairs, November 1957,
14 p.

It seems clear that there will be a major trend away from the approach adopted by Marshal Zhukov concerning the role of Party-political work in the Army, and that the Party will try to increase the authority of the political worker. There is also a major trend away from publicizing traditional Russian military heroes and toward Communist revolutionary heroes. Finally, the Party will try to drive home the theme that it directs the Army. The question remains open as to whether the Party will succeed in these efforts.

No. 571. Miller, David C.
"Soviet Armed Forces and Political Pressure."
Military Review Vol. 49 No. 12 (December 1969), pp. 63-68.

The Communist Party of the Soviet Union has gone to great effort to prevent the armed forces from becoming a threat to its political power. While the Soviet armed forces possess the potential strength to influence domestic and foreign decisions, there is no indication they have used this power unduly. The armed forces appear to have influenced policies in the limited sense of a subordinate group offering professional judgements. So long as the Party maintains its present control mechanisms and continues to treat the armed forces as a privileged class, there is no reason to assume that the military services will emerge as an independent political force.

No. 572. Odom, William E.
"The Party Connection."
Problems of Communism Vol. 22 No. 5 (September-October 1973), pp. 12-26.

Two questionable assumptions form the cornerstone of most Western analysis of Soviet Party-military relations. First, it is taken for granted that the civil-military boundary in the Soviet polity marks a potential cleavage. Thus far it has been forestalled by the Party's unique organizational control over the military, but one of increasing importance as a factor for eventual change in the political system. Second, it is assumed to be self-evident that autonomy in "military professionalism" is the source of military efficiency and a state's readiness for war; and that if the Party controls deny professional autonomy to the officer corps, there is ipso facto a loss of military efficiency. These misconceptions have underpinned the prognosis that the Soviet military would gain increasing autonomy vis-a-vis the Party -- for which no corraborative evidence has appeared. Secondly, they have encouraged proponents of "group theory" to treat the Soviet military as an incipient interest group. Thirdly, they have generally been associated with a dubious interpretation of the role of political controls over the military. Finally, they have kept the comparative study of the Soviet military's role in domestic politics from developing. The article offers an alternative conceptualization resting on five premises.

Response by Edward L. Warner, Problems of Communism Vol. 23 No. 2 (March-April 1974), pp. 78-79.

No. 573. Wolfe, Thomas W.
Signs of Stress in Soviet Political-Military Relations.
Santa Monica, Calif.: The RAND Corporation (P-2877), March 1964, 24 p.

The first of a two-part discussion of political-military relations in the USSR. The history of these relations is described as the search for a formula to reconcile political control with professional military efficiency, carried out against the background issue of what the proper extent of military influence should be on the formulation of Soviet policy and strategy. Examples of such stress and its implications are given.

Reprinted as "Political Primacy vs. Professional Elan," Problems of Communism Vol. 13 No. 3 (May-June 1964), pp. 44-52.

No. 574. Wolfe, Thomas W.
Impact of Khrushchev's Downfall on Soviet Military Policy and Detente.
Santa Monica, Calif.: The RAND Corporation (P-3010), November 1964, 38 p.

An examination of the impact of Khrushchev's downfall on Soviet military policy and the detente initiated during his regime. Discussed are: 1) military issues possibly involved in Khrushchev's downfall; 2) the new regime's first pronouncements on defense policy; 3) considerations affecting its military policy approach; and 4) prospects for detente under the new leadership.

Reprinted as the Appendix to Eleanor Lansing Dulles and Robert D. Crane (Eds.), Detente: Cold War Strategies in Transition (New York: Frederick A. Praeger, Publishers, 1965), pp. 280-303.

No. 575. Wolfe, Thomas W.
"Are the Generals Taking Over?"
Problems of Communism Vol. 18 Nos. 4-5 (July-October 1969), pp. 106-110.

Some Western observers argue that in recent years there has been a major shift of political power to the Soviet military leaders. It may be useful to examine some of the evidence on this matter and offer an appraisal of its significance. Since the rise of the Brezhnev-Kosygin regime, political-military relations appear to have involved three broad categories of problems: 1) those related to maintaining political control over the armed forces; 2) those of meshing economic and military planning to cope most effectively with the resource-consuming appetite of modern weapons systems; and 3) those of balancing military influence on Soviet policy formulation against the increasing need of political authorities to call upon the professional expertise of the military leadership. A review of the evidence does not support the proposition that the Soviet marshals have success-fully challenged the party leadership, or even that they aspire to do so.

7

Anthologies and Bibliographies

A. ANTHOLOGIES

No. 576. Baylis, John; and Gerald Segal (Eds.).
Soviet Strategy.
Montclair, N.J.: Allanfeld, Osmun, and Co., 1981, 236 p.

Analysis of the Soviet Union's military strategy has resulted in a wide expression of opinion on the crucial question -- what are the intentions of the USSR? The spectrum stretches from the "hawks" who see expansionism as the motivating force behind Soviet actions, to the "doves" who see defensiveness as the key element. This anthology of previously published articles seeks to combine the most important arguments from both sides, presenting a broad analysis of the key features of Soviet strategy. Beginning with an introduction to the subject, the book covers such topics as the Soviet approach to nuclear war, defense and deterrence in the nuclear age, and the calculation of risk in the use of the military instrument. One of the main themes running through the text is that although the Soviet Union clearly does not view military issues in the same way as does the West, its approach is not necessarily aggressive and dangerous in all respects.

Contents: Gerald Segal and John Baylis, "Soviet Strategy: An Introduction," pp. 9-54; Robert Arnett, "Soviet Attitudes Toward Nuclear War: Do They Really Think They Can Win?", pp. 55-74 [No. 101]; Ken Booth, "The Military Instrument in Soviet Foreign Policy," pp. 75-104; Benjamin Lambeth "How to Think About Soviet Military Doctrine," pp. 105-123 [No. 191]; Dennis Ross, "Rethinking Soviet Strategic Policy: Inputs and Implications," pp. 124-153 [No. 119]; Raymond Garthoff, "The Soviet Military and SALT," pp. 154-184 [No. 476]; Hannes Adomeit, "Soviet Risk Taking and Crisis Behavior," pp. 185-209 [No. 1]; Michael MccGwire, "The Rationale for the Development of Soviet Seapower," pp. 210-254.

Reviewed by Stanley Kober "Interpreting Soviet Strategic Policy,"
Comparative Strategy Vol. 4 No. 1 (1983), pp. 65-74.

No. 577. Bonds, Ray (Ed.).
The Soviet War Machine: An Encyclopedia of Russian Military
Equipment and Strategy.
London: Chartwell Ltd., 1976.

This book evaluates the forces and major weapons of the Soviet
Union, both individually and as part of a total force. Its
contributors describe how the Soviet Union and its Warsaw Pact
allies have organized themselves for defense and to carry out
offensive war or project power overseas into areas of vital
importance to the West. It includes numerous photographs,
charts, tables, and graphics depicting weapons and tactical
maneuvers.

Contents: Peter Vigor, "The Rise of Soviet Communism," pp.
10-17; and "Expansions in the Red Army," pp. 18-25; Christopher Donnelly, "The Organization of Soviet Forces," pp.
26-39; and "Modern Soviet Ground Forces," pp. 138-165; Shel-
ford Bidwell, "Soviet Global Policy in Peace and War," pp.
40-49; Stuart Menaul, "The Defense of Soviet Air Space,"
pp. 50-59; and "The Modern Soviet Air Force," pp. 60-71; Bill
Gunston, "Soviet Aircraft," pp. 72-95; "Soviet Warships,"
pp. 108-137; "Army Weapons," pp. 166-197; and "Soviet
Missiles," pp. 210-233; J. E. Moore, "The Modern Soviet Navy,"
pp. 96-107; James Dornan, "The Soviet Strategic Rocket Forces,"
pp. 198-207; John Erickson, "The Forces of the Warsaw Pact,"
pp. 234-243.

Second edition published as Russian Military Power (New York:
St. Martin's Press, 1980), 249 p. Reviewed by Thomas Sack,
Air Force Magazine Vol. 64 No. 3 (March 1981), p. 132.

No. 578. Brzezinski, Zbigniew; Richard Sincere, Martin
Strmecki, and Peter Wehner (Eds.).
Promise or Peril: The Strategic Defense Initiative.
Washington, D.C.: Ethics and Public Policy Center, 1986, 479 p.

President Reagan's 1983 announcement of the Strategic Defense
Initative has led to a fundamental reassessment of U.S. strategic
doctrine. The thirty-five selections in this book reflect both the
history of strategic defense thinking and a wide range of views
on the contemporary issues. Readers are left to decide for
themselves which arguments are most compelling. The book's
chapters are categorized into six parts: I) Origins of the
Strategic Defense Idea; II) Political and Technical Dimensions;
III) Soviet Initiatives in Strategic Defense; IV) SDI and the
Western Alliance; V) Strategic Defense and Arms Control; and
VI) Moral Aspects of Strategic Defense.

Contents (Part III): Nikolai Talensky, "Missile Defense: A
Response to Aggression," pp. 209-219; Alexei N. Kosygin,
"Missile Defense: For Saving Human Lives," pp. 219-220; Mikhail
Gorbachev, "SDI: A Threat to Peace," pp. 221-226; Daniel
Goure, "The Strategic Competition and SDI," pp. 227-236 [No.
304]; Hans Ruehle, "Gorbachev's 'Star Wars'," pp. 237-248 [No.
316]; Thomas Krebs, "Can the Soviets Counter SDI?", pp. 249-
263 [No. 309].

No. 579. Currie, Kenneth M.; and Gregory Varhall (Eds.).
The Soviet Union: What Lies Ahead? Military-Political Affairs
in the 1980s.
Washington, D.C.: Government Printing Office (Studies in Communist Affairs Vol. 6), 1985, 800 p.

In September 1980, nearly one thousand Soviet specialists from
government, the military, and academia gathered in Reston,
Virginia for a conference sponsored by the Assistant Chief of
Staff, Intelligence, U.S. Air Force. Panelists representing many
shades of the political spectrum were invited to the conference.
They presented a total of ninety-six papers in twenty-four
general subject areas, about half of which are included in this
collection.

Contents: Part I. The Soviet Military-Political Environment.
Richard E. Porter, "Soviet Military Decisionmaking: A Frame-
work for Analysis," pp. 6-20 [No. 494]; David R. Jones,
"Russian Military Traditions and the Soviet Military Establishment," pp. 21-47; Daniel Hannaway, "Principles of Soviet Military
Leadership," pp. 48-57; Howard Frost, "Soviet-Party-Military
Relations in Strategic Decisionmaking," pp. 58-74 [No. 472].
Part II. The USSR as a Global Power. Lincoln Landis, "Motives
and Perceptions in the USSR's Global Outreach," pp. 79-84;
Vojtech Mastny, "The Soviet Union and European Order," pp. 85
-105; Eugenia Osgood, "Soviet Perceptions of Arms Control," pp.
106-141 [No. 77]; George Kolt, "Soviet and American Perceptions
of Arms Control," pp. 142-147 [No. 75]; Edward L. Rowny,
"The Soviets Are Still Russians," pp. 148-153 [No. 257]; Rajan
Menon, "The Soviet Union, the Arms Trade, and the Third
World," pp. 154-172; Richard E. Bissell, "Soviet Aid to Africa,"
pp. 173-190; Michael M. Boll, "The 'Division of Labor' Within the
Soviet Penetration of the Third World: The Role of Bulgaria,"
pp. 191-211; Robert H. Donaldson, "The USSR in the Third
World: Opportunities, Obstacles, and Objectives," pp. 212-224;
Bruce D. Porter, "The USSR in Third World Conflicts," pp.
225-240; Robert Clute, "The Soviet Presence in Africa," pp.
241-159; Ray S. Cline, "Stabilizing the Beijing-Moscow-Washington
Triangle," pp. 260-266; H. Lyman Miller, "Chinese Foreign
Policy Coalitions and Sovet Options in China," pp. 267-291;
Stuart D. Goldman, "Soviet-Japanese Relations and the Strategic
Balance in Northeast Asia," pp. 292-311. Part III: Soviet Military
Capabilities. Stanley H. Kober, "Causes of the Soviet Military

Buildup," pp. 314-323 [No. 53]; Alan B. Smith, "Military Manpower Supply and Demand in the Soviet Union," pp. 324-335;
Martha Brill Olcott, "Soviet Muslims and the Military," pp.
336-349; Ivan Volgyes, "The Reliability of the Warsaw Pact
Armies," pp. 350-378; Gary L. Guertner, "Soviet Strategic
Vulnerability: Deterring a Multinational State," pp. 378-394 [No.
266]; Robert Kennedy, "Soviet Theater Nuclear Forces: Implica-
tions for NATO Defense," pp. 395-414 [No. 393]; Carl W.
Reddel, "The Soviet View of Human Resources in War," pp.
415-431. Part IV: The Soviet Military Economy. Norbert
Michaud, "An Epagog for an Increasing Soviet Defense Share,
1965-1979," pp. 434-451 [No. 534]; W.L. Morgan, "USSR Aircraft
Industry: Will Transfer of Work Practices to Non-defense Indus-
tries Promote Future Economic Growth?", pp. 452-459; Rebecca V.
Strode, "Soviet Design Policy and Its Implications for U.S.
Combat Aircraft Procurement," pp. 460-481; Robert L. O'Connell,
"The Soviet Tank and U.S. Weapon Acquisiton," pp. 482-487;
John W. Skipper, "An Estimate of the International Market Value
of the Soviet Navy," pp. 488-501; Haskell R. Scheimberg, "A
Cybernetic Approach to the Analysis of Soviet R&D Activity,"
pp. 502-513; Richard E. Thomas, "R&D in Soviet Military
Academies," pp. 514-519. Part V. The Soviet Armed Forces:
Their Organization and Training. Lynn M. Hansen, "Front
Aviation in Soviet Combined Arms Warfare," pp. 522-548; James
T. Reitz, "The Soviet Security Troops -- The Kremlin's Other
Armies," pp. 549-580; R.W. Barnett, "Soviet Strategic Reserves
and the Soviet Navy," pp. 581-605; Leon Goure, "Soviet Para-
military Training Programs," pp. 606-610; Gregory Lathrop,
"The Soviet Military National University," pp. 611-633. Part VI.
Soviet Military Strategy: Its Development and Its Future. John
C. Baker, "Continuity and Change in Soviet Nuclear Strategy,"
pp. 636-660 [No. 146]; Amoretta M. Hoeber, "Soviet Strategic
Intentions," pp. 661-669 [No. 127]; Gregory D. Foster, "Soviet
Perceptions of U.S. Strategic Activities: A Realtime Retrospec-
tion," pp. 670-692 [No. 263]; G. Paul Holman, "Deterrence vs.
Warfighting: The View From Moscow," pp. 693-705 [No. 129];
Tommy L. Whitton, "Soviet Strategic Wartime Leadership," pp.
706-729 [No. 500]; Kenneth C. Stoehrmann, "Perceptual Dif-
ferences in Thinking the Unthinkable: World War III," pp.
730-751 [No. 300]; Richard S. Soll, "The Soviet Union and
Protracted Nuclear War," pp. 752-773 [No. 181]; David T.
Twining, "Message From Sverdlovsk: The April 1979 Anthrax
Incident," pp. 774-788. Part VII: A Soviet Emigre's View of the
U.S.-Soviet Strategic Relationship. Andrei Amalrik, "Three
Western Approaches to the USSR," pp. 790-796.

No. 580. Erickson, John; Edward L. Crowley, and Nikolai
Galay, (Eds.).
The Military-Technical Revolution: Its Impact on Strategic and
Foreign Policy.
New York: Frederick A. Praeger, Publisher, 1966, 284 p.

The chapters in this volume grew out of the papers presented at an international symposium on "The Impact of the Modern Military Revolution on Strategy and Foreign Policy," held at the Institute for the Study of the USSR in Munich, Germany. The development and effects of nuclear strategy on the foreign policies and alliance systems of the major world powers and the dilemma posed by this strategy are examined; the underlying military, political, and technological problems are reviewed; and future prospects for the resolution of the dilemma are presented.

Contents: John Erickson, "Introduction; Nuclear Strategy: World Dilemma," pp. 1-19; Nikolai Galay, "The Soviet Approach to the Modern Military Revolution," pp. 20-31 [No. 157]; Ferdinand O. Miksche, "Is the Atomic Deterrent a Bluff?", pp. 35-51; Thomas W. Wolfe, "Trends in Soviet Thinking on Theater Warfare and Limited War," pp. 52-79 [No. 403]; David Rees, "Towards the McNamara Doctrine," pp. 80-92; William Rodney, "Neutralism and the West," pp. 93-113; Hellmuth Roth, "The Organizational Crisis in NATO," pp. 114-128; Richard V. Burks, "The Political Cohesion of the Soviet Bloc," pp. 129-141; Michel Garder, "The Impact on Land Warfare," pp. 142-147; Robert W. Herrick, "Soviet Naval Strategy," pp. 148-169; Martin Edmonds, "The Future of Manned Aircraft," pp. 170-186; John R. Thomas, "The Role of Missile Defense in Soviet Strategy and Foreign Policy," pp. 187-218 [No. 324]; N. Talensky, "Anti-Missile Systems and Disarmament," pp. 219-228 [No. 662]; Robert D. Crane, "Psychostrategy: A New Concept," pp. 229-238; Raymond Garthoff, "Military Power in Soviet Policy," pp. 239-257 [No. 11]; Malcolm Mackintosh, "Implications of the Sino-Soviet Dispute," pp. 258-269; Herbert S. Dinerstein, "The United States and the Soviet Union: Standoff or Confrontation?", pp. 270-284 [No. 4].

No. 581. Erickson, John; and E.J. Feuchtwanger (Eds.).
Soviet Military Power and Performance.
Hamden, Conn.: Shoestring Press (Archon Books), 1979, 219 p.

The military power of the Soviet Union and the possible danger it poses to the peace of the world is a matter of continuous debate in the West. This contribution to the debate deals with the nature of the Russian military system, with the arms and organization of the Soviet Army, Navy, and Air Force, with the men in the Soviet armed forces, and with the strategic doctrines prevailing in the USSR, in conventional warfare as well as in the area of nuclear weapons, deterrence, and arms control. The authors pay particular attention to the style and the attitudes which shape military behavior and doctrine in the Soviet Union. Russia is not by nature and experience an aggressive nation, and her great military effort is regarded by the authors as fundamentally defensive.

Contents: Norman Stone, "The Historical Background of the Red Army," pp. 3-7; John Erickson, "The Soviet Military System: Doctrine, Technology, and 'Style'," pp. 18-44; John Hemsley, "The Soviet Ground Forces," pp. 47-73; John E. Moore, "The Soviet Navy," pp. 74-87; Alexander Boyd, "The Soviet Air Force," pp. 88-98; Chris Donnelly, "The Soviet Soldier: Behavior, Performance, Effectiveness," pp. 101-128; Teresa Rakowska-Harmstone, "The Soviet Army As the Instrument of National Integration," pp. 129-154; Richard Burt, "Arms Control and Soviet Strategic Forces: The Risk of Asking SALT to Do Too Much," pp. 157-182; Peter Vigor, "The 'Forward Reach' of the Soviet Armed Forces: Seaborne and Airborne Landings," pp. 183-211.

Reviewed by Max Beloff "The Military Factor in Soviet Foreign Policy," Problems of Communism Vol. 30 No. 1 (January-February 1981) pp. 70-73; Dale R. Herspring, Slavic Review Vol. 39 No. 2 (June 1980), p. 314-315; Dallace L. Meehan, Air University Review Vol. 33 No. 2 (January-February 1982), p. 129.

No. 582. Haley, P. Edward; David M. Keithly, and Jack Merritt (Eds.).
Nuclear Strategy, Arms Control, and the Future.
Boulder, Colo.: Westview Press, 1985, 372 p.

This text assembles statements on nuclear strategy and arms control made by Soviet and U.S. policymakers, military thinkers, and opinion leaders during the past forty years. Major Soviet statements, rarely appearing in translations, reflect the disagreement over whether "victory" or "parity" is the goal of Soviet nuclear strategy and forces. The general introduction is structured to sort out the seemingly inchoate mass of ideas surrounding the arms race.

Contents of Part Two, The Two Faces of Soviet Nuclear Strategy: Chapter 17) "The Nature of Modern War," Marshal V.D. Sokolovsky, pp. 138-145; 18) "The Nature of the Offensive Under Conditions Where Nuclear Weapons are Employed," Colonel A.A. Sidorenko, pp. 146-150; 19) "Modern Means of Waging War and Operational-Level Strategy," Colonel-General N.A. Lomov, pp. 151-154; 20) "Military Strategy," Marshal N.V. Ogarkov, pp. 154-156; 21) "The Morale Factor in Modern War," General-Major S.K. Il'in, pp. 157-158; 22) "Contrasts in American and Soviet Strategic Thought," Fritz W. Ermath, pp. 159-165 [No. 282]; 23) "Remarks on the Objectives of Soviet Nuclear Strategy: 1," Leonid Brezhnev, pp. 166-167; 24) Remarks on the Objectives of Soviet Nuclear Strategy: 2," Leonid Brezhnev, p. 168; 25) "A Debate Between Raymond Garthoff and Richard Pipes on Soviet Nuclear Strategy," Richard Pipes and Raymond Garthoff, pp. 169-178 [No. 158]; Bibliography, Part Two, pp. 179-181.

No. 583. Jones, David R. (Ed.).
The Military-Naval Encyclopedia of Russia and the Soviet Union.
Gulf Breeze, Fla.: Academic International Press.

This work aims to bring together material from Western, Tsarist, and Soviet sources for the use of the general reader, the scholar, and the professional soldier. It includes entries on individual military, military-political, and military-industrial leaders, past and present; the lives of war heroes; the history of particular ships, regiments, and formations, both Tsarist and Soviet; the details of weapons systems and their development; accounts of battles, campaigns, and wars; and compact historical articles on Russian military institutions and the branches of the Soviet armed forces; the details of treaties and other diplomatic events that directly affected Russia's military situation, and the military-political history of non-Russian areas that are now part of the USSR. There are also entries on the use of certain terms, on military thought and practice, and geographic sites of military significance.

Vol. 1 (1978) "A" (Gliders) through Administration, Military, 247 p.
Vol. 2 (1980) Administration, Military Science of through Admiral Makarov (Ship), 245 p.
Vol. 3 (1981) Admiral Murgescu (Ship) through ADP, ADP-Tail, 247 p.
Vol. 4 (1984) Adrian i Nadezhda (Ship) to Adzhariia, 249 p.

No. 584. Jones, David R. (Ed.).
Soviet Armed Forces Review Annual.
Gulf Breeze, Fla.: Academic International Press.

This is an independent yearly publication with two basic sections. First, each volume includes surveys of the five branches of the Soviet armed forces as well as of other military-related topics. Second, the basic surveys are followed by a group of historical and contemporary essays, documents on the history of the Soviet armed forces and military thought, and bibliographic surveys. The purpose of this group is to provide a context for further analysis, and to contribute to ongoing research. Overall, the series is intended to assemble and organize in a standard format all basic relevant public information on Soviet military affairs, together with analytical topical discussion, documentation, and bibliography, and thereby make available one central reference source.

Vol. 1, 1977 (277 p.): Peter H. Vigor, "Soviet Military Questions in 1974," pp. 1-12; Richard T. Ackley, "Strategic Rocket Forces," pp. 13-26; Christopher N. Donnelly, "The Ground Forces," pp. 27-39; David R. Jones, "National Air Defense Forces," pp. 40-47; Alfred L. Monks, "Air Forces," 48-64; Michael MccGwire, "Navy," pp. 65-76; Jacob W. Kipp,

"Naval Air Forces," pp. 77-82; Donald C. Daniel, "Merchant Marine," pp. 83-88; Carl G. Jacobsen, "Military Developments in the Far East," pp. 89-93; John A. McDonnell, "Defense Industry," pp. 94-98; William H. Schauer, "Space Program," pp. 99-117; Jacob W. Kipp, "Russian Naval Reformers and Imperial Expansion, 1856-1863," pp. 118-148; Carl G. Jacobsen, "Soviet Think Tanks," pp. 149-152; John A. McDonnell, "Leadership Changes at the 25th Party Congress," pp. 164-175; David R. Jones, "The Officers and Soviets, 1917-1920," pp. 176-187; Donald E. David and Walter S.G. Kohn, "Lenin's 'Notebook on Clausewitz'," pp. 188-221; Donald E. Davis and Walter S.G. Kohn, "Bibliographic Notes on Marxist and Leninist Military Theory," pp. 222-229; P.A. Zhilin, "Soviet Military-Historical Literature, 1965-1969," pp. 230-243; David R. Jones, "Checklist of Soviet Military Literature, 1965-1971," pp. 244-277.

Reviewed by Shane Mahoney, "Posture and Purpose of the Soviet Military," Problems of Communism Vol. 28 No. 1 (January-February 1979), pp. 55-58.

Vol. 2, 1978 (372 p.): Peter H. Vigor, "The Strategic Balance Sheet, 1976," pp. 1-4; "Statistical Overview, 1965-1977," pp. 5-29; David R. Jones, "Military Manpower," pp. 30-45; Richard T. Ackley, "Strategic Rocket Forces," pp. 46-58; Christopher N. Donnelly, "Ground Forces," pp. 59-78; David R. Jones, "National Air Defense Forces," pp. 79-129; Alfred Monks, "Air Forces," pp. 130-153; Donald Daniel, "Navy," pp. 154-197; Jacob W. Kipp, "Naval Air Forces," pp. 198-211; Donald C. Daniel, "Merchant Marine," pp. 212-217; Leslie Symons, "Aeroflot," pp. 227-238; Philip Hanson, "Defense Spending and the Economy," pp. 239-243; John McDonnell, "Defense Industry," pp. 244-247; Patrick J. Rollins, "The USSR and Black Africa," pp. 248-261; Carl G. Jacobsen, "Developments in the Far East," pp. 262-274; William H. Schauer, "Space Program," pp. 275-288; David R. Jones, "Civil Defense," pp. 289-350; Carl G. Jacobsen, "Angola and the Evolution of Soviet Theory and Capability for Intervention in Distant Areas," pp. 351-363; David R. Jones, "Checklist of Soviet Military Literature, 1965-1976 (Part II)," pp. 364-372.

Vol. 3, 1979 (364 p.): Carl G. Jacobsen, "The Soviet Strategic Posture in 1978," pp. 1-4; Richard T. Ackley, "Strategic Rocket Force," pp. 5-14; Christopher Donnelly, "Ground Force," pp. 15-23; David R. Jones, "National Air Defense Force," pp. 24-44; Alfred L. Monks, "Air Force," pp. 45-65; Donald C. Daniel, "Navy," pp. 66-102; Jacob W. Kipp, "Naval Aviation," pp. 103-107; Graham H. Turbiville, Jr., "Airborne Troops," pp. 108-112; Philip Hanson, "The Soviet Economy and Defense in 1977-1978," pp. 113-115; Chistopher D. Jones, "The Warsaw Pact," pp. 116-133; "The USSR and Black Africa," pp. 134-143; Carl G. Jacobsen, "Developments in the Far East," pp. 144-155;

William H. Schauer, "Space Program," pp. 156-174; John A.
McDonnell, "The Soviet Weapons Acquisition System," pp.
175-203; Alfred L. Monks, "The Rise of Marshal Grechko," pp.
204-224; Jacob W. Kipp, "Sergei Gorshkov and Naval Advocacy:
The Tsarist Heritage," pp. 225-238; Edward H. Cabaniss, IV,
"The Soviet Tank Battalion in the Offensive," pp. 239-255;
David R. Jones, "Motives and Consquences of the Red Army
Purges, 1937-1938," pp. 256-264; Ronald R. Rader, "Anglo-
French Estimates of the Red Army, 1936-1937," pp. 265-280;
Christopher D. Jones, "Dubcek, Jan Palach and the Gottwald
Memorandum: Could Czechoslovakia Have Deterred Soviet Inter-
vention?", pp. 281-299; David N. Collins, "The Russian Red
Guards of 1917-1918: A Bibliographic Survey," pp. 300-315;
John A. McDonald, "Analyzing the Soviet Military Press: Morskoi
Sbornik, 1963-1975," pp. 316-345; John G. Neilson, "Select
Checklist of Articles of the Soviet Armed Forces in the Western
Military Press," pp. 346-364.

Reviewed by Joseph Thach, Jr., Naval War College Review Vol.
33 No. 1 (January-February 1980), pp. 100-101.

Vol. 4, 1980 (400 p.): Carl G. Jacobsen, "1980: The Return of
the Cold War," pp. 1-5; "Statistical Overview and Analysis,
1979-1980," pp. 5-65; Richard T. Ackley, "Strategic Rocket
Forces," pp. 67-75; R.A. Woff, "Ground Forces," pp. 76-107;
David R. Jones, "National Air Defense Forces," pp. 108-173;
Alfred L. Monks, "Air Forces," pp. 174-196; Donald C. Daniel,
"Navy," pp. 197-218; James T. Westwood, "The Navy's Surface
Logistical Force," pp. 219-227; Peter Hertel Rasmussen, "Naval
Infantry," pp. 228-238; Jacob W. Kipp, "Naval Aviation," pp.
239-254; Graham H. Turbiville, Jr., "Airborne Troops," pp.
253-263; Phillip Hanson, "The Economy and Defense," pp.
264-267; John McDonnell, "Defense Industry," pp. 268-271;
Patrick J. Rollins, "The USSR and Africa," pp. 271-283; Carl G.
Jacobsen, "The Far East," pp. 284-291; William H. Schauer,
"Space Program," pp. 292-306; Ronald R. Rader, "The Russian
Military and Afghanistan: An Historical Perpective," pp. 308-327;
Lee Dowdy, "Soviet Military Aid to Third World States," pp.
328-336; Daniel S. Papp, "Nuclear Weapons and the Soviet World-
view," pp. 337-352; Robert Kennedy, "The Strategic Balance in
Transition: Interpreting Changes in U.S./USSR Weapons
Levels," pp. 352-372; Michael MccGwire, "The Navy's Changing
Place in Soviet Policy," pp. 373-383; John McDonnell, "The SALT
II Agreements," pp. 385-400.

Vol. 5, 1981 (329 p.): "Statistical Overview and Indicators of
Soviet Military Power, 1980-1981," pp. 1-30; Ken Booth, "1931 +
50: It's Later Than We Think," pp. 31-49; Richard T. Ackley,
"Strategic Rocket Forces," pp. 50-60; Richard A. Woff, "Ground
Forces," pp. 61-80; David R. Jones, "Air Defense Forces," pp.
81-117; Alfred L. Monks, "Air Forces," pp. 118-133; Donald C.

Daniel, "The Navy," pp. 134-152; Peter Hertel Rasmussen, "Naval Infantry," pp. 153-157; Graham H. Turbiville, Jr., "Airborne Troops," pp. 158-162; Philip Hanson, "The Economy, 1980-1981," pp. 163-166; Patrick J. Rollins, "The USSR and Africa 1980-1981," pp. 187-199; William H. Schauer, "Space Program," pp. 200-213; Charles J. Dick, "Chemical and Biological Warfare," pp. 214-233; Keith A. Dunn, "Soviet Power Projection: Capabilities and Limitations," pp. 234-255; Robert L. Arnett, "The Consequences of World War III: The Soviet Perspective," pp. 256-265; Peter H. Vigor, "The Military Strategy of the Russian Civil War," pp. 266-274; K.J. Cottam, "Soviet Women in Combat During World War II: The Rear Services, Partisans and Political Workers," pp. 275-294; Gregory L. Lathrop, "The Soviet Military as a National University," pp. 295-316; David R. Jones, "VOENNAIA MYSL, 1940-1969: A Partial Author Index (Part 1)," pp. 317-329.

Reviewed by Joseph Thach, Jr., Naval War College Review Vol. 35 No. 3 (May-June 1982), pp. 96-98.

Vol. 6, 1982 (432 p.): David R. Jones, "The Soviet Military Year in Review, 1981-1982," pp. 1-54; "Statistical Analysis and Overview," pp. 55-98; Maurice Tugwell, "An Era of Political Warfare," pp. 99-104; Richard T. Ackley, "Strategic Rocket Force," pp. 105-117; William P. Baxter, "Ground Forces," pp. 118-131; David R. Jones, "Air Defense Forces," pp. 132-195; Alfred L. Monks, "Air Forces," 196-210; Donald C. Daniel, "Navy," pp. 211-230; Peter Hertel Rasmussen, "Naval Infantry," pp. 231-234; Graham H. Turbiville, Jr., "Airborne Troops," pp. 235-241; Philip Hanson, "The Economy," pp. 242-246; Carl G. Jacobsen, "The Far East," pp. 247-256; William H. Schauer, "The Space Program," pp. 257-278; James T. Reitz, "The Soviet Security Troops -- the Kremlin's Other Armies," pp. 279-326; Ken Booth and Lee Dowdy, "Soviet Security Interests in the Indian Ocean Region," pp. 327-377; Allen F. Chew, "Evolution of the Soviet Rifle/Motorized-Rifle Division," pp. 378-395; Raymond J. Graves, "Select Bibliography of Articles on the Soviet Military and Strategic Issues, 1978-1981," pp. 396-410; David R. Jones, "VOENNAIA MYSL', 1940-1969: A Partial Author Index (Part II: I-S)," pp. 411-426; Cumulative Topical Table of Contents to Soviet Armed Forces Review Annual: 1-5 (1977-1981), pp. 427-431.

Vol. 7, 1982-1983 (491 p.): David R. Jones, "The Soviet Military Year in Review, 1982-1983," pp. 1-47; "Statistical Overview and Analysis, 1982-1983," pp. 48-109; John L. Scherer, "Chronology of Soviet Military Events, January-March 1983," pp. 110-117; Richard T. Ackley and Craig Britton, "Strategic Rocket Forces," pp. 118-135; William P. Baxter, "Ground Forces," pp. 136-157; Russell G. Breighner, "Air Defense Forces," pp. 158-176; Alfred L. Monks, "Air Forces," pp. 177-213; Donald C. Daniel and

Howard M. Hensel, "Navy," pp. 214-235; Jacob W. Kipp and Christopher Lovett, "Naval Aviation," pp. 236-262; Graham Hall Turbiville, Jr., "Airborne Troops," pp. 263-273; David A. Dyker, "The Economy," pp. 274-286; Patrick J. Rollins, "The USSR and Africa," pp. 287-309; Carl G. Jacobsen, "The Far East," pp. 310-323; William H. Schauer, "Space Program," pp. 324-345; Ronald G. Purver, "Soviet Arms Control Policy in 1982," pp. 346-428; Christopher Jones, "Warsaw Pact Exercises: The Genesis of a Greater Socialist Army?", pp. 429-450; Matthew A. Evangelista, "The Evolution of the Soviet Tactical Air Forces," pp. 451-479; Raymond J. Graves, "Select Bibliography of Articles and Books on Soviet Military and Strategic Issues, 1982," pp. 480-490.

No. 585. Kolkowicz, Roman, Matthew P. Gallagher, and Benjamin S. Lambeth with Walter C. Clemens, Jr., and Peter W. Colm. The Soviet Union and Arms Control: A Superpower Dilemma. Baltimore, Md.: The Johns Hopkins Press, 1970, 212 p.

This discussion of Soviet attitudes to arms control examines the domestic and internal factors that mold Soviet policy -- the political, economic, strategic, and institutional pressures inside the Soviet Union, as well as the stresses imposed by China, the United States, and Europe. It reveals the dimensions of the hawk-dove debate within the Soviet Union and the context in which it perceives its strategic interests, looking beyond the SALT talks to the realities on which U.S.-Soviet negotiations must be based if arms limitations are to be achieved, the balance of terror stabilized, and the mad momentum of war technology arrested.

Contents: Matthew Gallagher, "The Arms Control Issue in the Soviet Political Context," pp. 1-20; Roman Kolkowicz, "Soviet-American Strategic Relations: Implications for Arms Control," pp. 21-69; and "Conclusions and Projections," pp. 181-202; Benjamin S. Lambeth, "Nuclear Proliferation and Arms Control," pp. 70-115; Peter Colm, "Sino-Soviet Relations and the China Factor in Soviet Arms Control Policies," pp. 116-148; Walter C. Clemens, Jr., "Soviet Policies Toward Europe: Implications for Arms Control," pp. 149-180.

No. 586. Kolkowicz, Roman; and Ellen Mickiewicz (Eds.). The Soviet Calculus of Nuclear War. Lexington, Mass.: Lexington Books, 1986, 320 p.

This book examines the Soviet view of war and peace in the nuclear age. Western approaches to Soviet-American military relations are badly distorted by ethnocentric bias and by a crippling ignorance of the Soviet Union. Although their weapons and technological capabilities are known, as well as the cost of their defense, the West remains dangerously unaware of the rest of their complex society: the who, how, where, and why of the political and strategic decision-making process.

Contents: 1) Roman Kolkowicz, "The Soviet Union: The Elusive Adversary," pp. 1-24; 2) Benjamin Lambeth, "Contemporary Soviet Military Policy," pp. 25-48; 3) Desmond Ball, "Soviet Strategic Planning and the Control of Nuclear War," pp. 49-68; 4) Jeffrey Richelson, "Ballistic Missile Defense and Soviet Strategy," pp. 69-84; 5) Rose E. Gottemoeller, "Soviet Arms Control Decision Making since Brezhnev," pp. 85-114; 6) Anne T. Sloan, "Soviet Positions on Strategic Arms Control and Arms Policy: A Perspective outside the Military Establishment," pp. 115-142; 7) Harold Brown, Ralph Earle II, Gerard C. Smith, and Helmut Sonnenfeldt, "Negotiating with the Soviets and Prospects for Arms Control Negotiations," pp. 143-170; 8) Abraham S. Becker, "Sitting on Bayonets: The Soviet Defense Burden and the Slowdown of Soviet Defense Spending," pp. 171-204 [No. 515]; 9) Stan Woods, "Weapons Acquisition in the Soviet Union," pp. 205-242; 10) Dale R. Herspring, "The Soviet Union and the East European Militaries: The Diminishing Asset," pp. 243-266.

No. 587. Lee, Asher.
The Soviet Air and Rocket Forces.
London: Weidenfeld and Nicholson, 1959, 311 p.

Until recently, information about Soviet air and rocket developments was hard to come by, and the most a writer could do was to be usefully speculative. But since the Korean War, information has been much more freely available, although sources of raw information are not adequately on all or even most subjects concerning Soviet air and rocket power. This book has drawn on most of the available information on Soviet air and rocket forces, using contributors from the United States, Britain, and Germany, as well as ex-Soviet officers. Its sketches the rise of the Soviet Union to the position of strategic air and rocket parity with the Western powers, analyzes the current state of the forces, and projects their probable future course.

Contents: 1) George Schatunowski, "The Civil War to the Second World War," pp. 21-46; 2) Walter Schwabedissen, "From Barbarossa to Stalingrad," pp. 47-60; 3) Peter Williams, "From Stalingrad to Berlin," pp. 61-74; 4) Hanson Baldwin, "Soviet Air Strategy in the Second World War," pp. 75-88; 5) Kenneth Whiting, "Post-War Strategy," pp. 89-100; 6) Phillip Joubert, "Long Range Air Attack," pp. 101-116; 7) Asher Lee, "Strategic Air Defense," pp. 117-129; 8) William Green, "The Development of Jet Fighters and Fighter Bombers," pp. 130-145; 9) Asher Lee and Richard E. Stockwell, "Soviet Missiles," pp. 146-159; 10) J.M. Mackintosh, "Soviet Airborne Troops," pp. 160-169; 11) Raymond L. Garthoff, "Soviet Air Power: Organization and Staff Work," pp. 170-187; 12) George Schatunowski, "The Training of Personnel," pp. 188-200; 13) Boris Kuban, "Politics in the Soviet

Air Force," pp. 201-215; 14) Boris Kuban, "Daily Life in the Soviet Air Force," pp. 216-228; 15) Richard E. Stockwell, "The German Legacy," pp. 229-240; 16) Richard E. Stockwell, "Soviet Aircraft Production," pp. 241-255; 17) Kenneth Whiting, "Soviet Civil Aviation," pp. 256-269; 18) Asher Lee, "The Air Allies of the USSR," pp. 270-286; and 19) Asher Lee, "The Future of Soviet Air Power," pp. 287-311.

Reviewed by Christopher R. Keegan, Military Review Vol. 39 No. 12 (March 1960), p. 112.

No. 588. Leebaert, Derek (Ed.).
Soviet Military Thinking.
London: George Allen and Unwin, 1981, 300 p.

This book brings together a number of prominent policy analysts to examine the influences affecting Soviet military planning and theory, and to ask what policy implications can be drawn from them. Their work offers an insight into the premises and calculations surrounding the Soviet conception of power. The book's assumption is that there has long been a missed connection in the United States between scholars focusing on Soviet studies and those who deal with military strategy, although the Soviets themselves have been far more attentive to the integration of these different disciplines.

Contents: Derek Leebaert, "The Context of Soviet Military Thinking," pp. 3-27; Robert Bathurst, "Two Languages of War," pp. 28-43; Fritz W. Ermarth, "Contrasts in American and Soviet Strategic Thought," pp. 50-69 [No. 282]; Stanley Sienkiewicz, "Soviet Nuclear Doctrine and the Prospects for Strategic Arms Control," pp. 73-91 [No. 80]; Raymond L. Garthoff, "Mutual Deterrence, Parity, and Strategic Arms Limitation in Soviet Policy," pp. 92-124 [No. 107]; Michael MccGwire, "Soviet Naval Doctrine and Strategy," pp. 125-181; Nathan Leites, "The Soviet Style of War," pp. 185-224 [No. 91]; Christopher Jones, "Soviet Military Doctrine and Warsaw Pact Exercises," pp. 225-258; David Holloway, "Doctrine and Technology in Soviet Armaments Policy," pp. 259-291.

Reviewed by Stanley Kober, "Interpreting Soviet Strategic Policy," Comparative Strategy Vol. 3 No. 1 (1983), pp. 65-74; Edgar O'Ballance, The Soviet Belief in Victory in a Nuclear War, Foreign Affairs Research Institute Report 13/1983, 7 p.; Francis Wright, Friday Review of Defense Literature 83-3 (21 January 1983), p. 6.

No. 589. Liddell Hart, Basil H. (Ed.).
The Red Army.
New York: Harcourt, Brace and Company, 1956, 480 p.

306

This appraisal of the modern Soviet military experience is made
by a group of noted military experts -- American, British,
French, Czech, German, and Russian -- some of whom fought
with the Soviet Union, and some against it. Present Soviet
strategy, espionage, guided missiles, chemical warfare, growth
of the navy and submarine fleet, threat to American air
superiority, and probable present dominance in airborne potential
are discussed, as well as current Soviet military equipment.
The history moves from the Czarist regime to the 1917 revolution,
and advances over 40 years to today's Soviet Army -- with its
many weaknesses and undisclosed strength.

Infantry: Recent Trends," pp. 328-336; 29) A. Niessel, "Caval-
ry," pp. 337-343; 30) Harold J. Gordon, "Artillery," pp. 344-
366; 31) Hellmuth Dorn, "Engineers and Technical Services," pp.
367-375; 32) Kurt Student, "Airborne Forces," pp. 376-383; 33)
V. Pozdnyakov, "The Chemical Arm," pp. 384-394; 34) Louis B.
Ely, "The Officer Corps," pp. 395-402; 35) J.M. Mackintosh,
"The Soviet Soldiers' Conditions of Service," pp. 403-410; 36)
Mikhail Koriakov, "The Military Atmosphere," pp. 411-419; 37)
G.C. Reinhardt, "Atomic Weapons and Warfare," pp. 420-438
[No. 397]; 38) J.M. Mackintosh, "The Satellite Armies," pp.
439-451; 39) Eric Ashby, "Science and the Soviet Army," pp.
452-460.

No. 590. MccGwire, Michael; and John McDonnell (Eds.).
Soviet Naval Influences: Domestic and Foreign Dimensions.
New York: Praeger Publishers, 1977, 698 p.

Although this book derives from the third annual seminar held
on Soviet naval developments held at Dalhousie University in
September 1974, it is actually made up of text submitted subsequently, up to mid-1976. It is the third volume in a series
produced through face-to-face discussions among some of the
most respected and well-informed specialists on the Soviet Navy
(also see the two following entries). The papers in this collection were heavily influenced by two works by Admiral of the
Fleet of the Soviet Union S.G. Gorshkov, "Navies in War and
Peace" (1972-73), and The Seapower of the State (1975).

Contents: 1) Vernon V. Aspaturian, "Detente and the Strategic
Balance," pp. 3-30; 2) Michael MccGwire, "The Overseas Role of
a 'Soviet Military Presence'," pp. 31-40; 3) John McDonnell,
"The Organization of Soviet Defense and Military Policy Making,"
pp. 61-106 [No. 491]; 4) James A. Barry, Jr., "Soviet Naval
Policy: The Institutional Setting," pp. 107-122; 5) David
Holloway, "Technological Change and Military Procurement," pp.
123-131 [No. 521]; 6) Michael MccGwire, "The Navy and Soviet
Oceans Policy," pp. 133-150; 7) K.J. Moore, Mark Flanigan, and
Robert D. Helsel, "Developments in Submarine Systems, 1956-
1976," pp. 151-184; 8) K.J. Moore, "Antisubmarine Warfare,"
pp. 185-200; 9) Jacob W. Kipp, "Soviet Naval Aviation," pp.
201-217; 10) Oles Smolansky, "Soviet Policy Toward Aircraft
Carriers," pp. 218-238; 11) James L. Moulton, "The Capability
for Long-Range Intervention," pp. 239-245; 12) Charles G.
Pritchard, "Soviet Amphibious Force Projection," pp. 246-277;
13) Graham H. Turbiville, Jr., "Soviet Airborne Troops," pp.
278-290; 14) Richard T. Ackley, "The Merchant Fleet," pp.
291-310; 15) Richard T. Ackley, "The Fishing Fleet," pp. 311-
321; 16) Robert P. Berman, "Soviet Naval Strength and Deployment," pp. 323-326; 17) Michael MccGwire, "Comparative Naval
Building Programs: East and West," pp. 327-336; 18) Michael
MccGwire, "Soviet Naval Programs," pp. 337-363; 19) James W.
Kehoe, Jr., "Warship Design: Ours and Theirs," pp. 364-386;

20) Herbert A. Meier, "Methodology for Analyzing Foreign Warships," pp. 387-401; 21) Robert G. Weinland, "The State and Future of the Soviet Navy in the North Atlantic," pp. 403-425; 22) Barry M. Blechman and Stephanie E. Levinson, "Soviet Submarine Visits to Cuba," pp. 426-443; 23) George Ginsburgs, "The Soviet Quest for Influence and Military Facilities in the Third World," pp. 445-459; 24) Ken Booth, "Warships and Political Influence," pp. 459-482; 25) Bradford Dismukes, "Soviet Employment of Naval Power for Political Purpose, 1967-1975," pp. 483-509; 26) Anne M. Kelly, "Port Visits and the 'International Mission' of the Soviet Navy," pp. 510-529; 27) Michael L. Squires and Ann R. Patterson, "Soviet Naval Transfers to Developing Countries, 1956-75," pp. 530-538; 28) Charles C. Peterson, "Soviet Mineclearing Operations in the Gulf of Suez," pp. 539-563; 29) James McConnell, "The Gorshkov Articles, the New Gorshkov Book, and Their Relation to Policy," pp. 565-620 [No. 448]; 30) Michael MccGwire, "The Soviet Navy in the Seventies," pp. 621-657.

Reviewed by: Robert J. Hanks, Strategic Review Vol. 5 No. 4 (Fall 1977), pp. 95-99; Gordon S. Brown, History, Numbers, and War Vol. 1 No. 4 (Winter 1977-1978), pp. 253-260; and Dov Zakheim, Air University Review Vol. 34 No. 5 (July/August 1978), pp. 90-91.

No. 591. MccGwire, Michael; Ken Booth, and John McConnell (Eds.).
Soviet Naval Policy: Objectives and Contraints.
New York: Praeger Publishers, 1975, 663 p.

This book is derived from a seminar on Soviet naval developments held at Dalhousie University in Nova Scotia in October 1973. It was the second in a series of seminars with an inter-disciplinary and cross-occupational approach, bringing several perspectives and analytical techniques to bear, with the emphasis always on the Soviet point of view. The purpose is to raise the level of informed analysis and debate on the subject by ensuring 1) that hard data on Soviet naval capabilities and deployments are made readily available, and 2) that analysis of Soviet naval policy is carried out within the full and proper context. Admiral S.G. Gorshkov's series of articles, "Navies in War and Peace," provided the backdrop to these discussions. The collection is intended to complement the first volume of the series (see the following abstract).

Contents: 1) Marshall D. Shulman, "Trends in Soviet Foreign Policy," pp. 3-22; 2) Malcolm Mackintosh, "The Soviet Military's Influence on Foreign Policy," pp. 23-39 [No. 22]; 3) Matthew P. Gallagher, "The Military Role in Soviet Decision-making," pp. 40-58; 4) John Erickson, "Soviet Defense Policies and Naval Interests," pp. 59-65; 5) Edward L. Warner, III, "The Bureaucratic Politics of Weapons Procurement," pp. 66-86; 6)

309

John McDonnell, "The Soviet Defense Industry as a Pressure Group," pp. 87-122; 7) Philip Hanson, "Analysis of Soviet Defense Expenditures," pp. 123-136; 8) John P. Hardt, "National Economic Priorities and Naval Demand," pp. 137-144; 9) Ken Booth, "Summary of Discussion in Part I," pp. 145-152; 10) Alvin Z. Rubinstein, "The Soviet-Egyptian Influence Relationship Since the June 1967 War," pp. 153-181; 11) Uri Ra'anan, "Soviet Decision-making in the Middle East, 1969-1973," pp. 182-210; 12) Robert O. Freedman, "The Soviet Union and Sadat's Egypt," 211-236; 13) George S. Dragnich, "The Soviet Union's Quest for Access to Naval Facilities in Egypt Prior to the June War of 1967," pp. 237-277; 14) Oles M. Smolansky, "Soviet Policy in the Persian Gulf," pp. 278-286; 15) Anne M. Kelly, "The Soviet Naval Presence During the Iraq-Kuwait Border Dispute," pp. 287-306; 16) Geoffrey Jukes, "Soviet Policy in the Indian Ocean," pp. 307-318; 17) Charles C. Petersen, "The Soviet Port-Clearing Operations in Bangladesh," pp. 319-340; 18) Robert L. Friedheim and Mary E. Jehn, "The Soviet Position at the Third U.N. Law of the Sea Conference," p. 341-362; 19) Ken Booth, "Summary of Discussion in Part II," pp. 363-373; 20) Robert G. Weinland, "Soviet Naval Operations: 10 Years of Change," pp. 375-386; 21) Michael MccGwire, "Foreign-Port Visits by Soviet Naval Units," pp. 387-418; 22) Robert Berman, "Soviet Naval Strength and Deployment," pp. 419-423; 23) Michael MccGwire, "Current Soviet Warship Construction and Naval Weapons Development," pp. 424-451; 24) Nigel D. Brodeur, "Comparative Capabilities of Soviet and Western Weapon Systems," pp. 452-469; 25) Peter H. Vigor, "The Semantics of Deterrence and Defense," pp. 471-478; 26) Geoffrey Jukes, "The Military Approach to Deterrence and Defense," pp. 479-485; 27) Michael MccGwire, "Soviet Strategic Weapons Policy," pp. 486-503; 28) Michael MccGwire, "The Evolution of Soviet Naval Policy: 1960-1974," pp. 505-546; 29) Robert Weinland, "Analysis of Admiral Gorshkov's 'Navies in War and Peace'," pp. 547-572; 30) Bradford Dismukes, "The Soviet Naval General Purpose Forces: Roles and Missions in Wartime," pp. 573-584 [No. 439]; 31) Harlan Ullman, "The Counter-Polaris Task," pp. 585-600; 32) Peter H. Vigor, "Soviet Understanding of 'Command of the Sea'," pp. 601-622; 33) Michael MccGwire, "Command of the Sea in Soviet Naval Strategy," pp. 623-636; 34) Franklyn Griffiths, "The Tactical Uses of Naval Arms Control," pp. 637-660.

Reviewed by: Orest M. Krause, Military Review Vol. 55 No. 11 (November 1975), pp. 107-108.

No. 592. MccGwire, Michael (Ed.).
Soviet Naval Developments: Capability and Context.
New York: Praeger Publishers, 1973, 555 p.

This collection of papers derives from a seminar held at Dalhousie University in October 1972. The need for such a gathering had been suggested by numerous contradictory assertions about the

310

substance and significance of Soviet naval developments, which were advanced during the public discussions on U.S. naval appropriations the previous spring. Although the seminar was intended to identify current trends and future possibilities in Soviet naval policy, its prior concern was to establish a reasonably solid frame of reference within which to assess contemporary developments. It must be stressed that these papers deliberately concentrate on the Soviet point of view. There is no attempt to discuss the implications of Soviet naval developments in terms of Western interests, except to the extent that Western actions have an effect on Soviet policy decisions.

Contents: 1) Franklyn Griffiths, "Forward Deployment and Foreign Policy," pp. 9-15; 2) P.H. Vigor, "The Soviet View of War," pp. 16-31 [No. 63]; 3) Ken Booth, "Military Power, Military Force, and Soviet Foreign Policy," pp. 31-56; 4) Malcolm Mackintosh, "Soviet Military Policy," pp. 57-69; 5) Thomas W. Wolfe, "Soviet Strategic Policy," pp. 70-81; 6) Charles Stockell, "Soviet Military Strategy: The Army View," pp. 82-92 [No. 430]; 7) Robert E. Athay, "Perspectives on Soviet Merchant Shipping Policy," pp. 93-108; 8) William E. Butler, "The Legal Dimension of Soviet Maritime Policy," pp. 109-124; 9) Michael MccGwire, "Naval Nomenclature," pp. 125-128; 10) Robert P. Berman, "Soviet Naval Strength and Deployment," pp. 192-135; 11) Michael MccGwire, "Current Soviet Warship Construction," pp. 136-143; 12) Michael MccGwire, "Comparative Warship Building Programs," pp. 144-150; 13) Michael MccGwire, "The Structure of the Soviet Navy," pp. 151-162; 14) Michael MccGwire, "Parallel Naval Developments," pp. 163-172; 15) Charles W. Stockell, "The Soviet Naval Infantry," pp. 172-175; 16) Michael MccGwire, "The Turning Points in Soviet Naval Policy," pp. 176-209; 17) Raymond Hutchings, "The Economic Burden of the Soviet Navy," pp. 210-227; 18) Michael MccGwire, "The Economic Costs of Forward Deployment," pp. 228-238; 19) Donald W. Mitchell, "Traditional Russian Maritime Strategy," pp. 239-244; 20) Thomas W. Wolfe, "Soviet Naval Interaction with the United States and its Influence on Soviet Naval Developments," pp. 245-276; 21) George E. Hudson, "Soviet Naval Doctrine, 1953-1972," pp. 277-291; 22) Robert G. Weinland, "The Changing Mission Structure of the Soviet Navy," pp. 292-305; 23) Robert W. Herrick, "The Gorshkov Interpretation of Russian Naval History," pp. 306-323 [No. 440]; 24) Robert G. Weinland, "Soviet Transits of the Turkish Straits, 1945-1970," pp. 325-343; 25) Michael MccGwire, "The Mediterranean and Soviet Naval Interests," pp. 344-357; 26) Oles M. Smolansky and Carey B. Joynt, "The Political Background to Soviet Naval Policy in the Mediterranean," pp. 358-381; 27) Michael MccGwire, "The Soviet Mediterranean Squadron, January 1968-June 1969: Deployment of Surface Combatants," pp. 382-388; 28) James M. McConnell, "The Soviet Navy in the Indian Ocean," pp. 389-406; 29) Oles M. Smolansky, "Soviet Entry Into the Indian Ocean: An Analysis," pp. 407-424; 30) Michael MccGwire, "The Pattern of Soviet Naval Deployment in the Indian Ocean, 1968-71," pp. 425-

441; 31) James M. McConnell and Anne M. Kelly, "Superpower Naval Diplomacy in the Indo-Pakistani Crisis," pp. 442-457; 32) Donald W. Mitchell, "The Strategic Significance of Soviet Naval Power in Cuban Waters," pp. 459-469; 33) Michael MccGwire, "Soviet Naval Interests and Intentions in the Caribbean," pp. 470-489; 34) Michael MccGwire, "Soviet Naval Policy: Prospects for the Seventies," pp. 491-519; 35) Barry M. Blechman, "Soviet Interests in Naval Arms Control: Prospects for Disengagement in the Mediterranean," pp. 520-534; 36) Michael MccGwire, "Soviet Maritime Strategy: Purposive or Preventive?", pp. 535-538; Michael MccGwire, "Epilogue: Western Naval Inputs to the Soviet Policy Process," pp. 539-540; Appendix A: Questions to be Answered, pp. 541-543; Appendix B: The Range of Naval Evidence, pp. 544-547.

No. 593. "Soviet Aerospace Almanac No. 1."
Air Force Magazine Vol. 58 No. 3 (March 1975), pp. 33-84.

Contents: William Scott, "Soviet Aerospace Forces and Doctrines," pp. 33-36; Edgar Ulsamer, "The Soviet Drive for Aerospace Superiority," pp. 44-48; Charles Sheldon "The Soviet Space Program," pp. 50-56; Harriet Scott, "Educating the Soviet Officer Corps," pp. 57-61; John Taylor, "Gallery of Soviet Aerospace Weapons," pp. 62-75; "Soviet Armed Forces -- Facts and Figures," pp. 76-84.

"Soviet Aerospace Almanac No. 2."
Air Force Magazine Vol. 59 No. 3 (March 1976), pp. 37-120.

Contents: William Scott, "Soviet Aerospace Forces: Continuity and Contrast," pp. 38-47; William Lee, "Military Economics in the USSR," pp. 48-55; Edgar Ulsamer, "The Soviet Juggernaut: Racing Faster Than Ever," pp. 56-68; Norman Polmar, "Soviet Naval Aviation," pp. 69-74; Harriet Scott, "The Military Profession in the USSR," pp. 75-81; Charles Sheldon, "Soviet Space Activities in 1975," pp. 82-87; Joseph Douglass, Jr., "Soviet Military Thought," pp. 88-92; John Taylor, "Gallery of Soviet Aerospace Weapons," pp. 93-107; "Soviet Armed Forces -- Facts and Figures," pp. 108-120.

"Soviet Aerospace Almanac No. 3."
Air Force Magazine Vol. 60 No. 3 (March 1977), pp. 35-110.

Contents: Edgar Ulsamer, "The USSR's Military Shadow is Lengthening," pp. 36-46; Leon Goure, "Soviet Military Doctrine," pp. 57-61; Harriet Scott, "The Soviet High Command," pp. 52-56; William Scott, "The USSR's Growing Tactical Mobility," pp. 57-61; Colin Gray, "Soviet Tactical Airpower," pp. 62-71; Charles Sheldon II, "Soviet Space Activities in 1976," pp. 72-77; David Smith, "Soviet Military Manpower," pp. 78-81; Frederick

Turner, "The Soviet G.I.," pp. 82-83; William Lee, "Trends in Soviet Military Spending," pp. 84-87; John Taylor, "Gallery of Soviet Aerospace Weapons," pp. 88-103; Harriet Scott, "Organization of Soviet Aerospace Forces," p. 104 and "Soviet Military Organization Charts," pp. 105-108; "Soviet Armed Forces Facts and Figures," pp. 109-110.

"Soviet Aerospace Almanac No. 4."
Air Force Magazine Vol. 61 No. 3 (March 1978), pp. 33-114.

Contents: Edgar Ulsamer, "The Accelerating Momentum of Soviet Military Might," pp. 34-41; Norman Polmar, "The Soviet SLBM Force," pp. 42-48; Colin Gray, "Strategic Rocket Forces: Military Capability, Political Utility," pp. 49-55 [No. 46]; William Scott, "Troops of National Air Defense," pp. 56-66 [No. 317]; Norman Polmar, "Soviet Naval Aviation," pp. 67-73; Charles Sheldon II, "Soviet Space Activities in 1977," pp. 74-77; Daniel Malone, "Air Defense of Soviet Ground Forces," pp. 78-83; Harriet Scott, "Universal Military Training in the USSR," pp. 84-87; John Taylor, "Gallery of Soviet Aerospace Weapons," pp. 93-114.

"Soviet Aerospace Almanac No. 5."
Air Force Magazine Vol. 62 No. 3 (March 1979), pp. 39-115.

Contents: Edgar Ulsamer, "World Hegemony Through Military Superiority," pp. 40-47; Peter Hughes, "SALT and the Emerging Strategic Threat," pp. 48-53; William Lee, "Soviet Military Policy: Objectives and Capabilities," pp. 54-59; Colin Gray, "Soviet Strategic Vulnerabilities," pp. 60-64; Norman Friedman, "The Soviet Mobilization Base," pp. 65-71; William F. Scott, "Soviet Perceptions of U.S. Strategy," pp. 72-75; William Schneider, Jr., "Trends in Soviet Frontal Aviation," pp. 76-81; Charles Sheldon II, "Soviet Space Activities in 1978," pp. 82-87; Harriet Fast Scott, "A Look at Soviet Military Recreation," pp. 88-93; John Taylor, "Gallery of Soviet Aerospace Weapons," pp. 99-115.

"Soviet Aerospace Almanac No. 6."
Air Force Magazine Vol. 63 No. 3 (March 1980), pp. 41-135.

Contents: Edgar Ulsamer, "Moscow's Goal in Military Superiority," pp. 42-53; Steve Kime, "How the Soviet Union is Ruled," pp. 54-59; William and Harriet Scott, "The Social Sciences Institutes of the Soviet Academy of Sciences," pp. 60-65; Colin Gray, "Arms Control in Soviet Policy," pp. 66-71; F. Clifton Berry, Jr., "Military Aircraft Exports: Soviet Foreign Policy Tool," pp. 72-79; William Schneider, Jr., "Soviet Military Airlift: Key to Rapid Power Projection," pp. 80-87; Charles Sheldon II, "The Soviet Space Program in 1979," pp. 88-93; Phillip Petersen, "Flexibility: A Driving Force in Soviet

Strategy," pp. 94-99; William Lee, "The Soviet Defense Establishment in the '80s," pp. 100-108; Harriet Scott, "Top Leaders of the Soviet Armed Forces," pp. 109-116; Gene Townsend, "A Charter for Better Understanding," pp. 117-118; John Taylor, "Gallery of Soviet Aerospace Weapons," pp. 119-135.

"Soviet Aerospace Almanac No. 7."
Air Force Magazine Vol. 64 No. 3 (March 1981), pp. 41-130.

Contents: Edgar Ulsamer, "The Politburo's Grand Design: Total Military Superiority," pp. 41-49; Paul Holman, "Deterrence vs. War-Fighting: The Soviet Preference," pp. 50-54 [No. 129]; Christina Shelton, "The Soviet System for Commissioning Officers," pp. 55-60; Jill Heuer, "The Role of the Soviet S&T Officer," pp. 61-67; Lynn Hanson, "Soviet Airpower: Behind the Buildup," pp. 68-76; Harriet Scott, "Top Leaders of the Soviet Armed Forces," pp. 77; Robert Kennedy, "Soviet Theater Nuclear Forces," pp. 78-83; William and Harriet Scott, "Space: Are the Soviets Ahead?", pp. 84-89; Nicholas Johnson, "Soviet Satellite Reconnaissance Trends," pp. 90-96; "Organization of Soviet Armed Forces," pp. 97-100; John Taylor, "Gallery of Soviet Aerospace Weapons," pp. 101-118; Peter Vanneman and Martin James, "Soviet Coercive Diplomacy: Saudi Arabia," pp. 119-123; David Twining, "Sverdlovsk Anthrax Outbreak," pp. 124-130.

"Soviet Aerospace Almanac No. 8."
Air Force Magazine Vol. 65 No. 3 (March 1982), pp. 38-110.

Contents: Edgar Ulsamer, "Military Power is the Root of Soviet Expansionism," pp. 38-42; William Scott, "Continuity and Change in Soviet Military Organization and Concepts," pp. 43-48; Harriet Scott, "Organization of the Soviet Armed Forces," pp. 49-61; Colin Gray, "The Idea of Strategic Superiority," pp. 62-63; Leon Goure, "The Soviet Scorecard on the Reagan Administration's First Year," pp. 64-73; Frank Dellerman, "STARTing from Reality," pp. 74-84; "Disinformation: War With Words," pp. 85-87; D.B. Lawrence, "Soviet Radioelectronic Combat," pp. 88-91; Kerry Hines, "Frontal Aviation: Committed to Air Superiority," pp. 92-94; John Taylor, "Gallery of Soviet Aerospace Weapons," pp. 95-110.

"Soviet Aerospace Almanac No. 9."
Air Force Magazine Vol. 66 No. 3 (March 1983), pp. 40-110.

Contents: Edgar Ulsamer, "Will Economic Weakness Increase Soviet Militancy?", pp. 40-47; Nicholas Johnson, "Soviet Strides in Space," pp. 48-52; Harriet Scott, "Top Leaders and Organization of the Soviet Armed Forces," pp. 53-57; Harriet Scott, "The Strategic Rocket Forces and Their Five Elites," pp. 58-63;

William Scott, "The Myth of Free Travel in the USSR," pp. 64-73; Alan Bergstrom, "Ivan is Only About 5'8"," pp. 74-78; John Taylor, "Gallery of Soviet Aerospace Weapons," pp. 79-110.

"Soviet Aerospace Almanac No. 10."
Air Force Magazine Vol. 67 No. 3 (March 1984), pp. 62-127.

Articles: Edgar Ulsamer, "Beyond Andropov," pp. 62-67; William F. Scott, "The Themes of Soviet Strategy," pp. 68-73 [No. 399]; Harriet Fast Scott, "Deadly Guardians of Soviet Airspace," pp. 74-82; Rana J. Pennington, "Closing the Tactics Gap," pp. 83-91; Sergei I. Sikorsky, "Make It Simple...Make it Work," pp. 92-95; Richard D. Ward, "The Structured World of the Soviet Designer," pp. 96-103; Harriet Fast Scott, "Organization of the Soviet Armed Forces," pp. 104-106; Harriet Fast Scott, "Top Leaders of the Soviet Armed Forces," p. 107; Dino A. Brugioni, "The Tyuratam Enigma," pp. 108-110; John W.R. Taylor, "Gallery of Soviet Aerospace Weapons," pp. 111-127.

"Soviet Aerospace Almanac No. 11."
Air Force Magazine Vol. 68 No. 3 (March 1985), pp. 48-113.

Contents: William F. Scott, "Soviet Concepts of War," pp. 48-52 [No. 180]; Harriet Fast Scott, "Top Leaders of the Soviet Armed Forces," p. 53; Harriet Fast Scott, "Organization of the Soviet Armed Forces," pp. 54-57; Harriet Fast Scott, "Red Stars in Motion," pp. 58-63; Richard D. Ward, "MiG-2000," pp. 64-73; James P. Coyne, "Frontal Aviation's One-Two Punch," pp. 74-77; Norman Polmar, "Soviet Naval Air Moves Up and Out," pp. 78-87; Sergei Sikorsky, "From Hind to Havoc," pp. 88-96; John W.R. Taylor, "Gallery of Soviet Aerospace Weapons," pp. 97-113.

"Soviet Aerospace Alamanc No. 12."
Air Force Magazine Vol. 69 No. 3 (March 1986), pp. 40-99.

Contents: William F. Scott, "The Soviets and Strategic Defense," pp. 40-45 [No. 318]; Harriet Fast Scott, "The Party Assembled," pp. 46-51; James Oberg, "The Sky's No Limit to Disinformation," pp. 52-58; Harriet Fast Scott, "Top Leaders of the Soviet Union," p. 59; Harriet Fast Scott, "Senior Military Leadership Changes for 1985," pp. 60-61; Harriet Fast Scott, "Organization of the Soviet Armed Forces," pp. 62-64; "Soviet Aerospace Almanac 1986," pp. 65-82; John W.R. Taylor, "Gallery of Soviet Aerospace Weapons," pp. 83-99.

No. 594. Vernon, Graham D. (Ed.)
Soviet Perceptions of War and Peace.

Washington, D.C.: National Defense University Press, 1981, 185 p.

The United States and the Soviet Union have widely different histories, cultures, and ideologies. Hence, it should not be surprising that the citizens and governments of both super-powers often approach, discuss, and resolve issues in fundamentally different ways. Although this thesis may be easy to accept in theory, it is often difficult for Americans to accept in practice. To suggest that it is useful for the United States to understand why the Soviets take a given stance is not to suggest acceptance of it. It is to suggest that because the two countries have contacts in various areas -- economic, cultural, military -- U.S. interests will be better served if we understand the "why" behind the "what" in Soviet policy. To that end, these studies present Soviet perceptions of certain political and military issues directly affecting the United States.

Contents: 1) John Dziak, "The Institutional Foundations of Soviet Military Doctrine," pp. 3-16 [No. 186]; 2) William P. Baxter, "Soviet Perceptions of the Laws of War," pp. 17-26 [No. 36]; 3) Dallas C. Brown, "Origins of the Cold War: The Soviet View," pp. 27-50 [No. 261]; 4) Steven F. Kime, "The Soviet View of War," pp. 51-66 [No. 51]; 5) William T. Lee, "Soviet Perceptions of the Threat and Soviet Military Capabilities," pp. 67-96 [No. 270]; 6) William F. Scott and Harriet Fast Scott, "Soviet Perceptions of U.S. Military Strategies and Forces," pp. 97-112 [No. 275]; 7) Graham D. Vernon, "Controlled Conflict: Soviet Perceptions of Peaceful Coexistence," pp. 113-142 [No. 28]; Nils H. Wessell, "Soviet Views of Multipolarity and the Emerging Balance of Power," pp. 143-172.

B. BIBLIOGRAPHIES

No. 595. National Security, Military Power, and the Role of Force in International Relations.
Washington, D.C.: Government Printing Office (DA PAM 550-19), September 1976, 171 p.

The 850 abstracts included in this publication were selected from a vast number of books, periodical articles, studies, and documents, which in their aggregate reflect on the complexities of National Security, Military Power, and the Role of Force in International Relations, covering the period from 1946 to 1976. They are arranged in seven chapers: I) Marxist-Leninist Dogma, Soviet Global Ambitions, and Strategies for War; II) National Security of States, Defense Policies, and Foreign Policies; III) National Military Preparedness and Force Postures; IV) Power and Force and International Relations; V) Doctrines and Strategies for Security and Survival: United States and Other

316

Western Nations; VI) National Power and the Control and Limita-
tion of Force; VII) Bibliographic Sources for Research and
Reference. The publication concludes with an essay by Fred C.
Weyand and Harry G. Summers, "Serving the People -- the Need
For Military Power."

No. 596. Parrish, Michael.
The Soviet Armed Forces: Books in English.
Stanford, Calif.: The Hoover Institution Press (Hoover Institu-
tion Bibliographical Series: XLVIII), 1970, 128 p.

This bibliography gathers and organizes a variety of publications
on the Soviet armed forces into twenty categories. It includes
books, journal articles (many not indexed previously), documents, and monographs and special studies gathered systematically from Western sources. It also includes translations from
leading Soviet sources published by the Joint Publications
Research Service of the U.S. Department of Commerce.

No. 597. Smith, Myron J., Jr.
The Soviet Navy, 1941-1978: A Guide to Sources in English.
Santa Barbara, Calif.: The American Bibliographic Company-Clio,
1980, 211 p.

This bibliography is intended to serve as a working guide to
English-language sources concerning the Soviet Navy. There
are eleven main sections to this work: 1) Reference Works; 2)
World War II; 3) The Balance of Power and Arms Control; 4)
Background and Naval Rivalry; 5) Government and Economics; 6)
Policy and Strategy; 7) Forward Deployment and Western
Responses; 8) Warships, Warfare, and Armaments; 9) the Naval
Air Force; 10) the Naval Infantry; and 11) Audiovisual Sources.
There are a total of 1741 entries.

No. 598. Smith, Myron J., Jr.
The Soviet Air and Strategic Rocket Forces, 1939-1980: A Guide
to Sources in English.
Santa Barbara, Calif.: The American Bibliographic Company-Clio,
1981, 320 p.

This bibliography is intended to serve as a working guide to
English-language sources concerning the Soviet Air Forces, the
National Air Defense Force, and the Strategic Rocket Force.
There are seven main sections to this work: 1) Reference
Works; 2) The Era of World War II; 3) The Soviet Economy and
Defense Establishment; 4) Soviet Aerospace Forces, 1946 to the
Present; 5) Soviet Aerospace Weapons Systems; 6) Arms Competi-
tion, Arms Control, and the Balance of Power; and 7) Soviet
Aerospace Arms and Assistance Around the Globe, 1945-1980.
There are a total of 3350 entries.

No. 599.   Smith, Myron J., Jr.
The Soviet Army, 1939-1980: A Guide to Sources in English.
Santa Barbara, Calif.: The American Bibliographic Company-Clio
(War/Peace Bibliography Series #11), 1982.

This guide is intended to serve as a working bibliography of
English-language sources concerning the Soviet Army. While not
definitive, it covers virtually all factors concerning Russian
ground forces, including the Soviet Navy-administered Naval
Infantry. There are five main sections to this work: 1)
Reference Works; 2) the Era of World War II, 1939-1945; 3) The
Soviet Economy and Defense Establishment; 4) The Soviet Ground
Forces, 1946 to the Present; and 5) The Soviet Army and Military
Assistance Around the Globe, 1945 to the Present. Within the
text, each section and many subsections have introductions.
There are a total of 5745 entries.

No. 600.   Soviet Military Doctrine: A List of References to
Recent Soviet and Free World Publications on Soviet Military
Thought.
Washington, D.C.: U.S. Department of State (External Research
Paper 141), August 1963, 39 p.

This is a selected list of Soviet and Western publications on
Soviet military thinking on strategic and tactical principles for a
future general war. At this time, Soviet military theory is in a
stage of revision. Therefore, not only authoritative pronouncements of policy, but also discussions and suggestions by military
officers are included. Selected statements of a political or
propagandistic character are listed insofar as they elucidate the
general attitude. Western publications include not only those
which explicitly analyze Soviet military theory, but also general
strategic works, which as a whole are conceived with a view to
Soviet doctrine and are studied and referenced by Soviet writers.
Discussion of the problems of disarmament are listed only insofar
as they reflect general principles.

No. 601.   Stanley, Zell.
An Annotated Bibliography of the Open Literature on Deception.
Santa Monica, Calif.: The RAND Corporation (N-2332-NA),
December 1985, 129 p.

This bibliography of deception includes twelve categories: 1)
Arms Control and Deception, which addresses agreements and
violations of agreements as well as compliance issues; 2) Behavior
of Targets of Deception, which analyzes methods of influencing
decision-makers; 3) Bibliographies of Deception; 4) China:
Military and Political Deception, recounting the role of deception
and strategm in China's history of warfare; 5) Countering
Deception, analytic procedures to detect and counter deception;
6) General Deception Studies, covering broad theoretical works

on aspects including persuasion, self-deception, and strategic deception from the perspectives of history, political science, psychology, and organization; 7) Historical Studies, encompassing works on World War II and groups in their role-enactment and deception methodologies; 8) Human Deception, on individual and groups in their role-enactment and deception methodologies, and involvement of interpersonal deception; 9) Interspecies Deception, which compares studies of mimicry and alarm systems in insects; 10) Surprise attack and Deception; 11) USSR Military Deception; and 12) USSR Political Deception.

No. 602. USSR: Analytical Survey of Literature.
Washington, D.C.: Government Printing Office (DA PAM 550-6-1), December 1976, 232 p.

The 1,000 selected and abstracted items in this publication are reflective of the political, military, economic, and sociological changes, shifts, and trends that have taken place within the Soviet Union since 1969. In selecting this material, the analysts attempted to present a balanced picture of the problems and prospects, and of the forces that influence and shape the various courses being taken by the Soviet Union. It is organized into three major sections: I) National Policy, Strategy, and Objectives; II) The Soviet Nation: Life, Politics, and Economics Under Communism; III) Bibliographic and Other Aids to Furnish Research on the Soviet Union -- these include a number of detached wall charts and maps.

8

Soviet Sources on Nuclear Weapons Policy

An important problem for analysts of Soviet nuclear weapons policy is the existence of contradictions between two important sources on Soviet strategic intent: writings emanating from the military and the publications and statements of representatives of the social science institutes of the Soviet Academy of Sciences. Until recently, these two sources of material differed on a number of important politico-military issues, and perhaps the greatest difference appears in discussions of nuclear weapons: under what conditions they would be employed, how they would be used, and what would constitute a meaningful "victory". Over the past decade these differences have lessened, but enough remains to trouble many analysts working with both sources.

Faced with this contradiction, a small number of analysts have rejected military writings as a useful source of information on Soviet intent. As a recent article in International Security asserted:

> ...some American analysts tend to claim as official Soviet doctrine the exhortations of military commissars whose primary function is to instill the "science of military victory" into raw recruits, ignoring political statements which imply a doctrine of deterrence. In the absence of more authoritative statements from the Soviet government, arms control advocates in the West often find it difficult to challenge these selected quotes from military propagandists.[1]

A second school accepts the military writings as authentic but regards the social science institutes of the Soviet Academy of Sciences as little more than centers for propaganda and disinformation. In this view, in any conflict with military literature the academic writings should be discarded. The majority of analysts, however, have chosen to regard both sets of material as possessing some validity. A common Sovietological

model postulates military "hawks" opposing academic "doves."
Actual Soviet policy, in this view, is forged by conflict, debate,
bargaining, and compromise between these two factions and their
allies and adversaries in the Soviet establishment.

To assess the validity of these competing views, an examination must be made of how the various types of Soviet writings
are produced, how widely they circulate, what purpose they
serve, and what the natures of the sponsoring institutions are.
Without such an examination, attempts to assess the comparative
utility of this material becomes little more than an exercise in
bolstering one prejudice over another.

A. THE SOVIET MILITARY PRESS

From shortly after the death of Stalin until the early 1960s,
the implications of the introduction of nuclear weapons upon
strategy, operational art, and tactics were thoroughly and widely
discussed in the Soviet military press. Partially as a result of
this discussion, the Soviet military was extensively reorganized
in 1959 into the form it still holds today: five branches of
service under the tripartite supervision of the Ministry of
Defense, the Main Political Administration, and the General Staff.
The Soviet military press was also reorganized: scores of
journals, magazines, and newspapers were consolidated into the
publications that exist today.

The Soviet military press differs markedly from military
publications and publishing houses in the West. It is subject to
tight censorship and editorial control from the Main Political
Administration of the Soviet Army and Navy (MPA), an organ of
the Communist Party (not the Soviet government) which operates
with the rights of a department (otdel') of the Central Committee. According to the Soviet Military Encyclopedia, the MPA:

> ...directs the central military newspaper, journals, and
> publishing houses, which are (all) under its authority; it
> controls the content and ideological direction of the
> entire military press; it publishes political and literary-
> artistic journals, approves the issuance of educational-
> methodological handbooks, manuals, and posters on questions
> of political and military education, and participates in
> the work of creating training and art films on military
> themes.[2]

Editorial staffers of Soviet military journals, newspapers,
and publishing houses, while holding military rank, are career
officers of the MPA. They do not rotate to other military duties,

and they generally spend their entire service career at the same military publication or publishing house.[3] The important work that they perform in assuring ideological and stylistic uniformity is backed up by Glavlit (The Main Administration for Safeguarding State Secrets in the Press). Glavlit censors, who are subordinate to the USSR Council of Ministers rather than to the Ministry of Defense or the Communist Party, give the final stamp of approval to media material before it is publicly released.

The most important military publishing house is Voyenizdat (literally MILPUB), the official publishing house of the Ministry of Defense. Voyenizdat produces between 350 and 500 titles annually; of these, at least a score address important doctrinal issues.[4] Other titles cover military history, foreign and technical military developments, and memoirs.[5] A press run can range from 5000 to over a million copies -- 20,000 is a rough average. The other important military publishing house is DOSAAF (Voluntary Society for Cooperation with the Army and Navy) Press. Its publications are similar to those of Voyenizdat, but tend to be more inspirational and less technical. Often, both publishing houses produce books in series, the most famous of which is the "Officer's Library."

In its present form, the Soviet military periodical press dates back to the last reorganization of the Soviet military, which took place between 1958 and 1960. The reforms of this period reduced the number of military journals published openly and nation-wide from roughly fifty to sixteen. Soviet military journals now include:

Kommunist vooruzhennykh sil (Communist of The Armed Forces). This monthly journal is the theoretical organ of the MPA. Kommunist vooruzhennykh sil was created in 1960 by the merger of a number of MPA journals and newspapers. It carries articles by high-ranking officers of all services, placing the Soviet policy line as determined by the Central Committee of the CPSU in a military context. It also carries articles by mid-level political officers on specific problems and techniques of party-political work. An important function of Kommunist vooruzhennykh sil is to present and analyze the "subjective and one-sided nature" of Western military and politico-military thought. The MPA also issues another monthly journal, Agitator, which focuses on specific techniques of agitation and propaganda for party-political work. Founded in 1942, it was named Bloknot agitatora (Agitator's Notebook), until 1976.

Voyenno-istoricheskiy zhurnal (Military-Historical Journal) is issued monthly by the Military Sciences Administration of the Soviet General Staff. This periodical was founded in 1939, but during the Second World War it was merged with Voyennaya mysl' (Military Thought), the journal of the Academy of the Soviet General Staff. At the end of the war the distribution of Voyennaya mysl', including its military-history section, was

restricted "only to admirals, generals, and officers." In 1959
Voyenno-istoricheskiy zhurnal resumed publication as a separate,
unclassified journal. The name of this journal can be misleading
to Westerners. Rather than restricting its focus to the study of
past military activities, the scope of Voyenno-istoricheskiy zhurnal is to examine the role of the military in the entire dialectical-
historical process. The Marxist-Leninist view of this process
includes the present and future as well as the past.

Voyennaya mysl' was founded in 1937 as the journal of the
Soviet General Staff. Originally it was unclassified, but in 1946
distribution was restricted. Throughout the 1950s copies
regularly reached the United States and were often cited in U.S.
publications. Since 1959 copies received by the U.S.
government have been classified, although in the 1970s an
incomplete set of English translations from Voyennaya mysl' was
declassified and later published by the U.S. Government Printing
Office.

Four of the five Soviet service branches (vidy Vooruzhennykh Sil) publish their own journals. These are Voyennyy
vestnik (Military Herald), for the Ground Forces; Aviatsiya i
kosmonavtika (Aviation and Astronautics), for the Air Force;
Vestnik PVO (Herald of Air Defense), for the Troops of Air
Defense; and Morskoy sbornik (Naval Digest), for the Navy.
Presumably, the journal for the Strategic Rocket Forces is
classified.

A number of specialized services of the Soviet Armed Forces
also have their own journals. These include Tyl i snabzheniye
(Rear and Supply), the journal of the Rear of the Armed Forces;
Tekhnika i vooruzheniye (Equipment and Weaponry), which
reports on technical developments and "propagandizes the
decisions of the CPSU on the further development of scientific-
technical progress in the Armed Forces";[6] and Voyennnyye
znaniya (Military Knowledge), which jointly serves the Troops
of Civil Defense and DOSAAF. Voyenno-meditsinskiy zhurnal
(Journal of Military Medicine) is the organ of the Central
Military-Medicine Administration. Zarubezhnoye voyennoye
obozreniye (Foreign Military Review) reports on developments in
foreign, primarily Western military forces; since January 1986 it
has not been available for export from the Soviet Union.
Pogranichin (Border Guard), is run by MPA for the Border
Troops of the KGB.

Four general publications covering the Soviet military are
also issued. Three are primarily inspirational and morale-
oriented: Znamenosets (Banner Carrier), a monthly magazine for
senior enlisted personnel; Sovetskiy voin (Soviet Fighting Man),
a biweekly for draftees; and Sovetskiy patriot (Soviet Patriot),
the organ of the Central Committee of DOSAAF, which appears
three times a week in newspaper format.

Soviet Military Review deserves special mention. It began monthly publication in 1965 in English and French. Editions were added in Arabic (1971), Spanish (1972), Portugese (1979), and Dari (the chief language of Afghanistan, 1983). A Russian edition did not appear until 1978. The publication is primarily oriented towards Third World military personnel, with a heavy emphasis on propaganda and on simple tactical employment of Soviet weaponry. However, since it has an English edition, some Western defense analysts rely on it more heavily than its contents merit.

Krasnaya zvezda (Red Star), a daily newspaper founded in 1924, is the main organ of the Ministry of Defense. It covers developments of all types throughout the Soviet military.

No comprehensive study of the Soviet military press has ever been made. Its role, function, clearance procedures, and editorial and censorship process are virtually unknown. Little more is known about the reasons why Soviet officers choose to publish articles and books, and what role they play in promotions, influencing debates, in interactions with discussion groups, etc. It is clear that the Party holds a firm hand on military publishing, that each publication has a clearly defined role and audience, and that primary purpose of each is professional and educational, rather than to influence the West. Published material is only part of the picture, however. It is used as a study guide, background to discussions, and as a background to fuller and more explict classified memoranda.

B.   SOURCES FROM AND ABOUT THE SOVIET MILITARY PRESS

Guides to and Discussions of Soviet Military Publications

No. 603.   Barnett, Roger W.; and Edward J. Lacey.
"Their Professional Journal."
U.S. Naval Institute Proceedings Vol. 108 No. 10 (October 1982), pp. 95-101.

The Soviet Union has a monthly naval journal entitled Morskoy Sbornik. This journal has regular features, such as reports on the forthcoming Communist Party Congresses and on the fleets. The substantive articles cover naval strategy, training, and history; the Communist Party; ordnance and engineering; natural phenomena and marine life; foreign navies; and critiques and bibliographies. The topics most common in the 1980 volume of the journal were naval strategy and art, the U.S. threat to the USSR, the requirements of controlling documents, technological developments, and the Law of the Sea.

No. 604. Dallin, Alexander.
"Red Star" on Military Affairs, 1945-1952: A Selected, Annotated
List of Articles in the Soviet Military Newspaper.
Santa Monica, Calif.: The RAND Corporation (RM-1637), Feb-
ruary 10, 1956, 49 p.

An annotated list of articles on military affairs appearing in the
Russian military newspaper Red Star, compiled as an aid to those
interested in recent discussions within the Soviet Union about
the military implications of nuclear weapons. The period covered
is July 1945 to the end of 1952, shortly before Stalin's death.

No. 605. Douglass, Joseph D., Jr.; and Amoretta M. Hoeber.
Index to and Extracts From "Voyennaya Mysl" (1963-1969).
Arlington, Va.: System Planning Corporation (SPC 464), Septem-
ber 1979, 506 p.

This report presents Tables of Contents, Author Index, Subject
Index, and selected extracts for declassified issues of Voyennaya
Mysl' from the time period 1963-1969.

No. 606. Erickson, John.
"Windows on the Soviet Military."
Problems of Communism Vol. 24 No. 5 (September-October 1975),
pp. 63-66.

This essay-review of the first four volumes of the "Soviet
Military Thought" series of translations (Sidorenko, The Offensive; Byely et al., Marxism-Leninism on War and Army; Lomov,
Scientific-Technical Progress and the Revolution in Military
Affairs; Savkin, Basic Principles of Operational Art and Tactics)
emphasizes the importance of these works and the U.S. Air
Force project of which they are a part. These four works fall
into two categories: tactical-technical works (Savkin and Sidorenko), and broader political-philosophical treatises (Marxism-
Leninism, Lomov). Even readers not interested in the tactics
and technical questions of the Soviet Military should pay heed to
the broader philosophical works.

No. 607. Scott, Harriet Fast.
"Insights Into the Soviet Military."
Problems of Communism Vol. 26 No. 1 (January-February 1977),
pp. 70-72.

This essay-review assesses the significance of the Soviet Military
Encyclopedia, the first volume of which appeared in the spring
of 1979. The full version of the eight volume encyclopedia is to
contain more than 10,000 entries. Western readers who expect it
to give a comprehensive treatment of military affairs will be
disappointed; data which in the West would be publicly available

fall in the category of "state" or "military" secrets in the Soviet Union. Nevertheless, the Soviet Military Encyclopedia contains information that is most instructive, especially in Russian and Soviet military history.

No. 608. Scott, William F.; and Harriet Fast Scott.
Soviet Sources of Doctrine and Strategy.
New York: Crane, Russak, and Co., 1975, 72 p.

This book identifies and discusses Soviet military-political spokes-men and their writings on military doctrine and strategy. It analyzes those Soviet publications which present basic tenets of Soviet military thought, as well as those intended for study by specific services within the Soviet Armed Forces. It also pro-vides an annotated bibliography of over 160 Soviet books published between 1960 and 1974 and used for the education, training, and indoctrination of the Soviet Armed Forces. Included is a brief list of Soviet writings that have been translated into English.

Reviewed by: Harold W. Nelson, Military Affairs Vol. 61 No. 4 (December 1977), p. 212; Peter Vigor, Slavonic and East Euro-pean Studies Vol. 55 No. 2 (April 1977), pp. 273-274.

No. 609. Weeks, Albert L.
"The New Soviet Military Encyclopedia."
Survey Vol. 26 No. 2 (Spring 1982), pp. 202-206.

The Soviet Military Encyclopedia is a gold mine of information for the Western student of Soviet military science, doctrine, and strategy. It provides some 11,000 articles on military history and theory, tactics, and strategy, biographies, polychromatic plates showing tsarist and Soviet medals and uniforms, insignia and uniforms of foreign nations, war maps of campaigns and battles, and a wealth of other material. Unlike any Western military reference work, the SME is interlaced with heavy doses of Marxist-Leninist ideology. Despite occasional disinformation, the new encyclopedia succedes in dispelling many of the mis-leading statements about Soviet military thinking and strategy that are distributed by the Soviet Union to the Western press for the purpose of disinformation.

Anthologies, Series, Features

No. 610. Current Digest of the Soviet Press is a weekly selec-tion of translations and abstracts from some ninety Soviet news-papers and periodicals, published in English as documentary materials with no elaboration or commentary.

No. 611. Douglass, Joseph D. Jr.; and Amoretta M. Hoeber.
Selected Readings From Soviet Military Thought (1963-1973).
Washington, D.C.: Government Printing Office (Studies in Communist Affairs, Vol. 5), 1983. Part I, 225 p.; Part II, 252 p.

Voyennaya Mysl' (Military Thought) is the classified journal of
the Soviet General Staff. Designed mainly for internal use, it is
one of the few Soviet journals in which problems and issues of
military and political-military strategy are regularly examined in
depth by senior military and Party officials. Recently the U.S.
government declassified and released for public use translations
from eight of the issues from July 1963 through December 1973.
These volumes contain a representative selection of the more
interesting articles from these translations, biographical information on the authors when available, and a detailed index to the
material. The selected articles span a wide variety of military
forces, combined arms operations, command and control, civil
defense, nuclear targeting, correlation of forces calculations,
and principles of military art.

Articles in Part I include: V. Sokolovskiy and M. Cherednichenko, "Military Strategy and Its Problems"; S. Ivanov,
"Soviet Military Doctrine and Strategy"; V. Zemskov, "Wars of
the Modern Era"; V. Zemskov, "Characteristic Features of
Modern Wars and Possible Methods of Conducting Them"; S.
Tyushkevich, "The Methodology for the Correlation of Forces in
War"; K. Stalbo, "The Significance of the Seas and Oceans in
Combat Actions"; L. Kuleszynski, "Some Problems of Surprise in
Warfare"; Z. Paleski, "Psychological Aspects of Surprise"; V.
Bestuzhev, "Combat Actions on the Sea"; M.V. Vetrov, "Problems
of War and Peace and the World Revolutionary Process"; I.
Zav'yalov, "Evolution in the Correlation of Strategy, Operational
Art and Tactics"; V.P. Chervonobab, "Principles of Military Art
and Their Development"; N. Zubkov, "General Principles of the
Approach to Appraising the Effectiveness of Combined-Arms
Control Systems"; H. Adam and R. Gebel', "Military Camouflage";
M. Ionov, "On the Methods of Influencing an Opponent's
Decisions"; A. Paliy, "The Status and Some Trends in the
Development of Radioelectronic Warfare"; A. Berezkin, "On
Controlling the Actions of an Opponent"; B. Bannikov, "Characteristic Features of Contemporary Naval Operations"; A.
Poltavets, "Use of Support Echelons and Reserves in Offensive
Operations"; V. Artamonov, "Supporting Combat Operations of
Submarines"; P. Korobkov, "Dispersed Basing of Aviation Under
Conditions of Waging a Modern War".

Articles in Part II include: V. Kruchinin, "Contemporary
Strategic Theory on the Goals and Missions of Armed Conflict";
V. Kulakov, "Problems of Military-Technical Superiority"; Kh.
Dzhelaukhov, "Augmentation of Strategic Efforts in Modern
Armed Conflict"; B. Golovchiner, "Encirclement and Annihilation
of Groupings of Defending Troops"; I. Kurnosov, "Development
of Radioelectronic Means of Troop Control and Methods of Their

Application"; K. Sevast'yanov and N. Vasendin, "Comments on
the Article 'Augmentation of Strategic Efforts in Modern Armed
Conflict'"; P. Kurochkin, "Operations of Tank Armies in Opera-
tional Depth"; Kh. Dzhelaukhov, "Combating Strategic Reserves
in a Theater of Military Operations"; I. Vorob'yev, "Forward
Detachments in Offensive Operations and Battles"; Kh.
Dzhelaukhov, "The Infliction of Deep Strikes"; K. Andrukhov
and V. Bulatnikov, "The Growing Role of Airborne Troops in
Modern Military Operations"; V. Kuznetsov, and B. Andreyev,
"Coordination Between Aviation and Tanks"; M. Shirokov,
"Military Geography at the Present Stage"; M. Skovorodkin,
"Some Questions of Coordination of Branches of Armed Forces in
Major Operations"; S. Krasovskiy, "Trends in the Use of Air-
craft in a Nuclear War"; I. Anureyev, "Determining the
Correlation of Forces in Terms of Nuclear Weapons"; B.
Samorukov, "Combat Operations Involving Conventional Means of
Destruction"; S. Shtrik, "The Encirclement and Destruction of
the Enemy During Combat Operations Not Involving the Use of
Nuclear Weapons"; G. Semenov, "The Content of the Concept of
an Operation"; N. Semenov, "Gaining Supremacy in the Air"; M.
Shirokov, "The Question of Influences of the Military and
Economic Potential of Warring States"; S. Begunov, "The
Maneuver of Forces and Materiel in an Offensive"; N. Vasendin
and N. Kuznetsov, "Modern Warfare and Surprise Attack"; B.
Khabarov, N. Bazanov, Ye. Orlov, and L. Semeyko,
"Methodology for Determining the Correlation of Nuclear Forces";
N. Svetlishin, "The Maneuver of National Air Defense Forces".

Also printed by System Planning Corporation (SPC 584), April
1980, 694 p.

No. 612. U.S. Foreign Broadcast Information Service. This
U.S. government agency produces a large volume of translations
from Soviet sources, many of which directly or indirectly touch
on the question of Soviet nuclear weapons policy. Unfortunately,
owing to changes in U.S. and Soviet copyright laws made in the
mid-1970s, very little of this material is available to the general
public. Instead, it is classified "For Official Use Only," which
is an administrative rather than a security classification. Soviet
materials published prior to 1973 do not have this protection.
Unclassified FBIS and JPRS publications may be ordered from the
National Technical Information Service (NTIS), Springfield,
Virginia 22161. Pertinant FBIS translations available to the
public include:

a. U.S.S.R. Report: Military Affairs. Published by the
Joint Publication Research Service (JPRS) on an occasional
basis (50-70 issues annually). It presents selected articles
or even entire issues of Soviet newspapers and journals of
military interest.

328

b.   USSR Report: The Soviet Union.   Produced daily by
FBIS, this publication includes selected articles from the
Soviet press as well as radio and television broadcasts.
Each issue generally has a military section.

No. 613.   Kintner, William R.; and Harriet Fast Scott.
The Nuclear Revolution in Soviet Military Affairs.
Norman, Okla.:   University of Oklahoma Press, 1968, 420 p.

While the Soviet Union exhibits an almost pathological concern for
secrecy about its nuclear weapons, military discussions of plans
for using those weapons have been published.   They are little
translated and virtually ignored by the English-speaking world.
Avoiding "propaganda and disinformation" sources, the authors
have collected from publications written by and for Soviet military leaders twenty-seven full or excerpted works published on
doctrine and strategy since the Cuban Missile Crisis of 1962.
These extensively annotated selections reveal the Soviet preoccupation with nuclear weapons and their impact on politics and
warfare -- a preoccupation that makes sense only in terms of the
plans and goal of the revolution in Soviet military affairs.
Soviet theoreticians have divided the military revolution into
three phases.   The first phase, creation of the nuclear weapon,
and the second phase, development of the weapon-carrying
missile, are now accomplished facts.   The third phase, sometimes
referred to as the "cybernetics revolution," is still underway,
and provides for perfection of guidance and control systems.
There is reason to believe that the Soviet Union is coming
increasingly close to this goal.   The Soviet orientation to an
all-out nuclear program and commitment to strategic superiority
have already provoked a crisis of strategy in the United States,
and one that will become more obvious in the next several years.

Contents: R.Ya. Malinovsky, "The Revolution in Military Affairs
and the Task of the Military Press," pp. 17-22; N.A. Sbitov,
"The Revolution in Military Affairs and its Results," pp. 23-33;
V.V. Larionov, "New Means of Fighting and Strategy," pp.
34-44; S.M. Shtemenko, "The Queen of the Battlefield Yields Her
Crown," pp. 46-55; V.V. Larionov, "New Weapons and the
Duration of War," pp. 56-64; K.S. Bochakarev, "On the
Character and Types of Wars in the Modern Era," pp. 65-82;
V.V. Glazov, "The Regularity of Development and Changes of
Methods of Armed Conflict," pp. 83-88; N.Ya. Sushko and S.A.
Tyushkevich, "National Liberation Wars," from Marxism-Leninism
on War and the Army, pp. 89-99; Ye.I. Ribkin, "On the Nature
of World Nuclear Rocket War," pp. 101-114; K.S. Bochkarev,
I.P. Prusanov, and A.A. Babakov, "The Modern Revolution in
Military Affairs and Its Meaning," from The Program of the CPSU
on the Defense of the Socialist Fatherland, pp. 115-145; V.V.
Molchalov, "Land Forces, Their Role and Future," pp. 146-152;
N.A. Lomov, "The Influence of Soviet Military Doctrine on the
Development of Military Art," pp. 153-169; S.V. Malyanchikov,

"The Character and Features of Nuclear Rocket War," pp. 170-183; V.I. Chuikov, "The Tasks are Important, Crucial," pp. 184-191; A.A. Strokov, "Military Art in the Postwar Period," from The History of Military Art, pp. 192-233; S.I. Krupnov, "According to the Laws of Dialectics," pp. 234-243; I.A. Grudinin, "The Time Factor in Modern War," pp. 244-258; V.D. Sokolovskiy and M.I. Cherednichenko, "On Contemporary Military Strategy," pp. 260-277; R.Ya. Malinovsky, "Address to the XXIII Congress CPSU," pp. 278-288; A.A. Yepishev, "Address to the XXIII Congress of the CPSU," pp. 289-301; V.V. Zagladin, "The Leninist Course of Foreign Policy of the USSR," pp. 303-319; V. Voznenko, "The Dialectics of Development and Change in Forms and Methods of Armed Conflict," pp. 320-323; V.D. Ivanov, A. Ovsyannikov, and M.I. Galkin; "The XXIII Congress of the CPSU on the Military Threat and the Problems of Strengthening the Defense Potential of the Country," pp. 324-339; I.A. Grudinin, "On the Question of the Essence of War," pp. 340-350; V.M. Bondarenko, "Military-technical Superiority: The Most Important Factor of the Reliable Defense of the Country," pp. 351-365; N.F. Miroshnichenko, "Changes in the Content and Nature of Modern Combat," pp. 366-373; I.G. Zavyalov, "On Soviet Military Doctrine," pp. 374-389.

No. 614. Lee, William T.
"Soviet Views of the ABM and Soviet Strategy."
Appendix A in William R. Kintner (Ed.), Safeguard: Why the ABM Makes Sense.
New York: Hawthorn Books, Inc., 1969, pp. 363-400.

This appendix presents articles and excerpts from articles and books written by Soviet military experts on the ABM issue. They are presented without any editorial comment, except for addition of emphasis where noted.

No. 615. Onacewicz, Wlodzimierz; and Robert D. Crane (Eds.).
Soviet Materials on Military Strategy: Inventory and Analysis for 1963.
Washington, D.C.: Georgetown University, Center for Strategic Studies, 1964, 139 p.

This collection of materials was prepared as a follow-on to a conference on Soviet military thought sponsored by the Center in 1963. Part I contains an essay by Robert D. Crane, "Possible Implications of Khrushchev's December Plenum Speech," U.S. reviews of Marshal V.D. Sokolovskiy's Military Strategy, and several Soviet reviews of the same work; and an essay by Thomas W. Wolfe, "Lomov on Soviet Military Doctrine" (q.v.). Part II consists of annotations of selected Soviet documents on military strategy, including books and monographs, journal articles, and speeches. Part III is a bibliography of selected Soviet documents on military strategy.

330

No. 616. <u>Progress Publishers</u> is a Soviet publishing house that provides translations of Soviet works for the export trade. Its selection of military titles is intended primarily for Third World nations with military ties to the Soviet Union or which have made important purchases of Soviet arms. A few representative titles from this publisher include:

a. I. Babenko, <u>Soviet Officers</u> (1976), 134 p.

b. B. Byely et al., <u>Marxism-Leninism on War and Army</u> (1972). Reprinted by the Government Printing Office (Soviet Military Thought No. 2), n.d. -- see No. 619b.

c. A. Grechko, <u>Liberation Mission of the Soviet Armed Forces in the Second World War</u> (1975).

d. A.Ya. Khmel, <u>Education of the Soviet Soldier: Party Political Work in the Soviet Armed Forces</u> (1973).

e. V. Ryabov, <u>The Soviet Armed Forces, Yesterday and Today</u>. (1976), 164 p.

f. S.M. Shtmenko, <u>The Soviet General Staff at War, 1941-1945</u> (1970).

g. A. Yepishev, <u>Some Aspects of Party-Political Work in the Soviet Armed Forces</u> (1975).

No. 617. Scott, Harriet Fast.
"Soviet Literature for 1966."
<u>Military Review</u> Vol. 46 No. 7 (July 1966), pp. 87-90.

Towards the end of each calendar year, representatives of Voyenizdat, the Military Publishing House of the Soviet Ministry of Defense, start advertising their planned publications for the next twelve months. This article reviews the publications announced for release in 1966. The program sounds impressive and should make a valuable contribution toward understanding Soviet views on warfare. However, when dealing with planned Soviet publications, one should be cautioned concerning expectations that may not be met.

No. 618. Scott, Harriet Fast, and William F. Scott (Eds.).
<u>The Soviet Art of War: Doctrine, Strategy, and Tactics</u>.
Boulder, Colo.: Westview Press, 1982, 325 p.

The purpose of this book is to document from basic Soviet sources the development of the Soviet art of war. Soviet military strategy, operational art, and tactics cannot be understood simply through the study and analysis of current Soviet publications. To evaluate Soviet military thought and to project trends in Soviet military affairs, it is necessary to start with the October Revolution and trace the evolution of the Soviet art of war from that time. This book contains excerpts from fifty-six key Soviet military works, along with annotation, introductory chapters, and a selected bibliography for further reading.

Reviewed by: Wynfred Joshua, Strategic Review Vol. 10 No. 2 (Spring 1982), pp. 85-88; James Hansen, National Defense Vol. 57 No. 382 (November 1982), p. 67; David R. Mets, Air University Review Vol. 31 No. 6 (September-October 1980), pp. 123-4.

No. 619. Soviet Military Thought is a series of translated military writings published by the U.S. Air Force Soviet Awareness Program. The dates given for the nineteen books thus far produced are their Soviet dates of publication; the Government Printing Office does not date its impressions of these works. They include:

a. Vol. 1. A.A. Sidorenko, The Offensive (1972). Volumes 1-4 reviewed by John Erickson, "Windows on the Soviet Military," Problems of Communism Vol. 24 No. 5 (September-October 1975), pp. 63-66.

b. Vol. 2. B. Byely et al., Marxism-Leninism on War and Army (1972). Reprinted from the Progress Publishers edition.

c. Vol. 3. N.A. Lomov, Scientific-Technical Progress and the Revolution in Military Affairs (1973).

d. Vol. 4. V.Ye. Savkin, Basic Principles of Operational Art and Tactics (1972).

e. Vol. 5. A.S. Milovidov and V.G. Kozlov, Philosophical Heritage of V.I. Lenin and Problems of Contemporary War (1972).

f. Vol. 6. V.V. Druzhinin and D.S. Kontorov, Concept, Algorithm, Decision (1972).

g. Vol. 7. A.M. Danchenko and I.F. Vydrin, Military Pedogogy (1973).

h. Vol. 8. V.V. Shelyag et al., Military Psychology (1972).

i. Vol. 9. A.A. Oleynik (Ed.), Dictionary of Basic Military Terms (1965).

j. Vol. 10. P.T. Yegorov et al., Civil Defense (1970).

k. Vol. 11. William F. Scott (U.S. Ed.), Selected Soviet Military Writings, 1970-1975. Reviewed by Dov Zakheim,

Air University Review Vol. 24 No. 4 (May-June 1978), p. 91.

l. Vol. 12. A.A. Grechko, The Armed Forces of the Soviet State (1975). Reviewed by Arnold L. Horelick, "The Strategic Mind-Set of the Soviet Military: An Essay-Review," Problems of Communism Vol. 26 No. 2 (March-April 1977), pp. 80-85.

m. Vol. 13. C.N. Kozlov (Ed.), The Officer's Handbook (1971).

n. Vol. 14. M.P. Skirdo, The People, the Army, the Commander (1970). Reviewed by Joseph E. Thatch, Jr., Air University Review Vol. 31 No. 2 (January-February 1980), pp. 109-112.

o. Vol. 15. B.A. Vasil'yev, Long-Range Missile-Equipped (1972).

p. Vol. 16. Yu.V. Chuyev and Yu.B. Mikhiylov, Forecasting in Military Affairs (1975).

q. Vol. 17. M.N. Kozhevnikov, The Command and Staff of the Soviet Army Air Force in the Great Patriotic War, 1941-45 (1977).

r. Vol. 18. D.A. Ivanov et al., Fundamentals of Tactical Command and Control (1977).

s. Vol. 19. S.A. Tyushkevich, The Soviet Armed Forces: A History of Their Organizational Development (1978).

The U.S. Air Force also produces a quarterly journal, Soviet Press: Selected Translations, which is classified "For Official Use Only." Prior to 1975 it was unclassified, but had to change its status for copyright protection purposes. It also produces an occasional publication, Soviet Military Concepts, which consists of translated articles from the Soviet Military Encyclopedia. However, to avoid problems with copyright regulations, the articles are often abridged, and are presented without full citation.

No. 620. The Soviet Strategic View is a regular feature of the quarterly journal Strategic Review, and has appeared since the Spring 1979 issue. It reports on published Soviet views of strategic issues, and includes lengthy quotes from source materials. It replaces an earlier journal feature, The Soviet View, which appeared from 1973 to 1977. This feature included translations of articles and exerpts from Soviet military books. It was discontinued for copyright reasons.

No. 621. <u>Soviet World Outlook</u> began publication in 1976. It was issued by the Advanced International Studies Institute, and offered a monthly report of views expressed in the Soviet press "on issues critical to U.S. interests." It was discontinued in December 1985.

No. 622. Weeks, Albert L.; and William C. Brodie. <u>War and Peace: Soviet Russia Speaks</u>. New York: National Strategy Information Center, 1983, 51 p.

To determine Soviet intentions, one must examine the statements Soviet officials and spokesmen issue as policy and doctrine to their own nation. To that end, this booklet has assembled some ninety-five short excerpts from Soviet statements and literature, covering a wide range of issues from arms and trade deals to political action and ideological conflict. It concludes with an essay by Frank R. Barnett.

Translations

Bashurian, P., "Frunze Military Academy," <u>Military Review</u> Vol. 50 No. 6 (June 1970), pp. 60-67. Condensed from <u>Voyennyy vestnik</u>, December 1968. [No. 623]

Baz, I., "Soviet Military Science on the Character of Contemporary War," Appendix A in Raymond L. Garthoff, <u>The Soviet Image of Future War</u> (Washington, D.C.: Public Affairs Press, 1959). From <u>Voyennyy vestnik</u> No. 6 (June 1958). [No. 624]

Dunin, A., "The Evolution of the Soviet Land Forces Since the End of World War II," <u>Survival</u> Vol. 30 No. 1 (January-February 1979), pp. 26-29. From <u>Voyenno-istoricheskiy zhurnal</u> No. 5, 1978. [No. 625]

"Excerpts from a Soviet Booklet on Nuclear War," <u>New York Times</u>, November 21, 1981, p. 4. [No. 626]

Glazov, V., "What is Local War?", <u>Survival</u> Vol. 3 No. 5 (September-October 1961), pp. 226-228. From <u>Krasnaya zvezda</u>, 16 May 1961. [No. 627]

Gorshkov, Sergei G., <u>Red Star Rising at Sea</u>. Annapolis, Md.: U.S. Naval Institute Press, 1974, 150 p. Articles from <u>Morskoy sbornik</u> (1972-1973), translated and printed in <u>U.S. Naval Institute Proceedings</u>, and collected in this book. [No. 628]

_____, <u>The Sea Power of the State</u>. New York: Pergamon Press, 1979, 290 p. Soviet date of publication, 1976. [No. 629]

334

_____, "The Sea Power of the State (Excerpts)," Survival Vol. 29 No. 1 (January-February 1977), pp. 24-29. [No. 630]

Grudin, I., "What Determines the Strength of the Army?", Military Review Vol. 40 No. 5 (August 1960), pp. 104-108, digested from an article in Krasnaya zvezda, 21 June 1960. [No. 631]

_____, "Man: The Principal Force in War," Military Review Vol. 40 No. 11 (November 1960), pp. 79-84. From Krasnaya zvezda, 16 February 1960. [No. 632]

Il'in, S.K., "The Morale Factor in Modern War," Chapter 21 in P. Edward Haley et al. (Eds.), Nuclear Strategy, Arms Control, and the Future (Boulder, Colo.: Westview Press, 1985), pp. 157-158. [No. 633]

Iovlev, A.M., "New Technology and Mass Armies," Survival Vol. 5 No. 3 (September-October 1961), pp. 233-234. [No. 634]

Isachenkov, N.V., "New Naval Weapons," Survival Vol. 4 No. 2 (March-April 1962), p. 89. From Krasnaya zvezda, 18 November 1961. [No. 635]

Kirin, I., "Raise the Offensive Tempos," Military Review Vol. 55 No. 2 (February 1975), pp. 51-55. From Voyennyy vestnik No. 7 (1973). [No. 636]

Korotkov, I., "On the Fundamental Factors Which Determine the Course and Outcome of Wars," Appendix B in Raymond L. Garthoff, The Soviet Image of Future War (Washington, D.C.: Public Affairs Press, 1959). From Soviet Aviation, August 12, 1958. [No. 637]

Kozlov, S., "Soviet Military Art and Science," Military Review Vol. 39 No. 6 (September 1959), pp. 93-100. From V pomoshch' ofitseram, izuchayushchim marksistsko-leninskuyu teoriyu (sbornik statey) (An Aid to Officers Studying Marxist-Leninist Theory: An Anthology). Moscow: Voyenizdat, 1959, pp. 200-220. [No. 638]

_____, "The Character of Modern War," Survival Vol. 3 No. 4 (July-August 1961), pp. 159-160. From Kommunist vooruzhennykh sil No. 2 (January 1961), pp. 13-15. [No. 639]

Kurasov, V.V., "On the Question of a Forestalling Blow," Military Review Vol. 39 No. 8 (November 1959), pp. 88-90. Reprinted from extracts in Survival, March-April 1959, of an article originally in Krasnaya zvezda. [No. 640]

Kurochkin, P.A., "Conventional Forces in the Nuclear Age," Survival Vol. 3 No. 6 (November-December 1961), p. 282. Partial translation from "Ob izuchenii istorii voyennogo iskusstva v sovremennykh usloviyakh" (On the Study of the History of War Under Modern Conditions), Voyenno-istoricheskiy zhurnal No. 8 (August 1961), pp. 3-12. [No. 641]

Larionov, V., "The Doctrine of Aggression in Doses," Survival Vol. 1 No. 4 (September-October 1959), pp. 135-136. From Krasnaya zvezda, 26 September 1961. [No. 642]

Lomov, N.A., "Modern Means of Waging War and Operational-Level Strategy," Chapter 19 in P. Edward Haley et al. (Eds.), Nuclear Strategy, Arms Control, and the Future (Boulder, Colo.: Westview Press, 1985), pp. 151-154. [No. 643]

Ogarkov, N.V., "The Fairytale Threat," Atlas World Press Review Vol. 26 No. 11 (November 1979), p. 51-54. [No. 644]

_____, "Military Strategy," Chapter 20 in P. Edward Haley et al. (Eds.), Nuclear Strategy, Arms Control, and the Future (Boulder, Colo.: Westview Press, 1985), pp. 154-156. From "Strategiya voyennaya" (Strategy, Military), Sovetskaya voyennaya entsiklopediya (The Soviet Military Encyclopedia) Vol. 7 (Moscow: Voyenizdat, 1979), pp. 555-565. [No. 645]

Pokrovskiy, Georgiy I. (Trans. and annotated by Raymond L. Garthoff), Science and Technology in Contemporary War. New York: Frederick A. Praeger, Publisher, 1959, 180 p. [No. 646]

Ponomarev, A.N., "Air to Air, Air to Ground," Survival Vol. 4 No. 2 (March-April 1962), pp. 8-89. Condensed translation from Krasnaya zvezda, 18 November 1961. [No. 647]

Reznichenko, V.G., "Troop Movements." An annotated chapter from Taktika (Tactics -- Moscow: Voyenizdat, 1966) produced by Oleg Hoeffding, Troop Movements in Soviet Tactical Doctrine (RAND, R-878-PR, November 1971). [No. 648]

Rybkin, Ye., "On the Nature of a Nuclear Missile War," Appendix A, The Red "Hawks" on the Rationality of Nuclear War. Santa Monica, Calif.: The RAND Corporation (RM-4899-PR), March 1966. From Kommunist vooruzhennykh sil No. 17 (September 1965), pp. 50-56. [No. 649]

Shtemenko, S.M., "The Land Forces in Contemporary War and Their Combat Training," Army, March 1963, pp. 47-56. From Krasnaya zvezda, 3 January 1963. [No. 650]

Sidel'nikov, I., "On Soviet Military Doctrine," Air University Quarterly Review Vol. 13 No. 4 (Summer 1962), pp. 142-150. From "O sovetskoy voyennoy doktrine," Krasnaya zvezda, 1 May 1962, pp. 2-3. [No. 651]

Sidorenko, A.A., "The Nature of the Offensive Under Conditions Where Nuclear Weapons Are Employed," Chapter 18 in P. Edward

336

Haley et al. (Eds.), Nuclear Strategy, Arms Control, and the Future (Boulder, Colo.: Westview Press, 1985), pp. 146-150. [652]

Sidorov, P., "The Creative Character of Soviet Military Science," Appendix C in Raymond Garthoff, The Soviet Image of Future War (Washington, D.C.: Public Affairs Press, 1959). From Sovietskiy flot, December 11, 1958. [No. 653]

_____, "Foundations of the Soviet Military Doctrine," Military Review Vol. 52 No. 12 (December 1972), pp. 89-91. Reprinted from Soviet Military Review, September 1972. [No. 654]

Smirnov, Mikhail V. et al., "On Soviet Military Science," Military Review Vol. 42 No. 3 (March 1962), pp. 78-87. From O Sovetskoy voyennoy nauke (Moscow: Voyenizdat, 1960). [No. 655]

Sokolovsky, V.D. (Ed.) (Raymond L. Garthoff, Ed. and Trans.), Military Strategy: Soviet Doctrine and Concepts. New York: Frederick A. Praeger, Publisher, 1963, 396 p. [No. 656]

Sokolovskii, V.D. (Ed.) (Herbert S. Dinerstein, Leon Goure, and Thomas W. Wolfe, Eds. and Trans.), Soviet Military Strategy. Englewood Cliffs, N.J.: Prentice-Hall, Inc., 1963. This and the Raymond Garthoff translation are reviewed together by: Hanson W. Baldwin, "The View From Red Army Headquarters," New York Times Review of Books Part VII, June 16, 1963, p. 3; Walter Darnell Jacobs, "Straight From the Horse's Mouth," National Review Vol. 15 (July 30, 1963), pp. 68-70; William Zimmerman, "Sokolovskii and His Critics: A Review," Journal of Conflict Resolution Vol. 8 No. 3 (September 1964), pp. 322-328. [No. 657]

Sokolovskiy, V.D. (Ed.) (Harriet Fast Scott, Ed. and Trans.), Soviet Military Strategy. New York: Crane, Russak and Company, Inc., 1975. Reviewed by: Ben Eiseman, Military Review Vol. 55 No. 11 (November 1975), pp. 108-109; and by Arnold L. Horelick, "The Strategic Mind-Set of the Soviet Military: An Essay-Review," Problems of Communism Vol. 26 No. 2 (March-April 1977), pp. 80-85. [No. 658]

Sokolovsky, V.D., "The Nature of Modern War," Chapter 17 in P. Edward Haley et al. (Eds.), Nuclear Strategy, Arms Control, and the Future (Boulder, Colo.: Westview Press, 1985), pp. 138-145. [No. 659]

Talenski, N., "The Character of Modern War," Survival Vol. 3 No. 1 (January-February 1961). [No. 660]

_____, "Missile Defense: A Response to Aggression," Bulletin of the Atomic Scientists, February 1965, and reprinted as Chapter 18 in Zbigniew Brzezinski et al. (Eds.), Promise or Peril (Washington, D.C.: Ethics and Public Policy Center, 1986), pp. 211-219. Originally published in International Affairs (Moscow). [No. 661]

_____, "Anti-missile Systems and Disarmament," in John Erickson et al. (Eds.), The Military-Technical Revolution. New York: Frederick A. Praeger, Publisher, 1966, pp. 219-228. [No. 662]

Varentsov, S.S., "Missiles on the Battlefield," Survival Vol. 4 No. 2 (March-April 1962), pp. 89-90. From Krasnaya zvezda, 18 November 1961. [No. 663]

Vershinin, K.A., "Rocket Vehicles -- the Basis of the Combat Might of the Soviet Air Force," Survival Vol. 4 No. 2 (March-April 1962), pp. 90-91. [No. 664]

Yefimov, Aleksandr N., "One Man Command," Military Review Vol. 55 No. 5 (May 1975), pp. 73-77. From Krasnaya zvezda, 5 September 1974. [No. 665]

C. THE SOCIAL SCIENCE INSTITUTES OF THE SOVIET ACADEMY OF SCIENCES

Publications and statements from representatives of the social science institutes of the Soviet Academy of Sciences have been followed closely in recent years by many analysts of Soviet strategic literature. There are over two dozen of these institutes. The two that receive the most attention from Western observers are the Institute for the Study of the U.S.A. and Canada (ISKAN), headed by Georgi Arbatov; and the Institute of World Economics and International Relations (IMEMO), until recently headed by the late Nikolay Inozemstev. Their output includes not only journal articles and books published in the Soviet Union, but also articles and books produced in the West, op-ed pieces, television and radio interviews, participation in academic conferences and political gatherings, and personal discussions with Western academics and political figures.

ISKAN (sometimes called IUSAC in the West) was founded in 1968 from a section of the Communist Party Central Committee staff. It remained under the direction of the Central Committee for a year before being transferred to the administration of the Academy of Sciences.[7] It publishes a monthly journal, SShA (USA). IMEMO has had a longer and more checkered career, being the successor to the Institute of World Economy and World Politics. This institute was part of the old Communist Academy, set up in the 1920s as a competitor to the Academy of Sciences. These two institutions merged in 1956, at which point IMEMO was formally established by the Presidium of the Academy of Sciences.[8] It also publishes a monthly journal, MEMO (World

Economics and International Relations). Both institutes publish books through "Nauka" (Science) Press, the Academy publishing house, generally in printings of less than 3,000 copies.

The social science institutes were founded to provide short factual reports to top Party officials. These reports are said to consist of little more than collated data. Production of such reports is still an important part of the work of the institutes.[9] In addition, the institutes publish journals, whose articles seem almost exclusively written by institute staffers, and they provide most of the Soviet government's interface with foreign scholars and political figures.

The institutes' staffs are composed of people with a great variety of backgrounds. In addition to a certain number of genuine academics, they include Party apparatchiki and ideologists, retired and active KGB and military officers, and children of the elite. While some foreign observers view these staffers as having great importance in the formulation of Soviet foreign and military policy, others see them as little more than purveyors of disinformation.

Following the ouster of Nikita Khrushchev in 1964, the entire infrastructure of Soviet "social science" was reorganized. Leonid Brezhnev personally critized Soviet social science in his address to the XXIIIrd Party Congress (in March 1966), emphasizing themes that had appeared in a number of pre-Congress Party journals. Chief among these was that the Academy of Sciences allowed too much "volunteerism," in that the research being conducted was of no direct benefit to the Party.[10] The military press also critized Soviet social science, pointedly referring to RAND and other Western "think tanks" under contract with the military as models for Soviet social scientists to emulate.[11]

The result of these attacks was the wholesale transfer of Party-sponsored research institutes to the Soviet Academy of Sciences. This move was probably welcomed by Party researchers eager to capitalize on the prestige of the Academy. The actual motive for this transfer, however, was probably to break the automony of the Academy. Owing to its high standards for admission and its custom of voting by secret ballot, the Academy of Sciences had been able to maintain a fair degree of independence from the Communist Party and the Soviet government. The admission of the Party institutes packed the Academy with political workers, and it has become increasingly subservient to Party directive.

An important effect of the creation of the Academy of Sciences' social science institutes has been to increase the sophistication of the Soviet Union's resources for dealing with Western centers of public opinion. One factor is that centers had been established in which academics, military officers, and

Party officals could pool their expertise. An early example of this new combination was an article by Igor Glagolev and Col. Larionov published in 1963 in International Affairs.[12] (This journal is published in Russian, English, and French, primarily for foreign and especially Third World audiences.) Glagolev was a staffer at IMEMO, and Larinov was a candidate of military science and officer-instructor at the Academy of the General Staff, who, among other things, was credited in each edition of Marshal V.D. Sokolovskiy's Military Strategy with "preparing the work for press." In his collaboration with Glagolev, Larionov refutes the conclusion of "foreign military analysts" that Soviet nuclear forces are "designed for a first and not a counterstrike," in spite of his involvement with the Sokolovskiy volume and with other military works which guardedly discuss preemption. At the time, such a collaboration between military and Party researchers was so rare that a prominent contemporary U.S. scholar of Soviet strategic literature, Thomas Wolfe, noted it as a "departure from customary Soviet practice."[13] Such collaborations are now common.

Affiliation with the Academy of Sciences also has enhanced the credibility of institute staffers in the West. These individuals have cultivated their Western connections and have become the Soviet Union's main resource for learning about Western intellectual prejudices. The exposure they receive in the United States has at times been great enough to give the Soviet Union a voice in the U.S. domestic political process. Institute representatives participate as speakers at nuclear freeze rallies, make regular appearances on American television, attend academic conferences, serve as visting fellows to U.S. university centers, sit on the editorial boards of U.S. academic journals, and contribute frequent op-ed articles for U.S. news-papers.

However, the articles and books published in Russian by ISKAN and IMEMO staffers cannot be dismissed as easily as their statements aimed at the Western public. Clearly, the institutes' writings are efforts to interpret U.S. policies and actions according to Marxist precepts and Soviet prejudices. As such, they can offer valuable insights into how other elements of the Soviet leadership view the United States, and their likely responses to U.S. initiatives.

D. SOURCES ON THE SOVIET SOCIAL SCIENCE INSTITUTES

About the Institutes

Beloff, Nora, "Escape from Boredom: A Defector's Story," Atlantic, November 1980, pp. 42-50. [No. 666]

Dash, Barbara L., A Defector Reports: The Institute of the USA and Canada. Falls Church, Va.: Delphic Associates, May 1982, 443 p. [No. 667]

Finkelstein, L., "Interview Given by First Defector from Arbatov's American Institute," American Bar Association Intelligence Report Vol. 3 No. 9 (September 1981). [No. 668]

Grant, Steven A., Soviet Americanists. Washington, D.C.: Office of Research, International Communications Agency (R-1-80), February 15, 1980, 24 p. [No. 669]

Jacobsen, Carl G., "Soviet Think Tanks," in David R. Jones (Ed.), Soviet Armed Forces Review Annual Vol. 1. Gulf Breeze, Fla.: Academic International Press, 1977, pp. 149-152. [No. 670]

Ruble, Blair; et al., Soviet Research Institutes Project. Vol. I: The Policy Sciences, 1980; Vol. II: The Social Sciences, 1981; Vol. III: The Humanities, 1981; Supplement to Vols. I and II, 1981. Washington, D.C.: Prepared for the U.S. Information Agency by the Kennan Institute for Advanced Russian Studies, Woodrow Wilson International Center for Scholars. [No. 671]

Scott, William F.; and Harriet Fast Scott, "The Social Sciences Institutes of the Soviet Academy of Sciences," Air Force Magazine (Soviet Aerospace Almanac No. 6) Vol. 63 No. 3 (March 1980), pp. 60-65. [No. 672]

Soll, Richard S.; Arthur A. Zuehleke, and Richard B. Foster, The Role of Social Science Research Institutes in Formulation and Execution of Soviet Foreign Policy. Arlington, Va.: Strategic Studies Center, SRI International (P-2625), March 1976, 98 p. [No. 673]

Thomas, John, "Militarization of the Soviet Academy of Sciences," Survey, Vol. 30 No. 2 (Spring 1985). [No. 674]

Representative Publications by Staffers of the Soviet Social Science Institutes

(The journals MEMO and SShA are translated by JPRS in full; the original Russian publications have a table of contents translated into English.)

Arbatov, Georgi A., "A Step Serving the Interests of Peace," Survival Vol. 14 No. 1 (January-February 1972), pp. 16-19. Reprinted from SShA, November 1971. [No. 675]

341

_____, "On Soviet-American Relations," Survival Vol. 16 No. 3 (May-June 1973), pp. 124-129. [No. 676]

_____, "The Dangers of a New Cold War," Bulletin of the Atomic Scientists Vol. 33 No. 3 (March 1977), pp. 33-40. [No. 677]

_____, "Challenge of the Next Two Decades: Dangers and Opportunities," in Norman C. Dahl and Jerome B. Wiesner (Eds.), World Change and World Security. Cambridge, Mass.: MIT Press, 1978. [No. 678]

_____, "A Soviet View of U.S. Policy," Wall Street Journal, April 29, 1980, p. 22. [No. 679]

_____, "You Americans Make it Difficult," Time Vol. 120 No. 23 (December 6, 1982), p. 30. [No. 680]

_____, "Relations Between U.S. and Soviet Union," in Burns Weston (Ed.), Toward Nuclear Disarmament and Global Security: A Search for Alternatives (Boulder, Colo.: Westview Press, 1984). [No. 681]

_____, and William Oltmans, The Soviet Viewpoint. New York: Dodd, Mead and Co., 1983, 219 p. [No. 682]

Austin, Anthony, "Moscow Expert Says U.S. Errs on Soviet War Aims: Interview with Lt. Gen. Mikhail A. Milshtein," New York Times, August 25, 1980. [No. 683]

Bogdanov, Radomir; and Lev Semeiko, "Soviet Military Might: A Soviet View," Fortune, February 26, 1978, pp. 46-53. [No. 684]

Davydov, Yuri, "Problems of Detente in Soviet-American Relations," Peace and the Sciences No. 2 (June 1977), pp. 92-104. [No. 685]

_____, "Why Detente Deteriorates: A Soviet View," Christian Science Monitor, February 8, 1980, p. 22. [No. 686]

Kozlov, Svyatoslav, "Soviet Views on Theater Nuclear Arms," Wall Street Journal, October 16, 1982. [No. 687]

Mil'shtein, Mikhail A. (Michael Milshtein), "Problems of the Inadmissibility of Nuclear Conflict," International Studies Quarterly Vol. 20 (March 1976), pp. 87-103. [No. 688]

_____, "Moscow Expert Says U.S. is Mistaken on Soviet War Strategy," International Herald Tribune, August 28, 1980. [No. 689]

342

_____, and L.S. Semijko, "U.S. Military 'R&D' Through Soviet Eyes," Bulletin of the Atomic Scientists Vol. 33 No. 2 (February 1977), pp. 32-38. [No. 690]

Proektor, Daniel, "Moscow on Geneva," New York Times, February 25, 1983, p. A31. [No. 691]

Trofimenko, Henry A., "Political Realism and the 'Realistic Difference'," in Robert J. Pranger and Roger P. Labrie (Eds.), Nuclear Strategy and National Security: Points of View. Washington, D.C.: American Enterprise Institute, 1977, pp. 38-53. From SShA, 1971, via Foreign Broadcast Information Service, Soviet Union (10 December 1971), pp. H1-H13. [No. 692]

_____, "Counterforce: Illusion of a Panacea," International Security Vol. 5 No. 4 (Spring 1981), pp. 28-48. [No. 693]

_____, "The 'Theology' of Strategy," Orbis Vol. 21 No. 3 (Fall 1977), pp. 497-515. [No. 694]

_____, Changing Attitudes Towards Deterrence. Los Angeles, Calif.: UCLA Center for International and Strategic Affairs (ACIS Working Paper No. 25), July 1980. [No. 695]

_____, "Moscow Isn't Worried," New York Times, September 22, 1980. [No. 696]

_____, "Strategic Metaphors," U.S. Naval Institute Proceedings, March 1980, p. 96. [No. 697]

_____, "The Third World and the U.S.-Soviet Competition: A Soviet View," Foreign Affairs Vol. 59 (Summer 1981), pp. 1021-1040. [No. 698]

_____, "Struggle for the Turf," World Politics Vol. 37 No. 3 (April 1985), pp. 403-415. [No. 699]

NOTES TO CHAPTER EIGHT

1. Jane M.O. Sharp, "Restructuring the SALT Dialogue," International Security Vol. 6 No. 3 (Winter 1981-82).

2. G.V. Sredin, "Glavnoye Politicheskoye Upravleniye" (The Main Political Administration), Sovetskaya voennaya entsiklopediya (The Soviet Military Encyclopedia) Vol. 2, Moscow, Voenizdat, 1977, p. 563.

3. Lilita Dzirkals, Thane Gustafson, and A. Ross Johnson; The Media and Intra-Elite Communication in the USSR. Santa Monica, Calif.: The RAND Corporation (R-2869) September 1982, esp. pp. 23-25.

4. The December listing of Tekhnika i vooruzheniye (Equipment and Weaponry) carries an annual survey of the most important of these works.

5. A Soviet guide to the usage and importance of military memoirs has appeared recently. Gen-Lt. V.S. Ryabov, Chitaya voyenniye memuary ... (On Reading Military Memoirs), Pravda, Biblioteka Ogon'ka, 1983, 48 p.

6. "Tyl i snabzheniye sovetskiykh vooruzhennykh sil" (Rear and Supply of the Soviet Armed Forces), Sovetskaya voyennaya entsyklopedia (Soviet Military Encyclopedia) Vol. 8. Moscow: Voyenizdat, 1980.

7. Leonid Finkelstein, "Interview Given by First Defector from Arbatov's "American Institute," American Bar Association Intelligence Report Vol. 3 No. 9 (September 1981), p. 6.

8. Richard S. Soll, Arthur A. Zuehlke, Jr., Richard B. Foster, The Role of Social Science Research Institutes in Formulation and Execution of Soviet Foreign Policy. Washington, D.C.: SRI International (Strategic Studies Center Project 2625) March 1976, p. 18.

9. Barbara L. Dash, A Defector Reports: The Institute of the U.S.A. and Canada. Washington, D.C.: Delphic Associates, Inc. (May 1982), pp. 24-30. (433 p.)

10. Soll, op. cit., pp. 5-9.

11. V.D. Sokolovskiy and M.I. Cherednichenko, "On Contemporary Military Strategy," Kommunist vooruzhennykh sil No. 4 (April 1966). See William F. and Harriet Fast Scott, "The Social Sciences Institutes of the Soviet Academy of Sciences," Air Force Magazine Vol. 63 No. 3 (March 1980), p. 61.

344

12. I. Glagolev and V. Larionov, International Affairs, November 1963.

13. Thomas W. Wolfe, "Shifts in Soviet Strategic Thought," Foreign Affairs Vol. 42 (April 1964) p. 477.

Index of Source Materials

Abshire, David M.; and Robert D. Crane, "Soviet Strategy in the 1960s: An Analysis of the Current Russian Debate Over Strategy," Army Vol. 13 No. 7 (July 1963), pp. 20-21, 84, 86. [No. 221]

Ackley, Richard T., "No Bastions for the Bear: Round 2," U.S. Naval Institute Proceedings Vol. 111 No. 4 (April 1985), pp. 42-47. [No. 438]

Adomeit, Hannes, Soviet Risk-Taking and Crisis Behavior: From Confrontation to Co-existence? London: International Institute for Strategic Studies (Adelphi Paper No. 101), Autumn 1973. [No. 1]

Alexander, Arthur J., The Process of Soviet Weapons Design. Santa Monica, Calif.: The RAND Corporation (P-6137), March 1978. [No. 508]

_____, Modeling Soviet Defense Decisionmaking. Santa Monica, Calif.: The RAND Corporation (P-6560), December 1980. [No. 465]

_____, "Research in Soviet Defense Production," NATO's Fifteen Nations Vol. 25 No. 5 (October-November 1981), pp. 52-64. [No. 466]

_____, Patterns of Organizational Influence in Soviet Military Procurement. Santa Monica, Calif.: The RAND Corporation (N-1327-AF), April 1982. [No. 467]

_____, Soviet Science and Weapons Acquisition. Santa Monica, Calif.: The RAND Corporation (R-2942-NAS), August 1982. [No. 509]

_____, A.S. Becker, and W.E. Hoehn, Jr., The Significance of Divergent U.S.-U.S.S.R. Military Expenditure. Santa Monica, Calif.: The RAND Corporation (N-1000-AF), February 1979. [No. 510]

Alexiev, Alex R., The Use of Force in Soviet Policy and the West. Santa Monica, Calif.: The RAND Corporation (P-6466), March 1980. [No. 33]

Alsop, Joseph, "Concern Stirred by Seeming Rise of Soviet Military Over Civilians," Washington Post, January 10, 1969. [No. 543]

Apel, Frank J., The Sokolovsky Strategy: A Paradigm for Future Conflict or Soviet Propaganda? Maxwell Air Force Base, Alabama: Air War College, 1972. [No. 222]

Arbatov, Georgi A., "A Step Serving the Interests of Peace," Survival Vol. 14 No. 1 (January-February 1972), pp. 16-19. [No. 675]

_____, "On Soviet-American Relations," Survival Vol. 16 No. 3 (May-June 1973), pp. 124-129. [No. 676]

_____, "The Dangers of A New Cold War," Bulletin of the Atomic Scientists Vol. 33 No. 3 (March 1977), pp. 33-40. [No. 677]

_____, "Challenge of the Next Two Decades: Dangers and Opportunities," in Norman C. Dahl and Jerome B. Wiesner (Eds.), World Change and World Security. Cambridge, Mass.: MIT Press, 1978. [No. 678]

_____, "A Soviet View of U.S. Policy," Wall Street Journal, April 29, 1980, p. 22. [No. 679]

_____, "You Americans Make It Difficult," Time Vol. 120 No. 23 (December 6, 1982), p. 30. [No. 680]

_____, "Relations Between U.S. and Soviet Union," in Burns Weston (Ed.), Toward Nuclear Disarmament and Global Security: A Search For Alternatives. Boulder, Colo.: Westview Press, 1984. [No. 681]

_____, and William Oltsmans, The Soviet Viewpoint. New York: Dodd, Mead, and Company, 1983. [No. 682]

Arbeiter, Jurgen B., "A Transparent Figleaf--The Offensive Nature of Soviet Military Doctrine," Air University Review Vol. 31 No. 6 (November-December 1980), pp. 93-98. [No. 122]

Arnett, Robert L., "Soviet Attitudes Toward Nuclear War: Do They Really Think They Can Win?", Journal of Strategic Studies Vol. 2 No. 2 (September 1979), pp. 172-191. [No. 101]

Aspaturian, Vernon V., "Detente and the Strategic Balance," Chapter One in Michael MccGwire and John McDonnell (Eds.),

347

Soviet Naval Influences: Domestic and Foreign Dimensions. New York: Praeger Publishers, 1977, pp. 3-30. [No. 2]

_____, "Soviet Global Power and the Correlation of Forces," Problems of Communism Vol. 29 No. 3 (May-June 1980), pp. 1-18. [No. 3]

Aspin, Les, "Soviet Civil Defense: Myth and Reality," Arms Control Today Vol. 6 No. 9 (September 1976), pp. 1-4. [No. 327]

_____, "What Are the Russians Up To?", International Security Vol. 3 No. 1 (Summer 1978), pp. 30-54. [No. 34]

Austin, Anthony, "Moscow Expert Says U.S. Errs on Soviet War Aims: Interview with Lt. Gen. Mikhail A. Milshtein," New York Times, August 25, 1980. [No. 683]

Babenko, I., Soviet Officers. Moscow: Progress Publishers, 1976. [No. 616a]

Baker, John C., "Continuity and Change in Soviet Nuclear Strategy," in Kenneth M. Currie and Gregory Varhall (Eds.), The Soviet Union: What Lies Ahead? Washington, D.C.: Government Printing Office, 1985), pp. 636-660. [No. 146]

Banerjee, Jyotirmoy, "Arms and Ideology in Soviet Foreign Policy," Institute for Defense Studies and Analyses Journal Vol. 5 No. 2 (October 1972), pp. 277-300. [No. 102]

Barber, Ransom E., "The Conventional Wisdom on Soviet Strategy: Is It Conventional?", National War College Forum No. 17 (Summer 1973), pp. 21-30. [No. 370]

_____, "The Myth of the Soviet Nuclear War Strategy," Army Vol. 25 No. 6 (June 1975), pp. 10-17. [No. 371]

Baritz, Joseph J., "The Soviet Strategy of Flexible Response," Bulletin of the Institute for Study of the USSR Vol. 16 No. 4 (April 1969), pp. 25-35. [No. 35]

Barlow, William J. "Soviet Damage-Denial: Strategy, Systems, SALT, and Solution," Air University Review Vol. 32 No. 5 (September-October 1981), pp. 2-20. [No. 147]

Barnet, Richard J., "The Soviet Attitude on Disarmament," Problems of Communism, May-June 1961, pp. 32-37. [No. 66]

Barnett, Roger W.; and Edward J. Lacey, "Their Professional Journal," U.S. Naval Institute Proceedings Vol. 108 No. 10 (October 1982), pp. 95-101. [No. 603]

348

Barry, James A., "Military Training of Soviet Youth," Military Review Vol. 53 No. 2 (February 1973), pp. 92-103. [No. 544]

Bashurian, P., "Frunze Military Academy," Military Review Vol. 50 No. 6 (June 1970), pp. 60-67. [No. 623]

Baxter, William P., "Survival, Fighting-on Stressed in Red Nuclear Defense Doctrine," Army Vol. 31 No. 7 (July 1981), pp. 59-61. [No. 406]

_____, "Soviet Perceptions of the Laws of War," Chapter 2 in Graham Vernon (Ed.), Soviet Perceptions of Peace and War. Washington, D.C.: National Defense University Press, 1981, pp. 17-26. [No. 36]

_____, Soviet Airland Battle Tactics. Novato, Calif.: Presidio Press, 1986. [No. 407]

Baylis, John; and Gerald Segal (Eds.), Soviet Strategy. Montclair, N.J.: Allanfeld, Osmun, and Co., 1981. [No. 576]

Baz, I., "Soviet Military Science on the Character of Contemporary War," Appendix A in Raymond L. Garthoff, The Soviet Image of Future War. Washington, D.C.: Public Affairs Press, 1959. [No. 624]

Becker, Abraham S., Soviet Military Outlays Since 1955. Santa Monica, Calif.: The RAND Corporation (RM-3886-PR), July 1964. [No. 511]

_____, Soviet Growth, Resource Allocation, and Military Outlays. Santa Monica, Calif.: The RAND Corporation (P-4135), June 1969. [No. 512]

_____, Strategic Breakout as a Soviet Policy Option. Santa Monica, Calif.: The RAND Corporation (R-2097-ACDA), 1977. [No. 67]

_____, CIA Estimates of Soviet Military Expenditure. Santa Monica, Calif.: The RAND Corporation (P-6534), August 1980. [No. 513]

_____, Guns, Butter, and Tools: Tradeoffs in Soviet Resource Allocation. Santa Monica, Calif.: The RAND Corporation (P-6816), October 1982. [No. 514]

_____, Sitting on Bayonets? The Soviet Defense Burden and Moscow's Economic Dilemma. Santa Monica, Calif.: The RAND Corporation (P-6908), September 1983. [No. 515]

Beloff, Max, "The Military Factor in Soviet Foreign Policy," Problems of Communism Vol. 30 No. 1 (January-February 1981), pp. 70-73. [No. 4]

Beloff, Nora, "Escape from Boredom: A Defector's Story," Atlantic, November 1980, pp. 42-50. [No. 666]

Berman, Robert P.; and John C. Baker, Soviet Strategic Forces: Requirements and Responses. Washington D.C.: The Brookings Institution (Studies in Defense Policy), 1982. [No. 199]

Betit, Eugene, "Soviet Tactical Doctrine and Capabilities and NATO's Strategic Defense," Strategic Review Vol. 4 No. 4 (Fall 1976), pp. 95-107. [No. 408]

Beukel, Erik, "Analyzing the Views of Soviet Leaders on Nuclear Weapons," Cooperation and Conflict Vol. 15 (June 1980), pp. 71-84. [No. 148]

Beumer, Robert S., "The Soviet Draft: Cornerstone of USSR Nuclear Strategy," Military Intelligence Vol. 5 No. 4 (October-December 1979), pp. 38-44. [No. 545]

Bladley, Stephen C., The New Soviet Civil Defense Program: A Warning for America. Maxwell Air Force Base, Ala.: Air War College (Professional Study No. 4288), 1971. [No. 328]

Bogdanov, Radomir; and Lev Semeiko, "Soviet Military Might: A Soviet View," Fortune, February 26, 1978, pp. 46-53. [No. 684]

Boileau, Oliver C., "Can Strategic Deterrence Prevent a Nuclear War?", National Defense, Vol 61 No. 2 (March-April 1977), pp. 370-373. [No. 123]

Bonds, Ray (Ed.), The Soviet War Machine: An Encyclopedia of Russian Military Equipment and Strategy. London: Chartwell Ltd., 1976. [No. 577]

Brodie, Bernard, The Communist Reach for Empire. Santa Monica, Calif.: The RAND Corporation (P-2916), June 1964. [No. 5]

Brown, Dallas C., "Conventional Warfare in Europe -- The Soviet View," Military Review Vol. 55 No. 2 (February 1975), pp. 58-71. [No. 372]

_____, "Origins of the Cold War: The Soviet View," Chapter 3 in Graham D. Vernon (Ed.), Soviet Perceptions of War and Peace. Washington, D.C.: National Defense University Press, 1981, pp. 27-50. [No. 261]

Brzezinski, Zbigniew, et al., Promise or Peril: The Strategic Defense Initiative. Washington, D.C.: Ethics and Public Policy Center, 1986. [No. 578]

Buchan, Glenn C., "The Anti-MAD Mythology," Bulletin of the Atomic Scientists Vol. 37 No. 4 (April 1981), pp. 13-17. [No. 277]

Byely, B. et al., Marxism-Leninism on War and Army. Washington, D.C.: Government Printing Office (Soviet Military Thought No. 2), n.d. [No. 616b]

Cade, David J., "Russian Military Strategy: A Fresh Look," Air University Review Vol. 29 No. 6 (September-October 1978), pp. 18-27. [No. 149]

Caldwell, Lawrence T., "The Soviet Union and Arms Control," Current History Vol. 67 No. 398 (October 1974), pp. 150-154, 178-180. [No. 68]

Caravelli, John N., "The Role of Surprise and Preemption in Soviet Military Strategy," International Security Review Vol. 6 No. 2 (Summer 1981), pp. 209-233. [No. 150]

Caron, Gerald C., Jr., "Soviet Civil-Military Relations: Conflict and Collaboration Among Comrades," Naval War College Review Vol. 24 No. 4 (December 1971), pp. 65-91. [No. 546]

Checinski, Michael, "The Soviet War-Economic Doctrine in the Years of Military-Technological Challenge (1946-1983): An Overview," Crossroads No. 12 (1984), pp. 23-51. [No. 516]

Chuyev, Yu.V; and Yu.B. Mikhiylov, Forecasting in Military Affairs. Washington, D.C.: Government Printing Office (Soviet Military Thought No. 15), n.d. [No. 619p]

Cimbala, Steven J., "Soviet Nuclear Strategies: Will They Do the Expected?", Strategic Review Vol. 13 No. 4 (Fall 1985), pp. 67-77. [No. 151]

_____, "Soviet 'Blitzkrieg' in Europe: The Abiding Nuclear Dimension," Strategic Review Vol. 14 No. 3 (Summer 1986), pp. 67-76. [No. 373]

Clark, Donald L., "Soviet Strategy for the Seventies," Air University Review Vol. 22 No. 1 (January-February 1971), pp. 3-18. [No. 6]

Clark, Richard W., Jr., Soviet Views on Tactical Nuclear Weapons. Oberammergau, West Germany: U.S. Army Institute of Advanced Russian Studies, 1 April 1962. [No. 409]

Clemens, Walter C., Jr., "The Soviet Militia in the Missile Age," Orbis Vol. 8 No. 1 (Spring 1964), pp. 84-105. [No. 239]

_____, "Kto Kovo? The Present Danger as Seen from Moscow," Worldview Vol. 20 No. 9 (September 1977), pp. 4-9. [No. 262]

Close, Robert, "Soviet Strategy, the Atlantic, and the Defense of the West," Atlantic Community Quarterly Vol. 18 No. 4 (Winter 1980-81), pp. 403-412. [No. 352]

Cockburn, Andrew, The Threat: Inside the Soviet Military Machine. New York: Random House, 1983. [No. 87]

Cohen, S.T.; and Joseph D. Douglass, Jr., "Selective Targeting and Soviet Deception," Armed Forces Journal, September 1983, pp. 95-101. [No. 278]

_____, and W.C. Lyons. "A Comparison of U.S.-Allied and Soviet Tactical Nuclear Force Capabilities and Politics," Orbis Vol. 19 No. 1 (Spring 1975), pp. 72-92. [No. 410]

Colton, Timothy, "Civil-Military Relations in Soviet Politics," Current History Vol. 67 No. 398 (October 1974), pp. 160-163, 181-182. [No. 547]

_____, Commissars, Commanders, and Civilian Authority. Cambridge, Mass.: Harvard University Press, 1979. [No. 548]

Crane, Robert Dickson, "The Cuban Crisis: A Strategic Analysis of American and Soviet Policy," Orbis Vol. 6 No. 4 (Winter 1963), pp. 528-563. [No. 235]

_____ (Ed.), Soviet Nuclear Strategy: A Critical Appraisal. Washington, D.C.: Center for Strategic Studies, Georgetown University, 1963. [No. 240]

Crommelin, Quentin, Jr.; and David Sullivan, Soviet Military Superiority: The Untold Facts About the New Danger to America (Los Angeles, Calif.: University of Southern California Defense and Strategic Studies Program, 1985). [No. 124]

Current Digest of the Soviet Press. Columbus, Ohio: weekly. [No. 610]

Currie, Kenneth M.; and Gregory Varhill (Eds.), The Soviet Union: What Lies Ahead? Washington, D.C.: Government Printing Office (Studies in Communist Affairs Vol. 6), 1985. [No. 579]

Dallin, Alexander, "Red Star" on Military Affairs, 1945-1952: A Selected, Annotated List of Articles in the Soviet Military Newspaper. Santa Monica, Calif.: The RAND Corporation (RM-1637), February 10, 1956. [No. 604]

352

_____, et al., The Soviet Union, Arms Control, and Disarmament: A Study of Soviet Attitudes (New York: Columbia University School of International Relations, 1964), 282 p. [No. 69]

Danchenko, A.M.; and I.F. Vydrin, Military Pedogogy. Washington, D.C.: Government Printing Office (Soviet Military Thought No. 7), n.d. [No. 619g]

Dash, Barbara L., A Defector Reports: The Institute of the USA and Canada. Falls Church, Va.: Delphic Associates, May 1982. [No. 667]

Davydov, Yuri, "Problems of Detente in Soviet-American Relations," Peace and the Sciences No. 2 (June 1977), pp. 92-104. [No. 685]

_____, "Why Detente Deteriorates: A Soviet View," Christian Science Monitor, February 8, 1980, p. 22. [No. 686]

Deane, Michael J., "The Soviet Assessment of the 'Correlation of World Forces': Implications for American Foreign Policy," Orbis Vol. 20 No. 3 (Fall 1976), pp. 628-636. [No. 37]

_____, "The Main Political Administration as a Factor in Communist Party Control Over the Military in the Soviet Union," Armed Forces and Society Vol. 3 No. 2 (February 1977), pp. 295-324. [No. 549]

_____, Political Control of the Soviet Armed Forces. New York: Crane, Russak and Company, 1977. [No. 550]

_____, and Mark E. Miller, "Science and Technology in Soviet Military Planning," Strategic Review Vol. 5 No. 3 (Summer 1977), pp. 77-86. [No. 517]

_____, Ilana Kass, and Andrew G. Porth, "The Soviet Command Structure in Transformation," Strategic Review Vol. 12 No. 2 (Spring 1984), pp. 55-70. [No. 374]

Deriabin, Peter (Ed.), The Penkovsky Papers. New York: Doubleday and Company, 1965. [No. 241]

Despres, J.H.; L. Dzirkals, and B. Whaley, Timely Lessons of History: The Manchurian Model for Soviet Strategy. Santa Monica, Calif.: The RAND Corporation (R-1825-NA), July 1976. [No. 411]

Dick, C.J., "Soviet Operational Manoeuver Groups: A Closer Look," International Defense Review Vol. 16 No. 6 (1983), pp. 769-776. [No. 412]

_____, "Catching NATO Unawares: Soviet Army Surprise and Deception Techniques," International Defense Review Vol. 19 No. 1 (January 1986), pp. 21-26. [No. 413]

Dinerstein, Herbert S., "The Revolution in Soviet Strategic Thinking," Foreign Affairs Vol. 36 No. 2 (January 1958), pp. 241-252. [No. 152]

_____, The Soviet Military Posture as a Reflection of Soviet Strategy. Santa Monica, Calif.: The RAND Corporation (RM-2102), 24 March 1958. [No. 153]

_____, "The Soviet Employment of Military Strength for Political Purpose," Annals of the American Academy of Political and Social Science Vol. 318 (July 1958), pp. 104-112. [No. 38]

_____, War and the Soviet Union: Nuclear Weapons and the Revolution in Soviet Military and Political Thinking. New York: Frederick A. Praeger, Publisher, 1958. [No. 184]

_____, "Soviet Strategic Ideas, January, 1960," Soviet Survey, October-December 1960. [No. 209]

_____, Introduction to the Second Edition of "War and the Soviet Union". Santa Monica, Calif.: The RAND Corporation (P-2620), August 1962. [No. 185]

_____, "Soviet Goals and Military Force," Orbis, Vol. 7 No. 4 (Winter 1962), pp. 425-436. [No. 39]

_____, The United States and the Soviet Union: Standoff or Confrontation? Santa Monica, Calif.: The RAND Corporation (P-3046), January 1965. [No. 40]

_____, Making of a Missile Crisis, October 1962. Baltimore, Md.: The Johns Hopkins University Press, 1976. [No. 236]

Dismukes, Bradford, Roles and Missions of Soviet Naval General Purpose Forces in Wartime: Pro-SSBN Operations? Alexandria, Va.: Center for Naval Analyses (PP 130), August 1974. [No. 439]

Donnelly, Christopher N. "The 'March' in Soviet Tactical Doctrine," RUSI Journal Vol. 119 No. 3 (September 1974), pp. 77-79. [No. 414]

_____, "Tactical Problems Facing the Soviet Army: Recent Debates in the Soviet Military Press," International Defense Review Vol. 11 No. 9 (1978), pp. 1405-1412. [No. 415]

_____, "The Development of Soviet Military Doctrine," International Defense Review Vol. 14 No. 12 (December 1981), pp. 1589-1596. [No. 154]

354

_____, "The Soviet Operational Maneuver Group: A New Challenge for NATO," International Defense Review Vol. 15 No. 9 (September 1982), pp. 1177-1186. [No. 416]

_____, Heirs of Clausewitz -- Change and Continuity in the Soviet War Machine. London: Institute for European Defense and Strategic Studies, 1986. [No. 353]

Douglass, Joseph D., Jr., The Soviet Theater Nuclear Offensive. Washington, D.C.: Government Printing Office (Studies in Communist Affairs Vol. 1), 1976. [No. 375]

_____, "Soviet Nuclear Strategy in Europe: A Selective Targeting Doctrine?", Strategic Review Vol. 5 No. 4 (Fall 1977), pp. 19-31. [No. 376]

_____, "Soviet Disinformation," Strategic Review Vol. 9 No. 1 (Winter 1981), pp. 16-25. [No. 279]

_____, "The Theater Nuclear Threat," Parameters Vol. 12 No. 4 (December 1982), pp. 71-81. [No. 377]

_____, "Strategic Planning and Nuclear Insecurity," Orbis Vol. 27 No. 3 (Fall 1983), pp. 667-694. [280]

_____, "The Theater Nuclear Threat," Defense Science 2001+, December 1983, pp. 23-37. [No. 378]

_____, and Amoretta M. Hoeber, "The Nuclear Warfighting Dimension of the Soviet Threat to Europe," Journal of Social and Political Studies Vol. 3 No. 2 (Summer 1978), pp. 107-146. [No. 379]

_____, and Amoretta M. Hoeber, Index to and Extracts From "Voyennaya Mysl" (1963-1969). Arlington, Va.: System Planning Corporation (SPC 464), September 1979. [No. 605]

_____, and Amoretta M. Hoeber, Soviet Strategy for Nuclear War. Stanford, Calif.: Hoover Institution Press, 1979. [No. 155]

_____, and Amoretta Hoeber, Conventional War and Escalation: The Soviet View. New York: National Strategy Information Center, 1981. [No. 380]

_____, and Amoretta M. Hoeber, Selected Readings From Soviet Military Thought (1963-1973). Washington, D.C.: Government Printing Office (Studies in Communist Affairs Vol. 5), 1983. [No. 611]

Druzhinin, V.V.; and D.S. Kontorov, Concept, Algorithm, Decision. Washington, D.C.: Government Printing Office (Soviet Military Thought No. 6), n.d. [No. 619f]

Dukes, William C., "Psychological Conditioning of the Soviet Soldier," Military Review Vol. 54 No. 12 (December 1974), pp. 69-78. [No. 551]

Dunin, A., "The Evolution of the Soviet Land Forces Since the End of World War II," Survival Vol. 30 No. 1 (January-February 1979), pp. 26-29. [No. 625]

Dyson, Freeman, "On Russians and Their View of Nuclear Strategy," Chapter Seven in Charles W. Kegley, Jr. and Eugene R. Wittkopf (Eds.), The Nuclear Reader: Strategy, Weapons, and War. New York: St. Martin's Press, 1985, pp. 95-99. [No. 281]

Dziak, John J. "The Institutional Foundations of Soviet Military Doctrine," International Security Review Vol. 4 No. 4 (Winter 1979-1980), pp. 317-332. [No. 186]

_____, Soviet Perceptions of Military Power: The Interaction of Theory and Practice. New York: National Strategy Information Center, 1981. [No. 187]

Dzirkals, Lilia. "Lightning War" in Manchuria: Soviet Military Analysis of the 1945 Far East Campaign. Santa Monica, Calif.: The RAND Corporation (P-5589), January 1976. [No.417]

Erickson, John, "Towards a New 'Soviet High Command': 'Rejuvenation' Renewed (1959-1969)," RUSI Journal, September 1969. [No. 468]

_____, Soviet Military Power. London: Royal United Services Institute for Defense Studies, 1971. [No. 469]

_____, "Soviet Command and Control," Military Review Vol. 52 No. 1 (January 1972), pp. 41-50. [No. 470]

_____, "The Soviet Military, Soviet Policy, and Soviet Politics: A Lecture at the U.S. Army War College," Strategic Review Vol. 2 No. 4 (Fall 1973), pp. 23-36. [No. 41]

_____, "Soviet Military Capabilities in Europe," RUSI Journal Vol. 120 No. 1 (March 1975), pp. 65-69. [No. 381]

_____, "Windows on the Soviet Military," Problems of Communism Vol. 24 No. 5 (September-October 1975), pp. 63-66. [No. 606]

_____, "Soviet Military Posture and Policy in Europe," in Richard Pipes (Ed.), Soviet Strategy in Europe. New York: Crane, Russak, and Company, 1976, pp. 169-209. [No. 354]

_____, "Soviet Theater-Warfare Capability: Doctrines, Deployments, and Capabilities," in Lawrence Whetten (Ed.),

356

The Future of Soviet Military Power. New York: Crane, Russak, and Co., 1976, pp. 117-156. [No. 382]

_____, "Soviet Military Capabilities," Current History Vol. 71 No. 420 (October 1976), pp. 97-100, 128, 135-137. [No. 42]

_____, "Trends in the Soviet Combined Arms Concept," Strategic Review Vol. 5 No. 1 (Winter 1977), pp. 38-53. [No. 418]

_____, "The Ground Forces in Soviet Military Policy," Strategic Review Vol. 6 No. 1 (Winter 1978), pp. 64-79. [No. 383]

_____, "The Chimera of Mutual Deterrence," Strategic Review Vol. 6 No. 2 (Spring 1978), pp. 11-17. [No. 103]

_____, "Soviet Military Policy in the 1980's," Current History Vol. 75 No. 440 (October 1978), pp. 97-99, 135-138. [No. 7]

_____, "The Soviet Military Press, 1978," Strategic Review Vol. 7 No. 3 (Summer 1979), pp. 83-96. [No. 471]

_____, "Soviet Combined Arms Operations: An Evalution," Armor, May-June 1980, pp. 16-21. [No. 419]

_____, "The Soviet View of Deterrence: A General Survey," Survival Vol. 24 No. 6 (November-December 1982), pp. 242-251. [No. 104]

_____, "Toward 1984: Four Decades of Soviet Military Policy," Air University Review Vol. 35 No. 2 (January-February 1984), pp. 30-34. [No. 200]

_____, et al. (Eds.), The Military-Technical Revolution: Its Impact on Strategic and Foreign Policy. New York: Frederick A. Praeger, Publisher, 1966. [No. 580]

_____, and E.J. Feuchtwanger (Eds.), Soviet Military Power and Performance. Hamden, Conn.: Shoestring Press (Archon Books), 1979. [No. 581]

Ermath, Fritz. "Soviet Military Politics," Military Review Vol. 48 No. 1 (January 1968), pp. 32-36. [No. 552]

_____, Internationalism, Security, and Legitimacy: The Challenge to Soviet Interests in East Europe. Santa Monica, Calif.: The RAND Corporation (RM-5909-PR), March 1969. [No. 8]

_____, "Contrasts in American and Soviet Strategic Thought," International Security Vol. 2 No. 2 (Fall 1978), pp. 138-155. [No. 282]

Evangelista, Matthew A., "Stalin's Postwar Army Reappraised," International Security Vol. 7 No. 3 (Winter 1982-83), pp. 110-138. [No. 355]

"Excerpts From a Soviet Booklet on Nuclear War," New York Times, November 21, 1981, p. 4. [No. 626]

Ferri, Albert Jr., Selections from the Soviet Military Press, 1968-71. Menlo Park, Calif.: Stanford Research Institution (SRI Project 8474, Technical Note SSC-TN-8974-70), 1973. [No. 553]

Field, Brian, "Soviet Military Expenditure Estimates: Meaning and Measurement," NATO Review Vol. 34 No. 4 (August 1986), pp. 28-31. [No. 518]

Finkelstein, L., "Interview Given by First Defector From Arbatov's American Institute," American Bar Association Intelligence Report Vol. 3 No. 9 (September 1981), pp. 1, 6. [No. 668]

FitzGerald, Mary C., "Marshal Ogarkov on the Modern Theater Operation," Naval War College Review Vol. 39 No. 4 (Autumn 1986), pp. 6-25. [No. 384]

"Five Keys to Soviet Strategy: A Special Report," Air Force Magazine Vol. 44 No. 10 (October 1961), pp. 29-32. [No. 9]

"Foremost Soviet Military Journal Emphasizes Crucial Role of War and Military Might," Soviet World Outlook, February 13, 1976. [No. 43]

Foster, Gregory D., "Soviet Perceptions of U.S. Strategic Activities: A Realtime Retrospective," in Kenneth M. Currie and Gregory Varhall (Eds.), The Soviet Union: What Lies Ahead? Washington, D.C.: Government Printing Office (Studies in Communist Affairs Vol. 6), 1985, pp. 670-692. [No. 263]

Frank, Lewis A., "Soviet Power After SALT I: A Strategic Coercive Capability?", Strategic Review Vol. 2 No. 2 (Spring 1974), pp. 54-60. [No. 156]

_____, Arms Limitations and Strategic Operations--A Soviet Perspective. Falls Church, Va.: Analytical Services Inc. (ANSER Strategic Division Note SDN 75-1), November 1975, revised January 1976. [No. 70]

Freedman, Lawrence, U.S. Intelligence and the Soviet Strategic Threat. Boulder, Colo.: Westview Press, 1977. [No. 283]

Frost, Howard, "Soviet Party-Military Relations in Strategic Decisionmaking," in Kenneth M. Currie and Gregory Varhall (Eds.), The Soviet Union: What Lies Ahead? Washington,

358

D.C.: (Studies in Communist Affairs Vol. 6), 1985, pp. 58-74. [No. 472]

Galay, Nikolai, "The Soviet Approach to the Modern Military Revolution," in John Erickson et al. (Eds.), The Military-Technical Revolution. New York: Frederick A. Praeger, Publisher, 1966, pp. 20-31. [No. 157]

Gallagher, Matthew P.; and Karl F. Spielmann, Jr., Soviet Decision-making for Defense: A Critique of U.S. Perspectives on the Arms Race. New York: Prager Publishers, 1972. [No. 473]

Garder, Michael, A History of the Soviet Army. New York: Frederick A. Praeger, Publisher, 1966. [No. 88]

Gareau, Frederick H., "Nuclear Deterrence: The Soviet Position," Orbis Vol. 8 No. 4 (Winter 1965), pp. (922-936). [No. 105]

Garrett, Banning N.; and Bonnie S. Glaser, Soviet and Chinese Strategic Perceptions in Peacetime and War. Washington, D.C.: Defense Nuclear Agency (DNA-TR-81-262), October 31, 1982. [No. 10]

Garthoff, Douglass F., "The Soviet Military and Arms Control," Survival Vol. 19 No. 6 (November-December 1977), pp. 242-250. [No. 474]

"A Garthoff-Pipes Debate on Soviet Strategic Doctrine," Strategic Review Vol. 10 No. 4 (Fall 1982), pp. 36-63. [No. 158]

Garthoff, Raymond L., "On Soviet Military Strategy and Capabilities," World Politics Vol. 3 No. 1 (October 1950), pp. 114-129. [No. 188]

_____, Soviet Military Doctrine. Glencoe, Ill.: The Free Press, 1953. [No. 189]

_____, The Soviet High Command and and General Staff. Santa Monica, California: The RAND Corporation (P-684), May 27, 1955. [No. 475]

_____, Recent Trends in Soviet Military Policy. Santa Monica, Calif.: The RAND Corporation (P-726), August 30, 1955. [No. 519]

_____, The Role of the Military in Recent Soviet Politics. Santa Monica, Calif.: The RAND Corporation (RM-1638), March 1, 1956. [No. 554]

359

_____, "The Role of the Military in Post-Stalin Politics," Russian Review Vol. 16 No. 2 (April 1957), pp. 15-24. [No. 555]

_____, Soviet Strategy in the Nuclear Age. New York: Frederick A. Praeger, Publisher, 1958. [No. 159]

_____, The Soviet Image of Future War. Washington, D.C.: Public Affairs Press, 1959. [No. 160]

_____, "The Soviet Challenge," Army Vol. 11 No. 2 (September 1960), pp. 30-32. [No. 106]

_____, "War and Peace in Soviet Policy," Russian Review Vol. 20 No. 2 (April 1961), pp. 121-133. [No. 11]

_____, "A Manual of Soviet Strategy," Reporter, February 14, 1963, pp. 34-36. [No. 223]

_____, Soviet Military Policy: A Historical Analysis. New York: Frederick A. Praeger, Publisher, 1966. [No. 44]

_____, "SALT and the Soviet Military," Problems of Communism Vol. 24 No. 1 (January 1975), pp. 21-37. [No. 476]

_____, "Negotiating With the Russians: Some Lessons from SALT," International Security Vol. 1 No. 4 (Spring 1977), pp. 3-24. [No. 71]

_____, "Mutual Deterrence and Strategic Arms Limitations in Soviet Policy," International Security Vol. 2 No. 1 (Summer 1978), pp. 112-147. [No. 107]

_____, "On Estimating and Imputing Intentions," International Security Vol. 2 No. 3 (Winter 1978), pp. 22-32. [No. 108]

_____, "The Death of Stalin and the Birth of Mutual Deterrence," Survey Vol. 25 No. 2 (Spring 1980), pp. 10-16. [No. 210]

_____, "Brezhnev's Opening: The TNF Tangle," Foreign Policy No. 41 (Winter 1980-81), pp. 82-94. [No. 356]

_____, Perspectives on the Strategic Balance. Washington, D.C.: The Brookings Institution, 1983. [No. 109]

_____, Detente and Cooperation. Washington, D.C.: The Brookings Institution, 1985. [No. 12]

Gervasi, Tom, The Myth of Soviet Military Supremacy. New York: Harper and Row, Publishers, 1986. [No. 89]

360

Ghebhardt, Alexander O.; and William Schneider, Jr., "The Soviet High Command: Recent Changes and Policy Implications," Military Review Vol. 53 No. 5 (May 1973), pp. 3-14. [No. 477]

_____, and William Schneider, Jr., "The Soviet Air Force High Command," Air University Review Vol. 24 No. 4 (May-June 1973), pp. 75-83. [No. 478]

Glagolev, Igor S., "The Soviet Decision-Making Process in Arms-Control Negotiations," Orbis Vol. 21 No. 4 (Winter 1978), pp. 767-776. [No. 479]

Glazov, V., "What is Local War?", Survival Vol. 3 No. 5 (September-October 1961), pp. 226-228. [No. 627]

Goldhammer, H., The Soviet Union in a Period of Strategic Parity. Santa Monica, Calif.: The RAND Corporation (R-889-PR), October 1971. [No. 13]

Gordon, Michael R., "Rubles for Defense -- Are the Soviets Really Outspending the Pentagon?", National Journal Vol. 13 No. 15 (April 11, 1981), pp. 601-604. [No. 520]

Gormley, Dennis M., "Understanding Soviet Motivations for Deploying Long-Range Theater Nuclear Forces," Military Review Vol. 61 No. 9 (September 1981), pp. 20-34. [No. 385]

_____, "A New Dimension to Soviet Theater Strategy," Orbis Vol. 29 No. 3 (Fall 1985), pp. 539-570. [No. 386]

_____, and Douglas M. Hart, "Soviet Views on Escalation," Washington Quarterly Vol. 7 No. 4 (Fall 1984), pp. 71-84. [No. 387]

Gorshkov, Sergei G., Red Star Rising at Sea. Annapolis, Md.: U.S. Naval Institute Press, 1974. [No. 628]

_____, The Sea Power of the State. New York: Pergamon Press, 1979. [No. 629]

_____, "The Sea Power of the State (Excerpts)," Survival Vol. 29 No. 1 (January-February 1977), pp. 24-29. [No. 630]

Goure, Daniel, "Strategic Offense and Defense: Enhancing the Effectiveness of U.S. Strategic Forces," Annals of the Academy of Political and Social Science Vol. 457 (September 1981), pp. 28-45. [No. 303]

_____, "The Strategic Competition and SDI," Chapter 21 in Zbigniew Brzezinski et al. (Eds.), Promise or Peril: The Strategic Defense Initiative. Washington, D.C.: Ethics and Public Policy Center, 1986, pp. 227-236. [No. 304]

361

_____, "Soviet Counters to SDI," NATO's Sixteen Nations Vol. 31 No. 2 (April 1986), pp. 34-37. [No. 305]

_____, "C³ and the New Soviet Nuclear Forces," Signal Vol. 41 No. 4 (December 1986), pp. 86-89. [No. 480]

_____, and Gordon H. McCormick, "Soviet Strategic Defense: The Neglected Dimension of the U.S. Soviet Balance," Orbis Vol. 24 No. 1 (Spring 1980), pp. 103-128. [No. 306]

Goure, Leon, Soviet Civil Defense. Santa Monica, Calif.: The RAND Corporation (P-1887), March 14, 1960. [No. 329]

_____, Civil Defense Training in Russia. Santa Monica, Calif.: The RAND Corporation (P-2340), March 8, 1961. [No. 330]

_____, Soviet Civil Defense. Santa Monica, Calif.: The RAND Corporation (P-2415), August 22, 1961. [No. 331]

_____, "Soviet Views on the Role of Civil Defense," Current History, November 1961. [No. 332]

_____, The Resolution of the Soviet Controversy Over Civil Defense. Santa Monica, Calif.: The RAND Corporation (RM-3223-PR), June 1962. [No. 333]

_____, Civil Defense in the Soviet Union. Berkeley, Calif.: University of California Press, 1962. [No. 334]

_____, Soviet Limited War Doctrine. Santa Monica, Calif.: The RAND Corporation (P-2744), May 1963. [No. 357]

_____, The Role of Civil Defense in Soviet Strategy. Santa Monica, Calif.: The RAND Corporation (RM-3703-PR), June 1963. [No. 335]

_____, Recent Developments in the Soviet Civil Defense Program. Santa Monica, Calif.: The RAND Corporation (P-2752), June 1963. [No. 336]

_____, Notes on the Second Edition of Marshal V.D. Sokolovskii's "Military Strategy". Santa Monica, Calif.: The RAND Corporation (RM-3972-PR), February 1964. [No. 224]

_____, Soviet Emergency Planning. Santa Monica, Calif.: The RAND Corporation (P-4042), February 1969. [No. 337]

_____, Soviet Civil Defense Revisited, 1966-1969. Santa Monica, Calif.: The RAND Corporation (RM-6113-PR), November 1969. [No. 338]

362

_____, Soviet Civil Defense, 1969-70. Coral Gables, Fla.: University of Miami (Center for Advanced International Studies), 1972. [No. 339]

_____, The Military Indoctrination of Soviet Youth. New York: National Strategy Information Center (Strategy Papers No. 16), 1973. [No. 556]

_____, Shelters in Soviet War Survival Strategy. Coral Gables, Fla.: University of Miami (Center for Advanced International Studies), 1974. [No. 340]

_____, War Survival in Soviet Strategy: USSR Civil Defense. University of Miami: Center for Advanced International Studies, 1976. [No. 341]

_____, Civil Defense in Soviet Strategic Perceptions. Washington, D.C.: Advanced International Studies Institute (DNA 5174 F), 1 January 1980. [No. 342]

_____, "The U.S. 'Countervailing Strategy' in Soviet Perception," Strategic Review Vol. 9 No. 4 (Fall 1981), pp. 51-64. [No. 264]

_____, "Nuclear Winter in Soviet Mirrors," Strategic Review Vol. 13 No. 3 (Summer 1985), pp. 22-38. [No. 265]

_____, Foy D. Kohler, and Mose L. Harvey, The Role of Nuclear Forces in Current Soviet Strategy. University of Miami: Center for Advanced International Studies, 1974. [No. 125]

Grant, Steven A., Soviet Americanists. Washington, D.C.: Office of Research, International Communications Agency (R-1-80), February 15, 1980. [No. 669]

Gray, Colin S., "Soviet-American Strategic Competition: Instruments, Doctrines, and Purposes," in Robert J. Pranger and Roger P. Labrie (Eds.), Nuclear Strategy and National Security: Points of View. Washington, D.C.: American Enterprise Institute (Studies in Defense Policy), 1977, pp. 278-301. [No. 45]

_____, "Soviet Rocket Forces: Military Capability, Political Utility," Air Force Magazine (Soviet Aerospace Almanac No. 4) Vol. 61 No. 3 (March 1978), pp. 49-55. [No. 46]

_____, "The Most Dangerous Decade: Historic Mission, Legitimacy, and Dynamics of the Soviet Empire in the 1980s," Orbis Vol. 25 No. 1 (Spring 1981), pp. 13-28. [No. 255]

Grechko, A.A., The Armed Forces of the Soviet State. Washington, D.C.: Government Printing Office (Soviet Military Thought No. 12), n.d. [No. 6191]

_____, Liberation Mission of the Soviet Armed Forces in the Second World War. Moscow: Progress Publishers, 1975. [No. 616c]

Green, Murray, "Soviet Military Strategy," Air Force Magazine Vol. 46 No. 3 (March 1963), pp. 38-42. [No. 225]

Green, William C., Civil Defense and the Strategic Balance. Claremont, Calif.: Public Research Syndicated Article No. 125 (February 4, 1981). [No. 343]

_____, "The Early Formulation of Soviet Strategic Nuclear Doctrine," Comparative Strategy Vol. 4 No. 4 (1984), pp. 369-386. [No. 211]

Ground Zero, What About the Russians -- And Nuclear War? New York: Pocket Books, 1983. [No. 110]

Grudin, I., "What Determines the Strength of the Army?", Military Review Vol. 40 No. 5 (August 1960), pp. 104-108. [No. 631]

_____, "Man: The Principal Force in War," Military Review Vol. 40 No. 11 (November 1960), pp. 79-84. [No. 632]

Guertner, Gary L. "Strategic Vulnerability of a Multinational State: Deterring the Soviet Union," Political Science Quarterly Vol. 96 No. 2 (Summer 1981), pp. 209-223. [No. 266]

Hahn, Walter F.; and Alvin J. Cottrell, "Ballistic Missile Defense and Soviet Strategy," Orbis Vol. 9 No. 2 (Summer 1965), pp. 316-337. [No. 307]

Haley, P. Edward; David M. Keithly, and Jack Merritt (Eds.), Nuclear Strategy, Arms Control, and the Future. Boulder, Colo.: Westview Press, 1985. [No. 582]

Hamlett, Bruce D., "SALT: The Illusion and the Reality," Strategic Review Vol. 3 No. 3 (Summer 1975), pp. 67-78. [No. 126]

Hansen, James H., "Countering NATO's New Weapons: Soviet Concepts for War in Europe," International Defense Review Vol. 17 No. 11 (November 1984), pp. 1617-1624. [No. 388]

Hanson, Donald W., "Is Soviet Strategic Doctrine Superior?", International Security Vol. 7 No. 3 (Winter 1982-83), pp. 61-83. [No. 284]

Harris, William R., "Arms Control Treaties: How Do They Restrain Soviet Strategic Defense Programs?", Orbis Vol. 29 No. 4 (Winter 1986), pp. 701-707. [No. 308]

Hart, Douglas M., "The Hermeneutics of Soviet Military Doctrine," Washington Quarterly Vol. 7 No. 2 (Spring 1984), pp. 77-88. [No. 285]

_____, "Soviet Approaches to Crisis Management: The Military Dimension," Survival Vo. 26 No. 5 (September-October 1984), pp. 200-234. [No. 481]

_____, and Dennis M. Gormley, "The Evolution of Soviet Interest in Atomic Artillery," RUSI Journal Vol. 128 No. 2 (June 1983), pp. 25-34. [No. 420]

Hasegawa, Tsuyoshi, "Soviets on Nuclear-War-Fighting," Problems of Communism Vol. 35 No. 4 (July-August 1986), pp. 86-79. [No. 250]

Heinlein, Joseph J., "The Main Political Administration in Today's Soviet Forces," Military Review Vol. 53 No. 11 (November 1973), pp. 55-64. [No. 557]

Hemsley, John, "Command Technology: Voennaya Sistemotekhnika. An Algorithmic Approach to Decision-making," RUSI Journal Vol. 125 No. 3 (September 1980), pp. 58-64. [No. 482]

_____, Soviet Troop Control: The Role of Command Technology in the Soviet Military System. Oxford: Brassey's Publishers Limited, 1982. [No. 483]

Herrick, Robert W., Gorshkov Makes the Case for Further Expansion of Soviet Navy: A Current Series of Articles in Morskoi Sbornik by Fleet Admiral Sergey Gorshkov Commander in Chief Soviet Navy. Alexandria, Va.: Center for Naval Analyses (M 1012), October 19, 1972. [No. 440]

_____, The USSR's "Blue Belt of Defense" Concept: A Unified Plan for Defense Against Seaborne Nuclear Attack by Strike Carriers and Polaris/Poseidon SSBNs. Alexandria, Va: Center for Naval Analyses (PP 111), May 1973. [No. 441]

_____, "Roles and Missions of the Soviet Navy: Historical Evolution, Current Priorities, and Future Prospects," in James L. George (Ed.), The Soviet and Other Communist Navies: The View From the Mid-1980s. Annapolis, Md.: Naval Institute Press, 1986, pp. 39-61. [No. 442]

_____, James M. McConnell, and Michael K. MccGwire, Admiral Gorshkov on the Soviet Navy in War and Peace. Alexandria, Va.: Center for Naval Analyses (M 1015), 1973. [No. 443]

Herspring, Dale R., "The CPSU and the Military," Problems of Communism Vol. 25 No. 2 (March-April 1976), pp. 71-75. [No. 558]

_____, "The Soviet Military in the Aftermath of the 27th Party Congress," Orbis Vol. 30 No. 2 (Summer 1986), pp. 297-316. [No. 559]

_____, "Marshal Akhromeyev and the Future of the Soviet Armed Forces," Survival Vol. 28 No. 6 (November-December 1986), pp. 524-535. [No. 251]

Heymant, Irving, "The Challenge of the Soviet Army," Military Review Vol. 40 No. 5 (August 1960), pp. 49-55. [No. 421]

Hickox, Joseph E., Party-Political Work in the Soviet Armed Forces. Maxwell Air Force Base, Ala.: Air Command and Staff College (Research Study), 1974. [No. 560]

Hines, John G.; and Phillip A. Petersen, "The Soviet Conventional Offensive in Europe," Military Review Vol. 64 No. 4 (April 1984), pp. 2-28. [No. 422]

_____, and Phillip A. Petersen, "Changing the Soviet System of Control: Focus on Theater Warfare," International Defense Review Vol. 19 No. 3 (March 1986), pp. 281-292. [No. 389]

_____, Phillip A. Petersen, and Notra Trulock, III, "Soviet Military Theory From 1945-2000: Implications for NATO," Washington Quarterly Vol. 9 No. 4 (Fall 1986), pp. 117-137.

Hoeber, Amoretta, "Soviet Strategic Intentions," in Kenneth M. Currie and Gregory Varhall (Eds.), The Soviet Union: What Lies Ahead? Washington, D.C.: Government Printing Office (Studies in Communist Affairs Vol. 6), 1985, pp. 661-669. [No. 127]

Hoeber, Francis, P.; and Amoretta Hoeber, "The Soviet View of Deterrence: Who Whom?", Survey Vol. 25 No. 2 (Spring 1980), pp. 17-24. [No. 128]

Hoeffding, Oleg, Troop Movements in Soviet Tactical Doctrine. Santa Monica, Calif.: The RAND Corporation (R-878-PR), November 1971. [No. 423]

Holloway, David, "Strategic Concepts and Soviet Policy," Survival Vol. 13 No. 11 (November 1971), pp. 364-369. [No. 484]

_____, "Soviet Strategists Attack Schlesinger," New Scientists Vol. 64 No. 926 (November 5, 1974), p. 707. [No. 267]

_____, "Technological Change and Military Procurement," Chapter 5 in Michael MccGwire and John McDonnell (Eds.), Soviet Naval Influences: Domestic and Foreign Dimensions. New York: Praeger Publishers, 1977, pp. 123-131. [No. 521]

_____, "Decision-Making in Soviet Defense Policies," in Prospects of Soviet Power in the 1980s, Part II. London: International Institute for Strategic Studies (Adelphi Paper No. 152), Summer 1979, pp. 24-31. [No. 485]

_____, "Research Note: Soviet Thermonuclear Development," International Security Vol. 4 No. 3 (Winter 1979-80), pp. 192-197. [No. 212]

_____, War, Militarism, and the Soviet State. New York: Institute for World Order (World Order Models Project Working Paper No. 17), 1981. [No. 72]

_____, The Soviet Union and the Arms Race. New Haven, Conn.: Yale University Press, 1983. [No. 201]

_____, "The View From the Kremlin," Wilson Quarterly Vol. 7 No. 5 (Winter 1983), pp. 102-111. [No. 14]

Holman, Paul, "Deterrence vs. War-Fighting: The Soviet Preference," Air Force Magazine (Soviet Aerospace Almanac No. 7) Vol. 64 No. 3 (March 1981), pp. 50-54. [No. 129]

Holst, Johan J., Comparative U.S. and Soviet Deployments Doctrines, and Arms Limitation. Chicago, Ill.: University of Chicago Center for Policy Studies, 1971. [No. 73]

Holzman, Franklyn D., Financial Checks on Soviet Defense Expenditures. Lexington, Mass.: Lexington Books, 1975. [No. 522]

_____, "Are the Soviets Really Outspending the U.S. on Defense?", International Security Vol. 4 No. 4 (Spring 1980), pp. 86-104. [No. 523]

Hopkins, M.M.; M.P. Kennedy, and M.F. Lawrence, The Tradeoff Between Consumption and Military Expenditures for the Soviet Union During the 1980s. Santa Monica, Calif.: The RAND Corporation (R-2927-NA), November 1982. [No. 524]

_____, and M.P. Kennedy, Comparisons and Implications of Alternative Views of the Soviet Economy. Santa Monica, Calif.: The RAND Corporation (R-3075-NA), March 1984. [No. 525]

Horelick, Arnold L., "Deterrence" and Surprise Attack in Soviet Strategic Thought. Santa Monica, Calif.: The RAND Corporation (RM-2618), July 1, 1960. [No. 213]

_____, "The Cuban Missile Crisis: An Analysis of Soviet Calculation and Behavior," World Politics Vol. 16 No. 3 (April 1964), pp. 363-389. [No. 237]

367

_____, "The Strategic Mind-Set of the Soviet Military: An Essay-Review," Problems of Communism Vol. 26 No. 2 (March-April 1977), pp. 80-85. [No. 268]

_____, and Myron Rush, Strategic Power and Soviet Foreign Policy. Chicago: University of Chicago Press, 1966. [No. 47]

Howell, Phillip D., "Divergent Doctrines Snarl Nuclear Face-Off: 'Unthinkable Weapon' Integral Part of Soviet Battle Philosophy," Army Vol. 31 No. 12 (December 1981), pp. 18-23. [No. 391]

Hsieh, Alice Langley, The Sino-Soviet Nuclear Dialogue: 1963. Santa Monica, Calif.: The RAND Corporation (P-2852), January 1964. [No. 15]

Hubbell, John G., "Soviet Civil Defense: The Grim Reality," Reader's Digest Vol. 112 No. 670 (February 1978), pp. 77-80. [No. 344]

Hughes, Peter C.; and M.R. Edwards, "Nuclear War in Soviet Thinking -- The Implications for U.S. Security," Journal of Social and Political Studies Vol. 2 No. 2 (April 1976), pp. 113-130. [No. 130]

Hyland, William G., "Soviet Theater Forces and Arms Control Policy," Survival Vol. 23 No. 5 (September-October 1981), pp. 194-199. [No. 392]

Il'in, S.K., "The Morale Factor in Modern War," Chapter 21 in P. Edward Haley et al. (Eds.), Nuclear Strategy, Arms Control, and the Future. Boulder, Colo.: Westview Press, 1985, pp. 157-158. [No. 633]

Iovlev, A.M., "New Technology and Mass Armies," Survival Vol. 5 No. 3 (September-October 1961), pp. 233-234. [No. 634]

Isachenkov, N.V., "New Naval Weapons," Survival Vol. 4 No. 2 (March-April 1962), p. 89. [No. 635]

Ivanov, D.A. et al., Fundamentals of Tactical Command and Control. Washington, D.C.: Government Printing Office (Soviet Military Thought No. 17), n.d. [612r]

Jackson, William D., "Soviet Images of the U.S. as Nuclear Adversary, 1969-1979," World Politics Vol. 33 No. 4 (July 1981), pp. 614-638. [No. 269]

_____, "Cold War Demonology," Bulletin of the Atomic Scientists Vol. 38 No. 8 (October 1982), pp. 52-54. [No. 286]

368

Jacobs, Walter Darnell., "The Leninist Revival in Soviet Military Doctrine," Military Review Vol. 38 No. 4 (July 1958), pp. 23-31. [No. 214]

_____, "Marshal Malinovskiy and Missiles," Military Review Vol. 40 No. 3 (June 1960), pp. 14-20. [No. 215]

_____, "Sokolovskiy's Strategy," Military Review Vol. 43 No. 6 (July 1963), pp. 9-19. [No. 226]

_____, "Soviet Strategic Effectiveness," Journal of International Affairs Vol. 26 No. 1 (1972), pp.60-71. [No. 526]

Jacobsen, Carl G., Soviet Strategy -- Soviet Foreign Policy: Military Considerations Affecting Soviet Policy Making. Glasgow: Robert Maclehose and Co., Ltd. (The University Press), 1972. [No. 486]

_____, "The Emergence of a Soviet Doctrine of Flexible Response?", Atlantic Community Quarterly Vol. 12 No. 2 (Summer 1974), pp. 233-238. [No. 48]

_____, "Soviet Attitudes to 'Controlled Strategic Conflict'," Current Comment No. 10 (May 1976), pp. 14-23. [No. 161]

_____, "Soviet Think Tanks," in David R. Jones (Ed.), Soviet Armed Forces Review Annual Vol. 1. Gulf Breeze, Fla.: Academic International Press, 1977, pp. 149-152. [No. 670]

_____, Soviet Strategic Initiatives: Challenge and Response. New York: Praeger Publishers, 1979. [No. 162]

_____, "The Soviet Military Reappraised," Current History Vol. 80 No. 468 (October 1981), pp. 305-308, 336-338. [No. 287]

_____, "Soviet-American Policy: New Strategic Uncertainties," Current History Vol. 81 No. 477 (October 1982). [No. 16]

Jenson, John W., "Nuclear Strategy: Differences in Soviet and American Thinking," Air University Review Vol. 30 No. 2 (March-April 1979), pp. 2-17. [No. 131]

Jonas, Anne M., "Changes in Soviet Conflict Doctrine," Chapter 13 in Walter F. Hahn and John C. Neff (Eds.), American Strategy for the Nuclear Age. Garden City, N.J.: Doubleday and Company, Inc., 1960, pp. 152-168. [No. 49]

Jones, Christopher D., "The 'Revolution in Military Affairs' and Party-Military Relations, 1965-70," Survey Vol. 20 No. 1 (Winter 1974), pp. 83-100. [No. 561]

_____, "Equality and Equal Security in Europe," Orbis Vol. 26 No. 3 (Fall 1982), pp. 637-664. [No. 358]

Jones, David R. (Ed.), The Military-Naval Encyclopedia of Russia and the Soviet Union. Gulf Breeze, Fla.: Academic International Press. Vol. 1 (1978), Vol. 2 (1980), Vol. 3 (1981), Vol. 4 (1984). [No. 583]

_____, (Ed.), Soviet Armed Forces Review Annual. Gulf Breeze, Fla.: Academic International Press. Vol. 1 (1977), Vol. 2 (1978), Vol. 3 (1979), Vol. 4 (1980), Vol. 5 (1981), Vol. 6 (1982), Vol. 7 (1982-1983). [No. 584]

_____, "Nuclear War and Soviet Policy," International Perspectives," November-December 1982, pp. 17-20. [No. 288]

Jones, Issac R., Soviet Military Strategy. Maxwell Air Force Base, Ala.: Air War College Professional Study, 1974. [No. 202]

Jones, W.M., Soviet Leadership Politics and Leadership Views on the Use of Military Force. Santa Monica, Calif.: The RAND Corporation (N-1210-AF), July 1979. [No. 50]

_____, Escalation Space and Assumptions about Enemy Motives: Elements in Warning Assessment. Santa Monica, Calif.: The RAND Corporation (N-1269-AF), January 1980. [No. 289]

Jorgensen, K., "The Rocket and Military Strategy," Military Review Vol. 37 No. 4 (July 1957), pp. 101-103. [No. 216]

Jukes, Geoffrey, The Development of Soviet Strategic Thinking Since 1945. Canberra: Australian National University Press (Canberra Papers on Strategy and Defense No. 14), 1972. [No. 203]

_____, "Soviet Strategy 1965-1990," Chapter 4 in Robert O'Neill and D.M. Horner (Eds.), New Directions in Soviet Thinking. London: George Allen and Unwin, 1981, pp. 60-74. [No. 204]

Kaiser, Robert G.; and Walter Pincus, "The Doomsday Debate: 'Shall We Attack America?'," Parameters Vol. 9 No. 4 (December 1979), pp. 79-85. [No. 290]

Kamoff-Nicolsky, G., "Voennaya Strategiya: Its Validity in the Eighties," Canadian Defense Quarterly Vol. 11 No. 2 (Autumn 1981). [No. 227]

Kaplan, Fred M., "The Soviet Civil Defense Myth," Bulletin of the Atomic Scientists Part I (March 1978), pp. 14-20; Part II (April 1978), pp. 41-58. [No. 345]

_____, "Soviet Civil Defense: Some Myths in the Western Debate," Survival Vol. 20 No. 3 (May-June 1978), pp. 113-120. [No. 346]

_____, Dubious Specter: A Skeptical Look at the Soviet Nuclear Threat. Washington, D.C.: Institute for Policy Studies, 1980. [No. 111]

Kassing, David, Changes in Soviet Naval Forces. Alexandria, Va.: Center for Naval Analyses (PP 183), November 1976. [No. 444]

Katzenbach, Edward L., "Russian Military Development," Current History Vol. 39 No. 231 (November 1960), pp. 262-266. [No. 256]

Keegan, George J., "An Editorial in the Form of a Letter," Strategic Review Vol. 5 No. 2 (Spring 1977), pp. 6-11. [No. 132]

Kennedy, Robert, "Soviet Theater Nuclear Forces: Implications for NATO Defenses," Orbis Vol. 25 No. 2 (Summer 1981), pp. 331-350. [No. 393]

Khmel, A.Ya., Education of the Soviet Soldier: Party Political Work in the Soviet Armed Forces. Moscow: Progess Press, 1975. [No. 616d]

Kime, Steve F., "The Soviet View of War," Comparative Strategy Vol. 2 No. 3 (1980), pp. 205-221.. [No. 51]

_____, "A Soviet Navy for the Nuclear Age," Parameters Vol. 10 No. 3 (March 1980), pp. 58-70. [No. 445]

_____, "Power Projection, Soviet Style," Air Force Magazine Vol. 63 No. 12 (December 1980), pp. 50-54. [No. 52]

King, Peter. "Two Eyes for a Tooth: The State of Soviet Strategic Doctrine," Survey Vol. 24 No. 1 (Winter 1970), pp. 45-56. [No. 133]

Kintner, William R.; and Harriet Fast Scott, The Nuclear Revolution in Soviet Military Affairs. Norman, Okla.: University of Oklahoma Press, 1968. [No. 613]

Kirin, I., "Raise the Offensive Tempos," Military Review Vol. 55 No. 2 (February 1975), pp. 51-55. [No. 636]

Kissinger, Henry A., Nuclear Weapons and Foreign Policy. New York: Harper and Brothers, 1957. [No. 190]

Kober, Stanley, "Interpreting Soviet Strategic Policy," Comparative Strategy Vol. 4 No. 1 (1983), pp. 65-74. [No. 112]

_____, "Causes of the Soviet Military Buildup," in Kenneth M. Currie and Gregory Varhall (Eds.), The Soviet Union: What Lies Ahead? Washington, D.C.: Government Printing Office (Studies in Communist Affairs Vol. 6), 1985, pp. 314-323. [No. 53]

Kolkowicz, Roman, Conflicts in Soviet Party-Military Relations: 1962-1963. Santa Monica, Calif.: The RAND Corporation (RM-3760-PR), August 1963. [No. 562]

_____, Soviet Strategic Debate: An Important Recent Addendum. Santa Monica, Calif.: The RAND Corporation (P-2936), July 1964. [No. 242]

_____, The Role of Disarmament in Soviet Policy: A Means or an End? Santa Monica, Calif.: The RAND Corporation (P-2952), August 1964. [No. 74]

_____, A General and the Apparatchiks. Santa Monica, Calif.: The RAND Corporation (P-3298), January 1966. [No. 563]

_____, The Red "Hawks" on the Rationality of Nuclear War. Santa Monica, Calif.: The RAND Corporation (RM-4899-PR), March 1966. [No. 243]

_____, Soviet Party-Military Relations: Contained Conflict. Santa Monica, Calif.: The RAND Corporation (P-3371), May 1966. [No. 564]

_____, The Impact of Modern Technology on the Soviet Officer Corps. Santa Monica, Calif.: The RAND Corporation (P-3380), June 1966. [No. 565]

_____, Political Controls in the Red Army: Professional Autonomy Versus Political Integration. Santa Monica, Calif.: The RAND Corporation (P-3402), July 1966. [No. 566]

_____, The Soviet Military and the Communist Party. Princeton, N.J.: Princeton University Press, 1967. [No. 567]

_____, "Interest Groups in Soviet Politics: The Case of the Military," Comparative Politics Vol. 2 No. 3 (April 1970), pp. 445-472. [No. 568]

_____, "Strategic Parity and Beyond: Soviet Perspectives," World Politics Vol. 23 No. 23 (April 1971), pp. 431-451. [No. 244]

_____, "Strategic Elites and Politics of Superpower," Journal of International Relations Vol. 26 No. 1 (1972), pp. 40-59. [No. 569]

_____, "On Limited War: Soviet Approaches," Chapter 5 in Robert O'Neill and D.M. Horner (Eds.), New Directions in Strategic Thinking. London: George Allen and Unwin, 1981, pp. 75-88. [No. 359]

_____, "U.S. and Soviet Approaches to Military Strategy: Theory vs. Experience," Orbis Vol. 25 No. 2 (Summer 1981), pp. 307-330. [No. 163]

_____, "The Military and Soviet Foreign Policy," Journal of Strategic Studies Vol. 4 No. 4 (December 1981), pp. 337-355. [No. 487]

_____, Matthew P. Gallagher, and Benjamin S. Lambeth with Walter C. Clemens, Jr. and Peter W. Colm, The Soviet Union and Arms Control: A Superpower Dilemma. Baltimore, Md.: The Johns Hopkins Press, 1970. [No. 585]

_____, and Ellen Mickiewicz (Eds.), The Soviet Calculus of Nuclear War. Lexington, Mass.: Lexington Books, 1986. [No. 586]

Kolt, George, "Soviet and American Perceptions of Arms Control," in Kenneth M. Currie and Gregory Varhall (Eds.), The Soviet Union: What Lies Ahead? Washington, D.C.: Government Printing Office (Studies in Communist Affairs Vol. 6), 1985, pp. 142-147. [No. 75]

Korotkov, I., "On the Fundamental Factors Which Determine the Course and Outcome of Wars," Appendix B in Raymond L. Garthoff, The Soviet Image of Future War. Washington, D.C.: Public Affairs Press, 1959. [No. 637]

Kozhevnikov, M.N., The Command and Staff of the Soviet Army Air Force in the Great Patriotic War, 1941-45. Washington, D.C.: Government Printing Office (Soviet Military Thought No. 17), n.d. [619q]

Kozlov, C.N. (Ed.), The Officer's Handbook. Washington, D.C.: Government Printing Office (Soviet Military Thought No. 13), n.d. [No. 619m]

Kozlov, Svyatoslav, "Soviet Military Art and Science," Military Review Vol. 39 No. 6 (September 1959), pp. 93-100. [No. 638]

_____, "The Character of Modern War," Survival Vol. 3 No. 4 (July-August 1961), pp. 159-160. [No. 639]

_____, "Soviet Views on Theater Nuclear Arms," Wall Street Journal, October 16, 1982. [No. 687]

Kramish, Arnold, The Soviet Union and the Atom: The "Secret" Phase. Santa Monica, Calif.: The RAND Corporation (RM-1896), April 11, 1957. [No. 217]

_____, The Soviet Union and the Atom: Toward Nuclear Maturity. Santa Monica, Calif.: The RAND Corporation (RM-2163), April 25, 1958. [No. 218]

Krebs, Thomas, Can the Soviets Counter SDI? Washington, D.C.: The Heritage Foundation (Backgrounder No. 454), September 17, 1985. [No. 309]

Kupperman, Charles M., "The Soviet World View," Policy Review No. 7 (Winter 1979), pp. 45-67. [No. 17]

Kurasov, V.V., "On the Question of a Forestalling Blow," Military Review Vol. 39 No. 8 (November 1959), pp. 88-90. [No. 640]

Kurochkin, P.A., "Conventional Forces in the Nuclear Age," Survival Vol. 3 No. 6 (November-December 1961), p. 282. [No. 641]

Laird, Robbin F.; and Dale R. Herspring, The Soviet Union and Strategic Arms. Boulder, Colo.: Westview Press, 1984. [No. 18]

Lambeth, Benjamin S., "Deterrence in the MIRV Era," World Politics Vol. 24 No. 2 (January 1972), pp. 221-242. [No. 113]

_____, Selective Nuclear Operations and Soviet Strategy. Santa Monica, Calif.: The RAND Corporation (P-5506), September 1975. [No. 164]

_____, "The Evolving Soviet Strategic Threat," Current History Vol. 66 No. 410 (October 1975). [No. 165]

_____, Selective Nuclear Options in American and Soviet Strategic Policy. Santa Monica, Calif.: The RAND Corporation (R-2034-DDRE), December 1976. [No. 166]

_____, How To Think About Soviet Military Doctrine. Santa Monica, Calif.: The RAND Corporation (P-5939), February 1978. [No. 191]

_____, "The Political Potential of Soviet Equivalence," International Security Vol. 4 No. 2 (Fall 1979), pp. 22-39. [No. 54]

_____, The Elements of Soviet Strategic Policy. Santa Monica, Calif.: The RAND Corporation (P-6389), September 1979. [No. 192]

_____, Soviet Strategic Conduct and the Prospects for Stability. Santa Monica, Calif.: The RAND Corporation (R-2579-AF), December 1980. [No. 76]

_____, Arms Control and Defense Planning in Soviet Strategic Policy. Santa Monica, Calif.: The RAND Corporation (P-6644), July 1981. [No. 488]

_____, Risk and Uncertainty in Soviet Deliberations About War. Santa Monica, Calif.: The RAND Corporation (R-2687-AF), October 1981. [No. 489]

_____, Trends in Soviet Military Policy. Santa Monica, Calif.: The RAND Corporation (P-6819), October 1982. [No. 90]

_____, On Thresholds in Soviet Military Thought. Santa Monica, Calif.: The RAND Corporation (P-6860), March 1983. [No. 167]

_____, The State of Western Research on Soviet Military Strategy and Policy. Santa Monica, Calif.: The RAND Corporation (N-2330-AF), October 1984. [No. 291]

Larionov, V., "The Doctrine of Aggression in Doses," Survival Vol. 1 No. 4 (September-October 1959), pp. 135-136. [No. 642]

Lee, Asher, The Soviet Air and Rocket Forces. London: Weidenfeld and Nicholson, 1959. [No. 587]

Lee, William T., "Soviet Views of the ABM and Soviet Strategy," Appendix A in William R. Kintner (Ed.), Safeguard: Why the ABM Makes Sense. New York: Hawthorn Books, Inc., 1969, pp. 363-400. [No. 614]

_____, "The 'Politico-Military-Industrial Complex' of the USSR," Journal of International Affairs Vol. 26 No. 1 (1972), pp. 73-86. [No. 527]

_____, "Soviet Defense Spending: Planned Growth, 1976-1980," Strategic Review Vol. 5 No. 1 (Winter 1977), pp. 74-79. [No. 528]

_____, Estimation of Soviet Defense Expenditures, 1955-75: An Unconventional Approach. New York: Praeger Publishers, 1977. [No. 529]

_____, "Soviet Targeting Strategy and SALT," Air Force Magazine Vol. 60 No. 9 (September 1978), pp. 120-129. [No. 168]

_____, Soviet Defense Expenditures in an Era of SALT. Washington, D.C.: United States Strategic Institute (USSI Report 79-1), 1979, 31 p. [No. 530]

_____, "Soviet Perceptions of the Threat and Soviet Military Capabilities," Chapter 5 in Graham D. Vernon (Ed.), Soviet Perceptions of War and Peace. Washington, D.C.: National Defense University Press, 1981, pp. 67-96. [No. 270]

_____, "The Shift in Soviet National Priorities to Military Forces, 1985," Annals, American Academy of Political Science No. 457 (September 1981), pp. 46-66. [No. 531]

_____, and Richard E. Staar, Soviet Military Thinking Since World War II. Palo Alto, Calif.: Hoover Institution Press, 1986. [No. 205]

Leebaert, Derek (Ed.), Soviet Military Thinking. London: George Allen and Unwin, 1981. [No. 588]

Legvold, Robert, "The Nature of Soviet Power," Foreign Affairs Vol. 56 No. 1 (October 1977), pp. 49-71. [No. 19]

_____, "Strategic 'Doctrine' and SALT: Soviet and American Views," Survival Vol. 21 No. 1 (January-February 1979), pp. 8-13. [No. 114]

Leitenberg, Millar, "The Counterpart of Defense Industry Conversion in the United States: The USSR Economy, Defense Industry, and Military Expenditure," Journal of Peace Research Vol. 16 No. 3 (1979), pp. 263-277. [No. 532]

Leites, Nathan, Soviet Style in War. New York: Crane, Russak and Company, 1982. [No. 91]

Lewis, K.N., The U.S.-Soviet Strategic Balance: Can We Meet the Challege? Santa Monica, Calif.: The RAND Corporation (P-6657), August 1981. [No. 169]

Liddell Hart, B.H., The Red Army. New York: Harcourt, Brace, and Company, 1956. [No. 589]

Lockwood, Jonathan S., The Soviet View of U.S. Strategic Deterrence: Implications for Decision-Making. New Brunswick, N.J.: Transaction Books, 1983. [No. 271]

Lomov, N.A., Scientific-Technical Progress and the Revolution in Military Affairs. Washington, D.C.: Government Printing Office (Soviet Military Thought No. 3), n.d. [No. 619c]

_____, "Modern Means of Waging War and Operational-Level Strategy," Chapter 19 in P. Edward Haley et al. (Eds.), Nuclear

Strategy, Arms Control, and the Future. Boulder, Colo.: Westview Press, 1985. [No. 643]

Long, J.F.L., "Shifts in Russia's Strategic Posture," Royal Air Force Quarterly Vol. 6 No. 4 (Winter 1966), pp. 297-302. [No. 245]

Lord, Carnes, "Taking Soviet Defenses Seriously," Washington Quarterly Vol. 9 No. 4 (Fall 1986), pp. 83-99. [No. 310]

Luce, Clare Booth, "Two Doctrines of War," Strategic Review Vol. 6 No. 4 (Fall 1974), pp. 12-14. [No. 134]

Mackintosh, J. Malcolm, Recent Developments in Political Instruction in the Soviet Army. Oxford: St. Antony's Papers on Soviet Affairs, November 1957. [No. 570]

_____, Juggernaut: A History of the Soviet Armed Forces. New York: MacMillan, 1967. [No. 92]

_____, "Soviet Strategic Policy," World Today Vol. 25 No. 7 (July 1970), pp. 269-276. [No. 20]

_____, "Russia's Defense: A Question of Quality," Interplay, February 1971, pp. 14-18. [No. 21]

_____, "The Soviet Military: Influence on Foreign Policy," Problems of Communism Vol. 22 No. 5 (September-October 1973), pp. 1-11. [No. 22]

Maddock, R.T., "Some Economic Constraints on Defense Spending in the Soviet Union," RUSI Journal Vol. 124 No. 3 (September 1979), pp. 38-43. [No. 533]

Mahoney, Shane E., "Posture and Purpose of the Soviet Military," Problems of Communism Vol. 28 No. 1 (January-February 1979), pp. 55-58. [No. 490]

MccGwire, Michael (Ed.), Soviet Naval Developments: Capability and Context. New York: Praeger Publishers, 1973. [No. 592]

_____, "Soviet Strategic Weapons Policy, 1955-70," Chapter 27 in Michael MccGwire, et al. (Eds.), Soviet Naval Policy: Objectives and Constraints. New York: Praeger Publishers, 1975, pp. 486-503. [No. 135]

_____, "The Overseas Role of the 'Soviet Military Presence'," Chapter 2 in Michael MccGwire and John McDonnell (Eds.), Soviet Naval Influences: Domestic and Foreign Dimensions. New York: Praeger Publishers, 1977, pp. 31-40. [No. 55]

_____, "Commentary: Soviet Intentions," International Security Vol. 4 No. 1 (Summer 1979), pp. 139-143. [No. 170]

_____, "Contingency Plans for World War," in James L. George (Ed.), The Soviet and Other Communist Navies: The View from the Mid-1980s. Annapolis, Md.: Naval Institute Press, 1986, pp. 61-81. [No. 446]

_____, Ken Booth, and John McDonnell (Eds.), Soviet Naval Policy: Objectives and Constraints. New York: Praeger Publishers, 1975. [No. 591]

_____, and John McDonnell (Eds.), Soviet Naval Influences: Domestic and Foreign Dimensions. New York: Praeger Publishers, 1977. [No. 590]

McConnell, James M., "Ideology and Soviet Military Strategy," in Richard F. Staar (Ed.), Aspects of Modern Communism. University of South Carolina Press, 1968. [No. 56]

_____, Military-Political Tasks of the Soviet Navy in War and Peace. Alexandria, Va.: Center for Naval Analyses (PP 148), February 1976. [No. 447]

_____, "The Gorshkov Articles, the New Gorshkov Book, and Their Relation to Policy," Chapter 29 in Michael MccGwire and James McDonnell (Eds.), Soviet Naval Developments. New York: Praeger Publishers, 1977, pp. 569-620. [No. 448]

_____, Strategy and Missions of the Soviet Navy in the Year 2000. Alexandria, Va.: Center for Naval Analyses (PP 206), November 1977. [No. 449]

_____, Soviet and American Strategic Doctrine: One More Time. Alexandria, Va.: Center for Naval Analyses (PP-271), January 1980. [No. 171]

_____, Briefing: Soviet Doctrine, Past, Present, and Future. Alexandria, Va.: Center for Naval Analyses (M 1050), March 1980. [No. 172]

_____, The Interacting Evolution of Soviet and American Military Doctrine. Alexandria, Va.: Center for Naval Analyses (PP 472), September 1980. [No. 173]

_____, Possible Counterforce Roles for the Typhoon. Alexandria, Va.: Center for Naval Analyses (PP-347), March 1982. [No. 450]

_____, The Soviet Shift in Emphasis from Nuclear to Conventional. Alexandria, Va.: Center for Naval Analyses (CRC 490), June 1983. [No. 174]

_____, "Shifts in Soviet Views on the Proper Focus of Military Development," World Politics, April 1985, pp. 317-343. [No. 193]

_____, "New Soviet Methods for Antisubmarine Warfare?", Naval War College Review Vol. 38 No. 4 (July-August 1985), pp. 16-27. [No. 451]

_____, "The Irrelevance Today of Sokolovskiy's Book Military Strategy," Defense Analysis Vol. 1 No. 4 (1985), pp. 243-254. [No. 228]

_____, "The Soviet Naval Mission Structure: Past, Present, and Future," in James L. George (Ed.), The Soviet and Other Communist Navies: the View from the Mid-1980s. Annapolis, Md.: Naval Institute Press, 1986, pp. 37-60. [No. 452]

McConnell, Robert B., Conventional Military Force and Soviet Foreign Policy. Monterey, Calif.: The Naval Postgraduate School, June 1978. [No. 23]

McDonald, Lawrence P., "On Defense: A Talk With Major General George Keegan," American Opinion Vol. 20 No. 8 (September 1977), pp. 1-4; 71-82. [No. 175]

McDonnell, John, "The Organization of Soviet Military Defense and Military Policy Planning," Chapter 3 in Michael MccGwire and John McDonnell (Eds.), Soviet Naval Influences: Domestic and Foreign Dimensions. New York: Praeger Publishers, 1977, pp. 61-106. [No. 491]

McGuire, Frank C., "Soviets Revert to ICBM Emphasis," Missiles and Rockets, December 2, 1963. [No. 246]

Meehan, John F. III, "Soviet Maneuvers, Summer 1971," Military Review Vol. 52 No. 4 (April 1972), pp. 14-21. [No. 424]

Mets, David R., "The Origin of Soviet Air Theory and Doctrine," Military Review Vol. 55 No. 8 (August 1975), pp. 36-48. [No. 425]

Meyer, Stephen M., "Soviet Military Programs and the 'New High Ground'," Survival Vol. 25 No. 5 (September/October 1983), pp. 204-215. [No. 311]

_____, Soviet Theatre Nuclear Forces. London: International Institute for Strategic Studies (Adelphi Papers Nos. 187 and 188), Winter 1983-84. [No. 394]

_____, "Soviet Perspectives on the Paths to Nuclear War," Chapter 7 in Graham T. Allison, Albert Carnesale, and Joseph S. Nye, Jr. (Eds.), Hawks, Doves, and Owls: An Agenda for Avoiding Nuclear War. New York: W.W. Norton and Company, 1985, pp. 167-205. [No. 176]

_____, "Soviet Strategic Programmes and the U.S. SDI," Survival Vol. 27 No. 6 (November-December 1985), pp. 274-292. [No. 312]

Michaud, Norbert, "An Epigog for an Increasing Soviet Defense Share, 1965-1979," in Kenneth M. Currie and Gregory Varhall (Eds.), The Soviet Union: What Lies Ahead? Washington, D.C.: Government Printing Office (Studies in Communist Affairs Vol. 6), 1985, pp. 434-451. [No. 534]

Miller, David C., "Soviet Armed Forces and Political Pressure," Military Review Vol. 49 No 12 (December 1969), pp. 63-68. [No. 571]

Miller, Mark E., "Soviet Strategic Thought: The End of an Era?", International Security Review Vol. 5 No. 4 (Winter 1980-1981), pp. 447-510. [No. 177]

_____, Soviet Strategic Power and Doctrine: The Quest for Superiority. Washington, D.C.: Advanced International Studies Institute, 1982. [No. 206]

Miller, Martin J., "Soviet Nuclear Tactics," Ordinance (May-June 1970), pp. 624-627. [No. 426]

Millett, Stephen M., Soviet Perceptions of Nuclear Strategy and Implications for U.S. Deterrence. Columbus, Ohio: Battelle Economics and Policy Analysis Occasional Paper No. 18 (April 1981). [No. 136]

Milovidov, A.S.; and V.G. Kozlov, Philosophical Heritage of V.I. Lenin and Problems of Contemporary War. Washington, D.C.: Government Printing Office (Soviet Military Thought Vol. 5), n.d. [No. 619e]

Mil'stein, Mikhail (Michael) A., "Problems of the Inadmissibility of Nuclear Conflict," International Studies Quarterly Vol. 20 (March 1976), pp. 87-103. [No. 688]

_____, "Moscow Expert Says U.S. is Mistaken on Soviet War Strategy," International Herald Tribune, August 28, 1980. [No. 689]

_____, and L.S. Semijko, "U.S. Military 'R&D' Through Soviet Eyes," Bulletin of the Atomic Scientists Vol. 33 No. 2 (February 1977), pp. 32-38. [No. 690]

Monks, Alfred L., "Evolution of Soviet Military Thinking," Military Review Vol. 51 No. 3 (March 1971), pp. 78-93. [No. 207]

_____, Soviet Military Doctrine: 1960 to the Present. New York: Irvington Publishers, Inc., 1984. [No. 208]

_____, and Kenyon N. Griffin, "Soviet Strategic Claims, 1964-1970," Orbis Vol. 16 No. 2 (Summer 1972), pp. 520-544. [No. 292]

Muehleisen, Dolf E., Changes in Soviet Military Strategy. Menlo Park, Calif.: SRI International (Research Memorandum SED-RM-316), July 1974. [No. 229]

Murray, J.E., An Approach to Long-Range Forecasting. Santa Monica, Calif.: The RAND Corporation (N-1609-01A), January 1981. [No. 293]

National Security, Military Power, and the Role of Force in International Relations. Washington, D.C.: Government Printing Office (DA PAM 550-19), September 1976. [No. 595]

Nicholson, Arthur Donald, Jr., The Soviet Union and Strategic Nuclear War. Monterey, Calif.: The Naval Postgraduate School, 1980. [No. 137]

Nunn, Jack H., The Soviet First Strike Threat: The U.S. Perspective. New York: Praeger Publishers, 1982. [No. 294]

Odom, William E., "Sokolovsky's Strategy Revisited," Military Review Vol. 44 No. 10 (October 1964), pp. 49-53. [No. 230]

_____, "Who Controls Whom in Moscow?", Foreign Policy No. 19 (Summer 1975). [No. 24]

_____, "The Party Connection," Problems of Communism Vol. 22 No. 5 (September-October 1973), pp. 13-26. [No. 572]

_____, "Soviet Force Posture: Dilemmas and Directions," Problems of Communism Vol. 34 No. 4 (July-August 1985), pp. 1-14. [No. 252]

_____, "The Implications of Active Defense of NATO for Soviet Military Strategy," Chapter 5 in Dan Quayle et al. (Eds.), Strategic Defense and the Western Alliance. Washington, D.C.: Center for Strategic and International Studies Significant Issues Series Vol. 8 No. 6 (1986), pp. 49-56. [No. 313]

Ogarkov, N.V., "The Fairytale Threat," Atlas World Press Review Vol. 26 No. 11 (November 1979), pp. 51-54. [No. 644]

_____, "Military Strategy," Chapter 20 in P. Edward Haley et al. (Eds.), Nuclear Strategy, Arms Control, and the Future. Boulder, Colo.: Westview Press, 1985, pp. 154-155. [No. 645]

Oleynik, A.A. (Ed.), Dictionary of Basic Military Terms. Washington, D.C.: Government Printing Office (Soviet Military Thought No. 9), n.d. [619i]

Olmstead, Freeman B., The Soviet Ministry of Defense: Some Aspects of Its Professional Behavior and Its Possible Reaction to United States Policy Initiatives. Maxwell Air Force Base, Ala.: Air Command and Staff College (Research Study No. 1460-71), 1971. [No. 492]

Olsen, Gerald E., The U.S. Concept of Deterrence--Versus the Challenging Soviet Military Power of the 1970's. Maxwell Air Force Base, Ala.: Air Command and Staff College (0527u-Research Study), 1972. [No. 138]

Onacewicz, Wlodzimierz; and Robert Dickson Crane (Eds.), Soviet Materials on Military Strategy: Inventory and Analysis for 1963. Washington, D.C.: Georgetown University Center for Strategic Studies, 1963. [No. 615]

Osgood, Eugenia V., "Soviet Perceptions of Arms Control," in Kenneth M. Currie and Gregory Varhall (Eds.), The Soviet Union: What Lies Ahead? Washington, D.C.: Government Printing Office (Studies in Communist Affairs Vol. 6), 1985, pp. 106-141. [No. 77]

Papp, Daniel S., "Soviet Perceptions of the Strategic Balance," Air University Review Vol. 32 No. 2 (January-February 1981), pp. 2-17. [No. 272]

Pappageorge, John G., "The Development of Soviet Military Policy," Military Review Vol. 52 No. 7 (July 1972), pp. 36-43. [No. 493]

Parker, T. Wood, "Theater Nuclear Warfare and the U.S. Navy," Naval War College Review Vol. 35 No. 1 (January-February 1982), pp. 3-16. [No. 453]

Parrish, Michael, The Soviet Armed Forces: Books in English. Stanford, Calif.: The Hoover Institution Press (Hoover Institution Bibliographical Series: XLVIII), 1970. [No. 596]

Payne, Keith B.; and Daniel L. Strode, "Arms Control: The Soviet Approach and Its Implications," Soviet Union/Union Sovietique No. 10 Pts. 2-3 (1983), pp. 218-243. [No. 78]

Payne, Samuel B., Jr., The Soviet Union and SALT. Cambridge, Mass.: The MIT Press, 1980. [No. 79]

Pelliccia, Antonio, "Clausewitz and Soviet Politico-Military Thinking," NATO's Fifteen Nations Vol. 20 No. 6 (December 1975-January 1976), pp. 18-21; 24-26; 28-29; 32. [No. 57]

Petersen, Charles C., Soviet Tactics for Warfare at Sea. Alexandria, Va.: Center for Naval Analyses (PP 367), November 1982. [No. 454]

382

Petersen, Phillip A., "American Perceptions of Soviet Military Power," Parameters Vol. 7 No. 4 (1977), pp. 71-82. [No. 295]

_____, "The Soviet Conceptual Framework for the Application of Military Power," Naval War College Review Vol. 34 No. 6 (May-June 1981), pp. 15-25. [No. 194]

_____, "The Soviet Conventional Offensive in Europe," Washington, D.C.: Defense Intelligence Agency (DDB-2622-4-83), May 1983. [No. 427]

_____, and John G. Hines, "Military Power in Soviet Strategy Against NATO," RUSI Journal Vol. 128 No. 4 (December 1983). [No. 395]

Pipes, Richard, Some Operational Principles of Soviet Foreign Policy. Washington, D.C.: Government Printing Office, 1972. [No. 58]

_____, "Why the Soviet Union Thinks It Could Fight and Win a Nuclear War," Commentary Vol. 64 No. 1 (July 1977), pp. 21-34. [No. 139]

_____, The Correlation of Forces in Soviet Usage -- Its Meaning and Implications. Menlo Park, Calif.: SRI International Technical Note (SSC-TN-43832), March 1978. [No. 25]

_____, "Militarism and the Soviet State," Daedalus Vol. 109 No. 4 (Fall 1980), pp. 1-12. [No. 59]

Pokrovskiy, Georgiy I. (Trans. and annotated by Raymond L. Garthoff), Science Technology in Contemporary War. New York: Frederick A. Praeger, Publisher, 1959. [No. 646]

Ponomarev, A.N., "Air to Air, Air to Ground," Survival Vol. 4 No. 2 (March-April 1962), pp. 8-89. [No. 647]

Pope, Ronald R., Soviet Views on the Cuban Missile Crisis: Myth and Reality in Foreign Policy Analysis. Washington, D.C.: University Press of America, 1982. [No. 238]

Porter, Richard E., "Correlation of Forces: Revolutionary Legacy," Air University Review Vol. 27 No. 3 (March-April 1977), pp. 24-32. [No. 60]

_____, Soviet Military Decision-making: A Framework for Analysis. Santa Monica, Calif.: The RAND Corporation (N-1515 -AF), June 1980. [No. 494]

Possony, Stefan T., "U.S. Intelligence at the Crossroads," Orbis Vol. 9 No. 3 (Fall 1965), pp. 587-610. [No. 296]

Prados, John, The Soviet Estimate: U.S. Intelligence Analysis and Russian Military Strength. New York: The Dial Press, 1982. [No. 297]

Proektor, Daniel, "Moscow on Geneva," New York Times, February 1977, pp. 32-38. [No. 691]

Questor, George H., "On the Identification of Real and Pretended Communist Military Doctrine," Journal of Conflict Resolution Vol. 10 No. 2 (June 1966), pp. 172-179. [No. 115]

Ra'anan, Uri, "Soviet Strategic Doctrine and the Soviet-American Global Contest," Annals, The American Academy of Political and Social Science No. 457 (September 1981), pp. 8-17. [No. 140]

Rand, Robert, Soviet Commentary on Winning a Nuclear War. Munich: Radio Liberty Research, 1980. [No. 141]

Record, Jeffrey, Sizing Up the Red Army. Washington, D.C.: The Brookings Institution, 1975. [No. 396]

Rehm, Allan S., An Assessment of Military Operations Research in the USSR. Alexandria, Va.: Center for Naval Analyses (AD 770116), September 1973. [No. 495]

Reinhardt, G.C., "Atomic Weapons and Warfare," Chapter 37 in B.H. Liddell Hart (Ed.), The Red Army. New York: Harcourt, Brace and Company, 1956, pp. 420-438. [No. 397]

Report of a Study Group of the Institute for the Study of Conflict. London: ISC Special Report, March 1978. [No. 142]

Reznichenko, V.G., "Troop Movements," in Oleg Hoeffding, Troop Movements in Soviet Tactical Doctrine. Santa Monica, Calif.: The RAND Corporation (R-878-PR), November 1971. [No. 648]

Richelson, Jeffrey T., "Soviet Responses to MX," Political Science Quarterly Vol. 96 No. 3 (Fall 1981), pp. 401-410. [No. 273]

Rivkin, David B., Jr., "No Bastions for the Bear," U.S. Naval Institute Proceedings Vol. 110 No. 4 (April 1984), pp. 36-43. [No. 455]

_____, "What Does Moscow Think?", Foreign Policy No. 59 (Summer 1985), pp. 85-105. [No. 314]

_____, and Manfred Hamm, In Strategic Defense, Moscow is Far Ahead. Washington, D.C.: The Heritage Foundation (Backgrounder No. 409), February 2, 1986. [No. 315]

Rose, John P., "The Battlefield Threat: Soviet Concepts, Doctrine, and Strategy," Air Defense, July-September 1978, pp. 24-29. [No. 428]

Rosefielde, Steven, False Science: Underestimating the Soviet Arms Buildup, An Appraisal of the CIA's Direct Costing Effort, 1960-80. New Brunswick, N.J.: Transaction Books, 1982. [No. 535]

_____, "Economic Foundations of Soviet National Security Strategy," Orbis Vol. 30 No. 2 (Summer 1986), pp. 317-330. [No. 536]

Ross, Dennis, Rethinking Soviet Strategic Policy: Inputs and Implications. Los Angeles, Calif.: UCLA Advanced Center for International Studies (Working Paper No. 5), June 1977. [No. 116]

Rowney, Edward L., "The Soviets are Still Russians," in Kenneth M. Currie and Gregory Varhall (Eds.), The Soviet Union: What Lies Ahead? Washington, D.C.: Government Printing Office (Studies in Communist Affairs Vol. 6), 1985, pp. 148-153. [No. 257]

Ruble, Blair, et al., Soviet Research Institute Project. Washington, D.C.: U.S. Information Agency, 1980-81. [No. 671]

Ruehle, Hans, "Gorbachev's 'Star Wars'," NATO Review Vol. 33 No. 4 (August 1985), pp. 26-31. [No. 316]

Ruggles, M.J.; and Arnold Kramish, The Soviet Union and the Atom: The Early Years. Santa Monica, Calif.: The RAND Corporation (RM-1711), April 2, 1956. [No. 219]

_____, and Arnold Kramish, Soviet Atomic Policy. Santa Monica, Calif.: The RAND Corporation (P-853), May 23, 1956. [No. 220]

Rupp, Ranier W., "Assessing Soviet Military Expenditure: A Complex and Controversial Task," NATO Review Vol. 29 No. 5 (October 1981), pp. 23-28. [No. 537]

Rush, Myron, "Guns Over Growth in Soviet Policy," International Security Vol. 7 No. 3 (Winter 1982-83), pp. 167-179. [No. 538]

Ryabov, V., The Soviet Armed Forces, Yesterday and Today. Moscow: Progress Publishers, 1976. [No. 616e]

Rybkin, Ye., "On the Nature of a Nuclear Missile War," Appendix A, The Red "Hawks" on the Rationality of Nuclear War. Santa Monica, Calif.: The RAND Corporation (RM-4899-PR), March 1966. [No. 649]

Sallagar, F.M., An Overview of the Soviet Strategic Threat. Santa Monica, Calif.: The RAND Corporation (R-2580-AF), February 1980. [No. 26]

Saunders, Richard M., "The Soviet Buildup: Why Does the Threat Grow?", Military Review Vol. 60 No. 4 (April 1980), pp. 61-71. [No. 398]

Savkin, Ye.V., Basic Principles of Operational Art and Tactics. Washington, D.C.: Government Printing Office (Soviet Military Thought No. 4), n.d. [No. 619d]

Scott, Harriet Fast, "Soviet Literature for 1966," Military Review Vol. 46 No. 7 (July 1966), pp. 87-90. [No. 617]

_____, "The Soviet Drive for Strategic Superiority," Air University Review Vol. 19 No. 4 (May-June 1968), pp. 59-62. [No. 178]

_____, "Insights Into the Soviet Military," Problems of Communism Vol. 26 No. 1 (January-February 1977), pp. 70-72. [No. 607]

_____, "The Soviet High Command," Air Force Magazine (Soviet Aerospace Almanac No. 3) Vol. 60 No. 3 (March 1977), pp. 52-56. [No. 496]

_____, and William F. Scott, The Armed Forces of the USSR. Boulder, Colo.: Westview Press, 1979. [No. 93]

_____, and William F. Scott, The Soviet Control Structure: Capabilities for Wartime Survival. New York: Crane, Russak, and Company, Inc., 1983. [No. 497]

_____, and William F. Scott (Eds.), The Soviet Art of War: Doctrine, Strategy, and Tactics. Boulder, Colo.: Westview Press, 1982. [No. 618]

Scott, William F., "The Contrast in Chinese and Soviet Military Doctrines," Air University Review Vol. 19 No. 2 (January-February 1968), pp. 57-63. [No. 179]

_____, "Soviet Military Doctrine and Strategy: Realities and Misunderstandings," Strategic Review Vol. 3 No. 3 (Summer 1975), pp. 57-66. [No. 274]

_____, "Changes in Tactical Concepts Within the Soviet Forces," in Lawrence Whetten (Ed.), The Future of Soviet Military Power. New York: Crane, Russak, and Co., 1976. [No. 429]

_____, (U.S. Ed.), Selected Soviet Military Writings, 1970-1975. Washington, D.C.: Government Printing Office (Soviet Military Thought No. 11), n.d. [No. 619k]

_____, "Troops of National Air Defense," Air Force Magazine (Soviet Aerospace Almanac No. 4) Vol. 61 No. 3 (March 1978), pp. 56-66. [No. 317]

_____, "The Themes of Soviet Strategy," Air Force Magazine (Soviet Aerospace Almanac No. 10) Vol. 67 No. 3 (March 1984), pp. 68-73. [No. 399]

_____, "Soviet Concepts of War," Air Force Magazine (Soviet Aerospace Almanac No. 11) Vol. 68 No. 3 (March 1985), pp. 48-52. [No. 180]

_____, "The Soviets and Strategic Defense," Air Force Magazine (Soviet Aerospace Almanac No. 12) Vol. 69 No. 3 (March 1986), pp. 40-45. [No. 318]

_____, and Harriet Fast Scott, Soviet Sources of Doctrine and Strategy. New York: Crane, Russak, and Co., 1975. [No. 608]

_____, and Harriet Fast Scott, "The Social Sciences Institutes of the Soviet Academy of Sciences," Air Force Magazine (Soviet Aerospace Almanac No. 6) Vol. 63 No. 3 (March 1980), pp. 60-65. [No. 672]

_____, and Harriet Fast Scott, "Soviet Perceptions of U.S. Military Strategies and Forces," Chapter 6 in Graham Vernon (Ed.), Soviet Perceptions of War and Peace. Washington, D.C.: National Defense University Press, 1981, pp. 97-112. [No. 275]

Scribner, Jeffrey L., "Soviet Military Buildup: A New Dimension in Foreign Policy," Military Review Vol. 51 No. 8 (August 1971), pp. 53-62. [No. 61]

Shelyag, V.V. et al., Military Psychology. Washington, D.C.: Government Printing Office (Soviet Military Thought No. 8), n.d. [No. 619h]

Shenfield, Stephen, "Soviet Thinking About the Unthinkable," Bulletin of the Atomic Scientists, February 1985. [No. 117]

Shtemenko, S.M., "The Land Forces in Contemporary War and Their Combat Training," Army, March 1963, pp. 47-56. [No. 650]

_____, The Soviet General Staff at War, 1941-1945. Moscow: Progress Publishers, 1970. [No. 616f]

Shulsky, Abram N., <u>Admiral Gorshkov on Naval Arms Limitations:</u>
<u>KTO KOGO?</u> Alexandria, Va.: Center for Naval Analyses (M
1024), January 1974. [No. 456]

_____, <u>Soviet Perceptions of the U.S.-USSR Rivalry</u>.
Alexandria, Va.: Center for Naval Analyses (P-1046), March
1976. [No. 276]

Sidel'nikov, I., "On Soviet Military Doctrine," <u>Air University</u>
<u>Review</u> Vol. 13 No. 4 (Summer 1962), pp. 142-150. [No. 651]

Sidorenko, A.A., <u>The Offensive</u>. Washington, D.C.: Government
Printing Office, n.d. [No. 619a]

_____, "The Nature of the Offensive Under Conditions
Where Nuclear Weapons Are Employed," Chapter 18 in P. Edward
Haley et al. (Eds.), <u>Nuclear Strategy, Arms Control, and the</u>
<u>Future</u>. Boulder, Colo.: Westview Press, 1985. [No. 652]

Sidorov, P., "The Creative Character of Soviet Military Science,"
Appendix C in Raymond Garthoff, <u>The Soviet Image of Future</u>
<u>War</u>. Washington, D.C.: Public Affairs Press, 1959. [No. 653]

_____, "Foundations of the Soviet Military Doctrine," <u>Military</u>
<u>Review</u> Vol. 52 No. 12 (December 1972), pp. 89-91. [No. 654]

Sienkiewicz, Stanley, "SALT and Soviet Nuclear Doctrine,"
<u>International Security</u> Vol. 2 No. 4 (Spring 1978), pp. 84-100.
[No. 80]

Simes, Dimitri K., <u>Detente and Conflict: Soviet Foreign Policy,</u>
<u>1972-1977</u>. Washington, D.C.: Center for Strategic and Inter-
national Studies (The Washington Papers No. 44), 1977. [No.
27]

_____, "The Anti-Soviet Brigade," <u>Foreign Policy</u> No. 37
(Winter 1979-80), pp. 28-42. [No. 298]

_____, "Deterrence and Coercion in Soviet Policy," <u>Inter-</u>
<u>national Security</u> Vol. 5 No. 3 (Winter 1980-81), pp. 80-103.
[No. 118]

_____, "Disciplining Soviet Power," <u>Foreign Policy</u> No. 43
(Summer 1981), pp. 33-52. [No. 62]

_____, "The Military and Militarism in Soviet Society,"
<u>International Security</u> Vol. 6 No. 3 (Winter 1981-82), pp. 123-
143. [No. 258]

Skirdo, M.P., <u>The People, the Army, the Commander</u>. Washington, D.C.: Government Printing Office (Soviet Military Thought
No. 14), n.d. [No. 619n]

388

Smirnov, Mikhail V. et al., "On Soviet Military Science," <u>Military Review</u> Vol. 42 No. 3 (March 1962), pp. 78-87. [No. 655]

Smith, Clyde A., "The Meaning and Significance of the Gorshkov Articles," <u>Naval War College Review</u> Vol. 26 No. 5 (March-April 1974), pp. 18-37. [No. 457]

Smith, Myron J., Jr., <u>The Soviet Navy, 1941-1978: A Guide to Sources in English</u>. Santa Barbara, Calif.: The American Bibliographic Company-Clio, 1980, 211 p. [No. 597]

_____, <u>The Soviet Air and Strategic Rocket Forces, 1939-1980: A Guide to Sources in English</u>. Santa Barbara, Calif.: The American Bibliographic Company-Clio, 1981. [No. 598]

_____, <u>The Soviet Army, 1939-1980: A Guide to Sources in English</u>. Santa Barbara, Calif.: The American Bibliographic Company-Clio (War/Peace Bibliography Series #11), 1982. [No. 599]

Snow, Donald M., "Strategic Uncertainty and Nuclear Deterrence," <u>Naval War College Review</u> Vol. 34 No. 6 (November-December 1981), pp. 27-41. [No. 119]

Snyder, Jack, <u>Soviet Strategic Culture: Implications for LNOs</u>. Santa Monica, Calif.: The RAND Corporation (R-2154-AF), September 1977. [No. 259]

Sokolovsky, V.D. (Ed.), (Raymond Garthoff, Ed. and Trans.), <u>Military Strategy: Soviet Doctrine and Concepts</u>. New York: Frederick A. Praeger, Pubisher, 1963. [No. 656]

Sokolovskii, V.D. (Ed.), (Herbert S. Dinerstein, Leon Goure, and Thomas W. Wolfe, Eds. and Trans.), <u>Soviet Military Strategy</u>. Englewood Cliffs, N.J.: Prentice-Hall, Inc., 1963. [No. 657]

Sokolovskiy, V.D. (Ed.), (Harriet Fast Scott, Ed. and Trans.), <u>Soviet Military Strategy</u>. New York: Crane, Russak, and Company, 1975. [No. 658]

Sokolovsky, V.D., "The Nature of Modern War," Chapter 17 in P. Edward Haley et al. (Eds.), <u>Nuclear Strategy, Arms Control, and the Future</u>. Boulder, Colo.: Westview Press, 1985, pp. 138-145. [No. 659]

Soll, Richard S., "The Soviet Union and Protracted Nuclear War," <u>Strategic Review</u> Vol. 8 No. 4 (Fall 1980), pp. 15-28. [No. 181]

_____, Arthur A. Zuehleke, and Richard B. Foster, <u>The Role of Social Science Research Institutes in Formulation and Execution of Soviet Foreign Policy</u>. Arlington, Va.: Strategic

Studies Center, SRI International (Project 2625), March 1976. [No. 673]

"Soviet Aerospace Almanac, Nos. 1-12," Air Force Magazine, March 1975-1986. [No. 593]

Soviet Civil Defense -- Post-Strike Repair and Restoration. Coral Gables, Fla.: University of Miami Center for Advanced International Studies (ASDIRS 4262), 1973. [No. 347]

"The Soviet Doctrine of War," Military Review Vol. 28 No. 9 (December 1948), pp. 79-82. [No. 195]

Soviet Military Doctrine: A List of References to Recent Soviet and Free World Publications on Soviet Military Thought. Washington, D.C.: U.S. Department of State (External Research Paper 141), August 1963. [No. 600]

Soviet Military Space Doctrine. Washington, D.C.: Defense Intelligence Agency (DDB-1400-16-84), 1 August 1984. [No. 319]

Soviet Strategic Defense Programs. Washington, D.C.: Departments of Defense and State, October 1985. [No. 320]

"The Soviet Strategic View," Strategic Review, Spring 1979 to date. [No. 620]

Soviet World Outlook, 1976-1985. [No. 621]

Spielmann, Karl F., "Defense Industrialists in the USSR," Problems of Communism Vol. 25 No. 5 (September-October 1976), pp. 52-69. [No. 539]

_____, Analyzing Soviet Strategic Arms Decisions. Boulder, Colo.: Westview Press, 1978. [No. 498]

Stanley, Zell, An Annotated Bibliography of the Open Literature on Deception. Santa Monica, Calif.: The RAND Corporation (N-2332-NA), December 1985. [No. 601]

Staudenmeier, William O., "Civil Defense in Soviet and American Strategy," Military Review Vol. 58 No. 10 (October 1978), pp. 2-14. [No. 348]

Stevens, Jennie A.; and Henry S. Marsh, "Surprise and Deception in Soviet Military Thought," Military Review Vol. 62 Nos. 6 and 7 (June and July 1982). Part I, pp. 2-11; Part II, pp. 24-35. [No. 299]

Stevens, Sayre, "The Soviet BMD Program," Chapter 5 in Ashton B. Carter and David N. Schwartz (Eds.), Ballistic Missile

Defense. Washington, D.C.: The Brookings Institution, 1984, pp. 182-220. [No. 321]

_____, "The Soviet Factor in SDI," Orbis Vol. 29 No. 4 (Winter 1986), pp. 689-700. [No. 322]

Stockell, Charles, "Soviet Military Strategy: The Army View," in Michael MccGwire (Ed.), Soviet Naval Developments: Capability and Context. New York: Praeger Publishers, 1973. [No. 430]

Stoehrmann, Kenneth C., "Perceptual Differences in Thinking the Unthinkable: World War II," in Kenneth M. Currie and Gregory Varhall (Eds.), The Soviet Union: What Lies Ahead? Washington, D.C.: Government Printing Office (Studies in Communist Affairs Vol. 6), 1985, pp. 730-751. [No. 300]

Strode, Dan L., "Arms Control and Sino-Soviet Relations," Orbis Vol. 28 No 1 (Spring 1984), pp. 163-168. [No. 81]

_____, and Rebecca V. Strode, "Diplomacy and Defense in Soviet National Security Policy," International Security Vol. 8 No. 2 (Fall 1983), pp. 91-116. [No. 253]

Strode, Rebecca V., "Soviet Strategic Style," Comparative Strategy Vol. 3 No. 4 (1982), pp. 319-339. [No. 260]

_____, "The Soviet Armed Forces: Adaptation to Resource Scarcity," Washington Quarterly Vol. 9 No. 2 (Spring 1986), pp. 55-69. [No. 540]

_____, et al., "The Soviet Response to U.S. Strategic Defense," in W. Bruce Weinrod, Assessing Strategic Defense: Six Roundtable Discussions. Washington, D.C.: The Heritage Foundation (The Heritage Lectures No. 38), 1985, pp. 37-64. [No. 323]

Talbott, Strobe, "The Dilemma of Nuclear Doctrine," Time Vol. 118 No. 22 (November 30, 1981), pp. 60-61. [No. 301]

Talenskiy, Nikolay, "The Character of Modern War," Survival Vol. 3 No. 1 (January-February 1961). [No. 660]

_____, "Missile Defense: A Response to Aggression," Bulletin of the Atomic Scientists, February 1965. [No. 661]

_____, "Anti-missile Systems and Disarmament," in John Erickson et al. (Eds.), The Military-Technical Revolution. New York: Frederick A. Praeger, Publisher, 1966, pp. 219-228. [No. 662]

Thomas, John R., "The Role of Missile Defense in Soviet Strategy," Military Review Vol. 44 No. 5 (May 1964), 46-58. [No. 324]

_____, "Limited Nuclear War in Soviet Strategic Thinking," Orbis Vol. 10 No. 1 (Spring 1966), pp. 184-212. [No. 360]

_____, "Militarization of the Soviet Academy of Sciences," Survey Vol. 30 No. 2 (Spring 1985). [No. 674]

Thompson, Andrew C., Civil Defense in the Soviet Union. Maxwell Air Force Base, Ala.: Air Command and Staff College (Research Study No. 1945-71), 1971. [No. 349]

Trapans, A., Logistics in Recent Soviet Military Writings. Santa Monica, Calif.: The RAND Corporation (RM-5062-PR), August 1966. [No. 431]

Tritten, James John, Soviet Naval Forces and Nuclear Warfare: Weapons, Employment, and Policy. Boulder, Colo.: Westview Press, 1986. [No. 458]

_____, "(Non)Nuclear Warfare," U.S. Naval Institute Proceedings Vol. 113 No. 2 (February 1987), pp. 64-70. [No. 459]

Trofimenko, Genrikh A. (Henry), "Political Realism and the 'Realistic Difference'," in Robert J. Pranger and Roger P. Labrie (Eds.), Nuclear Strategy and National Security: Points of View. Washington, D.C.: American Enterprise Institute, 1977, pp. 38-53. [No. 692]

_____, "Counterforce: Illusion of a Panacea," International Security Vol. 5 No. 4 (Spring 1981), pp. 28-48. [No. 693]

_____, "The 'Theology' of Strategy," Orbis Vol. 21 No. 3 (Fall 1977), pp. 497-515. [No. 694]

_____, Changing Attitudes Towards Deterrence. Los Angeles, Calif.: UCLA Center for International and Strategic Studies Affairs (ACIS Working Paper No. 25), July 1980. [No. 695]

_____, "Moscow Isn't Worried," New York Times, September 22, 1980. [No. 696]

_____, "Strategic Metaphors," U.S. Naval Institute Proceedings Vol. 106 No. 3 (March 1980), p. 96. [No. 697]

_____, "The Third World and the U.S.-Soviet Competition: A Soviet View," Foreign Affairs Vol. 59 (Summer 1981), pp. 1021-1040. [No. 698]

392

_____, "Struggle for the Turf," World Politics Vol. 37 No. 3 (April 1985), pp. 403-415. [No. 699]

Tyushkevich, S.A., The Soviet Armed Forces: A History of Their Organizational Development. Washington, D.C.: Government Printing Office (Soviet Military Thought No. 19), n.d. [No. 619s]

USSR: Analytical Survey of Literature. Washington, D.C.: Government Printing Office (DA PAM 55-6-1), December 1976. [No. 602]

"USSR: Atomic Tactics," Military Review Vol. 35 No. 10 (January 1956), pp. 73-74. [No. 432]

USSR Report: Military Affairs, Joint Publication Research Service. [No. 612a]

USSR Report: The Soviet Union, Foreign Broadcast Information Service. [No. 612b]

Van Cleave, William R., "Soviet Doctrine and Strategy: A Developing American View," in Lawrence L. Whetten (Ed.), The Future of Soviet Military Power. New York: Crane, Russak and Company, Inc., 1976, pp. 41-71. [No. 196]

_____, and Samuel T. Cohen, Tactical Nuclear Weapons: An Examination of the Issues. New York: Crane, Russak, and Company, Inc., 1978. [No. 433]

Van Oudenaren, J., Potential Threats to U.S. Soviet Deterrence: The Political Dimension. Santa Monica, Calif.: The RAND Corporation (P-6826), November 1982. [No. 120]

_____, Deterrence, Warfighting, and Soviet Military Doctrine. London: International Institute for Strategic Studies (Adelphi Papers No. 210), Summer 1986. [No. 121]

Varentsov, S.S., "Missiles on the Battlefield," Survival Vol. 4 No. 2 (March-April 1962), pp. 89-90. [No. 663]

Vasil'yev, B.A., Long-Range Missile-Equipped. Washington, D.C.: Government Printing Office (Soviet Military Thought No. 15), n.d. [No. 619o]

Vernon, Graham D., "Controlled Conflict: Soviet Perceptions of Peaceful Coexistence," Orbis Vol 23 No. 2 (Summer 1977). [No. 28]

_____, "Soviet Options for War in Europe: Nuclear or Conventional?", Strategic Review Vol. 7 No. 1 (Winter 1979), pp. 56-66. [No. 400]

_____, Soviet Perceptions of War and Peace. Washington, D.C.: National Defense University Press, 1981. [No. 594]

Verrier, Anthony, "The Red Army's New Strategy," The New Statesman, August 21, 1964, p. 238. [No. 231]

Vershinin, K.A., "Rocket Vehicles -- the Basis of the Combat Might of the Soviet Air Force," Survival Vol. 4 No. 2 (March-April 1962), pp. 90-91. [No. 664]

Vick, Alan J., "Soviet Military Forces and Strategy Come of Age: Implications for American Deterrence Theory," Vol. 32 No. 2 (January-February 1981), pp. 17-26. [No. 143]

Vigor, Peter H., "The Soviet Armed Forces on Exercise," Bulletin of the Institute for the Study of the USSR Vol. 18 No. 10 (October 1971), pp. 5-22. [No. 434]

_____, "Admiral Gorshkov's Views on Seapower," RUSI Journal Vol. 119 No. 1 (March 1974), pp. 53-60. [No. 460]

_____, "Strategy and Policy in Soviet Naval Warfare," Strategic Review Vol. 2 No. 2 (Spring 1974), pp. 68-75. [No. 461]

_____, The Soviet View of War, Peace, and Neutrality. London: Routledge and Kegan Paul, 1975. [No. 63]

_____, "Soviet Military Developments -- 1976," Strategic Review Vol. 5 No. 2 (Spring 1977), pp. 74-82. [No. 361]

_____, The Soviet Blitzkrieg Theory. New York: St. Martin's Press, 1983. [No. 435]

_____, and Christopher N. Donnelly, "The Soviet Threat to Europe," RUSI Journal Vol. 120 No. 1 (March 1975), pp. 69-75. [No. 401]

_____, and Christopher N. Donnelly, "The Manchurian Campaign and Its Relevance to Modern History," Comparative Strategy Vol. 2 No. 2 (1980), pp. 159-178. [No. 436]

Vincent, R.J., Military Power and Political Influence: The Soviet Union and Eastern Europe. London: The International Institute for Strategic Studies (Adelphi Paper No. 119), Autumn 1975. [No. 402]

Walt, Stephen M., Interpreting Soviet Military Statements: A Methodological Analysis. Alexandria, Va.: Center for Naval Analyses (CNA 81-0260.10), 5 December 1983. [No. 302]

394

Ward, Chester C., "The 'New Myths' and 'Old Realities' of Nuclear War," Orbis Vol. 8 No. 2 (Summer 1964), pp. 255-291. [No. 144]

Warner, Edward L., The Military in Contemporary Soviet Politics: An Institutional Analysis. New York: Praeger Publishers, 1979. [No. 499]

Weeks, Albert L., "The New Soviet Military Encyclopedia," Survey Vol. 26 No. 2 (Spring 1982), pp. 202-206. [No. 609]

_____, "The Garthoff-Pipes Debate on Soviet Doctrine: Another Perspective," Strategic Review Vol. 11 No. 1 (Winter 1983), pp. 57-64. [No. 182]

_____, and William C. Brodie, War and Peace: Soviet Russia Speaks. New York: National Strategy Information Center, 1983. [No. 622]

Weinland, Robert G., An Analysis of Admiral Gorshkov's "Navies in War and Peace". Alexandria, Va.: Center For Naval Analyses (PP 131), July 1974. [No. 462]

Weinstein, John M., "Soviet Civil Defense and the U.S. Deterrent," Parameters Vol. 12 No. 3 (March 1982), pp. 70-83. [No. 350]

Weiss, Peter, "Room at the Top for Ogarkov Again," International Defense Review Vol. 18 No. 10 (1985), pp. 1559-1560. [No. 254]

Welander, R.O.; J.J. Herzog, and F.D. Kennedy, The Soviet Navy Declaratory Doctrine for Theatre Nuclear Warfare. McLean, Va.: The BDM Corporation (DNA 4434T), 30 September 1977. [No. 463]

Wettig, Gerhard, "The Garthoff-Pipes Debate on Soviet Strategic Doctrine: A European Perspective," Strategic Review Vol. 11 No. 2 (Spring 1983), pp. 68-78. [No. 183]

Whitton, Tommy J., "Soviet Strategic Wartime Leadership," in Kenneth M. Currie and Gregory Varhall (Eds.), The Soviet Union: What Lies Ahead? Washington, D.C.: Government Printing Office (Studies in Communist Affairs Vol. 6), 1985, pp. 706-729. [No. 500]

Williams, E.S., "Soviet Military Thought and the Principles of War," Royal Air Forces Quarterly Vol. 15 (Spring 1975), pp. 17-22. [No. 437]

Wolf, Charles, Jr.; K.C. Yeh, E.D. Brunner, A. Gurwitz, and M.F. Lawrence, The Costs of the Soviet Empire. Santa Monica,

Calif.: The RAND Corporation (R-3073/1-NA), September 1983. [No. 541]

Wolfe, Thad A., "Soviet-United States Civil Defense: Tipping the Strategic Scale?", Air University Review Vol. 30 No. 3 (March-April 1979), pp. 40-55. [No. 351]

Wolfe, Thomas W., "Khrushchev's Disarmament Strategy," Orbis Vol. 4 No. 1 (Spring 1960), pp. 13-27. [No. 82]

_____, A First Reaction to the New Soviet Book 'Military Strategy'. Santa Monica, Calif.: The RAND Corporation (RM-3495-PR), February 1963. [No. 232]

_____, Some Factors Bearing on Soviet Attitudes Toward Disarmament. Santa Monica, Calif.: The RAND Corporation (P-2766), July 1963. [No. 83]

_____, Role of the Soviet Military in Decisionmaking and Soviet Politics. Santa Monica, Calif.: The RAND Corporation (P-2767), July 1963. [No. 501]

_____, A Postscript on the Significance of the Book "Soviet Military Strategy". Santa Monica, Calif.: The RAND Corporation (RM-3730-PR), July 1963. [No. 233]

_____, Comments on Lomov's "Soviet Military Doctrine". Santa Monica, Calif.: The RAND Corporation (P-2816), October 1963. [No. 502]

_____, Signs of Stress in Soviet Political-Military Relations. Santa Monica, Calif.: The RAND Corporation (P-2877), March 1964. [No. 573]

_____, "Shifts in Soviet Strategic Thought," Foreign Affairs Vol. 42 No. 2 (April 1964), pp. 475-486. [No. 234]

_____, Soviet Strategy at the Crossroads. Cambridge, Mass.: Harvard University Press, 1964. [No. 197]

_____, Soviet Strategic Thought in Transition. Santa Monica, Calif.: The RAND Corporation (P-2906), May 1964. [No. 247]

_____, "Some New Developments in the Soviet Military Debate," Orbis Vol. 8 No. 3 (Fall 1964), pp. 550-562. [No. 248]

_____, Soviet Influences on an Arms Control Environment. Santa Monica, Calif.: The RAND Corporation (P-2995), October 1964. [No. 84]

396

_____, Impact of Khrushchev's Downfall on Soviet Military Policy and Detente. Santa Monica, Calif.: The RAND Corporation (P-3010), November 1964. [No. 574]

_____, Note on the Naming of a Successor to Marshal Biriuzov. Santa Monica, Calif.: The RAND Corporation (P-3025), December 1964. [No. 249]

_____, Trends in Soviet Thinking on Theater Warfare, Conventional Operations, and Limited War. Santa Monica, Calif.: The RAND Corporation (RM-4305-PR), December 1964. [No. 403]

_____, Soviet Commentary on the French "Force de Frappe". Santa Monica, Calif.: The RAND Corporation (RM-4359-ISA), January 1965. [No. 362]

_____, The Soviet Union Six Months After Khrushchev's Fall. Santa Monica, Calif.: The RAND Corporation (R-3720), April 1965. [No. 29]

_____, "Problems of Soviet Defense Policy Under the New Regime," Slavic Review Vol. 24 No. 2 (June 1965), pp. 175-188. [No. 94]

_____, Soviet Military Policy Under Khrushchev's Successors. Santa Monica Calif.: The RAND Corporation (P-3193), August 1965. [No. 95]

_____, The Soviet Union and the Sino-Soviet Dispute. Santa Monica, Calif.: The RAND Corporation (P-3203), August 1965. [No. 363]

_____, Soviet Military Theory: An Additional Source of Insight Into Its Development. Santa Monica, Calif.: The RAND Corporation (P-3258), November 1965. [No. 198]

_____, The Soviet Union and Arms Control. Santa Monica, Calif.: The RAND Corporation (P-3337), April 1966. [No. 85]

_____, The Evolving Nature of the Warsaw Pact. Santa Monica, Calif.: The RAND Corporation (RM-4835-PR), April 1966. [No. 364]

_____, The Soviet Military Scene: Institutional and Defense Policy Considerations. Santa Monica, Calif.: The RAND Corporation (RM-4913-PR), June 1966. [No. 503]

_____, Soviet Military Power and European Security. Santa Monica, Calif.: The RAND Corporation (P-3429), August 1966. [No. 365]

397

_____, Soviet Military Policy Trends Under the Brezhnev-Kosygin Regime. Santa Monica, Calif.: The RAND Corporation (P-3556), May 1967. [No. 96]

_____, The Communist Outlook on War. Santa Monica, Calif.: The RAND Corporation (P-3640), August 1967. [No. 64]

_____, Soviet Military Policy at the Fifty-Year Mark. Santa Monica, Calif.: The RAND Corporation (RM-5443-PR), September 1967. [No. 97]

_____, The Soviet Quest for More Globally Mobile Military Power. Santa Monica, Calif.: The RAND Corporation (RM-5554-PR), December 1967. [No. 404]

_____, Evolution of Soviet Military Policy. Santa Monica, Calif.: The RAND Corporation (P-3773), February 1968. [No. 504]

_____, Soviet Power in the Setting of a Changing Power Balance. Santa Monica, Calif.: The RAND Corporation (P-4055), March 1969. [No. 30]

_____, "Are the Generals Taking Over?", Problems of Communism Vol. 18 Nos. 4-5 (July-October 1969), pp. 106-110. [No. 575]

_____, Statement by Dr. Thomas W. Wolfe at Hearings of the Subcommittee on National Security Policy and Scientific Developments, House Foreign Affairs Committee, July 22, 1969. Washington, D.C.: Government Printing Office, 1969. [No. 65]

_____, Soviet Foreign and Defense Policy Under the Brezhnev-Kosygin Regime. Santa Monica, Calif.: The RAND Corporation (P-4227), October 1969. [No. 31]

_____, "The Soviet Military Since Khrushchev," Current History, October 1969, pp. 220-227. [No. 98]

_____, Impact of Economic and Technological Issues on the Soviet Approach to SALT. Santa Monica, Calif.: The RAND Corporation (P-4368), June 1970. [No. 542]

_____, Soviet Power and Europe. Baltimore, Md.: Johns Hopkins Press, 1970. [No. 366]

_____, The Soviet Union's Strategic and Military Stakes in the GDR. Santa Monica, Calif.: The RAND Corporation (P-4549), January 1971. [No. 367]

_____, Soviet Interests in SALT: Political, Economic, Bureaucratic, and Strategic Contributions and Impediments to

398

Arms Control. Santa Monica, Calif.: The RAND Corporation (P-4702), September 1971. [No. 505]

_____, Role of the Warsaw Pact in Soviet Policy. Santa Monica, Calif.: The RAND Corporation (P-4973), March 1973. [No. 368]

_____, The Global Strategic Perspective from Moscow. Santa Monica, Calif.: The RAND Corporation (P-4978), March 1973. [No. 32]

_____, "Soviet Military Strategy and Policy," in Kurt London (Ed.), The Soviet Impact on World Politics. New York: Hawthorn Books, 1974, pp. 237-268. [No. 99]

_____, "Military Power and Soviet Policy," in William E. Griffith (Ed.), The Soviet Empire: Expansion and Detente. Lexington, Mass.: Lexington Books, 1976, pp. 145-216. [No. 100]

_____, "Soviet Military Capabilities and Intentions in Europe," in Richard Pipes (Ed.), Soviet Strategy in Europe. New York: Crane, Russak and Company, 1976, pp. 129-167. [No. 369]

_____, The Military Dimension in the Making of Soviet Foreign and Defense Policy. Santa Monica, Calif.: The RAND Corporation (P-6024), October 1977. [No. 506]

_____, "The Soviet General Staff," Problems of Communism Vol. 28 No. 1 (January-February 1978), pp. 51-54. [No. 507]

_____, The SALT Experience. Cambridge, Mass.: Ballinger Publishing Company, 1979. [No. 86]

Woolridge, E.T., Jr., "The Gorshkov Papers: Soviet Naval Doctrine for the Nuclear Age," Orbis Vol. 13 No. 4 (Winter 1975), pp. 1153-1175. [No. 464]

XXX, "The Adaptation of Soviet Ground Forces to Nuclear War," Military Review Vol. 46 No. 9 (September 1966), pp. 11-17. [No. 405]

Yefimov, Aleksandr N., "One Man Command," Military Review Vol. 55 No. 5 (May 1975), pp. 73-77. [No. 665]

Yegorov, P.T., et al., Civil Defense. Washington, D.C.: Government Printing Office (Soviet Military Thought No. 10), n.d. [No. 619j]

Yepishev, A., Some Aspects of Party-Political Work in the Soviet Armed Forces. Moscow: Progress Publishers, 1975. [No. 616g]

Yinon, Oded, "The Soviet Doctrine of Total War," Midstream Vol. 27 No. 10 (December 1981), pp. 7-11. [No. 145]

Yost, David S., "Soviet Ballistic Missile Defense and NATO," Orbis Vol. 29 No. 2 (Summer 1985), pp. 281-292. [No. 325]

_____, "Soviet Ballistic Missile Defense and the Atlantic Alliance," Chapter 7 in Dan Quayle, et al., Strategic Defense and the Western Alliance. Washington, D.C.: Center for Strategic and International Studies Significant Issues Series, Vol. 8 No. 6, 1986, pp. 70-85. [No. 326]